·*DIASPORA*·

Exile and the Contemporary
Jewish Condition

Editor
Étan Levine

STEIMATZKY
SHAPOLSKY
NEW YORK • JERUSALEM • TEL AVIV

Credits

I am grateful to *Forum* (Jerusalem) and its editor, Amnon Hadary, for permission to reproduce portions of papers presented to the World Zionist Organization by Salo W. Baron, Mordecai Kaplan, Golda Meir, A. B. Yehoshua, and Yitzhak Rabin, as well as Martin Buber's paper which was presented at the 1960 Paris Conference on Soviet Jewry. Jacob Agus' article was extracted from "Exceptionalism as Meta-Myth," which first appeared in the *CCAR Journal*, and my own study contains materials first published in *Conservative Judaism* and *Reconstructionist*.

This volume is an expanded and revised edition of my anthology, *Diaspora; Exile and the Jewish Condition* (New York 1983), and I sincerely thank the publisher, Jason Aronson, for allowing me to publish the materials contained in that volume.

A Shapolsky Book
Published by Shapolsky Books
a division of
Steimatzky Publishing of North America, Inc.

Copyright © 1986 by Étan Levine.
   All rights reserved under International Copyright Conventions. Published and printed in the U.S.A. by Shapolsky Books, a division of Steimatzky Publishing of North America, Inc. No part of this book may be used or reproduced in any manner whatsoever without written permission of Steimatzky Publishing of North America, Inc., except in the case of brief quotations embodied in critical articles or reviews.
   For any additional information, contact Steimatzky Publishing of North America, Inc., 56 East 11th Street, NY, NY 10003. (212) 505-2505

Cover design by The Great American Art Co., N.Y., N.Y.
Typography by Allen Wayne Communications, Inc., N.Y., N.Y.
10 9 8 7 6 5 4 3 2 1

1st Edition January 1986

Library of Congress Cataloging in Publication Data
Main entry under title:

Diaspora. Exile and the Contemporary Jewish Condition.

   Includes index.
   1. Jews — Diaspora — Addresses, essays, lectures.
   2. Israel and the Diaspora — Addresses, essays, lectures.
   3. Jews — Politics and government — 1948-   — Addresses, essays, lectures. I. Levine, Étan.

ISBN 0-933503-50-4

"And the Lord said to Abram:
Go forth
out of your country
and from your birthplace
and from your father's house
unto the land that I shall show you."

(Genesis 12:1)

◆ CONTENTS ◆

✦ PREFACE ✦

For two thousand years, exile has been the quintessential, normative Jewish condition. However, since 1948 diaspora is no longer an inevitability but an option: Jews have had the choice to continue to reside in the lands of the diaspora or to settle in the State of Israel. It is in our own day, consequently, that the issue of diaspora appears in a new perspective with heightened importance for Jews both in Israel and around the world.

These are the crucial questions: What has living in exile meant for Jews? What demands has diaspora life made on Jewish loyalty and identity? With the opportunity to life in Israel readily available, can living in the diaspora be justified? Are there reasons other than the obvious pragmatic ones that compel Jews to remain in the diaspora? Or perhaps an exile mentality is somehow an integral part of Jewishness—in which case, are all Jews, no matter where they live, in some way in exile?

This collection combines in one volume an interdisciplinary spectrum of ideas and opinions concerning this basic Jewish condition. The range of contributors includes academic experts, rabbis, and communal and political leaders. Their diverse experiences and insights shed light on various aspects of diaspora as a deeply rooted Jewish reality.

✦ CONTRIBUTORS ✦

Jacob Agus is a distinguished American Jewish rabbi in Baltimore, Maryland, and a historian of the Jews.

Salo W. Baron is former professor of Jewish history at Columbia University and a leading 20th-century Jewish historian.

Bernard Berofsky is professor of philosophy at Columbia University and an editor of the *Journal of Philosophy*. His published books deal largely with free will and determinism.

Dorothea Braginsky chairs the psychology department at Fairfield University. Her several well-known works on social psychology include *Mainstream Psychology*.

Martin Buber, the late philosopher, served as professor of social philosophy at the Hebrew University.

Jack J. Cohen is Hillel Director at the Hebrew University of Jerusalem and a leading figure in Reconstructionist Judaism. His books include *Judaism Without Supernaturalism*.

William Freedman is professor of English literature at the University of Haifa and a political and social activist on the Israeli scene.

Lee Bennett Gaber is head of psychology at Rambam Hospital, Haifa.

Morris Grossman is professor of philosophy at Fairfield University and a trustee of the American Aesthetics Society.

Amnon Hadary is editor of the Zionist journal *Forum* and a frequent contributor to both Israeli and American publications.

Hillel Halkin is the author of *Letters to an American Friend* and the foremost translator of modern Hebrew works into English.

Joseph Heckelman is the rabbi of the Conservative Synagogue of Safed and author of *American Volunteers and Israel's War of Liberation*.

Daniel R. Hershberg is a community activist in Albany, New York, and a leading advocate of American Jewish day-school education.

Arthur Hertzberg is rabbi of Temple Emanuel, Englewood, New Jersey. He has held many American Jewish leadership offices.

Abram Kanof is clinical professor of medicine at the University of North Carolina, Chapel Hill. He is past president of The American Jewish Historical Society. His published books include *Jewish Ceremonial Art and Religious Observance.*

Abraham Kaplan is a social philosopher of international repute who teaches at the University of Haifa.

Mordecai M. Kaplan is the founder of the Jewish reconstructionist movement.

Isaiah Leibowitz is professor of biology at the Hebrew University and Israel's best-known critic of both the religious and secular establishments.

Étan Levine is professor of biblical studies at the University of Haifa.

Nehama Lyn is an American-born writer living in Israel.

Golda Meir, the late Israeli political leader, held many positions, including that of Prime Minister of the State of Israel.

Jacob Neusner is a professor of religious studies, and the Ungerleider Distinguished Scholar of Judaic Studies at Brown University.

Yitzhak Rabin has held many military and political posts, including those of Israeli Ambassador to the United States and Prime Minister of Israel.

Roy A. Rosenberg is rabbi of the Temple of Universal Judaism in New York City and the author of articles dealing with the biblical period.

B. Z. Sobel is professor of sociology and Director of the Overseas Students Program at the University of Haifa.

Eugene C. Wiener is professor of sociology at the University of Haifa.

A. B. Yehoshua is one of Israel's leading fiction writers. His recent book, *Between Right and Right,* includes an analysis of the diaspora.

Walter P. Zenner is a professor of anthropology at State University of New York at Albany and the author of studies of dispersed Jewish communities.

◆ GLOSSARY ◆

Abot (var. Avot): literally "Fathers"; a tractate of the Mishnah which contains aphoristic ethical material

Aggadah: folklore; non-legal traditional Judaica

Aliyah: literally "ascent"; migration to Israel

Ashkenazim (pl.): Jews of Central and Eastern European descent

Apikorus: skeptic; one who rejects the tenets of Jewish belief

Ba'al Shem Tov: literally "Master of the Good Name"; eighteenth-century founder of the Hasidic movement; often abbreviated "Besht"

Bet Midrash (pl. Batei Midrash): place for Jewish study

B'rachah: blessing

Chuz la'aretz: literally "outside the land"; anywhere but Israel

Ein breira: there is no alternative

Eretz Yisrael: the Land of Israel

Golah (var. Galut): exile

Gornisht (Yiddish): nothing

Goy (pl. Goyim, adj. goyishe): literally in Hebrew "nation"; in Yiddish "non-Jew"

Hadith (Arabic): Islamic traditions describing the life of Muhammad

Haftarah: a reading from the prophets

Halakhah (adj. halakhic): literally "the way"; Jewish law

All terms are Hebrew unless otherwise indicated.

Halutz (pl. halutzim): pioneer, particularly associated with the early days of Zionist settlement

Hapoel Hatzair: literally "the young worker"; a Zionist periodical

Hasid (pl. hasidim): literally "devotee"; follower of the Ba'al Shem Tov emphasizing mystical over rational and legal religious experience

Havurah: a religious fellowship

Hesed: loving-kindness

Kabbalah: the Jewish mystical tradition

Kaddish: literally "sanctification"; a prayer praising God recited in memory of the deceased

Kashrut: Jewish dietary laws

Kenesset Yisrael: the community of Israel

Kelippah: literally "husk"; in mystical terminology an impediment that obscures God's presence

Kibbutz: Israeli agricultural collective

Kibbutznik (pl. Kibbutznikim): Kibbutz resident

K'lal Yisrael: the Jewish people in its entirety

Knessiah: Judicial religious body

Law of Return: Israeli law that grants eligibility for Israeli citizenship to everyone of Jewish birth

Maqom: literally "place"; also an epithet for God

Mellah (Arabic): North African ghetto

Mezuzah: a parchment scroll inscribed with the first two paragraphs of the Shema and placed on the doorpost of the home

Midrash: literary tradition that expounds Biblical texts or a specific example of this genre

Mishneh Torah: a legal code compiled by Maimonides (1135-1204)

Mishpachah: family

Mitnagdim: opponents of the Hasidim

Mitzvah (pl. mitzvot): a commandment from the Bible or rabbinic tradition or a good deed

Na'aseh V'Nishmah: literally "we will do and we will hear"; statement of the Jewish people at Sinai, on accepting the Ten Commandments

Neturei Karta (Aramaic): literally "guardians of the city"; an anti-Zionist religious Jewish sect

Ninth of Ab: fast day commemorating the destruction of the First and Second Temples

Oleh: literally "ascender"; one who immigrates to Israel

Pale: area in Czarist Russia to which Jewish settlement was restricted

Pesach (Passover): spring festival commemorating the exodus from Egypt

Responsa: rabbinic responses to legal questions

Sabra: a native-born Israeli

Sanhedrin: supreme rabbinic council and tribunal during post-exilic times

Sefirot: devine emanations; a kabbalistic term

Sephardim: Jews of Iberian and North African descent

Shalom Aleichem: literally "peace be unto you"; a greeting

Shekhinah: the divine presence

Shelilat Ha Galut: literally "negation of the Diaspora"; the attitude which denigrates the value of life in the diaspora (as opposed to Israel)

Shema: literally "Hear!"; the liturgical affirmation of belief in one God

Shikse (Yiddish): a non-Jewish woman

Shofar: a ram's horn blown on Rosh Hashanah and other occasions

Shtetl (Yiddish): a predominantly Jewish village in Eastern Europe

Shul (Yiddish): synagogue

Talmud: the law and lore of the rabbis compiled during the first to fifth centuries C.E.

Tefutsot: Diaspora

Torah: Pentateuch, also the body of Jewish learning

Tzores (Yiddish): troubles

Yeridah: literally "descent"; emigration from Israel

Yeshivah (pl. Yeshivot): traditional academy of Jewish higher learning

Yishuv: the Jewish settlement in the Land of Israel before the establishment of the state in 1948

Yored (pl. Yordim): literally "descender"; one who emigrates from Israel

Zohar: a classic mystical text

The Jews in Time and Space

Étan Levine

It has often been observed that in all the annals of recorded history, there is no chapter more romantic, more inspiring, yet more complex and more inexplicable than the 2,000-year episode of the Jewish people in exile. A numerically insignificant nation is banished from its ancestral homeland on the eastern shore of the Mediterranean and is then scattered over the face of the earth. These exiles possess no military power, no political autonomy, no religious hierarchy, no economic organization, no central authority, no common language. They are recurrently traumatized by repression, expulsion, and even physical destruction. Even in normal times these people constitute virtually the only outgroup in homogeneous Christendom and the lands of Islam. They must contend with being religiously stigmatized, mythologized as the incarnation of evil, and labeled the perpetrators of deicide.

Adversity notwithstanding, this exiled people—or part of it—keeps its faith. Not only does it maintain its separate identity, but it actually flourishes; not only does it become a creatively evolving religious civilization, but it contributes to its host cultures, and to human civilization at large, to a degree far in excess of its own numbers. In countless ways this people is the embodiment of paradox, and perhaps it is precisely due to the fact that the Jewish condition defies facile description that, although individual authors have written about exile from the perspectives of religion, philosophy, or nationalism, at no time was an interdisciplinary anthology of the Exile assembled.

In addition to the obvious diversity of Jewish experience in exile—a diversity which must, perforce, be reflected in any anthology concerning the Exile—the most basic elements of Jewish self-definition are not quite as clear as they are generally assumed to be. Thus, for example, despite the fact that Judaism is one of the oldest religions, it is not simply a religion to which one subscribes; it is a religio-ethnic concept. One belongs to the Jewish people.

1

Thus, exile (*Galut*)—the fundamental reality of Jewish life—is itself not only a religious but also an ethnic concept. The very concept of exile implies that the Jewish polity was not dissolved when it was separated from its homeland. It is no wonder, therefore, that classical Hebrew contains no word for religion; the medieval term *dat* signifies law, not religion. The Jews saw themselves as members of a people, and not simply as adherents to a religion.

Furthermore, in the 20th Century, although Jews may be considered by others and may often consider themselves to be a religious group, this definition is simply inadequate. Many Jews are not religious in any significant sense, in that they do not use the God hypothesis to explain nature or history. Their most powerful feelings and their most compelling loyalties are ethnic. Jews are bonded by a shared sense of destiny—past, present, and future. They share folkways, kinship ties, and elements of tribalism to no less a degree than they share theology or religious norms. Thus, to impose a religious definition on the Jewish people is to be reductionist in the extreme.

Not only is the essence of Jewishness fraught with paradox, but the very concept of exile is itself complex. A careful reading of Jewish history reveals that, by and large, until the present day the Jewish people chose to live in the diaspora. It is not simply the case that Jews could not have emigrated to the Land of Israel had they wanted to. Relocating to their ancestral homeland would not have invariably constituted a worsening of their condition; the Holy Land would not have provided a more dangerous, more impoverished, more precarious area in which to live, any more than it would have been a more inhospitable climate or inferior landscape as compared to many of the locales in which Jews chose to live. Suffice it to say that despite the yearning of the Jews to be redeemed and to return to their ancestral home, a marked ambivalence toward the Holy Land lay deep in the collective unconscious.

In surveying the Jewish condition—the individual Jew and the Jewish people, from whatever perspective—one is almost overwhelmed by the complexity of the realities. One quickly senses that no univocal posture, no single perspective, no individual discipline can adequately illuminate the Jewish past, the Jewish present, or the Jewish future. It is no wonder, therefore, that those individuals who attempted to do so merely confirmed what should have been sensed *ab initio*, that is, that insights into the Jewish condition must be as varied intellectually, spiritually, and emotionally as is the Jewish people itself.

Homelessness and Its Consequences

The most widely known yet least understood aspect of Jewish civilization is the fact that, for almost twenty centuries, Jews shared a common calendar and not a common country. Jewishness was expressed by means of experiences in time, whether they be the personal rites of passage, the marking of significant historical events, or the expression of religious concepts. Jewish living was encapsulated in time, whether the annual reenactment of the Exodus at Pesach, or the annual mourning over the destruction of Jerusalem at Tisha b'Ab. The Jewish day, week, month, and year constituted the structure of Jewish life. In fact, as several modern thinkers have observed, an interesting distinction exists between the ancient Greeks and the Jews: whereas the Greeks created their artistry in space, the Jews lived and created almost exclusively in the dimension of time.[1] Thus, rather than concretize abstractions, symbolize values, memorialize history, or reinforce aspirations by spacial means—for example, architecture, sculpture, painting, or tapestry —the Jews created artistic moments, poignant hours, and evocative days.

TIME VERSUS SPACE

It is not surprising, therefore, that the Talmud begins with the question, "From what time may the evening *Shema* be recited?"[2] The appropriate *time*, not the appropriate *place* is of paramount concern. For the most uniquely Jewish achievement, dictated by necessity after the destruction of the Second Jewish Commonwealth in 70 C.E., was precisely that: transcending space, and carving out an almost independent spiritual life in the dimension of time—past, present, and future. For almost 2,000 years Judaism survived, and even flourished, not only without benefit of Jewish space in the form of a self-governing and self-determining country, but with the barest benefit of shrines, sacred preserves, religious architecture, art, or statuary.

Contrary to popular belief, this was not due to religious antipathy to physical artistry[3] any more than lack of national autonomy was a function of Jewish apathy toward political power. Rather, the historical reality was that Jews did not control the dimension of space: the Christians and Moslems did. The Jew inhabited space solely by the erratic grace of his host, and therefore, to build spiritual foundations in the dimension of space would be to build upon precarious, shifting sand.

Diaspora living involved a long, arduous, painful process through which the Jewish people withdrew from the control of space, and learned to forego the multifaceted physical, spiritual, esthetic, and ethical benefits offered by territory. Thus, for almost twenty centuries the Jew was largely a non-participatory observer of the fundamental mission of both Christianity and Islam: the acquisition and control of space. The Jew was not involved in creating a map, whether it be the *Dar es Salaam*[4] of the Moslem lexicon, or Christendom in that religion's geography. Rather, the Jewish mission evolved into the sanctification of time; the Jewish vocation became the creation of a spiritual calendar constructed of timeless moments, sacred events, and religious imperatives, these largely ordered by the cycles of time, the passing of seasons, and even the hours of each passing day. Thus, while the host culture was engaged in the control of space, the Jews devoted themselves to the spiritualization of time.[5]

SPACELESSNESS AND SURVIVAL

Polemical historiography notwithstanding, the Jewish people's spacelessness was not an unrelieved liability; in fact, it proved to be an unparalleled survival mechanism. The Jewish people survived in large measure not despite spacelessness but because of it. Dispersal rather than concentration protected the Jews from physical annihilation, and it was the abandonment of space as a spiritual category which protected the Jews from spiritual destruction. Thus, for example, when the Crusaders destroyed virtually every synagogue standing in the Rhine valley, intending to destroy the roots of European Judaism, the effect was minimal, for they were striking at the wrong target. Quite naturally, they had drawn the analogy from their Christian religion as to where the life center of Judaism was to be found. But this was a faith which could function independent of a special place, national home, religious preserve, or institution. It could flourish in the humblest home, the most exposed field, or the most distant land. Judaism (and only Judaism) had succeeded in transcending space, and in that sense, in becoming truly universal.

FREEDOM IN TIME

The ultimate frustration for the anti-Semite was the fact that, from the first Christian century onward, there was no place to strike, no space to conquer. The only means of striking at Judaism was through the medium of time; to prevent the observance of the Sabbath and festivals, to end the lamenting over Jerusalem, to prevent the marking of rites of passage, the consecration of marriage, the celebration of adulthood, the marking of the seasons, and the passage of days—in short, all those moments in time which together constituted Jewish life. And this could not be achieved short of destroying the Jew's timespan itself, that is, his life. As long as the Jew inhabited the domain of time, his Judaism was inviolate. In time the Jews were free to live, feel, express, and create to the limit of their potential.

It was the good fortune of the diaspora Jew to have had a biblical warrant for this transition. For a uniquely biblical concept was that of the linearity of time.[6] Unlike the other ancients who conceived of time as cyclical, repetitive, and consequently purposeless, following a pattern of circularity similar to the seasons and the heavenly bodies, the Hebrews envisioned history, beginning with the Creation, as linear, meaning purposeful. It was going somewhere, it was part of a divine plan. Human life, history, and time itself were endowed with a divine purpose; it was man's role to join and to participate. The debilitating reality of diaspora existence, however, meant that the Jew did not control space, and it was precisely through the medium of space that many of these ideals could be translated into realities.

JUDAISM AND SPACE

Spacelessness was not an original characteristic of Judaism, of course. In the biblical period, Jews were very much involved with, and concerned about, Jewish space. There was the Holy Land with its unique sanctity and access to God. This territory had its boundaries, its unique institutions, and its special laws. The temple mount was endowed with even greater sanctity, and its inner space converged upon the Holy of Holies within. Even post-biblical Jewish law recognized the fundamental distinction between *terra sancta* and the lands of the Gentiles. The sanctity of space was so firmly a part of biblical religion that centuries after the ancient Hebrews transcended the territorial circumscription of God, the epithet *HaMaqom* (The Place) remained, as it continues to remain, a standard Jewish circumlocution for the name of God.[7]

One distorts diaspora theology beyond recognition if one does not include its spacial dimension, its nostalgia for the Land of Israel of antiquity, its geocentric conception of Jerusalem manifest by the thrice daily direction of prayer toward that center, and its formulation of redemption as the ultimate physical enshrinement and reconstruction of the people of Israel in the Land of Israel.

JEWS ALWAYS OCCUPIED THE LAND OF ISRAEL

On a demographic level, it is simply not true that all Jews were banished from their land in the first Christian century, not to return until the advent of political Zionism in the 19th Century. This myth was created by Christian theologians who interpreted the diaspora as divine retribution to the Jews for their not having accepted Jesus as the Messiah. This pernicious myth which flies in the face of all archeological and textual evidence has recently been revived by Arab polemicists to support their depiction of the Jews as usurpers who forfeited their rights to the land by virtue of a 2,000-year absence. The fact is that Jewish settlement throughout the Land of Israel changes his place changes his fortune"; rather, it was complete change of

The fact is, therefore, that as an ideal, the Jew never renounced the category of space completely. Just as the traditional prayer book is replete with references to the Holy Land, so did Jewish communities, both in Israel and in the diaspora, endow particular places with sanctity: shrines, houses of worship, and cemeteries. Of course, here too, the reason for the sanctity is not the space *per se*, but rather the events in time which once occurred there, or which would, through divine grace, occur there in the future.[8] Suffice it to say, therefore, that a proto-Zionism, or an appreciation of the role of Jewish space, was a fundamental component of diaspora Judaism through the ages. And this despite the fact that the Jewish people lived outside of space, and that space was a conceptual category, limited to a sacred history of the distant past and future.

THE REEMERGENCE OF SPACE

The reemergence of space as a primary category of the Jewish psyche of the 20th Century constitutes the greatest, most radical shift in Jewish history since the Hellenistic period. This fundamental challenge to the very underpinnings of diaspora Judaism emerged from both philosophical and historical cataclysms, and it currently constitutes the major issue which Jewish thinkers and thinking Jews must confront.

The philosophical basis for the emergence of a consciousness of Jewish space is deeper than the nationalistic ideologies and movements of 19th Century Europe, as is often claimed. Zionism emerged not simply as a Jewish equivalent of, or alternative to, exclusivistic ethnocentric politicization of Europe; rather, the Zionists as well as the other Jewish territorialists espousing Jewish political autonomy in Russia, Argentina, Uganda, or even Grand Island were all responding to a pervasive claim of modern Western thought. Technological civilization concerns itself with man's control of space, for things exist in space, and the assumption of Western man is that objective reality is physical: that anything nonmaterial can be reduced to material phenomena and explained in exclusively physical terms. By this definition, whoever refuses to equate the real with the physical may be dismissed as a mystic. Obviously, then, since only the quantitative aspects of physical phenomena refer to the real world, the religious experiences of diaspora Judaism are illusory, without objective counterpart. Living in time, rather than space, Judaism had no object of physical experience, and therefore its existence was both meaningless and powerless. In brief, Zionists, as well as Jewish institutional leaders of other persuasions, equated space with power, and confused the control of space with the control of destiny.

The Jewish experience of the 20th Century lent powerful credence to this concept. Recurrent traumas produced mass migrations to the United States, to Israel, and elsewhere where space was more controllable. The problems of place replaced the problems of time in the hierarchy of Jewish concerns. It was not merely acting on the Talmudic adage (Ta'anit 24b), "He who changes his place changes his fortune"; rather, it was complete change of emphasis—whether involving the State of Israel, the United States, or other countries, whether through the synagogue, the community center, the retreat or summer camp—the Jewish people, in a neobiblical leap, translated its spiritual arena from the realm of time to the realm of space.

SPACE AND ETHICS

The Jewish reemergence into space is proving more difficult than anticipated, and one can ascertain this most clearly in the realm of ethics. For almost 20 centuries, the spacelessness of the Jewish people absolved it of most moral responsibility. The Jews were powerless, and they could negotiate with the sources of power only by a moral plea. Now it is well and proper to castigate the armies of other nations if one is pacifistic, to abhor police brutality if one has no law-enforcement agencies of one's own, and to criticize the foreign and domestic policies of the nations of the world if one has no space under one's own control; and criticism, by and large, was the primary mode of the Jewish contribution to Western morality. But this is all a thing of the past. The Jewish people, through that segment of it which has reconstituted itself in the State of Israel, now controls a space, and has an army, police, a judiciary, a penal system, and the entire gamut of spatial concerns both inside Israel's borders and abroad. Therefore, Israel's behavior, ethics, policies, and values can and must be compared to those of other nations, as well as to those which the Jews espoused when they were powerless.

The Jewish people now controls a national space, and is now, for the first time in many centuries, ethically responsible for delivering all of those ethical, political, judicial, and societal goods, to minorities, to the disenfranchised, and to the helpless that it espoused and yearned for when it was banished from a homeland. In sum, the Jews now have a greater ethical function and challenge than simple moralizing.

THE ISRAEL DILEMMA. The Zionist movement and the creation of a Jewish state, in creating Jewish space on a national level, have also created a dilemma: now the existential Jewish question is not only how to sanctify a moment in time, but how to sanctify a point in space as well. By way of illustration one may consider Jerusalem. As a concept in time—an entity of sacred history in the distant past and the anticipated future—Jerusalem pervaded Jewish thought and feeling. It was a symbol of heavenly felicity, divine sanctity, human justice, and religious faith in redemption. But unlike the Jerusalem of time, today's Jerusalem of space requires garbage disposal among other, less lofty, concerns. And if today's Judaism which has embraced spatial Jerusalem has nothing compelling to say regarding garbage disposal, organized crime, grinding poverty, social injustice, exploitation of minorities, rampant consumerism, etcetera, then it has nothing to say to the actual Jewish condition. Like the Jerusalem of biblical antiquity from time to time, today's Jerusalem is literally staggering under the burdens of existence. And like the religious establishment against which the prophets railed, today's Judaism in Israel is speaking in an irrelevant idiom. Contemporary religious leaders continue to think along the anachronistic lines of Jewish time—to the virtual exclusion of Jewish space.

INVESTING SPACE WITH SANCTITY. The transition from living in time to living in space is proving to be unanticipatedly difficult, on many levels, precisely because of its radical nature. Every identifying Jew has a fairly clear (albeit perhaps *sui generis*) idea of what to do with Jewish time; but what should be done with Jewish space? The question itself has an alien ring. Thus, for example, the Orthodox mentality was traditionally attuned to expressing Judaism through a plethora of *mitzvot*, or religious imperatives. But deeds exist in time, with only tangential reference to place. The liberal mentality sought the religious experience; here, too, what is experienced by the soul is a moment of insight, rather than a place, where the event transpired. Yet at this point in its history, the Jewish people is faced by the unavoidable need to invest not only time but also space, with sanctity, ethics, esthetics, and ultimate significance.

Without belaboring the issue, one can merely cite an example: how does Judaism relate to the Jewish space of Israel? It is not enough to decry, as even some Israeli religionists have, the Wailing Wall cultism that has emerged: the spiritually un-Jewish shrine attachment, the crassness and the squalor attached to this holy place. Rather, one must ask how can the Jewish tradition engage in constructive dialogue with Israeli architecture and urban planning? How does Jewishness relate to such spacial aspects as pollution, fragmentation, compartmentalization, and the spiritual diminution of man in Israeli cities? Can Judaism say nothing more to urban transit than the adage, posted in Israeli buses, "Rise before the aged"? Israel as a spatial reality consists of hospitals, prisons, army camps, kindergartens, universities, ball fields, factories, hotels, and restaurants, as well as homes. In general terms, these quite properly follow patterns similar to those found among all nations of the world. But where is the voice of Jacob guiding the hands of Esau? Where is the Jewish dimension of this Jewish space?

THE DIASPORA DILEMMA. Jewish space today is not limited to Israel; it involves specific loci in the diaspora as well. If one is to lend credence to the analytical observers of the scene, Jewish civilization is hanging by a thread. At this point in time, the largest American Jewish denomination is not the Orthodox, the Conservative, the Reform, or the Reconstructionist; rather it is the unaffiliated. If we speculate as to the future, the process of assimilation, disaffection, and trivialization will continue, for the young have discovered the cruelest of truths: that the most effective way of punishing their parents is by imitating them. It is, quite simply, the acceleration of an inherited process.

To reverse this trend will require addressing both the dimension of time and of space, for it is precisely through Jewish space—through such various Jewish institutions as synagogues, community centers, summer camps, old-age homes, and so on—that Jewish involvement is expressed. The acquisition, structuring, financing, maintaining, and enhancing of Jewish space is what keeps Jews busy. And we must now ask how much of these is truly

Jewish space.[9] I do not mean to simply compare the aura of the synagogue to that of a cathedral or church, but rather to compare the synagogue's space to the way in which a hospital is medical space, a library is reading space, and a playground is recreational space. To be is to stand for, and each of these spaces is faithful to a certain idea, plan, purpose, and value system. It is embarrassing, yet essential, to pose the obvious query: what commitments, passions, values, and ideas characterize Jewish institutional space? In what way does it serve to address the existential posture of the Jew and his need to ascertain who he is and what he should endeavor to become: if time is a measure of change, and if life is the process of becoming, how does Jewish space in its various forms relate to Jewish time?[10]

On the most intimate level, of course, Jewish space involves the home, and modern Jews invest unprecedented expense and emotion into their private living space. However gratuitous it may be to ask, I ask: other than the mandatory Chagall print and Epstein copy flanking the grandparents' candelabrum, how much Jewishness informs this space? The question is whether the door, with or without benefit of *mezuzah*, opens on Jewish space in any meaningful, significant sense. Does it frame, through Jewish books, art, traditions, practices, and norms, an authentic Jewish character? Will it evoke the nostalgia and commitments which characterized the much humbler Jewish spaces of yesterday? In most cases, the answer is painfully obvious; the affluent split-level home bears few traces of the tents of Jacob. The Jewish home has conquered space by the prevailing technological, functional, and perhaps esthetic standards, but in so doing it has sacrificed its soul.

RECONSTRUCTING JEWISH SPACE

The central, critical challenge now facing the Jewish people is the need to reconstruct Jewish space. This will require fundamental shifts in Jewish thought, for it is not enough to have space; one must control, mold, and sanctify that space. A religion which embraces space as well as time cannot be a religion of mere inwardness, for space involves the use and abuse of power, and this necessitates the adoption of a reconstructionist concept of ethical peoplehood, whether as a minority in a culturally pluralistic society or as a majority in a Jewish state.[11]

Perhaps conceptual thinking was adequate for people living exclusively in time, but living in space requires situational thinking that has as its object not simply mental constructs, but the actual situation of man. A relevant Judaism will perforce be tentative and evolving. It will proceed from the realization that we are involved in a new situation which requires understanding and action. A Judaism creatively interacting with both time and space will unite a tolerance based on its own relativity with a commitment based on the magnitude of its concern. Now that the Jewish people has emerged into space, in many respects today's Jew is a person in search of a soul. For better or for worse the Jewish people has reemerged into the dimension of space; for nearly twenty centuries Jews have survived space-lessness; they must now learn to survive space.

Notes

1. See A. J. Heschel, *The Sabbath*. New York: Farrar, Straus, and Young, 1951, *3 et seq*. For balance, cf. Ira Eisenstein, What it means to be a Jew today. In *Varieties of Jewish Belief*. New York: Reconstructionist Press, 1966, pp. 63–71.

2. Babylonian Talmud, *Berakhot* I:1. Note the answer which itself refers to time, i.e., an event encapsulated in sacred history: the temple cult.

3. Witness the archeological finds dating from the first Christian centuries and onward (e.g., Bet Alpha and Dura Europos synagogues) containing physical, and even human representations. Cf. Hershel Shanks, *Judaism in Stone: The Archeology of Ancient Synagogues*. New York: Biblical Archeology Society 1979, pass.

4. The Arabic term is best translated as "the pacified abode," i.e., the conquered region, rather than as "the peaceful abode." This area is contrasted with the *Dar el Harb*, i.e., the rest of the world, where the sword of Islam must yet be wielded.

5. Note the category of religious imperatives time-linked (*mitzvot shehaze-man geraman* in Hebrew).

6. This to the exclusion of Ecclesiastes, of course. See Étan Levine, *The Aramaic Version of Qohelet*. New York: Sepher Hermon Press, 1978, and Robert Gordis, *Koheleth, The Man and His World*. New York: Bloch Publishing Co. 1955.

7. It is also true that in the Hellenistic period the epithet "Eternal" is applied to God (*Ribbon 'Olam, Ribbon Ha'olamim, Mar'Alma*, etcetera). Cf. W. Bousset, *Die Religion des Judentums*. Berlin: Reuter and Reichard, 1906.

8. Interestingly, the biblical term for cemetery is "Eternal Home" (in Hebrew *Bet'Olam*) in Qoh. XII, 5. In fact, even the Jewish people is given the epithet "Eternal People" (*'Am 'Olam*) in Is. 44:7. Ezek. 36:20, etcetera.

9. Parenthetically, one may consider contemporary Jewish art. To my mind, there is nothing shameful in Jewish tradition not having created a fine repository of architecture, statuary, or art. The Jewish contribution to civilization need not be all-embracing! But now, as part of the spatial emphasis, Jewish art has inundated homes and institutions in Israel and in the diaspora; these generally fail the minimal criteria of what constitutes Jewish and what constitutes art!

10. The question was powerfully put by Mordecai M. Kaplan, *The Meaning of God in Modern Jewish Religion*. New York: Reconstructionist Press, 1962. A partial response is provided by Eli Ginzberg, *Agenda for American Jews*. New York: Reconstructionist Press, 1964.

11. For a schematic analysis of the theoretical benefits and limitations of the State of Israel, cf. Étan Levine, Toward a logic of *aliyah* discourse, *Reconstructionist* XXXIV 14, 1968, pp. 1–6.

·I·
The Origins of Exile

·1·
Exile as a
Neurotic Solution

A. B. Yehoshua

The Jews and the Golah

The demographic balance of the past year shows that in the State of Israel there are 3,300,000 Jews and 570,000 Arabs. The population growth among the Arabs is astounding (when the State was established the Arabs numbered only 120,000). They increased fivefold in 30 years, without immigration, in spite of a small but steady emigration of intellectuals and others. The natural growth of the Jews last year was about 50,000. There were also 21,000 new immigrants, and 17,000 people left the country. Thus the Jewish population increase through *aliyah*, was a net of 4,000. This is our demographic condition, at a time of peace talks, when the government wishes to incorporate an additional 1,250,000 Arabs from the West Bank and Gaza Strip, and when the refusal of the Jewish people to come and settle in Israel is becoming more adamant. One ought to publish these figures as part of a chart, noting the proportion of the world's Jews living in Israel and abroad. In fact, it would be worthwhile to make a slide of such a chart, screening it from time to time on television, before or after the news, or as a backdrop for rabbis, with or without army rank, politicians, professors steeped in the sources, or impassioned authors making their routinely inflammatory speeches about "the eternal, deep, and wondrous bonds which tie the Jewish people to the Land of Israel."

I begin with these few concrete facts because people shy away from abstract questions irrelevant to their immediate situation. Yet, the question of the *golah* lies at the root of a great many practical questions. The *golah* and our attitude to it constitutes the most Jewish of questions because it clearly and reliably defines the essence of the Jew. When people talk about Jewish values, I do not know what they mean. When pressed they usually

15

say: to have Jewish values means to love the Land of Israel and the Jewish people. This is like saying, to have Danish values means to love Denmark and the Danish people. But when I talk about the *golah* I know that I am talking about something totally Jewish, something specifically Jewish. I am touching on the heart of the problem.

In the past 15 years, discussion of questions about the *golah* has been of a descriptive character. The central problems were how to enhance the affinity between Israel and the *golah*, what was the situation with regard to assimilation there, and so forth. But the primary issue that has always been at the root of the intramural struggle of Zionism among the people is still why have a diaspora at all? It is as though people are now ashamed to ask this question.

There are two attitudes toward the *golah*. One regards the *golah* as a kind of accident that befell the Jewish people, a tragedy wrought upon the Jews by the nations of the world. According to this view the *golah*, although it has lasted for a long time, is essentially transient, and the nation yearns for redemption. It simply awaits more favorable conditions that will enable its return. All roads lead either to Israel or to assimilation. When peace comes, and with it some respite, then the *golah* will gradually disintegrate and the nation will stream to Israel. This conception ignores the basic fact that the dispersion was not forced upon us; it was, rather, something we forced upon ourselves. It should not be viewed as an accident or a tragedy, but rather as a distortion—a basic deviant trait in our national makeup—and that is why any solution must be different from what is commonly imagined.

The other attitude views the *golah* as a permanent, almost natural state. If one accepts this view, it is remarkable that other nations do not also maintain diasporas worthy of the name, scattered throughout many countries. People with this attitude sense the depth of Jewish people's need for the *golah*, how closely woven the *golah* is to the essence of the Jew, and they try to see exile as a legitimate and normal state. As a consequence of this attitude the question sometimes arises: why bother to have a state? And even when the necessity for an independent national center is not rejected, there is a duality in which the *golah* and the center are seen as equal in value. This framework of ideas ignores the simple fact that the *golah* was the source of the most terrible disasters to befall the Jewish people; that because of the *golah* the nation was almost completely wiped out in our generation; that in spite of the existence of the State of Israel, the *golah* constitutes a threat to a large community of Jews in the Soviet Union and is likely to pose a grave threat to the Jews of South America; and that the *golah* is the root cause for that infamous Jewish fate which is a given in any discussion on Jewish questions. I shall try to synthesize these concepts. To that end I shall divide my remarks into three parts.

Historical Facts

I shall begin by noting some simple and well-known historical facts, the juxtaposition of which are intriguing and sometimes even astounding (Gen. 12:1 et seq.). Abraham, the founder of the nation, was born outside *Eretz Yisrael*. He left his native land and went to Israel as the most distinguished of new immigrants, and it was he who received the promise which bound the land and the nation together. It transpires that the first new *oleh* was also the first *yored* (emigrant from Israel) for as soon as economic conditions in the land began to deteriorate, Abraham went down to Egypt. It is strange to think that this man, who gave up so much in leaving his father's house, having finally reached the Promised Land, could leave it so easily and choose to go into exile.

Jacob died in exile. He followed his sons to Egypt, although he did ask to be reburied in *Eretz Yisrael*. Could it be that herein lies the hidden purpose of the land—to be a burial ground for Jewish bones? Or is it also the land of the living? Abraham and Jacob were founding fathers, and they brought forth a new nation. Yet the attitude of these patriarchs, which ought to have served as an example to the generations to come, was already ambivalent. The nation was created in the *golah*. Have we grasped the full significance of this? The Jewish people was neither created nor born in its land. Thus, the elementary association between nation and land is not natural for the Jews.

Then came the 40 years of wandering in the desert. Where was the law given to us if not in the wilderness? This is another fact of which the implications are not always fully understood. The Law—the system of values which were to define our identity and establish our goal—was not given to us in the Land of Israel. That special bond forged between the people and God was not established in the Land of Israel, but in the desert, in that no-man's land between the *golah* and *Eretz Yisrael*. We shall see how throughout its history the Jewish people seeks that no-man's land time and again, especially when it seeks spiritual renewal.

In the desert we are both alive and dead. The wilderness is a place of death, and in this place of death the new nation was born. The wilderness is also a sterile, untouched, pure place. It is there that the people prepares itself before entering the land. But there is always a fear of *aliyah*, for this act of *aliyah* is highly significant. It is not simply conquest of any country by a nomadic people, but a conquest with a spiritual significance.

The promise of the land to the people is accompanied by stringent conditions. Force alone will not ensure continued possession of the land. The people will remain in possession of their land only if they heed the word of the Lord, and obey His commandments. If they do not, they will suffer grave penalties, of which the most severe will be expulsion and exile.

In the earliest of the scriptures, this basic principle is laid down: the people takes precedence over the land in every sense. Remaining in the land and retaining possession of it is conditional, but there are no conditions attached to the survival of the people as people. The people can commit the most terrible sins, but its continued existence is never in question. It may be punished, but never exterminated. It is true that the *golah* will emerge, but that is not the end of the matter; it is possible to survive there, and it is possible to return.

The books of Numbers and Deuteronomy are worth reading. The people had not yet realized its independence for a single moment. It had not yet set foot in the Promised Land. Yet it is already being told about exile and the return therefrom. There are already clear signs that it is possible for the nation to exist without *Eretz Yisrael*, without a country.

All the important national-religious festivals that we celebrate—Sukkot, Pesach, Shavuot (as distinct from the purely religious holidays such as Rosh Hashana and Yom Kippur)—are concerned with the experiences of the people in the wilderness rather than in the Land of Israel. The people arrives, conquers the land, and establishes its kingdom. After some time the kingdom is split in two. Hundreds of years pass, the Kingdom of Israel is destroyed, and its ten tribes are exiled and vanish. That part of the nation which apparently always behaved in a more natural and normal fashion than the more Jewish part in Judea, also behaved normally when it was exiled. It lost its identity and nationality. It behaved as other nations do.

When the kingdom of Judah was destroyed and the people went into exile in Babylon, it survived. It preserved its identity and behaved according to the precepts laid down in the book of Deuteronomy. It proved that the people comes before the land and that it possesses a formula for survival as a nation without a country. It demonstrated the tenacity and power of the spirit and the imagination. Following the decree of Emperor Cyrus in 537 B.C.E. (Ezra I, iff. and Nehemiah I, iff.), part of the people came home to build the Second Commonwealth and gradually reestablished its independence. Part of the nation did not return, preferring to remain of its own volition in the first *golah*. That part of the people that did not return belonged to the upper strata, dignitaries who maintained their Jewish affinity. Nevertheless, they did not join those returning home, preferring to remain in exile. Perhaps it was convenient for them that part of the nation was returning and setting up a national home which could serve as a haven for them in time of need. Or perhaps they already perceived the possibility that the national center might be destroyed again. If that were to be the case, they may have felt that it would perhaps be better to keep the land as a dream, a hope, and a mission rather than to see it once more as a disappointing reality.

On the eve of the destruction of the Second Temple, one-third of the people was already abroad. They left of their own choice and settled in various parts of the Roman Empire, and outside it. This *golah* had a deep affinity for the Land of Israel, supported it financially and politically, and, to a degree, even encouraged a rebellion against the Romans. This insane and hopeless uprising, which had not the slightest chance of success and brought nothing but disaster (the sack of Jerusalem accompanied by the most fearful slaughter), this pointless and unnecessary rebellion was actually encouraged to a certain extent by the Jews of the *golah*. These Jews living in a totally non-Jewish ambience, surrounded by idolatry and abominations, in the midst of defilement itself, who voluntarily gave up any vestige of Jewish national life, actually encouraged the extremists and the zealots in Jerusalem to demand full political independence—something that not one people in the Roman Empire had been granted.

Rabban Yohanan Ben-Zakkai's departure from Jerusalem on the eve of the destruction—to establish the School of Yavneh—was already informed with the perception that the Jews would have to give up their country. His purpose was to create an alternative Jewish way of life for the *golah*, and to prepare the people for survival there. Ben-Zakkai was carried out of the city in a coffin, in the guise of a corpse; this legend is vividly symbolic of Jewish life in the *golah*. The Jewish people must disguise itself—this is the key to understanding the diaspora. Whoever assumes the guise of a corpse remains very much alive in his inner being, for he has to devise the most sophisticated means of looking like a dead man. The new doctrine which was created was, in effect, a return to a Sinaitic situation. That is to say, the people that had twice been found wanting had to prepare once again for the test. This time, however, it would be a serious preparation, perhaps even an infinite, eternal preparation, for the test had also become most serious—complete redemption, the culmination of history, the end of days. After such a test, a man has no more need of anything.

Thus began two thousand years of exile, and I do not think I err if I claim that in 1,800 years—from the destruction of the Second Temple until the birth of Zionism—the Jewish people did not make one serious or significant effort to return to *Eretz Yisrael* and restore its lost independence. This people, with the resourcefulness, flexibility, and cunning to reach almost every point on the face of the earth—from the Atlas Mountains to the Indian Desert, from Tierra del Fuego to the Siberian steppes—did not make one real effort to come back and settle in *Eretz Yisrael*. Further, the Jews settled in masses in every country around the Mediterranean basin, except *Eretz Yisrael*. In their wanderings the Jews circled around and about the Land, drawn to it yet fearing it. It is depressing to hear ideologues telling us with pride how many Jews there were in *Eretz Yisrael* throughout the generations, or to hear tribute paid to the one family of Peki'in (who reputedly never left the country at all, remaining in the land since the destruction of the Second Temple), and to hear praise of every rabbi who made *aliyah* with his flock of disciples. Had the Jews become as attached to *Eretz Yisrael* as they became to Poland, for example, or Babylon, or had the Jews fought for their right to live in *Eretz Yisrael* as they fought for that right in an England from which they were, in any case, later expelled this need to prove that Jews did live in *Eretz Yisrael* or to recount the story of Rabbi Yehuda Halevi being smitten with such yearning that he went to Israel in spite of everything, would not be necessary. It is true that Jews were sometimes forbidden to come and live in Israel, and that there were many harsh edicts. But in what country was the habitation of Jews not subjected to constraints, expulsions, and prohibitions? And just as the Jews succeeded in finding loopholes in the barriers erected against them in so many countries, they could have done the same in *Eretz Yisrael*, in which the regime changed hands no less than six times after the destruction.

ZIONISM

Zionism was born at the end of the last century, not out of a new yearning for *Eretz Yisrael*, nor out of a sudden hatred of the *golah*, but from fear of the *golah*. It suddenly became clear just how dangerous and terrible the *golah* could be. Zionism was a movement with only a few isolated adherents, and they were violently opposed by the Orthodox, the Socialist *Bund*, and the assimilationists. The mass of the people did not believe in Zionism and did not want it. When the Balfour Declaration was issued in 1917, and a powerful nation like Great Britain gave its blessing to the possibility of establishing a Jewish state in *Eretz Yisrael*, the Jews *still* did not come to Israel en masse. No sharp-witted sophistry can evade this decisive fact, the consequences of which have been so disastrous. We could have established a Jewish state in *Eretz Yisrael* in the 1920s. While hundreds of thousands of Jews were emigrating from Eastern Europe to the West in the years from 1917 to 1921, only 30,000 Jews came to Israel, and this was *after* the Balfour Declaration. At that time the Jewish people numbered 15 million. Had but one-tenth of them come to Israel, we could have established a Jewish state before the Holocaust. One-and-a-half-million Jews living in *Eretz Yisrael* at that time would have established that state as a decisive fact in a Middle East which was then only awakening from its long slumber. And if we had had a state before the Second World War, the Holocaust would never have attained such appalling proportions. Thus, indirectly, the Jewish people itself was responsible for its own terrible fate in this century.

However, if anyone needs final and absolute proof of the dubious attitude of the Jewish people toward *Eretz Yisrael*, of the fact that it made no serious attempt to return to the land, of its fear of the return to the land, of its attachment to the *golah*, he has only to look to the first 30 years of the existence of the Jewish state. The gates are open, the possibilities are many, but the immigrants do not come. Most of the waves of immigration consisted of people fleeing persecution in the *golah*: survivors of the Holocaust, Jews from Arab countries, refugees from the Communist countries. Only a small minority came here of its own free will, and this minority is dwindling still further.

Ambivalence toward Israel and the Golah

What are the common denominators that deter Jews of such varying social background from going to Israel? These must be the same common factors which deterred Jews from coming for hundreds of years. Russian Jews who risk their lives to get out of the Soviet Union would rather live in a German city, on charity from a Jewish or even a Christian organization, than come to Israel, which offers them better conditions if only from an economic point of view. The Jews of Lebanon prefer to live a hundred yards from the headquarters of the Popular Front for the Liberation of Palestine, close to the centers of anti-Israel hatred and propaganda, beside the vipers' lair, in a city marked by hostility and strife and subject to attacks by the Israel Air Force— all this rather than come to Israel. The Jews of Argentina prefer life in a fascist country whose economy is crumbling, where anti-Semitism is on the upsurge, rather than come to Israel. And now Iran.

There are endless examples: the Jews of Syria up until 1967; the Jews of Morocco and Algeria. Each community ostensibly had its own explanation for not coming to Israel. Some cite economic grounds, some the security situation in Israel. Others say it is hard for them to leave the country in which they were born. Some give reasons of a religious nature. But it is precisely because the reasons given for staying are so varied and sometimes contradictory, and because of the fact that the face of Israel and her attractions have altered so radically in the past 30 years (from a cooperative pioneering society to a capitalist state, from a state with a secular character to one with a national–religious emphasis) that an underlying, basic reason must be found for this determination: to remain in the *golah*. It is inconceivable that such a variety of deterrents could so consistently produce the same result.

I sometimes stand amazed at those who try to explain the Jews remaining in the *golah* on economic grounds, as if the most important thing to the Jews were the fleshpots, as though Marx were right when he said Mammon is the god of the Jews.[1] This argument, sometimes adopted by serious people, is not only insulting in that it accepts the basest anti-Semitic theories; it is also fundamentally invalid. This concept presents the Jews throughout history as rich merchants.

Others would have the reasons for the lack of emigration to Israel as being fear of the security situation. But this theory, too, explains the excuse rather than the essence. One has only to see how Jews flock to Israel when it is threatened, and the way that Jewish students fight to get on planes to take them straight to war, to realize that this theory is not true either. And, of course, there are Jewish communities that live in far greater physical danger than does Israel.

Faced with the diversity of phenomena of 2,500 years of *golah* and with many Jewish communities so different from each other, one cannot settle for explanations valid for a particular time or place. One must seek the underlying causes. Such a common denominator is called for because of the decisive fact that in all its prayers and other spiritual expressions, the Jewish people rejected permanent existence in the *golah*. Normative Judaism never legitimized the *golah*. On the contrary, the diaspora was always regarded as a national disaster, a temporary situation, a *fall*, and the root of all evil. Even the *Shekhinah*—the Divine Presence—was considered to be in exile. The world, it was felt, would not be right until the *golah* disappeared. That is to say (and I put this briefly and in general terms in order to get to the essence), hatred and total rejection of the *golah* situation is coupled with an intense compulsion to preserve it and live in it. The few attempts to legitimize the diaspora failed. For example, in the 19th Century, reform Jewry in the United States attempted to build a legitimate system of diaspora existence and to place the link with *Eretz Yisrael* in the same light as the religious ties of the Catholics with the Vatican. Reform Jews changed their minds after the Second World War, and today they can, without hesitation, be described as part of the Zionist movement.

When such a fundamental and difficult question as this ambivalence is examined, what emerges is behavior of a palpably neurotic nature. (I am using a clinical term to describe collective behavior, *façon de parler*, for lack of appropriate terms to describe collective neuroses and pathologies.) The nation hates the *golah* and dreams of *Eretz Yisrael*. At all levels of its authentic spiritual activity, the nation rejects the *golah*; on the other hand, throughout its historical activity it has been preoccupied with the one problem of how to survive in the *golah*, how to go on maintaining that hated existence.

Suppose, for example, that we had an unmarried friend who hated and suffered from his unmarried status, proclaimed that he believed in family life, and avidly sought it; this man wanted children as a continuance of himself. Suppose that despite this he spoiled—almost intentionally—all possibilities of marriage, that everytime we arranged a union between him and any woman, he did everything to get out of it, not because he did not like the woman or was incapable of love, but out of fear of marriage, in which he so fervently believed. Would it not be our duty to this friend to try to find out, by therapeutic or other means, the underlying motives for his profound neurotic conflict? The Jewish people are in need of just such therapy; and the first step in any course of treatment is diagnosis—in this case insight.

Thus the basic question is, why? What is the reason for this neurotic, painful, and compulsive choice of the *golah*? Why does the entire people fear sovereign, normal life in *Eretz Yisrael?* That, in my view, is the ultimate question for the Jewish people, and it is appropriate that we devote all our intellectual and spiritual powers to its clarification. In this framework, I shall try to postulate two answers, albeit speculative, as working hypotheses.

The Golah
THE SOLUTION TO THE CONFLICT
OF RELIGION AND NATIONALITY

The Jewish people is a most interesting and original compound of nationality and religious groups, of a natural system (family, tribe, people) with a value system. The national system is very open and flexible. The very ancient definition of a Jew as one born of a Jewish mother stretches the limits of nationality very far indeed. The fact that the Jew belongs to the people does not by definition obligate him—and this is very important—to inhabit a particular territory, to speak a particular language, or to adopt particular cultural and spiritual values. His biological attachment in itself is sufficient to identify him as a Jew. On the other hand, the value system is clear, well-defined, and distinguished by thousands of precise details. At one time, of course, the two systems were bound up with each other, but not to such a degree that it was impossible to perceive the two distinct elements that made up the identity and way of life of the people.

It was precisely because the religious identity was so specific that the national identity could be so blurred. For example, because the distinctive qualities of Yom Kippur are common to all Jews, those observing it could be far from each other, scattered, speaking different languages, living in different landscapes and in varying community situations. The religious basis made it possible to have a very indistinct national existence. Nationality, however, limited the religion. That means that the religious message and content did not hold good for the entire world, but only for the Jewish people, which was defined by a national criterion (born of a Jewish mother) and not a religious criterion. In other words, Judaism as a religion endows the identity of the Jew with legitimacy, even if he does not maintain any connection with it. The religion provides legitimacy for even the most tenuous identity. The Jew can be a complete assimilationist (even an apostate), lacking any connection with the Jewish people from a national point of view. Yet the religious system will still identify him as a Jew with a religious potential, or, in other words, as a permanent candidate for repentance. Were the Jewish people to identify itself exclusively as a national entity, it would never be able to live with such a loose definition.

Between the national and religious systems there exists a constant tension, arising out of the permanent contradiction between their aims. On the one hand, there is a normal national system functioning in accordance with the basic needs of national existence in a territory, and, on the other hand, there is the religious system, which sets spiritual goals for the people and tries to subordinate the people's existence to religious and spiritual demands.

As we examine our history, we shall see how the contradiction between these two systems gives constant rise to bitter conflicts—for example, the conflict between Moses and the people in the wilderness, the conflicts between priest and king, and the conflicts between prophet and king. At first Samuel refused to anoint a king over Israel, seeing it as a betrayal of himself (I Sam. 8:4ff.). Like him, the prophets in their sermons were constantly chastising kings, for they were incapable of accepting the fact of monarchy as a natural, national dynamic. They saw it as a tragedy, as a betrayal and a disavowal of the mission of the commonwealth of priests, of a holy people. One could say that there has been conflict in all nations between the spiritual and the temporal powers, and that this was not uniquely Jewish. This is true. However, with the Jewish people the phenomenon assumed a particularly grave aspect because the theater of conflict was confined to the Jewish people alone. The other great monotheistic religions broke out of national confines, finding other outlets for the energies fueling the conflict. Unable to force themselves on national regimes, these religions set out to spread their message among other peoples. The victory of the state over the church at the close of the Middle Ages led the Christian church to embark upon a campaign of missionary conquest. Among nations other than the Jews, the religious system always found available detours for the ideological struggle. The universal option of Christianity and Islam released them from the need to enter into an overt struggle over power in a particular nation. In contrast, the Jewish religion has no universal aims. It is intended solely for the Jewish people and has no stake in other peoples. It cannot, therefore, forego its authority over the Jewish people. Its success or failure can be tested only in the Jewish context. Consequently, the intervention of religion in polity is unavoidable.

This endless friction between the religious and national systems ignited constant controversy, and threatened to split the nation. All the other conflicts—spiritual, class, and power struggles—are pale beside this one. The solution lay in the *golah*, because life in the *golah* is not a total Jewish existence requiring an unequivocal resolution of this dichotomy. The Jewish framework in the *golah* is essentially voluntary. The Jew is, in essence, free to direct the fervor of his Judaism in any way he desires. The power of coercion is limited. A Jew is expected to observe the commandments, but he cannot be forced to do so. He can be ostracized, even excommunicated, by the Jewish community, but he cannot be put to death.

Thus, the struggle was directed outward rather than inward. Since the constant attack on the Jews was from outside it was desperately important to survive and preserve the identity of the people as such; all parties rallied around this cause. Disputes over the content of Jewish identity were of secondary importance. That is, of course, a broad generalization. There were internal conflicts over the components of Jewish identity: for example, the controversy between the Hasidic movement and its opponents, the *Mitnagdim*, and other controversies between religious world views. But these were theoretical controversies, not struggles for real control over assets and political centers of power. In all other nations, real civil wars were fought because the objectives in the conflict were tangible. Among the Jews, the parties to the dispute were always at the mercy of a third party, foreign and essentially hostile, which was recognized as the genuine threat.

The *golah* freed the national and religious systems from the need to disavow each other. It blunted and restrained the conflict. For example, the Lubavitcher Rabbi who lives in New York can only ask the Jews of New York to refrain from traveling on the Sabbath, to send their children to Jewish schools, and to eat only kosher food. But if the Lubavitcher Rabbi were to come to Israel, he would in principle be able to compel the Jews to refrain from traveling on the Sabbath, to study Judaism, and to eat only kosher food, and it would be his religious duty to do so. The holistic national–religious framework makes coercion obligatory. In the *golah* one can preach, cajole, educate, or persuade, but in a totally Jewish ambience there comes a moment of truth, and at that moment the choice must be either religious or secular. Life in the *golah* postpones that moment of truth. It is as if the people senses how dangerous is its conflict with itself and therefore tries to put off the condition to full sovereign life which can exist in *Eretz Yisrael*. There the conflict must break out into the open. A religious Jew is ready to put up with desecration of the Sabbath in the *golah*, but desecration of the Sabbath in *Eretz Yisrael* outrages him. He prefers to come to *Eretz Yisrael* where he will be unable to avoid seeing this desecration with his own eyes, for if he does see it, and if he does nothing about it, he risks becoming responsible for it. Any other value system would fare exactly like religion. For example, a Jew who believes in a decent progressive society and wishes to define Judaism as the value system of a just society, will always nurture his dream of progressive Judaism abroad rather than come to Israel where he would have to see to what extent the historical reality of Jewish sovereignty contradicted his dream. When he lives in Paris or Buenos Aires he cannot engage in a real conflict of values with other Jews because that conflict would not take place in a total Jewish reality. He can only endeavor, ask, persuade, or educate Jews to be pacifists, socialists, or humanists. When the system under which Jews live as Jews is not total but partial, the central questions are not theirs to decide. They do not have to confront tangible realistic decisions, but only theoretical ones.

THE SOLUTION FOR THE NEED TO BE DIFFERENT:
A CHOSEN PEOPLE

Among the elemental atoms that constitute our identity lies the need to be different, unique, special, set apart from the entire family of nations. This need stems from our inherently diasporic nature. Because Jewish national identity was often blurred and the land in which one was born was perceived as being alien, there was a compulsion to be different. The religious system sanctified isolation and otherness with the phrase: "Thou hast chosen us,"[2] which runs like a leitmotif throughout the spiritual levels of the national-religious activity. It is a people that shall dwell alone, a different people. The House of Israel shall not be like all the nations. "To be like all the nations" carries a negative connotation in Judaism.

However, is it not basically impossible to be different from all the nations? Indeed, is the concept "all the nations" real at all? Cast in individual terms we would immediately discern the absurdity of wanting to be different from all other people. When anyone says that he is different from all other people, we agree. We are all different in a different sense. On the individual level this desire to be chosen and different from all other people appears to be absurd, but it is astonishing to see how far we are prepared to adopt this concept and aspiration on the national level. Such pretentiousness places the billions of people throughout the world in one category—the category of "behaving like all men"—and places Jews in a separate category, different from everyone else. Time and time again I have been unable to believe my ears when people of varying positions expressed the view: "we must not be like the other nations."

Can all the variations of nationality be placed in one category? Can it be said that all the tribes and peoples in the proliferation of their behavior, religion, and culture are like all the nations, and that only the Jewish people stands apart from them? Over the years, Professor Yishayahu Leibowitz has reiterated that the Jews eat, dress, and copulate differently from other peoples—as though the Japanese, Indians, Nepalese, or Eskimos do not eat, dress, or copulate differently from other peoples. All nations share this relative difference, but the Jewish people is told in unequivocal terms that it should be different from all the nations. Vast quantities of commentary have been written on the question of otherness. The Jewish people groans under this burden, which it was unable to live up to when living a normal sovereign existence in its own country. The only way to put it into practice was to go into exile. When you are in the *golah* you are indeed different from other peoples.

Imagine an artist's palette. Each color is equally distinguishable from the others, but none is more different than any other. If I wish to make the red more different without altering its essence, I must change its situation. If I take the red, break it up, and splatter it like drops onto the other colors, it will indeed be different from the other colors—but not in its essence. That is the Jewish *golah* solution—it creates differences between us and other peoples. Since it is apparently impossible to make ourselves different in essence, we make ourselves different in a technical sense, as it were, and this technical differentiation generates a substantive state, which we may not like, and which causes us physical and spiritual suffering, but which also constitutes a solution—albeit a neurotic one—to an impossible aspiration.

I have offered two hypotheses to explain the basic nature of the attraction which exile holds for the Jew. I am sure these two hypotheses will arouse resistance because they are so abstract. Yet is it conceivable that Jews came to *Eretz Yisrael* from any number of countries, from a variety of circumstances, for just such spiritual or intellectual—which is to say abstract—reasons? I venture to answer yes. The answer to this question must be sought in intrinsic causes since all the extrinsic ones do not explain anything. One cannot describe Jewish history as a unique case of dedication on the part of a people to spiritual and religious principles, and in the same breath claim that the fleshpot was of paramount importance to that same people. If we strip away layers of time and place—the particulars of historical situations throughout the generations—we find certain transcending structures, myths, and basic concepts that motivate all of us; we all line up according to a few basic patterns. The backdrops may change constantly, the actors may change, and the style may be different, but the text, in its essence, repeats itself. If we wish to grapple with the exiled essence within us, we shall have to change some of the fundamental Jewish concepts. The fate of the Third Jewish Commonwealth will be like that of the other two unless we deal with the root of the problem. In the early days of Zionism, some experiments in long-range intellectual reexamination of certain basic concepts were begun. To people with insight, simple continuity seemed dangerous and futile. Atavistic survivalistic tendencies of the Jewish people were considered to be too powerful for Zionism to ignore, but the physical struggle for the establishment of the state drained all the spiritual and intellectual energies that ought to have been expended in a fundamental examination of the basic questions. And the Holocaust created the illusion that the great debate with the forces of the *golah* had been unequivocally settled by a cruel history.

The most astonishing aspect of the *golah* condition is that the Holocaust, while destroying a third of our people, did not destroy the *golah* in the collective Jewish mind, and with astonishing rapidity, the people went back to the old ways. Zionism thought that at long last history had provided final and absolute proof of the terrible dangers of the diaspora, but an overwhelming majority of the people thought otherwise. It viewed the Holocaust as merely another station along the bitter path guided by the meaninglessness of Jewish destiny.

The Jewish people is a permanent remnant of itself. The *golah* now, once again, grows steadily stronger, though not in absolute terms, since the process of assimilation continues. Still the *golah* is growing stronger, relative to Israel. Consequently, the *golah*, which is regarded as the champion of Israel, is at the same time a threat to her. The not inconsiderable group of Israeli Jews who staked their identity on the survival of the State of Israel has to maintain itself in the face of the *golah* which threatens to undermine the sovereign existence won at the cost of so much effort. The great debate about *aliyah* to Israel which Ben-Gurion tried to arouse on an emotional and instrumental plane should be renewed and pursued in even greater depth.

The *golah* condition is authentic and lies at the basis of our history. It is the womb from which the Jewish people emerged. To put it in psychoanalytic terms, the people have an urge to return to the womb, particularly when it has to face up to the imperatives of national sovereignty, when reality begins to weigh heavily. There is no way of knowing ontologically what came first, but it is almost certain that all components—a religio–nationality, the sense of chosenness, and the *golah*—merged.

The Exile—an abnormal reality—was found to be an efficient reality from the viewpoint of Jewish existence. It posits suffering but prevents an explosion of a more serious kind, forestalling a crisis which the people cannot handle. As with every neurotic solution, this one, too, cannot bring happiness and should not be regarded as permanent. Better a known and manageable neurosis with which the people can live than a dark unknown where it would have to stand exposed and alone before a jealous and demanding God, and prove that it is a people chosen above all others, a priestly and holy people. The people fears that its emptiness and impotence will be exposed; or perhaps it is the other way around, and it fears an exposure of the emptiness and insignificance of God. However, in this century the pathology of the neurotic solution suddenly became apparent. It became manifest as a source of suffering which was too great and which detracted from our ability to cope with reality. At the end of the 19th Century, in the countries of secular, modern Europe, Jews began to sense the first unpleasant signs of modern anti-Semitism. The Holocaust revealed the true depth of the abyss on whose edge the Jews had been walking (where they had intended to continue walking until the end of time). This mortal conflict with the external environment appeared much more terrifying than the internal conflicts in the Jewish people, including those conflicts which the people had always tried to avoid or postpone.

Zionism is a process of self-liberation from the fears of independence, and its method is mainly to demonstrate that the alternative to independence is worse. At its most profound and at its best, Zionism was a beginning of a process of self-consciousness, a process of breaking the vicious cycle of diaspora to being a chosen people, to national religion in which the people was trapped. The vitality of Zionism stemmed from the plight of the people.

The *golah* could be a viable alternative only for an unnatural life. The spectacular success of Zionism is due first and foremost to the help it derived from the objective situation—the suffering of the Jews. Strangely, the peoples of the world, too, helped the Zionist cause. They had their reasons; they understood how abnormal Jewish existence in their midst was, and they were afraid of the murderous confrontation into which the existence of the Jews was likely to drag them. The decisive step was taken. A total Jewish reality was reestablished. Independence was renewed. But a mere thirty years after the establishment of the State of Israel, there are already disturbing signs of the revival of the *golah*. The most flexible people in the world has already learned the laws of the new, modern reality, and is adjusting the *golah* condition to it. The existence of a center frees people to strike deeper roots in the *golah*, for it now has an insurance policy. In Israel this arouses strange, almost heretical reflections. As it constitutes an ongoing presence, many young people are suddenly becoming aware that the *golah* posits a real alternative to life in Israel. What are we to do to prevent the collapse of the Third Jewish Commonwealth? How can we ensure that the 20 percent of the Jewish people living in a state of national independence can be assured of the continuity of their way of life and of a long-term future of this round of the return to Zion?

Underlying Concepts

In my article "In Praise of Normality,"[3] I tried to establish the urgent need for stressing normality as a value, and to conduct an intramural Jewish struggle against the concept of chosenness. We must see ourselves as an integral part of humanity, neither superior nor inferior. We must adopt this position as an unequivocal value, without evasions or sophisticated interpretations. Declaring that we are better has three adverse effects: (1) it causes people to suspect us; (2) it imposes upon us criteria which we oursleves cannot live up to; and (3) it causes us, consequently, frustration and self-recrimination. The State of Israel has a basic right to exist, even if it has organized crime, corruption, and social injustice. We wish to improve the quality of our existence, not because we have to prove our moral superiority, nor to justify our existence to someone, but simply because we want to improve ourselves. Once and for all we must get rid of the slave mentality, which turned an inferiority complex into a sense of mission, superiority, and elitism. The more conscious we are of the negative instincts which underlie our sense of superiority, the more chance we have of uprooting it.

THE RELIGIOUS QUESTION

Secular Zionists always sensed that the religious question was one of the most dangerous traps lying in wait for them, so they always preferred to bind the sleeping tiger in the fetters of political coalition agreements. The status quo is, however, a highly explosive concept. The potential for conflict is frightening because the emotions pent up on both the secular and religious sides are immensely powerful. These tensions have to be placated and shored up in agreements, for the slightest breach in the dam could lead to a deluge. Perhaps in the early days of statehood there was a misguided notion that the days of religion were numbered, and its sting could be blunted by means of agreements and the status quo, and by the legitimacy with which the secular system would endow it; subsequently, religion would become institutionalized and gradually lose its vitality until it died a quiet death; or alternately perhaps it was felt that it would be better to erect a network of agreements precisely because a religious revival was in the offing and it threatened to be so uncontrollable as to sweep away the entire system. Whatever the reason, the purpose of the status quo was in one way or another to suspend the struggle between religion and state. The status quo in Israel was intended to replace the *golah* experience as the salient factor which had muted the eternal conflict in the total Jewish system of life. The difficult security situation always served as a convenient excuse for preserving the status quo. However, there was always an unspoken assumption among Israelis that when peace came, the wars of the Jews would break out over the religious question. Historically the most violent clashes between the citizen and the authorities, or between rival groups of citizens, were always over religious questions.

I have no wish at present to go into the complex questions aroused by the conflict between religion and state. I shall only say that this conflict always induces an escape to the *golah*. If we really want to eliminate the *golah* as a viable possibility—at least for the Jews now living in Israel—we must consider changing the religion from within. What is needed is a religious reform. Some of the basic values of the religion must be questioned, the national horizon of the religion must be made more flexible, and above all, new and separate sources of authority must be created inside the religion. We are in need of some new and genuine religious reformers. We need a Jewish Luther. These reformers could come from the margins of Orthodoxy and could receive powerful support from the Reform and Conservative movements, which, for their part, will have to undergo a process of "Israelization." To put it bluntly, religion is too important to be left to the religious. Secular Jews, or those who are known as secular, must become involved in religious affairs, not as romantic penitents, but as daring reformers.

It is astonishing to see what a cool reception the secular element in Israel's leadership gave movements of religious reform and how totally insignificant was the help it extended to them. There were two particular reasons for this: (1) The subject was highly sensitive for the religious parties. They were ready to make concessions on many issues, provided their exclusive authority in the field of religion went unchallenged. (2) The American coloration of these movements appeared artificial and lacking in authenticity to Israel's leaders, who grew up on notions of authenticity delimited by the Eastern European Jewish experience. Had Ben-Gurion at the height of his power, intellectual influence, and enormous authority gone to pray on Yom Kippur in an Israeli-style Reform synagogue instead of shutting himself up in his house for the day to pore over Spinoza or Aristotle, he would have endowed reformist thought with a decisive measure of legitimacy. In addition, reformist thought would have undergone a radical process of Israelization. It is only now that some time has elapsed—since Begin came to power—that one of the profound differences has emerged between the present administration and the previous one: that is, namely, the inner attitude toward religion. The leaders of the Labor movement had been much more secular than the average Israeli of today.

There can be no realistic hope for a normalization of the Jewish people without a radical approach to the religious questions. If we want to see any significant change in the next 100 years, we shall have to start rethinking the religious question right now. A total war against religion will be meaningless because the Jewish people has a profound collective psychological need for religion, although this impulse is governed by a cyclical pattern of ebb and flow. The only reform that secular Jews want is the kind that will make things easier by granting them freedom *from* religion. This way of thinking is basically misguided. The problem is not to make the commandments less burdensome, but to expose them to the complexity of life and to fulfill them while changing them. It is astounding to see to what extent the Jewish religion has managed to resist change and to survive without changing its essence even in *Eretz Yisrael* under Jewish sovereignty. Since Jewish orthodoxy is not capable of changing and does not want to the change will come only through the creation of additional centers of authority.

In summary, in order to get right to the source of the *golah* virus within us, there is a need for profound thought, involvement, and courage on our part. Brenner once said: "That is the question. In order that our character may be changed as far as possible, we must have an environment of our own. Yet in order that we may create that environment with our own hands—our character has to change completely." We already possess the environment. We do not wish to change our character merely for the sake of changing it, but in the clear context of the unending war against the *golah* potential lurking inside each one of us.

A Program for the Immediate Future

A number of practical conclusions emerge as courses for action in the immediate future. If Israel's Prime Minister were to appear at the opening conference of the Bond drive in the United States and, instead of speaking once again about Israel, the territories, and relations with the United States, he were to announce ceremonially that this year the State of Israel refused to accept money from the *golah* out of anger over the fact that only the money immigrates to Israel, not the Jews; if Israel's Prime Minister or her senior representatives were, by a dramatic and demonstrative act, to condemn the *golah* for the absence of *aliyah* and were to announce that the money was being sent back to the *golah* for the sole purpose of boosting *aliyah*; if the State of Israel were to stop sending teachers, educators, and community emissaries to a Jewish community that does not fulfill even minimal *aliyah* quotas; perhaps some impression would be made, and perhaps the question of the *golah* would be placed at the center of things. I do not claim that millions, or even hundreds of thousands would come, but even if only a few extra thousands came, it would be sufficient. That in itself would constitute a revolution.

At present approximately 2,000 American Jews per year immigrate to Israel. Even if the number increased to 20,000, not even a half of 1 percent of American Jewry would be represented. But from the point of view of Zionist fervor, it would be a drastic change. On the one hand, such an *aliyah* would put a stop to the catastrophe of Jews leaving Israel, and on the other, an additional 100,000 Jews would be bound in the *golah* to Israel through family connections and friendships. From a scientific and cultural point of view, it would bring about a most important occurrence. But can it be done? One can at least begin intending to do it. One can try to believe that it is possible.

Recently Israel has become a too-familiar presence in the *golah*, especially in the United States. Paradoxically, it is no longer necessary to immigrate to Israel to live in Israel, and it is possible to acquire scraps of significant Israeli reality in the *golah* itself. The aura of distance and mystery surrounding Israel has become blurred, if it has not vanished altogether. The media contributed to this, but they are not the only ones to blame. The constant deepening of relations between the *golah* and Israel has obscured the dividing line between them. Perhaps it was thought that in this way people's hearts would be prepared for *aliyah*, but the reverse is true. What has been created is a legitimate reality of substitutes for *aliyah*—of quasi-*aliyah*. We must at all costs reestablish a certain feeling of alienation between the *golah* and Israel— a controlled disengagement, as it were.

A not inconsiderable group of Jews abroad has forged a network of very intimate relations with the leadership of the State of Israel. This group is party to more of Israel's state secrets than are parallel groups of Israelis. At the cost of a 5 percent contribution to the national budget, the *golah* has become a recognized intermediary in our relations with foreign governments—a service we rightly chose to do without in the early years of statehood. The mutual dependence of Israel and the *golah* has greatly increased. Spiritually the *golah* needs Israel. Our political conflicts, our economical problems, and, in a certain sense, Israeli culture provide the spiritual nourishment for Jewish identity in the *golah*. These have replaced the Talmud, the Kabbalah, and the Responsa. Hence the *golah* will not abandon Israel at the moment when it initiates an ideological conflict over *aliyah*. Of course a few such attempts will be made, but that part of the Jewish people (which for the sake of convenience we shall call Jewish People A), which accounts for 3 million out of the 11 million Jews in the *golah*, which nurses a very profound affinity to Israel and Judaism, and which supplies Jewish services to the other 5 or 6 million (Jewish People B), can never sever its link. It is now in our power (Jewish People B), before it is too late, to cause group A a certain shock, and to demand that it make a choice to end the eternal schizophrenia from which it suffers. At present the *golah* and Israel tightly clasp each other's hands. But if we were to upset the inertia of this stability by quickly withdrawing our hands from group A's grasp, the resulting imbalance would pull them sharply towards us. A state of peace could free us from our dependence on the *golah*, and would restore our upright stance. But even before full peace comes, we must begin to develop a different attitude and posture with regard to the *golah*. Instead of engaging in Jewish education in the *golah*, we must engage exclusively in the promotion of *aliyah*. Too much Jewish education obscures the need to come to Israel. Instead of trying to tempt and induce Jews to come here, we must coldly expose the pathology, immorality, and hypocrisy of the *golah*. We must start a quarrel with the most warmhearted of Jews, the Jews who are most loyal to Israel, for they are our public. It is true that this will be a quarrel among brothers, but it seems to me that this would be preferable to the condition of peace that exists at present.

According to the most optimistic studies, in the year 2000, only about 50 percent of the population in the borders of greater Israel will be Jewish and this assumes an *aliyah* of 25,000 a year, with only a small *yeridah*. There is the very real danger that in another 50 years we will lose our majority even inside the Green Line (pre-1967 Israel). With peace, of course, there will be the opportunity and the hope for large-scale *aliyah*. But let us not forget that there is also a possibility of emigration and the scattering of the Jews throughout the region. In conditions of economic prosperity, and in a world in which distances are becoming less significant, Jews could live in the *golah*—in Tunis, for example—and teach their children Judaism by means of Israeli television programs.

The virus of the *golah* is in our blood. Let us not forget that. We are descendants of those Jews of whom, at the time of the Second Temple, and in the difficult conditions of the ancient world, the famous Greek geographer Strabo wrote: "It is hard to find a place in the entire world in which this people does not live." Gershom Scholem once said that it is as if Israel by its very existence had absorbed the sparks of the redemption imprisoned in the *golah*, and as if it thereby freed the *golah* from the need for redemption and from the guilt of nonredemption. It is up to us to do everything in our power in order not to exculpate the *golah* from the guilt of nonredemption. (The absolute criterion in our relationships with the *golah* must be guided by what increases *aliyah* and what limits it.) It goes without saying that *yordim* are to be condemned and should on no account be given jobs in Israeli institutions abroad; however, there is no moral validity in condemning the *yordim* without condemning life in the *golah* in general.

Do we really need another internecine quarrel? Will it do any good? My answer is yes. The conflict with the *golah* will uncover what we in Israel have in common, as distinct from those living abroad. It will show once again what the cardinal things are—the things for which we are fighting: freedom and independence. Instead of fighting with each other tooth and nail over the issue of an acre more or an acre less territory, we shall see that the real issues lie elsewhere. The essence of our life in Israel is different from that of *golah* life, and the differences should not be obscured. Spiritual life in the *golah* is like that of a man who has built his house on the water's edge, is preoccupied with the question of whether the water will inundate his home, and is engaged in endless efforts to keep it out. We in Israel, on the other hand, are like a man who has removed his house far from the erosive powers of the waves. The problem of the water no longer preoccupies him. He is able to build his house, cultivate his land, and create something new.

I believe that deep inside every man lies a desire for redemption, and each man possesses a latent vitality. I shall never forget a wonderful story from the time of the "illegal" *aliyah* from Morocco. It happened early in the 1960s, when ships were collecting Jews from Morocco, which was already completely under Moslem control. One day a ship arrived in one of the ports to pick up some Jews from a remote village. For various reasons the expected immigrants did not arrive and the ship could not wait. The Jewish agency representatives on the ship went to the nearest Jewish community, knocked on the doors and said: "Are you prepared to leave for Israel, right now, without further ado? Take whatever you can. Take your chance." And, in fact, quite a number of Jews got up and left, then and there. This impulsive component can be found in every one of us.

I am always astounded to rediscover in conversations with Jews abroad— intellectuals and others well-established in their jobs and their business—that they do not rule out the possibility that one day they might come to Israel. It is not just talk aimed at making an impression on others; "the redemption gland" exists in every Jew. A thousand obstacles, personal and collective, lie in the path of anyone who wishes to make *aliyah*; yet the decisive fact is that there is a minority that has done so of its own free will.

One of the most compelling reasons for peace has not been heard: namely that peace is likely to increase *aliyah* and to reallocate resources for *aliyah*.

Peace is likely to release Soviet Jews from their prison. Our historical responsibility is not toward land. It lies first and foremost with people. History will never forgive us if, because of our attachment to the ideal of settlement in all parts of *Eretz Yisrael*, we abandon a huge Jewish community in the Soviet Union to anti-Semitism and assimilation.

For thousands of years the Jews have said: "Next year in Jerusalem," meaning it, yet not meaning it. The same is true today; however, in the past generation a new group has emerged that cannot say "next year in Jerusalem," because it is already living in the real down-to-earth Jerusalem. This group will never again be satisfied with the abstract concept of celestial Jerusalem (a Christian concept that first appears in the New Testament: Galatians 4:25, Revelations 3:12 and 21:2).

The great debate between Israel and the *golah* must be resumed at once, without hypocrisy, with all its fierceness and honesty.

–– *Notes*

1. D. Runes (Ed.), *A World Without Jews*. New York: Philosophical Press, 1959.

2. I. Singer, *Standard Prayer Book*. New York: Bloch Publishing Co., 1943.

3. A. B. Yehoshua, *Between Right and Right*. New York: Doubleday, 1981.

·2·
Exile, Mysticism, and Reality

Roy A. Rosenberg

According to the biblical account, originally the people of Israel had no land of their own. But then, in the desert, they encountered a deity who took them as his people in exchange for their taking him as their God. Deuteronomy preserves the memory of this desert meeting:

Yaweh came from Sinai
  and dawned from Seir upon them;
He shone forth from Mount Paran
  and came from Meribath-Kadesh. (33:2)

He found him in a desert land,
  in the howling waste of the wilderness;
He engirdled him, he cared for him,
  he kept him as the pupil of his eye. (32:10)

Thus a people was born; a deity had found a band that would find him a home at the same time that it would find one for itself. Together Yahweh and Israel conquered the land of Canaan. The people that had been nomadic shepherds became settled tillers of the soil, and the tenacious, loving linkage of this people to this land began, to continue through the centuries to this day. Yahweh, for his part, took possession of the sacred precinct of Jerusalem, a locus that remains linked to him, too, to this day.

Along with the rooting of the people of Israel in its land, came the official theology that Yahweh would never permit the removal of his people nor the destruction of his own holy house in Jerusalem. Jeremiah, however, following the tradition handed down by some of his prophetic predecessors, challenged this assertion. "Go now to my place which was in Shiloh, where I established my name at first, and see what I did to it because of the wickedness of my people Israel. Now . . . I will do to the house which is called by my name, and in which you trust . . . as I did to Shiloh, and I will cast you out of my sight" (Jer. 7:12ff., c. 600 B.C.E.). Jeremiah's assertion was scandalous because it flew in the face of the common beliefs of his day. But it flowed out of the historic memory that Yahweh and the people of Israel had at one time been migrants into the land. If Yahweh had led his people to the land, he could just as surely force them out. Since Yahweh had at first been a deity without a permanent abode, he could surely, if he chose, exile himself from his home.

History proved Jeremiah to be right. Jerusalem was destroyed, and the Jews were exiled to Babylon. Had they been like the other people of antiquity, they would have forsaken their ancestral cult and embraced the gods of the land in which they lived. But Jeremiah, perhaps singlehandedly, saved the cultic tradition, and through it an entire people. He wrote to the exiles in Babylon: "Build houses and live in them, plant gardens and eat their produce. Take wives and have sons and daughters . . . Seek the welfare of the city where I have sent you into exile and pray to Yahweh in its behalf, for in its welfare will you find your welfare" (29:5ff.). These words made possible a Jewish life outside of the land of Israel, and the continued worship of the Jewish God even in the absence of his Temple. This concept is one of the most significant in all of scripture, for without its influence there would be no Judaism, no Christianity, and no Islam. It created diaspora Judaism.

With the end of the Babylonian captivity in 538 B.C.E., the exiled Jews had the opportunity to return and rebuild Jerusalem, including the house of the God of Israel. Nonetheless, many Jews did not avail themselves of this opportunity. Even a century later, Ezra and Nehemiah, the leaders of the Jerusalem community, could not convince large numbers of those who remained in Babylon to go home. Although they retained a spiritual attachment to their ancestors' land, and though they paid for the support of the House of God, they preferred to remain in Babylon as an autonomous community. Out of this community came the Babylonian Talmud, the text on which Judaism to this day is based.

The complexion of life throughout the Near East changed radically when the conquests of Alexander the Great brought Greek culture and forms of social organization to this part of the world. Such great cities as Alexandria and Antioch grew up, and commercial life developed as never before. Jews from the very beginning flocked to these new cities. They did not regard themselves as sinners for having left their homeland. Large, Greek-speaking Jewish communities established themselves in the Hellenistic cities on the Mediterranean. They had a major degree of autonomy and were granted various privileges by the ruling powers. They constituted an organized ethnic body within these cities, similar to the situation of Babylonian Jewry. This is the pattern that persisted into the days of the Roman Empire, and thereafter in the cities of Europe to the dawn of modern time. The Jews looked upon the Land of Israel as their spiritual home, to which they were destined to return in the end of days under the Messianic king. They looked upon the holy mountain in Jerusalem as the veritable abode of their God, the most sacred spot on earth. But, for the most part, they had no desire to go there to live.

The idea of exile as punishment for sin had, of course, been emphasized in a number of biblical passages. The Babylonian captivity was regarded as a chastisement of the Jewish people, but the voluntary migration of Jews to the Hellenistic cities was not. What caused the dispersion of the Jews throughout the Mediterranean world to be interpreted as punishment for sin was the destruction of the Temple of Jerusalem by Rome in 70 C.E. Jews leaving the homeland could be accepted with equanimity. What could not be accepted was the destruction of the House of God, the one place on earth which Judaism regarded as uniquely His. While the God of Israel, in accordance with Jeremiah's insight, could be worshipped anywhere in the world, the destruction of his Temple meant that He was in exile. It was, therefore, understood that the sinfulness of the Jewish people had caused not only their own dispersion, but the exile of the *Shekhinah*, the Divine Presence. She was visualized as both accompanying the Jewish people on their wandering, and also as hovering above the temple's Western Wall, awaiting the return not only of her people but of her people's God. Hence the prayer on the festival days:

> On account of our sins were we exiled from our land and removed far from our country. We are unable to go up, to appear and to worship you, and to fulfill our obligations in your chosen house, that great and holy house called by your name, because of the hand that is stretched out against your sanctuary. May it be your will, Lord our God and God of our fathers, merciful king, that you return and have mercy upon us and upon your sanctuary, and that you rebuild it speedily and magnify its glory.[1]

The most profound theology of exile in Judaism made its appearance in Kabbalah, the mystical tradition. The classic text of this tradition is the Zohar, dating from 13th-Century Spain. In the Zohar the *Shekhinah* is the female aspect of deity that must unite with her male counterpart in order for the universe to remain in equilibrium and not revert to chaos. While the Temple of Jerusalem stood, the *Shekhinah* and the Holy King were in perpetual union, but with the destruction of the Temple they are able to come together only on the Sabbath. (Hence in kabbalistic thought and in Hasidism, the Sabbath is the marriage feast of God and his *Shekhinah*.) In the Zohar the *Shekhinah* is also called *Kenesset Yisrael*—the community of Israel—for she is embodied in the Jewish people. The exile of the Jewish people from the Holy Land is a reflection of the exile of Adam and Eve from

Paradise, and both adumbrate the separation of the Holy King from his Queen. The Jewish people, by performing the commandments with proper mystical intention, can bring about the reunion of God and his *Shekhinah*, which on earth will be manifested by an end to exile. In this way the verse will be fulfilled, "On that day shall the Lord be One and his name One." While during the period of exile the world is in thrall to the Tree of Knowledge of Good and Evil, in which the realms of good and evil struggle between themselves so that there is both holiness and impurity, permitted acts and forbidden acts, life and death, at the time of redemption dominion will pass to the Tree of Life, which is perfection and immortality.[2]

The Kabbalah of Isaac Luria, which flourished in 16th Century Safed, was built on the imagery of the Zohar. It held that everything has been in exile since the beginning of Creation, and that the task of restoring everything to its proper place has been given to the Jewish people, whose destiny symbolizes the state of the universe at large. The sparks of divinity are dispersed everywhere, but they are held captive by the *kelippah*—the power of evil—and must be redeemed. This process of redemption is called *tikkun*—restoration—and is the task of the Jewish people. Those who live a holy life, fulfilling the commandments with the proper concentration and intention, help to hasten the arrival of this world of *tikkun*. Since Lurianic Kabbalah taught that almost the whole process of restoration had been completed and that only the final stages had to be undergone, it is quite understandable that it could spawn the Messianic movement of Sabbetai Zevi in the 17th Century, agitating Jewry throughout the world for years.[3]

The Lurianic Kabbalah and its offspring, the Sabbatian movement, were not able to end the exile of the *Shekhinah* and her people, the Jews. But the Enlightenment of the 18th Century, culminating in the French Revolution, brought in its wake the most drastic change in the condition of the Jewish people, at least in western and central Europe, since the days of antiquity. Since Alexander, the Jews had constituted a distinct ethnos wherever they lived in Europe, Asia, and North Africa. But the Revolution called for an end to all ethnic distinctions, seeking instead a society based on liberty, equality, and fraternity, in which each individual would have a direct relationship to the state, not mediated through religious or ethnic institutions. This new attitude was codified by the Sanhedrin and Assembly of Notables convoked by Napoleon in 1807.[4] These bodies declared that every Jew is religiously bound to consider his non-Jewish fellow citizens as brothers, to aid, protect, and love them in the same measure as if they were Jews, and that the Jew is required to consider the land of his birth or adoption as his fatherland, to love and defend it when called upon. Thus the secular society was born, in which each individual is expected to participate, both emotionally and bodily, in the civic and social life of the land in which he resides, transcending any religious or ethnic loyalties that he may have. Nothing like this had ever before existed during the long sweep of Jewish history. Small wonder, then, that many felt that the redemption had finally dawned. The days of exile were ended, not by a return of the Jews to Jerusalem but by the acceptance of Jews into full civic equality by the societies in which they lived. Reform Judaism grew up in central Europe, a movement giving religious expression and validation to this new way of life, thought, and feeling.

Not all Jews wished to give up the consciousness of exile, but perhaps more significantly, not all non-Jews were willing to embrace the ideals of the French Revolution and regard the Jews of their land as their brothers and sisters. Doctrines of romantic nationalism took root in central Europe and France as a reaction against the liberal and egalitarian ethos of the Revolution, and anti-Semitism was born. This is the teaching that there is something inherently noxious and evil in Jewish blood, that Jews by their very presence act as a corrupting influence on the peoples and cultures of the lands in which they live. The Holocaust was the inevitable culmination of these ideas. If it is thought that Jews, not so much in their religious doctrines and practices as in their biological endowment, corrupt and despoil the people among whom they live, then of course their total elimination becomes not only thinkable but even obligatory. From the latter part of the 19th Century, through the terrible days of Nazism and the Second World War, the sense of exile was reborn among the Jews of the world, perhaps with an intensity unmatched in any previous age.

The response of the Jewish people to anti-Semitism was Zionism, which taught that the only way in which the Jewish people can find a true home is in its return to its ancestral home—the Land of Israel. The culmination of Zionism is the State of Israel, risen out of the ashes of the Holocaust. The existence of Zionism and the State of Israel causes every Jew who lives outside the boundaries of the state to face the question, "Am I in exile from my true home?" And then the question: "Ought I return to my true home or can I fulfill my destiny as a Jew in other lands?" The answer of classical Zionism is that all Jews are in exile unless they live in the Land of Israel, and that a fulfilling Jewish life is impossible outside of the Land. Ideologies deriving from the Enlightenment and the French Revolution maintain that where Jews have full rights of citizenship and freedom to promulgate their religion and culture, they are not in exile. The tension between these two approaches continues to exist, as it has for 200 years.[5]

What can be said without contradiction is that if there had been no exile, and particularly no destruction of the Temple of Jerusalem, there would be no Judaism today—at least as we know it. The cult of the Jewish people would still revolve around the animal sacrifices offered at the Holy Place in the Holy City, and the spiritual progress of the Jewish religion would have been impossible. The Hebrew word for exile—*galut*—is derived from the same root as is the word for revelation—*gillui*: it is exile, then, that reveals the nature of reality to humanity. In exile we are able to mature and grow. Exile is challenge.

One might also say that the only true end to exile is death, for it is only then that we are at rest in the womb of earth, whence we came. According to psychoanalytic theory, death is sometimes acceptable as a final reunion with the mother. The unconscious may long for reunion with the primordial mother, even if it is the terrible mother who is death herself. This is hinted at by Kabbalah, for when the exile of the *Shekhinah* is finally ended, she will be united not only with the Holy King but also with the Mother, that emanation of deity that is the womb of all existence, and all will return at the Great Jubilee to its proper place. Then all will be as it was before creation, and "Yahweh alone will be exalted on that day."[6] But until that day comes, we have been taught to choose life, that we and our children might live wherever we be found, whether it be at home or in exile.

Notes

1. I. Singer, *Standard Prayer Book*. New York: Bloch Publishing Co., 1943, p. 339.

2. G. Sholem, *Kabbalah*. New York: Quadrangle, 1974, p. 166.

3. Ibid., p. 245.

4. David Philipson, *The Reform Movement in Judaism*. New York: Ktav Publishing, 1967, pp. 18ff.

5. Ibid., p. 5.

6. See Book of Concealment, Zohar 2:179a. Cf. Rosenberg, R., *The Anatomy of God*. New York: Ktav Publishing, 1973, p. 33.

The Land Flowing With Milk and Honey

Étan Levine

Introduction

The story of the Jewish People begins in the biblical land of Israel. One of the most familiar and most cherished descriptions of the Promised Land is that of "a land flowing with milk and honey." This phrase appears no less than 15 times in the Pentateuch and five times thereafter.[1] From the earliest biblical translations and commentaries until the modern era, exegetes have been virtually unanimous in understanding the phrase, "flowing with milk and honey" as an Eden-like hyperbole stressing the abundant fertility and lushness of the land assigned to the People of Israel.

Many reasons contribute to this universal understanding of the phrase. Thus, the Bible itself refers to milk (or milk products) and honey as luxury items.[2] These are high-energy foods used by people who camp in the wilderness (II Sam. 17:29), articles of trade (Ezek. 27:27), contributions to priests and Levites (II Chr. 31:9), and worthy gifts (Gen. 43:11, 1Ki 14:3). Honey is described as being both pleasurable and healthful (Pr. 16:24),[3] and is used by biblical authors as symbolic of such diverse pleasures and benefits as God's commands (Ps. 19:11, 119:103), wisdom (Pr. 24:13, 16:24), and, along with milk, sexuality (Cant. 4:11, 5:1). It is, therefore, not surprising that the divinely-bestowed mannah in the wilderness has the taste of honey (Ex. 16:31), nor that God will deny the sinner milk and honey in the future (Job 20:17).

In brief, just as the answer to the rhetorical question, "What is sweeter than honey? (Ju. 14:18)" was regarded by the biblical author as self-evident, so have biblical scholars regarded the meaning of the phrase, "a land flowing with milk and honey." In the following study, however, an attempt will be made to demonstrate that the real meaning is extremely different; that in the interpretation of this phrase (as with many biblical expressions), familiarity has substituted for understanding.[4] Furthermore, this represents not only a fundamental mistake about the Land of Israel, but also about the divine covenant concerning that land.

The Topological Realities

In order to understand biblical civilization generally, and biblical semantics specifically, some awareness of topology is essential. By 'topology,' of course, we mean the role of the topography, the actual physical environment, in the shaping of that civilization, including its economy, religion, technology, jurisprudence, language, art and literature. As a case in point, let us consider how manifoldly misleading has been the widespread translation of the Hebrew *midbar* as 'desert' or 'wilderness.' Today we recognize that although it may be, in certain parts, arid, uninhabited wasteland, the *midbar* includes pasture, and its inhabitants live in settled towns as well as in nomadic encampments.[5] In fact, much of biblical topography consisted of *midbar*: a land mass which sustained large populations before, during and after the Israelite period. Thus, to conceive of *midbar* as being actual desert waste is to significantly distort the topography of biblical civilization, and everything associated with that culture.

When our thinking conforms to the topographical realities, and when we think not of "milk and honey" in the abstract, but of "a land flowing with milk and honey," we can quickly ascertain that a helpful clue to its real meaning is contained in Samson's famous riddle: it is a case of "out of the strong there came forth sweet (Ju. 14:14)." For in biblical Palestine as everywhere, both milk and honey are products not of rich, cultivated farmlands, but of poor, uncultivated grazing areas. The milk-producing flocks and herds are "led" (Heb. *dbr*) into the "marginal land" (Heb. *midbar*): not actual desert or wilderness, but not suitable for agriculture. And it is there, amidst the wild thickets, rocks and bushes, that the wild honey is also found.[6]

Biblical diction paired 'milk and honey' not simply because of their gastronomical or culinary affinity, but because both milk and honey are products of the very same topographical-economic conditions. And these are the conditions of bare survival: almost the very opposite of a Garden of Eden, Paradise or the like.

Textual Evidence

The biblical text itself alludes to the essential characteristics of "a land flowing with milk and honey." Thus, it warns the Israelites as they depart from Egypt, "Therefore shall you keep all the commandments which I command you this day, that you may be strong, and go in and possess the land which you are going over to possess. And so that you may prolong your days upon the land which the Lord swore unto your fathers to give to them and to their seed, a land flowing with milk and honey." The text explains, "For the land which you are going in to possess is not like the land of Egypt from whence you came out, where you would sow your seed, and where you would irrigate it with your foot, as an herb garden. Rather, the land which you are going over to possess is a land of hills and valleys, and it drinks water according to the rainfall of heaven: a land which the Lord thy God must care for. The eyes of the Lord are upon it always, from the beginning of the year Until the end of the year (Dt. 11:8–12)."

After comparing the fertile lushness of Egypt to the precarious marginality of the "land flowing with milk and honey," there follows a stern warning. The people must obey God's will, "lest the anger of the Lord be kindled against you, and He shut up the heavens so there be no rain, and the ground shall not yield her fruit, and you perish quickly from off the good land which the Lord is giving you (vv. 16f.)." This is hardly a 'rose garden' being promised to the People of Israel!

There are numerous biblical passages which testify to the authentic meaning of a land which produces milk and honey. One of the most revealing is found in Isaiah's description of young Immanuel, who will eat "curd and honey (Is. 7:15)." What exegetes have failed to realize is that this is *not* intended to symbolize blessing or affluence; it is the divine 'sign' (v. 10) symbolizing the aftermath of destruction and destitution!

As expressly stated by Isaiah, the Lord will bring the hosts of the enemy to raze the land, "And it shall come to pass that a man shall rear a young cow and two sheep. And it shall come to pass, for the abundance of milk that they shall give, he shall eat curd; for curd and honey shall everyone that is left in the land eat (v. 21f.)." What previously had been a thriving, agricultural area will become a wasteland fit only for grazing: "And it shall come to pass on that day, that every place where there used to be a thousand vines at a thousand pieces of silver, there shall be briers and thorns. With arrows and bows shall one venture there, because all the land shall be briers and thorns. And all the hills that had been cultivated with the mattock you will not go to, because of fear of the briers and thorns, except for the leading forth of sheep and the treading of oxen (vv. 23ff.)."

However familiar and entrenched the commentaries' concensus may be, in no way can the eating of milk and honey in this Isaiah passage be interpreted to symbolize comfort and wealth! In fact, Isaiah is using imagery familiar from the Pentateuch (Ex. 33:3, Lev. 20:24), wherein the eating of milk and honey is the aftermath of military destruction. Rather than constituting a blessing, it represents a marginal economy of bare subsistance: a recurrent reality in the land of Israel in the biblical period and thereafter.

There is one case in the Bible where "a land flowing with milk and honey" may well signify lushness and fertility *par excellence,* and it is interesting to note that it is used in nostalgic allusion to Egypt, not to the land of Israel! Thus, "And Moses sent to summon Dathan and Abiram the sons of Eliab. And they said: We will not come up. Is it a small thing that you have brought us up out of a land flowing with milk and honey, to kill us in the wilderness . . . (Nu. 16:20f.)" Yet here too, when the malcontents complain of being led neither to grazing ground nor to agricultural land, they use the phrase with its literal meaning: "Moreover, you have not brought us into a land flowing with milk and honey, nor have you given us inheritance of fields and vineyards (v. 14)."

Having recognized that milk and honey are products of uncultivated pasture areas, and that the eating of milk and honey represents marginal subsistance due to sparse vegetation or even the aftermath of destruction, we must somehow reconcile those biblical verses in which the phrase "a land flowing with milk and honey" is clearly an encomium. These are passages in which the author's lauditory intention is clear, due to the usage of terms such as 'goodly' (Nu. 13:27, 14:8, 16:3) or 'beautiful' (Ez. 20:6, 15). To resolve this apparent contradiction, and to arrive at a precise understanding of the intent of "a land flowing with milk and honey," several aspects of biblical semantics, society and culture must be recalled.

Nomad's Blessing and Farmer's Curse

Biblical civilization spans a period during which there was a general evolution from pastoral to agricultural occupations. And a "land flowing with milk and honey," i.e. grazing land, means very different things to a nomad and to a sedentary farmer. For the nomad who leads his flocks between the wilderness wastes and the farmed fields, it is the source of his livelihood. It is a joyous gift, enabling him to feed his flocks and herds, find honey amidst the bushes, and pick the various spices, berries and fruits of the wild. And both the milk and honey products will constitute his merchandise for trade. But for a thriving agricultural community, the eating of milk and honey is a frightening symbolization of catastrophe. The wild brush, untilled thickets and sparse vegetation constitute the dislocation of agrarian economy: desolation brought on by either war or natural disasters. It is the wilderness reaching out to destroy settled civilization.

Biblical scholarship, like rationality itself, must know its own limits. And the fact is that we don't even know the precise identity of the ancient Hebrews, or whether the term signifies an ethnic group or a class! What is clear, however, is that during the biblical period, Israelite society was 'Dimorphic,' with interaction between the nomadic and the sedentary, the pastoral and the agricultural.[7] Further, we know that there was an outcast group: elements outside of structured society (e.g. mercenaries, vagrants, outlaws, robbers) who belonged neither to the established tribal society nor to the established agricultural society.[8] And, of course, each of these groups had very different attitudes toward "land flowing with milk and honey." However cherished the felicitous idiom may be, the actual implications of wild, grazing land can only be ascertained by the context: whether it is used in contrast to desolate wilderness, or in contrast to lush farm land. Then, and only then, can we determine whether that particular milk and honey represents a blessing or a curse.

And to compound the difficulties, there is the well-attested conservatism of language, so that biblical Hebrew retained traces of nomadism for generations after that period had been largely eclipsed by agriculture and even city dwelling. Thus, for example, long after the conquest of "the land flowing with milk and honey," a stone house was called a 'tent,'[9] demobilized soldiers were sent 'each man to his own tent' (I Sam. 4:10, 2 Sam. 18:17), and the cry 'To your tents, Israel,' was the rebellion call under David (2 Sam. 20:1) and after Solomon's death (I Ki. 12:16). The language of Israel itself was dimorphic, witness the contemporary texts in which every man returned 'to his house' (I Ki. 22:17) or to 'his town' (I Ki. 22:36).

Metaphors borrowed from nomadic life are found throughout biblical literature, long after their ideal was not "milk and honey," but the more affluent, luxurious sitting "every man under his vine and his fig tree." To cite a few examples,[10] death is represented as a tent blown away (Is. 38:12) or a cut tent rope or a peg removed (Job 4:21). Disaster is represented by a tent blown down or its ropes broken (Jer. 10:20), whereas security is described as a tent with taut ropes and firm pegs (Is. 33:20). An expanding nation is a tent being widened (Is. 54:2). And the familiar representation of the savior of the people, be it God or his Messiah, is that of a shepherd.[11] Suffice it to say that the myriad allusions to pastoral motifs long after the nomadic period, makes the dating of these texts on purely semantic grounds, a virtual impossibility. Therefore we cannot ascertain whether the economy of the period is genuinely nomadic-pastoral or sedentary-agricultural.

Milk and Honey vs. Affluent Society

One of the universally recognized phenomena of ancient civilization is the fact that only in the transition from nomadic to sedentary life is there the immense concentration of energy no longer needed exclusively for sustaining basic nutrition and reproduction. The coalition of both military-administrative power and religious myth conspire to create a powerful social organism involving storage areas, irrigation ditches, religious shrines, recreational areas, military fortresses, recreational sites, cultural institutions, and all of the immense practical functions of distributing agricultural plentitude, defending against marauders, diverting population growth, creating collective wealth, enforcing communal jurisprudence, etc. The centralization of power, and the ability to make new community decisions changed earlier tribal norms and created vast communal changes beyond even the imagination of pastoral communities.

Unlike the survival economy of the nomad, the social organism produced by settled civilization could create such wonders as the Great Pyramid of Giza, where one hundred thousand workers would perform a colossal task with precision. No earlier level of civilization could marshall the human power, undeviating discipline and order required for projects such as these. The transition from nomadic to sedentary life required submission to a central authority, inflexible regimentation, specialization of vocation, constant readiness for war, and a number of other liabilities, but it vastly expanded the scope of human capability. It may well have obliterated or debased precious human elements that even the humblest nomadic groups possessed, but the economic benefit was astounding. The engineered community, whose perfected order derives not from an idealized conception of man, but from a pursuit of social unity as a material imperative, was a community which provided wealth, security and high culture. Compared to these, the life of even the most successful nomad who achieved his dream of having "a land flowing with milk and honey," was meagre and sparse in the extreme.

To summarize the economics, the pastoral life was one of economic survival. Only the sedentary agrarian or urban economy could produce the kind of wealth which 'milk and honey' symbolized to later generations who lived far removed from these realities. It is no wonder that there is no case of biblical communities opting for a reversion back to nomadism as a means of enhancing their material well being!

Relation to the "Desert Ideal"

It is initially tempting to hypothesize that the description "a land flowing with milk and honey" is merely another metaphor retained from an earlier period. For during this past century there has developed the theory of the "Desert Ideal." This theory holds that Israelite culture, and the prophets specifically, considered the desert period to be the ideal age of Israelite history: an era when the relationship between the People and its God was most intimate. The desert period, supposedly, was considered both the past ideal and the future goal. But this entire theory reflects more of nineteenth and twentieth century Romanticism than it does biblical reality, as the following points, merely listed *brevitatis causa,* quickly indicate:

First, nowhere in the Bible is there the slightest attempt to apply the "Desert Ideal" to all Israel as a program. Second,[11] the desert and the desert period are conceived in the Bible not as intrinsically valuable, but originally and basically as a punishment and a necessary transitory stage in the restoration of Israel to its ideal setting, which is an organized fully developed society, with a deep appreciation of civilization, settled in the cultivated Land of Israel."[12] Third, those verses (which include Jer. 2:2!) which have been cited as 'proof texts' of Israel's loyalty to God, have been shown to be indicating the very opposite, i.e., God's loyalty to Israel even during the period of punishment. For "to say that Israel went after Yahweh in the desert is simply another way of saying that Yahweh went before Israel, i.e., led her in the desert. This shows kindness in the guide, not necessarily loyalty in the guided. After all, Israel did not follow Yahweh in the desert of her own free will. The forty-years wandering was imposed on Israel as a punishment and a test, as Dt. 8:2-6 stresses. Yahweh is aware of Israel's hardship, and this calls forth his sympathy and kindness (Dt. 2:7). The wondering is paternal punishment for the sake of instruction (Dt. 8:2-6), and a father may maintain his kindness even during the time of punishment."[13]

Even in those biblical authors supposedly representing a "Desert Ideal," the ideal future rapprochement between Israel and God is represented not in desert terms, but in terms of sedentary agriculture! Thus, Hosea describes God as threatening Israel with the punishment of the cessation of all her harvest festivals and the destruction of her vines and fig trees (2:13f.) And subsequently He will restore her vineyards and fertility. This is the identical agricultural motif found in Jeremiah, the supposed advocate *par excellence* of a "Desert Ideal": "I will again build you securely, O virgin Israel, you shall again adorn yourself with your timbrels and shall go forth in the dance of the merrymakers. Again you shall plant vineyards on the mountains of Samaria. The planters shall plant and shall enjoy the fruit (Jer. 31:4-5)." On textual grounds alone, it is clear that the desert in itself has no value as an ideal or a goal for the establishing or renewal of a union with God.[14] Thus, "a land flowing with milk and honey" cannot be a 'Desert Ideal' metaphor because the 'Desert Ideal' *itself* does not exist in the Bible!

The So-called 'Nomadic Ideal'

Even modern writers who have articulately demolished the erroneous 'Desert Ideal' accept the concept of a 'Nomadic Ideal' in ancient Israel.

Thus, "For all that, there seems to have been a "nomadic ideal," or rather — a "semi-nomadic ideal," in ancient Israel. The institution of Nazirites, the Rechabites, and perhaps Elijah's hairy cloak and leather girdle seem to show that certain groups in the population did idealize the semi-nomadic way of life."[15] The distinction to be drawn is that, "this idealization was apparently oriented not to the period of Israel's trek in the desert, but to the non-civilized way of life in itself. . ."[16] Yet this 'nomadic ideal' itself requires correction.

First, the desert itself, and the 'nomadic' lifestyles lived in the desert, can be, and must be, divided. The true desert, i.e., areas with a mean annual rainfall of less than 10 cm. a year, is the domain of the camel breeders who can survive in, or at least cross these barren wastes. These people have almost no contact with sedentary society, and they are constantly travelling great distances in search of grazing. At no time were the Israelites such people, nor were the Patriarchs themselves, who lived before the domestication of the camel in the Middle East. The median desert region receives 10–25 cm. of precipitation a year, and here nomads breed goats and sheep which are less hardy than camels, and which require the richer vegetation. Distances between water holes and grazing grounds are less, and the nomads have ongoing contact with the settled communities, since the grazing areas skirt their settlements. A third category is the marginal desert: not quite suited for intensive agriculture, but able to sustain cattle as well as flocks, and capable, in good years, of being sown with grain. In such areas, the nomad divides his time and efforts: part of the year (winter and spring) he lives as a tent-dwelling nomad, and part of the year he lives in a permanent settlement. And this third category included Israelites throughout the biblical period.

Consequently, when encountering terms such as "land flowing with milk and honey," one must recall that nomadism or semi-nomadism was not an *ideal* but a *reality* throughout the biblical period, despite the ongoing progression to the stages of agriculture, commerce and urbanization.[17] A land flowing with milk and honey does not sustain the agriculture whereby a man can settle contentedly beside his vine and his fig tree, but it is the most luxurious grazing ground that a nomad can hope to have.

From biblical literature itself as well as from general anthropology we know of the conflicts which accompany the evolution of Man, be it the conflict between the sheep (i.e., *rahel*) tribes and the kine (i.e., *leah*) breeders, be it the conflict between the roaming shepherds and the settled villagers, be it the conflict between the country folk and the urbanized city-dwellers. And we also know of the inner conflicts: the sense of disappointment with a specific way of life and nostalgic memories (or illusions) about an earlier life style. Much of the ills that the classical prophets speak against would, in today's categories, be referred to as urbanization. For "this transformation of man has an ugly side: civilized man, if more law-abiding, is likewise more calculating: if he is more skillful and intelligent, he is more selfish. If he is stirred by ambitions and desires that were foreign to the modest expectations of archaic culture, he is also subject to perverse derangements and criminal insubordinations: as a result, civilization has often brought about gigantic miscarriages of life, in bestialities and butcheries that simpler communities lack the animus as well as the power to inflict."[18]

In biblical Israel as elsewhere, the progressive economic-social-cultural transformation of Man increased the attributes of isolation, fixation, stratification, regimentation, standardization and militarization. And if a 'nomadic ideal' is extrapolated from biblical literature, it is because millenarian images, along with pastoral motifs from the 'classical' past are part of these writings. In any relatively continuous culture, older utopian fantasies are never entirely obliterated, and semantic elements from the past survive, albeit with somewhat altered meanings.[19] Still, it must be emphasized, in biblical Israel, nomadism, or semi-nomadism, was very much a part of the *real*, not the *fantasy* lifestyle of much of the populace. And it is to *reality* that we must look, if we are to understand the Covenant of Milk and Honey as biblical man understood it.

The Covenant of Milk and Honey

As explicitly admitted by the biblical text itself (e.g. Dt. 11:8ff.), the Promised Land is a marginal, precarious one. Although it can sustain the people, were there to be a reduction of precipitation the drought would cause them to 'perish quickly.' This omnipresent danger is, of course, the most serious threat to any pastoral community. In light of this, it is not surprising to discover that the description, "a land flowing with milk and honey" is almost invariably used in reference to Israel's obeying or disobeying God's commandments.[20] In fact, in the Book of Joshua and in the Prophets, it is the *exclusive* context in which the phrase is used.[21] Living in the 'Land of Israel' is conditional upon a certain mode of behavior.

The People of Israel, whatever their individual occupations be, at the time, or in the future, are given a message from "The God of your fathers," or "The God of Abraham, Isaac and Jacob," i.e., from the god of the pastoral patriarchs.[22] The message is clear: the Lord has taken (or is taking, or will take) his people back to their 'roots': to a subsistence economy in a marginal land that is totally dependent upon his ongoing supervision. Maintaining the grace of God by observing the covenant is literally a matter of life and death, because of the precariousness of "a land flowing with milk and honey." This motif is one of the essentials in biblical religion: there is no divine guarantee in perpetuity, for the People can cause their life-sustaining land to become an arid waste. And since it is only a 'milk and honey land,' there is no reserve of water or warehoused agricultural products that can take them over a season of divine wrath.

These realities were common knowledge in the biblical period, of course, despite whatever idealization of the land of Israel, the 'good old days' of nomadic life, and 'the land flowing with milk and honey' which may have existed. But it is in the post-biblical period that this idealization continued, reaching unnatural, fantastic proportions: an unreal image of *terra sancta* in every respect. Exaggerated descriptions of the dimensions and attributes of the Land of Israel abound in post-biblical literature, feeding the fantasy engendered by the misunderstanding of the meaning of 'a land flowing with milk and honey.' It is not difficult to ascertain the reason for these illusions: should not the Holy Land be the embodiment of wealth, security and blessing, if it is, in fact, the land that God has established for his Chosen People? Would anything less than the most desirable be appropriate for the covenant between God and His people?

Yet the realities of the situation are quite different: Israel was a marginal society living on the precipice of catastrophe. In virtually every dimension, they faced every crisis that could confront a People. However, they did continue to exist, albeit an existence which was conditional, problematic and difficult. This was the Promised Land: nowhere near as fertile or secure, by any definition, as Egypt, Babylon or other lands which they knew, and to which they even migrated. The covenant assures survival, not affluence; one of the lessons painfully learned by biblical man is that, despite the thorns and thistles, there are many worse diets than milk and honey! But however it is perceived, the covenant of a land flowing with milk and honey offers the People of Israel subsistance, not Paradise!

In retrospect, we may well say that the story of the Jewish People has *two* beginnings. One involves their life in 'the land flowing with milk and honey.' The other involves their two-thousand year march through history in the Diaspora. For whether through choice or of necessity, the major part of the Jewish People lived their lives in other lands. For them, the Land of Israel was both memory and fantasy, as they kept the basic article of Faith, "Thou art One and Thy name is One, and who is like Thy People Israel, One People Throughout the World."

Notes

1. Ex. 3:8,17; 13:5; 33:3; Lev. 20:24; Nu. 13:27; 14:8; 16:13f.; Dt. 6:3; 11:9; 26:9,15; 27:3; 31:20; Josh. 5:6; Jer. 11:5; 32:22; Ezek. 20:6, 15. I am conforming to common usage and translating the Heb. *zb.* as 'flowing,' although I think 'oozing' is more accurate. For initial study, cf.

my "The Milk and Honey Diet," *Forum on the Jewish People, Zionism and Israel* 49 (1983), 89–94.

2. E.g., Gen. 43:11, Ju. 14:14, Ezek. 27:27.

3. Parenthetically, the characteristic *caveat* of Pr. 25:16,27 warns that this most desirable of nutrients should be eaten in moderation.

4. I am indebted to my father, the late Prof. Samuel H. Levine, for this interesting observation.

5. Cf. F. Brown, S. R. Driver and C. A. Briggs, *A Hebrew and English Lexicon of the Old Testament* (henceforth *BDB*), Oxford 1907, 184f.

6. See Dt. 32:13, Ps. 81:17 for literary references. Natural grassland grows in climates where available moisture is insufficient to encourage the growth of forest, or to reward human agriculture. Here, of course, water is the critical, limiting factor, and periods of drought alternate with more favorable years. Yet whatever the extreme be, these lands, unlike cultivated croplands, do produce something. Thus, during the growing season, successive waves of flowering and fruiting occur; when dry years occur, the foliage is dominated by those plants which have been suppressed during the richer times. In these marginal lands, as in forest, tundra and all natural areas, life, i.e., continuity, or integrity, is based upon variety.

By interesting coincidence, in *BDB* the entry for 'honey' (*dbs*) immediately follows the entry *dbr*, the land we are discussing which is so widely translated as 'wilderness' or 'desert'!

7. I am grateful to Prof. Jack M. Sasson for drawing my attention to M. B. Rowton, "Dimorphic Structure and the Problem of the 'Apiru — 'Ibrim," *Journal of Near Eastern Studies* 35:1 (1976), 13–20.

8. Cf. J. T. Luke, *Pastoralism and Politics in the Mari Period* (Ann Arbor 1975) and R. De Vaux, *Ancient Israel* (New York 1965), I, 5ff.

9. Ju. 19:9; 20:8; I Sam. 13:2; I Ki. 8:66.

10. Cf. listing of similar usages in R. De Vaux, *op. cit.,* 13.

11. The 'Good Shepherd' motif is found, e.g., in Is. 40:11, Jer. 23:1ff., Ezek. 34, Ps. 23 and widely throughout scripture.

12. S. Talmon, "The 'Desert Motif' in the Bible and in Qumran Literature," A. Altman, ed., *Biblical Motifs,* Cambridge, Mass. (Harvard University Press) 1966, 37.

13. M. V. Fox, "Jeremiah 2:2 and the 'Desert Ideal'," *Catholic Biblical Quarterly* 35:4 (1973), 446.

14. Cf. Fox, *op. cit.,* 441–450 for a thorough exposé of the 'Desert Ideal' and a correct rendering of the verses on which it is based.

15. See De Vaux, *op. cit.,* 14f. and this conclusion of Fox, op. cit. 450.

16. Fox, *loc. cit.* Of course, nostalgic allusion to an idealized past is commonplace in both individuals and societies. See, e.g., Mircea Eliade, *Patterns in Comparative Religion,* New York (Sheed & Ward) 1958, Lloyd

Morgan, *Life, Mind and Spirit,* New York (Holt) 1926, Pierre Teilhard de Chardin, *The Phenomenon of Man,* New York (Harper) 1959, Norman O. Brown, *Life Against Death; The Psychoanalytical Meaning of History,* New York (Vantage) 1959, and A. H. Maslow, *Religions, Values, and Peak-Experiences,* Columbus (Ohio State U. Press) 1964, as well as the classical psychological and anthropological sources.

17. For relevant data, see Lewis Mumford, *The Transformations of Man,* New York (Harper & Row) 1956.

18. L. Mumford, *op. cit.,* 43.

19. On the pervasive utopian ideal, cf. Frank E. Manuel, "Toward a Psychological History of Utopias," L. Mumford, "Utopia, the City and the Machine," and George Kateb, "Utopia and the Good Life," in *Daedalus; Journal of the American Academy of Arts and Sciences* 94:2 (1965).

20. Ex. 13:5; Lev. 20:22ff.; Nu. 14:8; Dt. 6:3; 11:9f.; 26:15; 27:3; 31:20.

21. Josh. 5:6; Ezek. 20:6,15; Jer. 11:5; 32:22.

22. Ex. 8:17; 33:3; Dt. 6:3; 26:5f.

·4·
The Ba'al Shem Tov and the Flaming Sword

Hillel Halkin

In the opening pages of the *Shivḥei ha-Besht*, the 19th Century Hasidic compilation of stories about the Ba'al Shem Tov, there occurs a brief tale that, at first glance, appears to be simply one more wondrous legend about the founder of the Hasidic movement, yet that strikes me as a telling comment on Jewish life in exile in the Ba'al Shem's time and in our own. The story is set in the early, concealed period of the Ba'al Shem's career, when he was living alone, his true powers unrevealed, in a remote mountain district of the Carpathians. It goes:[1]

> Once [two] thieves came to him and said, "Master, we know of a short route to the land of Israel through underground caverns and tunnels. If you wish, come with us and we will be your guides." So he agreed. And as they were walking they came to a great bog of water, filth and mud which they had to pass by means of a plank laid from one shore to the other, supporting themselves on a long pole that they thrust against the bottom of the bog. Thus, the thieves crossed safely over, but when the Ba'al Shem sought to follow he saw before him a flaming sword that turned every which way, and so he turned back. For he would have been in great danger had he continued on his way.

What is one to make of this tale? Like many of its counterparts in the *Shivḥei ha-Besht* it apparently has a historical point of departure, since there is reason to believe that, at one point in his life, the Ba'al Shem Tov did contemplate settling in the Holy Land. His reason for changing his mind is

55

unknown, but even if it was purely pragmatic, his disciples, who attached a deep inner significance to all his actions, would hardly have construed it as such. To them its nature must have been spiritual, having a mystical cause and meaning, and our story is evidently their attempt to explain it in this fashion.

What then is the explanation offered? The Ba'al Shem Tov, we are told, did wish to journey to the Land of Israel—wished it so intensely, in fact, that in order to do so he was willing on the spur of the moment to follow two thieves through a frightening subterranean passage. (The popular belief in a network of such passages connecting all countries to the Holy Land was a traditional one, dating back to the Mishnaic times, yet these tunnels or *meḥilot* were thought to be reserved for the use of the dead at the time of the resurrection, and one does not, previous to this tale, hear in Jewish legend of their being traversed by the living.) Halfway there, however, he encountered an obstacle and turned back. Thus, his failure to proceed was not of his own volition, since a force greater than he barred the way.

So far the story is a simple one. It becomes less so, however, the moment we seek to understand what this force was. For the image of the sword that barred the Ba'al Shem Tov's ways is taken from the Bible, from the story of the expulsion from Eden, at whose gates, the Book of Genesis tells us, the Lord stationed Cherubim with "a flaming sword that turned every which way." Thus, our tale implies, it is God Himself who has prevented the Ba'al Shem Tov from reaching the Land of Israel, just as He prevented Adam and his descendants from returning to their primeval home. Moreover, He has prevented the Ba'al Shem alone, since the two thieves continue on their way unharmed, as they have done in the past. Indeed, it is only the Ba'al Shem who sees the flaming sword, the thieves being apparently unaware of it.

Was the Ba'al Shem Tov then being punished like Adam, since, unlike the thieves, he was not allowed to reach the Holy Land? This hardly seems to be the story's point—in the first place because, like all the tales in the *Shivḥei ha-Besht*, its purpose is to praise the Ba'al Shem, and second since it concludes that, had he not turned back, "he would have been in great danger." Far from being a punishment, then, the flaming sword seen by him alone is a sign of grace, a vision vouchsafed him to save him from some unsuspected peril.

But what was this peril? And why did it threaten only the Ba'al Shem Tov and not the two thieves as well? The *Shivḥei ha-Besht* does not tell us. It does not even inform us how the Ba'al Shem returned home again except to mention that on his way he met a huge frog that was the transmogrified soul of a lapsed Talmud scholar doing penance for a dissolute life that had begun with one small sin. The Ba'al Shem, we are told, took pity on this imprisoned spirit and released it from its loathsome incarnation—and with that our story is done.

And yet we are not done with it. For there are stories, particularly folk tales and myths, that tell us far more than the teller of them is aware of and that, being at once tantalizingly simple and oddly enigmatic, pose the problem of an undeciphered dream; such, I believe, is this legend from the *Shivḥei ha-Besht*. It is, in other words, an only partly conscious production, that part of it that is not conscious being the more revealing, as is suggested by its very terrain—its underground caverns and tunnels, archetypical symbols in folk tale and myth of the human unconscious.

Let us then examine its latent, dream content. Two thieves invite the Ba'al Shem Tov to travel with them through a hidden passage to the Land of Israel. Why thieves rather than ordinary men? Of course, it is the business of thieves to know of such secret ways, but there is more to them than this, for the thief commonly stands in dream life and myth for that lawless part of the self that would seize forbidden opportunities and act out inner desires in defiance of social convention. Indeed, it is not at all clear in our text whether the thieves are even Jews, and, as Gentiles enticing the Ba'al Shem to accompany them to the Holy Land, their illicit function is further strengthened.

But surely a Jew is not forbidden to live in the Land of Israel? No, certainly not; and in fact, in 1746, some years after the period of our story, the Ba'al Shem Tov's brother-in-law, Rabbi Abraham Gershom of Kitov, settled in Palestine himself. Yet Abraham Gershon's *aliyah* was highly unusual for its time and place, when returning to the Holy Land was universally considered to be an act best left for Messianic times. (Significantly, the one organized group of Ashkenazi Jews to attempt such a return before the Ba'al Shem Tov's time, that of Yehudah he-Hasid and his followers who took up residence in Jerusalem in 1700—the conjectured year of the Ba'al Shem's birth—was composed of heretical Sabbatians, for whom the Messiah had already come.) Indeed, in the underground caverns and tunnels of the Ba'al Shem Tov's mind a problem clearly exists, for the way that leads to the Land of Israel is via passages reserved for the dead; that is, despite his desire to live there, he too has doubts whether such a thing is permissible or better postponed until the resurrection.

Yet the thieves convince him to set out. No sooner has he done so, however, than he comes to "a great bog of water, filth and mud," that is, to a deep, unconscious crisis. Here he and the thieves must part. The latter forge ahead, but the Ba'al Shem sees a flaming sword in his path and understands that he must not proceed. The way to the promised land is closed to him.

But what is the nature of this crisis and what is the role in it of the flaming sword? Here, it would seem, lies the key to the puzzle of our story. The sword that bars the Ba'al Shem Tov's way is the same as that which bars the return to paradise. And indeed, for the Jew in exile the Land of Israel is paradise, or rather, paradise lost—a land blessed above all others, luminous with God's presence, sanctified by Him for His people and for His divine abode. For it, Jews yearned for centuries, endlessly recounting its virtues, lauding its holiness, praying for their triumphant return to it on the day of their redemption, which would be the final, irrefutable proof that they were indeed God's Chosen People and that their long, humiliating absence from the land had not been in vain. Indeed, the longer their exile lasted, the further they wandered from Israel, and the more remote their memories of it grew, the more paradisiacal a place it seemed to them—a land in which no miracle was impossible and every wonder was to be found. Little by little it ceased to be a real, tangible country, a land of ordinary hills and valleys, stones and earth, and it transformed itself into a fabulous dream in which the grief of loss and the promise of restoration mingled indiscriminately. For hundreds of years this dream sustained the Jew, bestowing solace on his suffering and hope on his travail.

And to this dreamed-of land the Ba'al Shem Tov is warned not to go. But why? What is the danger facing him if he disobeys the warning? Is it really because the divine will has decreed that no Jew shall enter it until the time of the Messiah? Yet nowhere in Jewish tradition is such a thing ever suggested; on the contrary, for all the notable failure to implement it, the commandment of *yishuv Eretz Yisrael*—of resettling the Land of Israel—is repeatedly stressed. Is it because Yehuda he-Hasid and his followers have tainted this commandment with the sin of the false Messiah, which threatens to infect the Ba'al Shem too? Although he may have conceivably been inspired by the heretics' example, the Ba'al Shem certainly never harbored Sabbatian tendencies himself, nor was his plan to settle in the Holy Land part of any Messianic scheme. It was, as our story tells us, a purely private decision, made in isolation and far from the public eye.

One must make, then, a different assumption. What causes the Ba'al Shem to turn back cannot be his fear of divine displeasure. It must be his fear of something else.

Of what, though? The answer is: of the Land of Israel itself, for paradise is a human myth, one of the most haunting; it is an expression of human longing and lack, one of the most powerful ever devised. But it is not a real place on earth, certainly not such a place as 18th Century Palestine. Or rather, it can be such a place only when seen from afar. One can never return to it, not because the way is barred, but because as soon as one enters it, it ceases to exist.

Now, I believe, we can interpret our story correctly. At some point early in his life, when he was not yet a public figure and still had no disciples, the Ba'al Shem Tov made up his mind to settle in the Land of Israel. Perhaps the idea was suggested to him by the *aliyah* of Yehuda he-Hasid, or perhaps it sprang directly from his own great inner need for an immediate, spontaneous relationship with the elements of Jewish experience, for piercing the shells of religious symbols to the core of the reality for which they stood. Others might pray for an end to the Exile; he would shake its dust from his feet; others might dream of the Promised Land; he would inhabit it. Such a plan might be deemed mad by any Jews who heard of it, but in those days the Ba'al Shem Tov was not considered normal by those who knew him anyway, nor was it his habit to consult with them. And so he resolved to undertake the journey. Yet having done so, he was immediately thrown into deep conflict. On the one hand, his excitement at soon being in the land of his forefathers was intense. On the other hand, the more imminent the prospect, the greater grew his fear of what awaited him there. Suppose that the lost paradise of the Promised Land should turn out to be an ordinary land like any other? Suppose that its hills and valleys, stones and earth, were only hills and valleys, stones and earth? Suppose that he was unable to experience them as anything else? Beautiful sights and natural splendors there would be there, of course, but the Carpathians had these too. Suppose that there was nothing more?

This then was the danger: not that he was unworthy to enter the Promised Land, but that it might be unworthy of its promise. And if it was, what would happen to the entire structure of Jewish belief that rested on that promise? If the Holy Land itself was merely a symbol dreamed in exile that could not withstand the encounter with the reality, what in Jewish life was safe from challenge? Once begun, where would the disillusionment end? (It is surely no accident that, in the linked story of the transmogrified talmudic scholar, we are told that the latter was originally a pious Jew who carelessly committed one sin which inexorably led to another and another until he had violated practically the whole Torah. He stands, in other words, for the fear of such a concatenation in the Ba'al Shem's own mind, from which he can exorcise himself only once he has abandoned his plan.)

The Ba'al Shem Tov's turmoil is underground, since he cannot possibly admit the full extent of it to himself. And then suddenly, as the bog of doubt deepens, he reverses himself. The Jews who counsel against returning to the Land of Israel are right; it is too dangerous. The conventional wisdom of the ages against which he has rebelled is now realized to be, in an unconscious flash of insight, far wiser than he has thought. The Jews who for centuries dreamed of the Holy Land, yearned for the Holy Land, grieved for the Holy Land, yet made no attempt to live in the Holy Land, knew exactly what they were about. In order to protect its holiness, in order to protect oneself as a Jew, one must never set foot in it. Only a thief may do so with impunity, perhaps because he is so spiritually gross that he has no expectations to be shattered; perhaps because he is not even a Jew. But the Ba'al Shem Tov is not a thief. And a flaming sword that turns every which way bars his path. It is a divine sign to him not to go on.

And so he remains in exile. In time he emerges from his concealment; he gathers disciples around him; his fame as a seer and worker of wonders spreads far and wide; he becomes the founder of one of the great spiritual movements in Jewish history. And long afterwards he tells his followers how once, when he was young and unencumbered, he nearly set out for the Holy Land but turned back at the very last minute. They ponder the meaning of this tale. Was our story invented by one of them out of some deep intuitive understanding of the crisis that his master had passed through? Or did the Ba'al Shem himself tell it in some form to his students? And if he did, could it have been in the form of a revelatory dream that he dreamed and later related to them, until in the telling and retelling it became the legend that appears in the pages of the *Shivḥei ha-Besht?* The phantasmal logic of its imagery suggests as much.

In any event, once the decision was made there was no going back on it. Years later the Ba'al Shem Tov's brother-in-law, Rabbi Abraham Gershom of Kitov, who was then living in Hebron, wrote to him: "The learned Jews here beseech me to write you and urge you to come live here, but what can I do? I know your nature . . . and I have despaired of your ever coming to the Holy Land before the time of the Messiah, may it be soon."

V'hamevin yavin.

Notes

1. My translation is from Sh. H. Horodetsky's edition of *Shivḥei ha-Besht.* Tel Aviv, DVIR, 1947, p. 48. The story also appears without comment as a chapter heading in the original Hebrew version of A. B. Yehoshua's excellent essay, Exile: the neurotic solution, in *Between Right and Right*. New York: Doubleday, 1981. (It was I who first pointed it out to Yehoshua during a conversation between us.)

·II·
The Psychology
of Exile

·5·
Jewish Exile and Jewish Redemption

Joseph Heckelman

Exile is our natural and initial situation. The trauma of birth propels the infant from a secure, warm, quiet, dark shelter to a bright, hostile, noisy, strange world. Much of our subsequent energy is devoted to attempting to transcend this exile. An individual can fully replicate the all-encompassing womb only in death, enfolded by Mother Earth in the all-encompassing tomb.

People reach out through various connecting networks: family (both the family one is born into and the family one creates), work, hobbies, professional associations, friends, neighbors, religious community, sports associations, etcetera, all of which may be compared to horizontal circles. And where they overlap stands the individual. Each circle has substance: some are relatively solid and firm, and some are light and wispy. The greater the accumulated weight of overlapping circles, the more redeemed is the individual. In addition there is vertical outreach upward to God and downward into history and land (individual peasantry, and group identification).

All motion is not outward, however, there is also retreat within a protective wall, a wall that both isolates and shields one from possible hurts that come from the outside. Some people are involved in more of these outreach areas, some fewer; some more completely, some less thoroughly. Redemption is the opposite of the lost sense of exile. With redemption one achieves awareness of peace, belonging, enlightenment (in the religious rather than intellectual sense). It is not then unreasonable to suggest that a major goal in life is individual redemption from universal initial alienation.

How is such redemption achieved? It may occur through major successful identification with just one of the above areas. More often, however, Western man will identify with a good number of these areas in a shallow way; limits tend to be culturally determined. Overt concern with self, for example, sets up walls which block and limit the extent of outreach that is possible. Thus, for example, while bonds of affection are strong in enlightened Western families, individual, scattered households are more often found. Even when family members work together they often receive individual salaries and are individually held accountable; each subunit is totally independent of every other. In contrast, the pre-Enlightenment Middle Eastern family (with some carry-over into the first couple of "liberated" generations) is most often characterized as an extended family functioning as an organic whole. Thus, when elderly parents buy or build a home, even the married sons reflexively set aside their normal obligations and freely help their parents. A joint business is run rather like a commune, with the father dispensing proceeds in accordance with need as he perceives it. Regardless of the inequities in such a pattern and the impossibility of its surviving intact under the impact of Western conceptions of rights, this structure provides a far more emotionally and psychologically secure place than does the Western nuclear family: the Middle Eastern extended family is far more substantial than its Western equivalent.

Every human being exists somewhere on the continuum between exile and redemption, and where depends on the number and intensity of subjectively significant involvements. Some areas of significance are universal and some are culturally determined. Whether or not the atheist who, by definition, denies God is existentially deprived because of his estrangement may be argued; but all agree that the religious individual who loses a sense of contact with God is indeed deprived. Similarly, an individual raised with no awareness of a relevant religious/political homeland may or may not be sustaining an actual loss; but the individual raised with such a consciousness —indeed with emphasis on its enormous importance for his individual and collective wholeness—surely is deprived when such a place is unattainable, even (or all the more so?) when it is not attained only because he chooses to live elsewhere.

How do the above generalities apply to the specific Jewish condition? It is a truism that "Jews are like everyone else, only more so." Jews are disproportionately visible in virtually every area of human endeavor. In other words, Jews are disproportionately successful. A variety of not entirely successful explanations have been offered to explain this phenomenon. It is, however, best explained in terms of Jewish expectations.

Perhaps an unperceived need produces an expectation (perceived or unperceived)? Certainly a perceived expectation—whether or not it is grounded in reality—produces a stimulus. Such a stimulus leads to a generating of more energy, which may function directly toward the stimulus or it may function in some roundabout way. It is this writer's suggestion that Jews, in general, have had more expectations, resulting in more stimuli, and thus energy output, than have non-Jews. The very concept of chosenness—of being, as it were, God's selected first-born (although clearly appearing on the stage of history relatively late)—both expresses and creates expectations.

The status "Chosen People" involved a system of rules and regulations, of standards which seem to be impossible for the people as a whole to achieve. This condemned the Jews to a cycle of frustration, punishment (the most severe being exile from the Promised Land), and reconciliation. The always-somewhat-out-of-reach goal was a continuous stimulus. While it was not possible to live completely according to the rules and regulations, the ongoing obligation was to both study this complex system and to basically live by its general requirements.

The expectation dimension is most powerfully involved in the Jew's haunting consciousness of exile. For homeland or redemption through return lies at the core of the Jewish psyche. Jewish history begins with a dynasty founder who is on the move. Abraham passes through and lives in a new Promised Land, the promise of that land being an aspect of new religious revelation. His son Isaac lives his entire life in that land; his grandson Jacob (renamed Israel) turns to retrace his grandfather's footsteps. He goes north and later returns southward as did Abraham. Later, as an old man going to Egypt, Israel regards his residence and that of his progeny as a temporary separation from their proper promised home, the land of Caanan (later to be called the Land of Israel). The fourth generation of sojourners in Egypt struggled out, having grown and made the transition from extended family to an agglomeration of tribes. As such—that is, as a people—they experience the theophany at a desolate mountain in Sinai. There is no Jewish tradition as to which particular mountain this is because it was never intended to be a sacred mountain; rather, it is a deliberately anonymous mountain in a deliberately anonymous wilderness—an unowned no-man's land. Revelation can take place anywhere.

The children of Israel were held in Egypt until they had undergone transformation, in a manner somewhat analogous to the gestation of the fetus. It is quite interesting that the Hebrew letters that spell "Egypt"—*mzrym*—also make up the words narrow water; the Jews passed through a narrow channel in the sea and were, as it were, born as a people. Their special fate was certified at the start in the "cutting of the Covenant" at the mountain in the Sinai: just as each individual male Jew has his fate affirmed by the circumcision, or "cutting of the Covenant" in his flesh at a rather early age. This special people carrying a special message in its manner of existence was not fated to wander anonymously in a barren no-man's land; had that happened the message would have been private, secret, withheld; rather, the Jews were to be rooted in the land promised to the Patriarchs as a sign of this special Covenant. Moses, the mediator, brought to the Jewish people in the wilderness a series of laws, rules, and regulations—written and oral. Living in accordance with this special framework will serve to characterize, identify, and preserve this people.

The Jewish religion, carried by the Jewish people, had to root itself in a particular place. They settled at the confluence of three continents, a place selected for the Jews by God. Before the Jewish conquest, the land was a collection of city-states, inhabited by a variety of different ethnic groups. Only with its later pacification under King David did the country live under unified rule for the first time in its history. At no other time in world history do we find a people, a religion, and a land starting out together and developing together for the first several hundred years. Thus, the Land of Israel has an experiential importance to the people of Israel and the religion of Israel is of a totally different order than any other religion. For other expatriates there may be ties of community, nostalgia, and so on, strengthening the connection with the ancestral homeland; but in no case is it the total religious, national, historic homeland—the place where religion, nation, and people were born.

Further, this place is also the anticipated future gateway to the transformed world to be called the Messianic era. This long-anticipated era is to be accompanied by a physical ingathering of Jews from all over the world in this same land. Even for those who choose to metaphorically view the Messiah, earthly Jerusalem is the way to the heavenly Jerusalem. Therefore, during the millennia that Jews were in exile—that is, not in the Land of Israel—whether the exile was forced or voluntary, the prayers recited every day of the week for all of the years of one's life included a prayer for a physical return to a restored Land of Israel.

Beginning with Joshua's conquest some 3200 years ago, some Jews did live in the Land of Israel. Beginning a few centuries later, some Jews did return to the Land of Israel in every generation. In our day, a combination of factors came to supplement the ongoing return to the homeland. Nineteenth- and twentieth-century nationalism, transmuted Messianic ideology, the Holocaust experience, modern means of communication and transport, and so on, led, in 1948, to the reestablishment of a Jewish state in the Land of Israel. Surely, all Jews should have been expected to flood to the now available homeland with its many redemptive associations.

However, Jewish redemption was defined, traditionally, as living in the Land of Israel under the rule of the Messiah descended from the house of King David in a transformed world of universal contentment! According to this definition, in the age of redemption human nature will be changed: we will all be living in the world to come. Although all Jews will be gathered in the Land, there will be room for all non-Jewish people to come to Jerusalem and acknowledge that God who chose the Jewish people as His special message bearers and His partners in the Covenantal relationship, is indeed the God of all people and of all the world. Not only will this be a time of peace among nations but there will be a sense of wholeness, security, enlightenment, and peace in every human soul. Anything short of this is, by definition, not ultimate redemption: it is, rather, at least a partial exile, even if one lives in the homeland. The non–Messianic political Jewish state of Israel potentially climbs several steps on the ladder toward redemption in many ways: it allows Jews in Israel to be part of a Jewish majority; provides a natural awareness of all religious holidays (even if one chooses not to observe them) in the press and on the street; insures the absence of the impact of other religions' major holidays; gives shelter behind the Jewish citizen army; and provides the metaphysical rootedness of living in the Land and being aware of the history that has been lived here. All of these provisions should make of Israel the place of highest redemptive potential for every Jewishly conscious person.

However, if a voluntary immigrant from a Western country has great difficulty learning Hebrew, cannot earn a living, feels pushed around by officials, treated with indifference by most of his neighbors, and finds the mix of people and customs strange, he may well feel more deeply at home in the exile country where he was born and raised. Further, he may well have a stronger support group (family and friends) back there, and not in the Land of Israel.

It does require particular initiative to implement the urge to return to the homeland that represents redemption. The State of Israel and the Land of Israel appear to be at best only the beginning of redemption. To live there is to experience a deeper rootedness, a more enveloping positive Jewish presence, but not a state of Messianic grace! Thus two-way Jewish traffic will continue; some people will come to live in Israel because it is Israel while some of those people born and raised in Israel will leave.

In summary, at birth the condition of every man is a state of exile, and life involves attempts to move somewhere in the direction of redemption. The infant Jew is no more lost than anyone else, but as he develops, because his expectations and the expectations of him are higher, his subconscious sense of exile is greater. When unfulfillable demands are an inseparable aspect of chosenness, chosenness itself adds to exile. When the physical homeland is a uniquely inseparable aspect of one's metaphysical past, and of the unattainable metaphysical future, deep metaphysical exile must accompany physical exile. And the unattainable expectations on return to the homeland perpetuate some sense of exile, even when one has returned to the ancestral soil. As long as one does not succumb to despair, such exile serves—as it was probably meant to serve—as a special spur to Jewish creativity. Indeed, exile is fundamental to the Jewish condition.

6

The Psychological Phenomenology of Exile

Lee Bennett Gaber

Throughout history the Jewish people have been characterized as feeling a nebulous longing, and this longing has acted as a common bond. One expression of this is heard in the closing phrase of the ritual Passover meal: "Next year in Jerusalem." This expressed desire to be in Jerusalem is at once a wish for unification, belongingness, a sense of security, and an end to exile. However, further consideration reveals the Exile to be not only a physical reality but also an inner feeling.

The feeling of exile, with its accompanying longing, transcends time and place; it is both temporary and permanent. The sensation has existed for the Jews since biblical times, punctuated by various banishments, wanderings, and homecomings. It was evident in the feelings of suffering and despair during the Spanish Inquisition, as well as during the Holocaust. This feeling was a force that helped to create the modern State of Israel, and it has sustained Israel through its short yet perilous existence.

Paradoxically, however, this longing and feelings of exile continue to be prevalent despite the existence of a national homeland. Although the longing and exile seem to be philosophically always present, as well as historically permanent, Jews have, for generations, related to it as if it were a temporary phenomenon which could be partially eradicated. Apparently, on a physical level, exile may be eradicated, but it remains psychologically an elusive motivating factor in both the individual and collective behavior of the Jewish people.

One may view the inner sense of exile with its concomitant longing as having been historically inbred—integrated into the psychological space of the Jewish people. Successful attempts at dealing with this inner sense of longing foster adaptive processes; unsuccessful attempts foster insecurity, pain, and assimilation through loss of Jewish identity. Implicit in this view is the notion that an inner sense of exile and its resultant longing are essential components of Jewish identity.

The development of individual and collective inner roots and resources may be seen as one way of coping with the insecurity that emanates from the inner sense of exile. These resources not only compensate for the feelings of inner exile, but can, if need be, be carried into states or periods of physical homelessness. This expansion of inner space includes the expansion of such values as love of knowledge, importance of education, dependence on faith, and emphasis on acts of kindness toward others. In the modern era these values are manifested in and realized through the arts and sciences, technology and business, and social institutions. They serve as inner sustenance, counter-balancing the effect of the feelings of loneliness and helplessness. Further-more, the Jewish people have always nurtured adaptability, flexibility, and creativity as necessary and valuable mechanisms for coping with states of exile (inner and outer).

When these inner roots—both of the individual and of the community—have become steadfast, increased awareness and investment in the non-Jewish social environment have evolved as complimentary coping mechanisms. Involvement and commitment to social causes and betterment have always characterized the Jewish community. Moreover, an identification with the feelings of exile and longing in others, more often than not with minorities, has motivated work toward social reform and equality. Jews have attempted to integrate into the culture of the country of residence and to usefully contribute—as Jews with an inherent sense of exile. This has helped to lessen the weight of the inner sense of exile; yet its remnants remain. Only when this sense is emotionally understood and accepted as an inner reality can a productive *modus vivendi* be achieved. A balance between the longing and insecurity resulting from the inner exile and the strengths derived from the Jews' moral values and social contributions can then be reached.

When the feeling of exile is phenomenologically too threatening, and therefore excessively painful, attempts may be made to deny its very exist-ence. This denial promotes a false sense of security and forces a relinquish-ing of Jewish identity. Attempting to deny the inner reality of exile causes the forfeiture of a unique heritage and values and the striving to be accepted as something one is not. This may well be the beginning of a self-defeating process both in terms of the individual psyche and in terms of Jewishness.

If the inner sense of exile is too pervasive, it becomes paralyzing, and the feeling of a painful isolation leads to a fragmented existence.

The Jewish people have traditionally yearned and prayed for an end to exile. When in the diaspora the prayers are conducted facing east; in Israel one faces toward Jerusalem; in Jerusalem the Western or Wailing Wall of the temple mount is faced. To an extent, these yearnings and prayers have been fulfilled by the reestablishment of Israel. If, however, the end of the Jewish people's physical exile causes them to neglect the inner sense of exile, the meaning of Jewish experience will be endangered.

The Jewish people today need to successfully recognize the inner components of exile and must relate to rather than avoid these inner components. Returning to the land of our Fathers does not, *ipso facto*, ensure Jewish psychological survival and identity. In Israel, as anywhere else, Jewish identity may be forfeited unwittingly. If the psychological aspects of exile are regarded seriously and consciously dealt with in the education and life-style of the state, then Israel will prove to be a valuable link to and a catalyst of Jewish culture. If this education does not occur, Israel will become a state devoid of historical Jewish ideas, insights, sensitivities, and values: another amorphous wasteland in which disillusioned people grope for personal meaning and identity.

7

Exiled from Exile: Existential Reflections

Morris Grossman

What Is Exile?

To be in exile, with a religious or historical sense that one is exiled, is to have already a mission and purpose in life. One's clear project then is to end the exile and to return to one's home, one's roots, one's authentic nature, one's place of proper being. To know, or to think one knows, where home is, must give the exile comfort and perhaps even a gratifying sense of destiny. I do not share this historical Jewish sense of exile, but the metaphor of exile is singularly applicable to the Jewish condition—including mine—and it is relevant to the human condition, which I am not adverse to sharing. I see exile in personal, psychological, even metaphysical terms, rather than in terms of geography, history, and destiny. Exile is a condition to be endured, or partially overcome, by internal travel and meditation, rather than a condition to be overcome by external travel of *aliyah*. I have no impulse toward *aliyah*, though I can imagine threats and dangers which might generate such an impulse. I do not disapprove of those for whom the impulse is genuine and enthusiastic. I am wary of arguments either for or against *aliyah*, including those I will offer in this chapter.

I was brought up "without religion," without the ritual, biblical, and Talmudic devotions which are, for many Jews, so large a part of being Jewish, and which, indeed, are seen as defining characteristics. When my parents made allusion, in Yiddish, to the coming of the Messiah, I heard only a tone of sardonic disbelief. I had to learn, rather belatedly, that for some

Jews the Messiah was a real expectation and a real power. My father's interest in Israel, through the labor Zionist organization *Poale Zion* and through friendship with many of Israel's founders, was not religiously based, and he partook of no sense of cosmic destiny. He and my mother never visited Israel, as I have, though they made the much longer and harder trek from Koidenov (near Minsk) to New York.

I consciously resent being exiled from Koidenov, where my family lived and worked for generations. Doesn't that give me a juridical claim? Yet I cannot return, and if my family had not left I would not have survived. Those members of my mother's family who never left Koidenov were shot in front of their own graves by the Nazi *Einsatzgruppen*, before the Holocaust became gaseous, efficient, and impersonal. Though Koidenov exists no longer, even barely in the dwindling memories of fewer and fewer people, I choose to claim it and to feel exiled from it. Koidenov is an appropriate if absurd reminder of the disparity between juridical and factual claims, and the frequent futility of the former.

In any case, my real exile is not from any historical homeland—familial, juridical, geographical, biblical—but from any sure sense of a cosmically moral or divine purpose. Hence my exile from Exile. This latter exile is endemic to the modern intellectual experience, shared by Jews and non-Jews alike, but, because of historical circumstances, perhaps known by Jews with special poignancy. My reflections here are deliberately personal, intended as much to reveal my condition as to justify it. Since my overall point is that our circumstances determine our attitudes as much as our reasoned choices, it is not inappropriate to explore those formative factors. I suspect that they are widely shared.

Israel and the Law of Return

Whatever idiosyncracy there is in my Jewishness, it does not keep me from a sense of identity with world Jewry, and with concern about its safety and well-being. I am delighted that Israel exists, and I want it to remain viable and strong. Its existence gives political strength to world Jewry, just as world Jewry gives political strength to Israel.

When I visited Israel I admired it, but from a distance. Moving there, on balance, would bring me to a more alien world than the one I am in now. My lack of a knowledge of Hebrew would be devastating and would hardly make up for some tribal affinities I might experience, such as the opportunity to speak Yiddish to people in Tel Aviv.

I am pleased nonetheless that there is a Law of Return. It is an available option, and the value to us, as Jews, of available options that are not likely to be exercised should not be underestimated. A sense of historic danger, and a concern for survival, generated that need for options which has always enlivened the Jewish imagination. But a desire to move to Israel could only come about for me as a result of anti-Semitic repression. The impulse to go there to settle would not be associated with values, with history, or with a sense of peoplehood, but with desperation. Although this does not sound much like a tribute to Israel, I believe these are feelings that are relevant in the dispersed Jewish world. Without a desire to live in Israel or an ideological commitment to it, I have sometimes wondered about the Law of Return as it applies to me. What right do I have to be taken in by Israel in view of my feelings and my dubious Jewish identity? Where is the juridical element? The Law of Return is like mother love—at once generous and possessive. It brings advantages and burdens to Israel, as it brings advantages and burdens to those who fall under its rule. The law is a gratuitous and unconditional beckoning hand; it is extended to any prodigal and will receive him without reference to active merit—other than the merit of being nominally identified as one of the tribe. I am pleased that the option exists even if I never exercise it—as people are pleased that they can return to a parental home, knowing that the occasion of such a return might be an escape from problems and misfortunes. It is a family thing, and family gestures (particularly Jewish ones, as we know) are as full of loving and undeserved welcomes as they are marked, at times, by undeserved rejections.

Seeing the matter in this tribal way, the various arguments about whether only Orthodox conversions (and not Conservative or Reform) should be the basis for admitting Jewish converts to Israel take on a comic, or tragicomic, cast, particularly in view of Israel's willingness to welcome secular and unaffiliated Jews like me. But this only confirms the tribal quality of it all. I am part of the family, if only a dubious part.

The Morality of Exile

Having touched upon initial matters of attitude and feeling, I turn to some questions. First, what is exile for the Jew? and is living in exile natural? Exile means many things, both natural and unnatural. Much of Jewish experience has meant risky habitation in lands of unfriendly non-Jews, and it can be said that such experience has become part of the Jewish psyche. To forget such experience, or in its abeyance not to fear its return, would be to lose some traditional Jewishness. So exile, or the exile mentality, is natural. It is particularly natural for Jews and natural in varying degrees for many peoples. But it is unnatural, morally undesirable, to live threatened and scapegoated the way Jews have lived. And so they have sought safety through immigration, sometimes to the Land of Israel. Who would not want to escape the defining characteristics, discriminated against; persecuted; wandering, in order to live normally and unthreatened in one promising place?

However, the moral and intellectual issues are more complicated. Exile has not meant only danger. It has meant possibility, challenge, venturesomeness, excitement, insight, and accomplishment. Alienation, whether from self or from tribal brethren, contributes to intellectual liberation and psychological emancipation. The resultant tension, sometimes bordering on the unbearable, produced many great works of knowledge and of art that were the very direct consequences of exile. Mahler, Freud, Kafka, Benjamin, Einstein—the 19th and 20th Centuries are filled with Jewish achievements or, if one prefers, achievements of Jews, which were inextricably bound up with the condition of exile. Of course Jews were not the only exiles; Joyce and Santayana were exiles, too, and the predicament of being exiled—what has almost come to be the modernist predicament—is intimately connected with the pain and glory of so many intellects and artists. The categories of natural and unnatural simply cannot be applied to special lives and accomplishments. Perhaps they ought not to be applied even to ordinary lives and accomplishments.

The view that Jewish culture can only, or primarily, flourish in a Jewish homeland begs the essential question. It is based on the distinction between Jewish culture proper and the accomplishments of merely cultured Jews—such as those named above. However, the enormous flowering of culture—Jewish culture it could be called—depended in part on attention to traditional Jewish themes but largely on the circumstances of Jewish thinkers. They were partly assimilated and partly unassimilated; they were outsiders subjected to "the ordeal of civility," to Gentile pressures to conform and belong. Jewish response, in so many important instances, was neither to give in to this ordeal by attempts at total assimilation, nor to try to revert to tribal isolation, separateness, or escape from exile. Jews managed to be beneficially involved in, but critically detached from, the cultures in which they lived. This made possible remarkable outpourings of creativity and originality, just possibly a greater cultural achievement in the last century than in any comparable period of Jewish history.

I take it as evident that the kind of adversity which in excess is merely destructive can in moderation function as a stimulus to all kinds of energy and effort. Nietzsche recommended that we live dangerously. Jews have not had to make a special effort. What for others has been a choice, a deliberate departure from the ordinary, for Jews has been an ongoing state of being—unstable, metastatic, hazardous, ambiguous, in a word, the dangerous condition of exile.

SAFETY VERSUS SECURITY

Does exile mentality or exile behavior manifest itself in Jews without reference to the realities of their surroundings? What are the realities of one's surroundings? Are they the cultural and intellectual opportunities of a pluralistic society (which we have looked at) as compared to the devotional, religiously focused opportunities of an ingathered society? Let us look at the blunter realities—the possible threat and danger in the lands of exile against the possible safety and security in the Land of Israel.

The realities having to do with danger and safety are not always readily apparent. Jewish preoccupation with history serves as a reminder that the immediate reality, the here-and-now political situation, may not be the most relevant. Potential for change, particularly change for the worse, is part of the deeper, hidden, time-binding reality. But in its utmost depths this reality remains obscure, and it is often well nigh impossible objectively to assess safety and danger. This has been the nearest thing to Jewish reality: the presence of risk and precariousness that cannot be weighed and quantified. The reality of the pervasive uncertainty of the degree of danger has led to painful, difficult, and contradictory Jewish responses. Our friends, as well as our enemies, tell us that we are oversensitive in the absence of provocation, and that we walk to the slaughter when we should know better. And we often say the same things to ourselves. What we should know better is that we can at least liberate ourselves from the illusion of knowability. Such absence of knowledge does not free us of the need for decision and action; and the questions that cannot be answered force existential responses. For Jewish survival, or the survival of Jews, should we cooperate and be doves? Or should we fight and be hawks? The Timerman case has reawakened Holocaust memories.[1] If the Argentinians will turn out to be as bad as the Nazis, certain risks and actions should be taken. If they are not as bad, and are subject to wholesome influence, then other actions ought to be taken. One cannot know when the common garden variety of anti-Semitism will veer toward the violent and insane. One cannot know when Jewish defensiveness and militancy give insufficient regard to the reasonableness of enemies. Should Argentinian Jews react with fury or with restraint, remain in Argentina or go to Israel? In their situation I doubtless would be driven to decision, in fear and trembling. The real division in these matters is not between Jews and other Jews, but within the Jewish psyche. The division is there because answers cannot be objectively found, and because decisions have to be made repeatedly.

Messianism

When the realities are difficult or impossible to comprehend, they are best encountered by avoiding Messianic illusions and by looking at the available facts with as cold an eye as possible. Messianic hopes arise and are perpetuated when the facts look grim or confusing and cannot generate in us sure, hopeful decisions. Still, if the concern is safety, I opt for intellectual detachment and uncertainty over pious dreams.

I realize that there are learned and sophisticated arguments for Messianism. The last one I saw was "Israel and the Messiah" by Jacob Katz in *Commentary*, January 1982. It attempts to show a linkage between historical Messianism and Zionism, with the assurance that "this is as it should be." Katz scolds "secular ideologues" for thinking otherwise, but it is in fact religious ideology which increases dangers and which loses touch with what little reality is sometimes available.

A bad argument can sometimes have useful public clout, and may be a dubious means (as in the Moral Majority's support of Israel) to a desirable end. But overall, the risks of self-deception and blindness override the practical gains generated by religious and other such attempts at self-fulfilling prophecy. I deplore any truck with the Messiah (*any* anointed one) as I am sure He does with me. He is not a cosmic power but an occasion for a human and sardonic joke about cosmic power. If we do not understand this distinction we are in trouble. We are also in trouble if we *do* understand it, but real trouble, Jewish trouble—*tsoris*—should at least have the imprint of some knowledgeable grounding and be worthy of us. There is a difference between recognizing on the one hand that reality is unknowable or elusive, and on the other hand filling the cosmos, and our ignorance, with the figments of a strained and pained imagination. To know that we do not know, as Socrates taught us, is a great advance over thinking that we know when we do not.

Un-Messianic Realities
ALIYAH

A further look at the un-Messianic realities invites some speculation about the general prospect for world Jewry. What about the *aliyah* option? The motives for ending exile are complicated, personal, and not readily connectable to reality. But from the point of view of world Jewry, is it better to end the diaspora or to sustain it? Given larger concern about survival, total *aliyah*, insofar as it is the Zionist aim, is a misguided eggs-in-one-basket approach. Massive anti-Semitism is possible anywhere in exile, even in the United States, where Jews for a long time have enjoyed a good measure of freedom and prosperity. But Israel too is under threat; it is a ghetto state surrounded by massive hostile powers which would mercilessly destroy her if they could. Israel is as beleaguered as many other historical Jewish ghettos were in their moments of ascendancy. Calling it a God-promised nation adds absolutely nothing to its power to survive beyond its military and political strength.

Because of this beleaguered condition and the possibility of total destruction, it would be prudent and preferable that all Jews not go to Israel. We would lose that final desperate option of "seed" Jews dispersed around the world. The self-destruction of the diaspora (presuming that the necessary exit visas were available) would offset the shorter-term gain of strength and viability which *aliyah* would bring to Israel. I acknowledge that my attempt to think the impossible—a frequent Jewish way of arguing—has little bearing on actual motives, feelings, and options. But I present it as a reminder to those who see in *aliyah* a sure sanctum and protection for world Jewry, and whose religious illusions blind them to possible outcomes.

FANTASY VERSUS REALITY: THE JURIDICAL CLAIM

Some argue that the concept of exile means that the Jewish nation was not dissolved when it lost its territorial homeland. They claim that unless the Jew maintains that the Jews are an autonomous nation, there is no juridical claim to a national homeland. This typically Jewish Kafkaesque fantasy logic attributes to juridical powers more force than they have to create facts, and it gives facts less power than they have to foster juridical claims. A concept, even one as grandiose as exile, cannot guarantee and sustain Israel; only living effort and ongoing victory can. There have been many govern-ments in exile over the years. Whether or not they reestablished their traditional geographies depended on politics and force. Nations come into being and pass away. Where are the Carthaginians? Did they lack a concept of Carthage, a Messiah, a sufficient sense of destiny? No nation, big or small, is destined for survival, and to believe otherwise is to turn a forgivable tribal emotion into an absurd claim. It is to say, without irony, "Koidenov lives." While hopes grounded in fantasy sometimes animate extraordinary efforts and cooperate with chance, such hopes are unworthy of free minds. Even proper God hypotheses, as articulated by Spinoza with careful philosophical effort, avoid such fantasies.

The minimal juridical claim to Israel, based as it is on religion and the concept of exile, neglects other more pertinent claims. One does not have to appeal to ancient history and God for claims to nationhood. One can pro-claim nationhood, and generate the here-and-now claims in the process of proclaiming it. The colonists did this at the time of the American Revolution, and, to look at a more painful example, the PLO is now attempting to do the same. The United Nations is a hodgepodge of national entities; many rose from the earth like mushrooms, and almost as speedily. They have no history, but they do have votes—"juridical" votes. Israel's juridical claims, too, had better be closely connected with current clout and current circumstances.

The Refugee Dilemma

But having made the above remarks, let me venture my own sense of the relevant claims of Jews to Israel, and indulge some of my own fantasies about justice. Jews have lived in the Middle East for a long time, but it is the recent facts that are important. Jews immigrated to Israel, bought land, cultivated it, settled on it, fought for it. For me, the crucial, modern juridical fact is that there are Jewish refugees from Arab countries as well as Arab refugees from Israel. Those Jewish refugees were badly treated, and in the process of becoming refugees lost claims to lands and communities in which they lived for a long time—as I have lost my claim to Koidenov. Certainly, Arabs were forced out of what is now Israel and suffered individual injustice. But there are more Jewish refugees from Arab countries than there are "Palestinians" who left Israel, and so the refugee situation, group for group, remains enormously in favor of the Arabs. A proper balancing out of the respective group claims would involve reparations to Jews in Israel and a cessation of Arab territorial claims. I realize that this vision veers toward fantasy, given the current political climate; but pleading for reasonableness in the face of force is the secular Jewish way of hoping for the Messiah; and there is widespread ignorance of the facts about refugees among people who assess the situation.

Assimilation

Concern about exile is directly connected with concern about assimilation, since exile is a condition of partial assimilation in the Gentile world. The vicissitudes of assimilation—the degrees and kinds of exile from exile—deserve some final comment.

The process of assimilation takes place, when it does, by a series of modulations, sometimes through a number of generations. With each modulation—or shift toward assimilation—the prospect of the next shift seems less drastic. We share a group—or tribal—history, but we also have individual histories. These histories are so variable that Jews of different exile cultures can be strangers to each other, and sometimes remain estranged even when gathered in Israel. Members of a single family, especially those of different generations, may live in different mental, if not physical, worlds and may lack common experience. Each individual carries within himself his own past and his own future, as well as the pressures and the urgings of his people. The change, the loss, the modulation for each individual is seldom total, and residues and memories remain. But to surrender some of the past in the process of acquiring some of the future is the perennial human condition. With respect to assimilation and the dilemmas it has created, Jews are truly Chosen People as well as choosers. We learn the languages, obey the laws, grapple with the opportunities, relate to the people who are around us—and inevitably we become part of, if not one with, them.

The metaphor of modulation is intended to suggest the subtle mix, through gradual stages, of choosing and chosenness. In assimilating, we are by no means necessarily acquiescent and accepting of our surroundings.

While assimilation sometimes manifests itself as a kind of passivity, an evasion of self and dignity, it is sometimes an active, affirmative process—deliberate, principled, and positive. It will inevitably be a gain from some perspectives, and a loss from others.

The active and passive factors in these processes are enormously complicated and can be endlessly explored and interpreted. It always seemed to me that many 19th Century Jews who converted to Christianity should not have, and that it was an undignified yielding. Yet at the time it must have seemed natural, promising, and perhaps not too agonizing a thing to do.

Scolding does not help and is not to the point. It cannot help if we do not know where we have been and where we ought to go. Koidenov was once a lively, real place, then it became a memory, and then, devoured by history, became a haunting illusion of a home away from home. The modulation analogy now fails, since in classical music we do know when we are modulating away from, and when toward, home. Modern life and music is less clear; we move about and touch many keys, but we cannot be sure of the desirable direction. That is why Jews are wanderers, and why our deepest fantasy—and it is only a fantasy—is that there is a home.

Many secular Jews like myself are not unsympathetic to Jewish militancy, even when that militancy is linked to doctrines (exile, religion, etcetera) to which we cannot give assent. Such prerational militancy, or tribal vehemence, gives direction to life and produces clear-cut emotional and practical gains just as eschewing such impulses brings clear-cut intellectual gains. Ambivalence is inevitable.

I was once stopped by a Hasidic Jew near the Metropolitan Museum of Art on Fifth Avenue, in New York City; he asked me if I were a Jew. (How did he know to stop me?) He then proceeded to lecture me on the rudiments of proper worship. If part of me felt emancipated from the likes of him—his narrowness, his dedication, and his single-mindedness—another part of me admired him—his narrowness, his dedication, his single-mindedness. He is a brother, which is to say that some of his many children and grandchildren might turn out to be as much like me as like him. He is a mysterious bearer of the sundry seeds of our common, and mixed, heritage. I feel the same about the militant Zionist who would escape exile. May he remain in his home if he is sure he is there, and may he find it if he thinks he knows where it is.

Notes

1. J. Timmerman, *The Longest War*. New York: Knopf, 1982.

· III ·

Exile in Jewish Theology

·8·
Meta-Myth: The Diaspora and Israel

Jacob B. Agus

Sometime ago the late Henry Hurwitz and I coined the term *meta-myth* to stand for the notion that the Jewish people are mysteriously and metaphysically different from the rest of humanity. This myth is, of course, deeply imbedded in the romantic and naive currents of ancient and medieval Judaism. We called it a myth because in itself it is a vestige of ancient, precritical thought, though it is frequently associated in Judaism with the noblest ideals of self-sacrifice. Myths have a life and even a logic of their own, since they draw their power from the collective unconscious. In mythology, the "will to believe" is directed toward concrete things—in this case, an empirical people of flesh and blood. Also, myths reflect the drive of instincts, which were developed in the struggle for survival, rather than the outreach of ideals—in this case, the hurt of injured pride and ethnic prejudice. Again, as Émile Durkheim and Lucien Levy-Bruhl pointed out, primitive, pre-culture peoples worshipped "collective representations" of their own corporate being, in effect deifying the life of the tribe or the folk. In all its brute power, this kind of myth has been reincarnated in the "folkist" movements of our own day. And its power is not yet spent.

The meta-myth is not identical with the Chosen People concept which could be interpreted in historical and rational terms; that is, as a fact of history, the Jews became the first bearers of monotheism: "My first-born Israel" (Ex. 4:22)—first in a family of many sons. This priority doubtless imposes upon Israel special obligations, in accordance with the famous "therefore" of Amos (Amos 3:2). But, apart from the initiative of God, the character of the Jewish people may not be different from that of other nations. Indeed, they may well be "stiff-necked" people (Ex. 32:9). Furthermore, the Jews could be "chosen," in the sense of *example*, rather than *exception*; that is, the career of Israel dramatizes the turbulent love affair between God and mankind. In its liberal interpretation, Israel represents both the greatness and the littleness of humanity, according to whether it turns toward or away from God.

The meta-myth, on the contrary, stresses Jewish *exceptionalism*. It insinuates the nightmarish fog of mystery into the public image of the Jew of our day. It transfers the secret of the purpose of God, which was not revealed to any man—not even to Moses—to the mundane struggles of the marketplace. A whole community is either chosen or rejected, predetermined for salvation or for perdition. A fantastic theology becomes an invidious biology. Our so-called uniqueness is made to depend on our blood. The Jews are "a people apart that is not counted among the nations" (Num. 23:9). Halevi puts them in a unique domain extending between humanity and the angels.[1] This mode of thinking became axiomatic in the vast literature of *Kabbalah*, and in the folk-imagination it drew immense power from the dispersion of the Jewish people—their ghost-like unity, in spite of their utter fragmentation.[2]

The Christian religion took over the meta-myth but changed its valence from plus to minus. The Chosen People, favored by divine fiat, were now the rejected people, living under a curse until the end of days. The pro-Semitic theologians labored hard to prove that Israel's fate was distinguished from that of mankind in two ways, a plus and minus, chosen, rejected, to be chosen again. But even in the more favorable view, the Jew was not to be seen as just another human being, to be judged by the same standards, praised and condemned in the same light. The historical categories of nationality and religion, cultural amalgamation and segregation, rationality and romantic fantasy do not apply to him. Superhuman and sub-human, he is accordingly in a class apart.[3]

The historical consequences of the meta-myth were inevitable—about the Jews, the wildest charges were believable. After all, they were an enigmatic mystery, akin to that of the Incarnation; only unlike the latter, they were incarnate; in the Christian view, God's love turned into wrath.

It is hardly necessary to pass in review the various expressions of the meta-myth in the long and dismal record of Christian anti-Semitism. Jules Isaac has put us all in his debt by his collection of material from French Catholic sources.[4] The Vatican Council had made a valiant effort to inhibit, if not to completely destroy, the dragon's seed of anti-Jewish mythology still rampant in the Christian world. The Christian task is far from completed, however. Christian writers still speak of the rejection of the Jewish people as a result of the Crucifixion—as if God had intervened in the course of history to put Jews, and only Jews, under His continuing "wrath." Even Augustin Cardinal Bea, who authored and defended the *Schema* calling on Christians to desist from acting as "avengers of Christ," nevertheless claimed that a cosmic guilt somehow persisted within Jewry. *All* Jews must not be condemned for the crime of deicide.[5] However, the guilt "falls upon any one, who in some way *associates* himself with the 'perverse generation', which is primarily guilty. . . ."[6] And "the refusal to believe in the Gospel and in Jesus is a factor in this judgment, and so, in one way or another, is a free decision to ally oneself with the 'perverse generation', with the powers opposed to God."[7] Accordingly, Jews are left in an ambiguous position. Their "refusal" is *a* factor, not *the* factor. The meta-myth is suspended, not dissipated.[8]

It is exceedingly difficult for an orthodox faith, claiming infallibility, to move clearly and unequivocally to a new position. Its protagonists have to back obliquely into the future, while protesting that they cling to an unchanged past. Nevertheless, I believe that in the contemporary dialogue, the humanist position can be asserted and developed in a way that will eventually result in the total repudiation of the meta-myth. This assurance is based on the fact that the humanist outlook is itself part of the Judeo–Christian heritage. The very concept of dialogue derives from the irresistible momentum of the humanist ideal within both Judaism and Christianity. In a meaningful dialogue, this common heritage is likely to be reinforced in numerous and intangible ways.

However, this blessing will surely elude us if our own ideologists continue to move within the shadowed underbrush of mythology. We live today in continuous interaction with our Christian neighbors, so that a dialogue, implicit and many-sided, is constantly in progress. Indeed, we speak loudest when we think we speak to ourselves alone. Unfortunately, in recent years the meta-myth in our tradition has gathered fresh force and a massive worldwide impetus. Within three decades our generation was cast into the darkest depths and exalted to the loftiest heights. Such a fantastic chain of events fits better into the mold of mythology than within the compass of a reasonable world view. But our destiny depends on the growing power of reason in human affairs. Say our sages, "If a person devotes himself to understanding, it is as if the Holy Temple were built up in his day" (Sanhedrin 99a).

By way of clarifying the general posture that an authentic life of dialogue implies, I wish to call attention to the exchange of letters which took place in 1916 between Franz Rosenweig and Eugen Rosenstock-Heussey. These letters illustrate vividly what a dialogue must not be—since both parties were possessed by the meta-myth, as by a *dybbuk*. This historical dialogue is especially significant because of the stature of the two exponents. Rosenweig continued to grow as a Jewish theologian, with his best insights appearing in his minor essays.[9] Rosenstock-Heussey was a formidable philosopher, who, as a Jew, could not be accused of anti-Semitism. He was converted at age 16, ten years or so before this debate. Nor, as his later life demonstrated, could he be accused of self-hate.

Alexander Altmann extols this dialogue as an epoch-making event:

> . . . one of the most important religious documents of our age. . . . Unlike the medieval disputations, in which dogma was arrayed against dogma, verse set against verse, this discussion is a true dialogue. It is indeed the most perfect example of a human approach to the Jewish–Christian problem. It is also an exemplification of what is called the "existential" attitude to theological problems. . . .[10]

The meta-myth, wherever we find it, is the invariant catalyst of mythological anti-Semitism. This awareness is a timely warning, for while the meta-myth in its Christian form has been allayed in recent years, it appears to have been born in a fresh guise in the Moslem world. Indeed, as the Islamic nations see the dawn of a Golden Age in their newly found oil wealth, they are impelled by daily headlines to see the State of Israel as their collective enemy. Naturally, the antagonist must be worthy of the steel of so mighty a horde; hence, the stature of Israel must be blown up to mythic proportions. Even now, we see the ancient myth taking on an Islamic shape. Moslem writers see Israel as the body of a mythical octopus-like monster, with tentacles, visible and invisible, extending into the mighty capitals of the world, pulling the wires of the marionettes of parliaments and congresses. Soon enough, they will resurrect forgotten *Hadiths*, depicting the Jew as the inveterate minion of Satan. Hold on to your copies of *The Jewish Encyclopedias* and to the classic Jewish works on the Moslem faith, for in a little while we shall be inundated with tracts demonstrating that Islam was always and everywhere wedded to mythological anti-Semitism! So, *ein beraira*, we never have an alternative.

In Greek legend, ghosts are reincarnated when they drink blood. Even now, this particular ghost has drawn blood and behold—it is materializing before our very eyes.

As Jews, we are all too prone to be fascinated and even intoxicated by the meta-myth, with all its dark and heartwarming pathos. Only now the myth is centered around the State of Israel rather than around the widely scattered diaspora. Everything about Israel is seen in an eerie light, so that it is either bathed in Messianic, unearthly glory, or in the dark colors of pseudo-Messianic despair. Overblown rhetoric resounds all about us, as if we were standing at the Eschaton. In the past, we have prided ourselves on our capacity to reject the hold of myths upon our faith. Ezekiel Kaufman sought to demonstrate this thesis with an amazing display of erudition and brilliance. Reform thinkers in particular have been the stout champions of an antimythological mentality. The renowned 20th-Century philosopher, George Santayana, wrote, "Hebraism is a striking example of a religion tending to discard mythology and magic."

But have not some of us turned ourselves into a myth, uprooted from humanity and endowed with a unique, mysterious sanctity? Have we allowed the momentum of this historic myth to seduce us to the worship of blood and soil? Have we joined in the chorus of the Israeli chant of despair, "the whole world is against us?" Has the Messianic mood, in all its millennial depth, distorted our perception of reality, like a psychedelic drug? Have we lost the capacity to glory in the imageless absolute, the source of the ideals of rationality and humanism? These are some of the questions that we should ponder, as the future rushes upon us with the speed of jets.

Notes

1. See H. Hirschfeld, *Kitab al Kharizi*. New York: Richards, 1967.

2. It is axiomatic in *kabbalistic* writings that the higher souls of Jewish people are derived from the divine *pleroma*—the realm of *Sefirot*—whereas the souls of all other nations are derived from the "shells." Rabbi Hayim Vital does not exempt converts from this rule (*Aitz Hayim* 7,10, 7) (*Aitz Hadaat, Bemidbar*). The "Tanya" of Rav Sheneur Zalman was written for the general public. Its view of Gentile souls is in Chapter 6. The Zohar follows the same line, save that in the *Midrash Haneelam*, we note a certain effort to account for this difference. Before Adam sinned, he possessed the higher soul; after his sin, only his animal soul remained. Thereafter, the divine soul comes only to those who are preoccupied with Torah, entering the body of the Jewish male at age 13 (*Zohar Hodosh, Bereshit 18b–19a, Midrash Hane'elam*).

3. The basis of this belief is in Rom. 11:25. Jacques Maritain, the recently deceased Catholic theologian, undertook to combat anti-Semitism in a number of addresses. Yet, he continued to represent Israel as "a mystery": "Thus from the first Israel appears to us a mystery of the world and the mystery of the Church." We recall that the "mystery of the world" is satanic in character. So, Maritain continues, "But, since the day, when because its leaders chose the world, it stumbled, it is bound to the world, prisoner and victim of that world, which it loves, but of which it is not, shall not be, and never can be. This is the mystery of Israel understood from a Christian viewpoint." Jacques Maritain, *A Christian Looks at the Jewish Question*. New York: Arno Press, 1973, pp. 25, 27.

4. Jules Isaac, *Genèse de l'antisemitisme*. Paris: Calmann-Levy, 1956.

5. Augustine Cardinal Bea, *The Church and the Jewish People*. New York: Harper and Row, 1966, p. 69.

6. Ibid., p. 78.

7. Ibid., p. 85.

8. Eric Werner points to the fact that the deicide charge is the theme of a poem called *Improperia* that is still part of the Catholic service. See his article, Melito of Sardes, the first poet of deicide. *HUCA Hebrew Union College Annual*, XXXVII, 1966, 191–210.

9. *Kleinere Schriften*. Berlin: Schocken, 1937.

10. *Judaism Despite Christianity*. Schocken Press, University of Alabama, 1969, pp. 26–27.

11. G. Santayana, *The Life of Reason* (Condensed Edition). New York: C. Scribner's and Sons, 1922, p. 258.

·9·
Exile and Redemption in Modern Jewish Theology

Jack J. Cohen

Throughout the centuries, efforts were made to find a theoretical basis for the connection between the Jewish people and *Eretz Yisrael* beyond the compelling but not very informative claim that God had decreed the eternal marriage of the two. One of the most notable efforts of this kind was the attempt of Yehuda Halevi (1086–1140 C.E.) to demonstrate that *Eretz Yisrael* is like the people of Israel, supernaturally endowed with qualities that raise it above all other lands. The very air, earth, and sky of *Eretz Yisrael* are prerequisites for the emergence of prophecy.[1] Furthermore, "All who prophesied did so only in *Eretz Yisrael* or in behalf of it."[2] In other words, it is told that a special relationship subsists between the Jewish people and its land, such that only in that land can the people attain its unique fulfillment in prophecy.

The Maharal (R. Judah Loew ben Bezalel of Prague c. 1525–1609 C.E.) attributed Israel's title to *Eretz Yisrael* to the fact that every people has its natural habitat and only in its own land can it fulfill its destiny. For Israel to live in exile is unnatural, and the exile, therefore, must inevitably come to an end. No condition which defies the demands of nature can last beyond an appointed time. Thus, despite the supernaturalism which underlay the thinking of Halevi and Maharal, their description of election as based on certain inherent qualities of land and people opens the way to more objective analysis of the relationship between these two factors in the evolution of Judaism.

Maimonides, the rationalist, also recognized the central role which *Eretz Yisrael* must play in Jewish creative survival. His philosophy of the land is best outlined in several passages of the "Laws of Kings" in his massive code, the *Mishneh Torah*. Maimonides summarized rabbinical law concerning Jewish settlement in *Eretz Yisrael* and the diaspora. As a realist he was aware of the many subjective and objective considerations which might require a Jew to dwell abroad for a period of time.[3] But while such temporary residency was permissible everywhere (except in Egypt),[4] Maimonides declared in his *Mishneh Torah* that under no circumstances should a Jew settle permanently except in *Eretz Yisrael*.

Maimonides highlighted the deep emotional attachment of the Jewish people to *Eretz Yisrael* when he recalled how the great sages would kiss its stones and roll around in its soil, apparently in order to experience physically as much as possible of its holiness. He did not go beyond this mystical hint except to maintain that according to the sages, the sins of he who dwells in *Eretz Yisrael* are forgiven, and that life in the world to come is guaranteed to a person who walks in the land at least four cubits.

Both of the foregoing visions of land and people flow from the supernaturalist view of God which was deep in Yehudah Halevi and from which Maimonides might, in the opinion of some interpreters, have departed just a step. In this state of thinking, Israel's claim to *Eretz Yisrael* is theological, and the land itself, whether because of its inherent natural qualities or as a result of the function which God has chosen for it, is an inseparable element in the doctrinal complex of election. Indeed, I believe that it is the fulcrum on which the whole doctrine rests. The following cursory survey should help us find our way through the maze of problems connected with the present-day Jewish presence in Israel and in the diaspora.

Harav Kook

Abraham Yitzhak HaKohen Kook (1865–1935) was passionately in love with the God of Israel, with the Jewish people, and with its land. While no love, in his conception, had a right to stand on the same level with the supreme love of God, the Jew's attachment to God, the people of Israel, and the Land of Israel are of one piece, for to love Israel is to love God's people; to love the Land of Israel is to love God's soil.

Kook's Zionism is an indispensable element of his theology. That theology, in turn, finds a logical application in a political program for the Jewish people. The redemption will not be brought about by the one-sided initiative and action of God; the Jews themselves have to become activists. On the other hand, such activity must be aimed at only one objective—to make manifest Israel's love for God.

We, our entire people, feel within us that it is worthwhile to yearn for absolute good, good for all. On this basis, it is worthwhile to establish a state and to engage in politics. We ourselves have witnessed that absolute good is the eternal goodness of God in all reality, and we always strive to pursue it collectively as people. Therefore, the love of God and devotion to Him are of the very essence to us and cannot be erased or changed.[5]

Kook's political theory involves a theological rejection of the lands of the Exile and an affirmation of Israel's oneness with *Eretz Yisrael*. At the basis of Kook's theology is the idea that the universe is simultaneously united and divided. Because God is one, so too must all of creation be unified. But in accepting the kabbalistic doctrine that Creation came about as a result of God's self-contradiction, Kook had to adopt the idea that during this process, the created world became divided. Only Israel maintains the inherent capacity to understand the divine secret of unity and embody it in its life. But while Israel possesses this capacity, there are stumbling blocks in its way, the main one being its state of exile. As long as Israel remains scattered among the nations, it cannot restore its true sense of God's unity.

In the impure lands of the nation, it is impossible for the unified *Weltanschauung* to be revealed, for the divided world dominates, and its individualistic, splintered, divided and alienated view overwhelms all of life's concerns. As a result, despite every effort to draw an Israelite breath and to understand the secret of cosmic unity, the atmosphere of a foreign land stands in the way. Therefore, the impure earth of the diaspora is filled with the stench of idolatry and Jews abroad are idolaters, however pure their motives. The only escape from the disgrace of idolatry is for Israel to be gathered together in the Land of Israel . . .[6]

In contrast to the lands of the exile,

The air of *Eretz Yisrael* makes wise, illuminating the soul's ability to grasp the foundation of the united world. In *Eretz Yisrael*, we draw sustenance from the light of Israelite wisdom, from the quality of the spiritual life which is peculiar to Israel, and from the Jewish conception of the cosmos and of life, which are basically the triumph of the united world over the divided one.[7]

Thus, in Kook's mind, the return to *Eretz Yisrael* and the establishment there of a Jewish polity, are prerequisite to the fulfillment of what inheres in Israel as God's people. In the divine unity Israel has a unique affinity to God; in the cosmic disparity, only Israel possesses the potential for helping to restore the pristine unity.

Blessed is our lot that we have been chosen to restore the great and simple truth to the world, on which the life of every soul depends and with which the removal of the light of the whole universe is bound up. We have this aptitude in our individual and collective essence, in the contour of our history, in the nature of our physical substance, in the quality of our land and in the souls of our great ancestors.[8]

Israel's affinity to *Eretz Yisrael* constitutes only one facet, albeit of transcendent importance, of its God-given character. The idolaters and heretics know only themselves and the drives of their crass, materialistic pleasures. Even the spiritual pleasures serve only their own egos and that "which is baser and uglier, that which is condensed within the narrow confines of the private interest is, for them, basic."[9] In contrast, Israel's love of God's goodness is no tangential matter but the inherent nature of the people. It follows that

> Our relationship to *Eretz Yisrael* is not accidental; it is, rather, a natural, divine tie. All our being and essence are tied to the land of our desire, so that even every removal from the land because of our sins did not cause any change in our essential character. . . .[10]

Exile, however, does mute the ability of the Jewish people to live up to its inherent spiritual ability. Israel is born with the divine quality of *hesed* (lovingkindness) which, according to Kook, is lacking in other peoples. To regain its ability to act according to its true nature, Israel must return to *Eretz Yisrael*.

The return, however, would bring no automatic salvation. Kook was caught up with the mood of the time, and he articulated from his *halakhic* perspective the new vision of work which Aaron David Gordon conceived in his own form of humanistic mysticism. Kook understood that the first step toward eliciting from *Eretz Yisrael* its nation-building powers would have to be its physical reconstruction. Spirit had to be tied to the body. This conception explains why Kook believed that the antireligious *halutzim* were performing an important function in the scheme of redemption. Eventually, he hoped, they would also find their way to an *halakhic* existence. But meanwhile, Kook's *halakhic* vision embraced physical labor and the settlement of *Eretz Yisrael* as a normal working, agricultural, and industrial society. Kook was caustic in his criticism of those traditional Jews who failed to participate fully in the physical reconstruction of *Eretz Yisrael*, but who, instead, thought that work could only be an interruption to the true vocation of the Jew—the study of the Torah.

Kook stood on the borderline between pre-modernity and modernity. His conception of election was drawn from the deep well of Jewish theological tradition, from its faith in a supernatural God who conferred upon Israel a unique set of spiritual qualifications to which other peoples could aspire but could not attain until Israel had carried out its mission to educate. This view of election was patently racial, albeit with a humane purpose in mind. The purpose—the unity of mankind and the universal love of God—informs the whole course of Jewish history. One can disagree with Kook as to the paternalistic way in which this goal will be achieved, but the goal itself bespeaks a genuine love of man. Kook's anthropology, however, stemming both from a longstanding and normative theological supernaturalism that characterized pre-modern western religions and from a benighted conception of human physiology, psychology, and social development,[11] prevented him from stepping completely into the modern world. As it was, his toleration of the *kibbutz* humanists never encompassed a realization, let alone an acceptance of the new vision of man and work which both guided and resulted from the endeavors of the *halutzim*. Kook could tolerate the idealistic workers, because he believed that ultimately they would accept the life of *mitzvot* which God had commanded. He could not, however, accept the legitimacy of any Jewish orientation which rejected historical revelation. The return from exile could never be complete without the full restoration of Torah in the life of every Jew. The Jew's membership to the Chosen People obligated him to observe the Torah, and no matter what might be his contribution to the building of *Eretz Yisrael*, in the long run he could never be a "kosher Jew" (a designation which appears several times in Kook's writings) unless he undertook the full burden of his election.

Kook rarely, however, pressed the logic of his position to its bitter end. His personal warmth and tolerance frequently served as a brake on any fanaticism that might have been inherent in its view of things. It is of course conjecture, but it seems to me unlikely that Kook would have approved the direction in which his son, Rabbi Zvi Yehudah Kook, has pressed the logic of *Eretz Yisrael* as the Promised Land of the Chosen People. Yet it was Harav Kook's personality and not his philosophy which might have raised a barrier between the members of *Gush Emunim* and him. For him as for them, the ethical and spiritual role of the land was defined for Israel before it became a people, and the people had no right to reject their responsibility to live in *Eretz Yisrael* and to fulfill the Jewish mission in all its borders.

While Kook's humanity and patience might have prevailed over the pressure of the doctrine of election, he was never able to address himself directly—and certainly not systematically—to the role of land in the development of nationhood. For that endeavor we turn to Mordecai M. Kaplan.

Mordecai M. Kaplan: Eretz Yisrael, Exile, and Jewish Election

For all his intellectual distance from Harav Kook, Mordecai Kaplan (1881–) is amazingly close to Kook's points of departure. Both Kook and Kaplan begin with a deep emotional attachment to the Jewish people.

They both emphasize the moral purpose of Torah, and they both accept the primacy of the Pentateuch and its legalism in the scheme of Judaism. For both Kook and Kaplan, *Eretz Yisrael* is cherished for itself and for what it can elicit from the Jew. Yet despite these similarities, the two thinkers are poles apart in the rationales on which they base their common commitments and on the substance of those commitments.

Kaplan's intellectual problem as a Zionist has been threefold: (1) to provide an understanding of why land is so essential to Jewish continuity; (2) to explain why that land must be *Eretz Yisrael*; and (3) to state the case that would justify the right of the Jewish people to this spot of earth. Note that while Kook could, given his system of election, have avoided all these questions, he was too much of a modernist to have ignored them completely. In the end, however, his ultimate response was theological: *Eretz Yisrael* has a divine nature; it was given to Israel, and only there can the Jewish people live naturally; Israel's right of possession, being God-given, is indisputable. Nonetheless, when Kook finds it necessary to proclaim the unity of matter and spirit, when he espouses the prophetic ethic of moral nationalism, and even when he tries to prove that the wastes of *Eretz Yisrael* can be redeemed only by the Jewish people, he demonstrates that dogmatic assertion about election is insufficient. At some point the human experience has to be brought into the picture. In contrast, human need and social experience are the keys to Kaplan's view of the role of *Eretz Yisrael* in Jewish life.

> Judaism could neither have arisen, nor continued to exist apart from the land that gave it birth. . . . A common country molds an aggregate of human beings into a people. . . . Mere physical propinquity is sufficient to give rise to common language, common customs, laws, forms of worship, ethical standards and social aspirations. What soil is to the life of a tree, a land is to the civilization of a people.[12]

This short paragraph summarizes Kaplan's conception of the making of Jewish peoplehood and a hint of what the role of *Eretz Yisrael* must be in its future.

Kaplan knows full well that the emergence of the Jewish people and its civilization in *Eretz Yisrael* is an insufficient explanation as to why, after two millennia of survival under oppressive conditions in the diaspora, it once again has become necessary to root Jewish life in the soil of the ancient homeland. Not being able to fall back on election, which he rejects, Kaplan has to provide a different rationale for his Zionism. He has no difficulty with the history of Jewish survival. The Jews were able to survive in exile for a number of reasons, a principal one being that

> No matter where the Jews lived, culturally and spiritually they moved in a Palestinian milieu. Even the climate and other physical conditions of the countries

they lived in did not seem to interest them. We do not find that they prayed for rain or dew for the countries of their dispersion. . . . The memory of having once lived in Palestine, and the certainty of occupying it again, could not be considered the equivalent of actually living there, but they were at least effective anodynes for his *Heimweh*. The Jew remembered that he was in exile and bitterly deplored his condition.[13]

In other words, according to Kaplan, the Jews were successful alchemists who were able to transform the dross of exile into the gold of Jerusalem simply by acting out the dream of return. However improbable, the Jews had learned the secret of survival as a nation even though they were uprooted from their natural home.

Of course Kaplan cites other factors to account for the survival of an uprooted Jewish people, but the desire to be a nation in *Eretz Yisrael* provided, in his opinion, a stronger bond of unity than could be attained even by most other peoples living unmolested on their own soil. Thus, students of the *Halakhah* continued throughout the centuries to study and to elaborate on the laws which applied only to *Eretz Yisrael*, while ordinary Jews have prayed daily for the return to the land and thank God for its bounty every time they eat a meal.

All this is history, in which the mystique of *Eretz Yisrael* has provided the motive for the world view of Jews who believed and still believe in their election and in God's choice of the land to be the home of their people. Kaplan, however, cannot rest his case on such premises. Why, after the Emancipation, does the Jewish people need *Eretz Yisrael*? One obvious answer is that the Emancipation for Jews is far from complete. Only in a few democratic countries have Jews acquired human and civil rights to a significant degree. But even there pockets of anti-Semitism are to be found and their latent virulence to be feared. Jews still need a place of refuge. Kaplan argues that such a role can be played only by an autonomous Jewish state; nevertheless, while this explanation of the need is necessary it cannot be sufficient. Jewish unity might be preserved as long as there is a serious threat to Jewish existence, but Jewish creativity under freedom has to be derived from more diverse and positive considerations.

The Zionist movement is thus not merely the outcome of the need of Jews for a haven of refuge from persecution or discrimination. It is principally a response of the Jewish People to its inner drive to metamorphose itself into a new corporate entity, by transposing its spiritual heritage into the key of naturalistic and thus worldly salvation.[14]

In contrast to Kook, Kaplan has understood the career of the Jewish people as a natural phenomenon, subject to the same laws of social development and change that characterize the histories of other nations. This is not to deny the uniqueness and even genius of the Jewish struggle for survival, but these qualities are no more or less explainable than are such more negative characteristics of men and nations as bland normalcy or deficiency. Recourse to supernatural election can only lead to distortion of historical fact and the kind of theological gymnastics that have been employed in order to explain why it is necessary for God to play favorites. Kaplan will have none of this style of thinking. Jews need a land because they are a civilization, which Kaplan defines as "the product of a group commonly known as a nation, whose life is rooted in a specific part of the earth."[15] "Each civilization has its own landscape which it conceptualizes and thus makes an object of consciousness."[16] Why is it no longer possible for the Land of Israel to continue to function in the consciousness of the Jewish people, as it has for two millennia, without having to be occupied again by a large, autonomous Jewish population?

Kaplan's answer can be summed up in his remark that "Jewish unity can no longer be merely a tradition which served mainly to qualify all who lived by it for bliss in the hereafter. What Jews need now is living collective experience that they can share in common."[17] Only in a sovereign community founded in a land which the group recognizes as its own can such living experience be fully realized. The conditions of modern life, particularly in the free world, are hardly conducive to the long-range survival of ethnic sub-groups. Nor can such minority entities ever hope to achieve the level of collective experience for their groups which would guarantee the preservation and creative enhancement of their traditions.

In adopting this basic premise of the Zionist analysis, Kaplan nevertheless does not then draw the conclusion of *Shelilat HaGolah*: denying the value and even possibility of Jewish survival in the diaspora. He adopts the position of the Israeli educator, Eliezer Rieger, who wrote: "*Eretz Yisrael* and the *Golah* are mutually indispensable. Without the *Golah* to encompass it, *Eretz Yisrael* will become parochial; and without *Eretz Yisrael* as its center the *Golah* is apt to deteriorate."[18] A land, then, according to Kaplan, is necessary in order to enable the Jewish people to realize the potential of its civilization. But for all its magnificence as the instrument of Jewish survival from the destruction of the ancient Jewish state until the Enlightenment and Emancipation, the exclusivity of *Eretz Yisrael* is insufficient. The Jewish people requires a theory of and strategy for survival in the diaspora and a new conception of society in *Eretz Yisrael* that will accord with modern standards of autonomy, democracy, and pluralism.

Modern Jews need a land in order to stir their imaginations and to provide them with an outlet for their creative energies as members of the Jewish people. Building an autonomous Jewish community in *Eretz Yisrael* not only serves the needs of those Jews who live there and participate in the daily collective experience of the *yishuv*, but it also provides the Jews of the diaspora with an agenda of supportive activities and of mutual criticism and dialogue with the majority group of Israeli Jews, as well as with new founts of Jewish cultural and spiritual expression that spring up in *Eretz Yisrael*.

Why does this land have to be *Eretz Yisrael*? In Kaplan's response we can see a naturalistic transposition of the thesis of election. According to his doctrine, *Eretz Yisrael* can be the only possible land for the people of Israel because of the divine chemistry of their interaction. True Judaism can be composed only in the laboratory which God has prepared especially for his cosmic experiment. Kaplan revalues this traditional view by exploring the natural process within which the attachment between a people and its historical homeland is cultivated. It is in a land which a group of people identifies as its home that it first acquires a we-feeling.[19] Inevitably, the group identity is associated with that land alone. Obviously, this process is a complicated one, involving responses to a number of interrelated problems. What initially draws a group of people to a land? Why did the nomadic Hebrews decide to settle down, and why assuming that the call to Abraham was historical fiction, did they select Canaan for settlement? Why was no other people, apparently, able to galvanize the same creative energies in Canaan that the Hebrews succeeded in doing? How was *Eretz Yisrael* able in modern times to evoke this same creativity among Jews that no other land was able to do—even though there are lands in which modern Jews feel very much at home?

Kaplan is aware of all these questions. To some of them, answers can only be educated guesses. But the fact remains that any love relationship has about it elements of chance (how do couples meet?) and mystery or arbitrariness (what draws a lover and beloved together?). The connection between a people and its land is basically founded on love. However, with all its undefinable qualities, love is nonetheless a natural human experience whose absence or presence requires no recourse to supernatural explanations. *Eretz Yisrael* is necessary for the Jewish people, argues Kaplan, because it is the only land which can awaken the people's full power of creativity. Perhaps the best way to articulate what Kaplan sees as the power of *Eretz Yisrael* is to quote a few verses, taken from writings of latter-day Zionists which he helped his co-editors to prepare for their Sabbath prayer book:

Not as a gift is a homeland acquired, nor through claims
    based on statutes and charters;
It cannot be bought for gold, not taken by force,
By the sweat of pioneers, by the toil of workers
    with brawn and brain, it is built,

By men and women armed with invincible will and
   prepared to link their destiny to a sublime purpose.
A homeland is a creation, the collective achievement of a people,
The fruit of its physical, mental and moral labors for
   many ages.[20]

The above describes what a homeland can and must do for any people.
For the Jews, only *Eretz Yisrael* can serve this purpose. Before the establishment of the State of Israel, Kaplan and his colleagues put these sentiments
into the form of prayer; some of these sentiments were uttered by so-called
secularist Jews:

> Whenever some memory of the Land is kindled in the heart of the Jew, his blood
> flows more exultantly; all his being is aroused to new heroism, new fortitude, a
> new thirst for God. Every contact with the Land works a complete revolution in
> his outlook on life, an uplift which is a return to God, a veritable redemption.
> Every contact with the Land heals the soul of the people and brings to life all the
> good that is latent in the hidden recesses of its spirit. The great joy of creation now
> throbs through the arteries of all Jewry, the creation of a people risen to full
> stature, vigorous, thriving, responsible.[21]

In these passages, Kaplan presents a plausible substitute for election both
as an explanation for the historic relationship between the Jewish people and
Eretz Yisrael and as a means of spurring a continuous creative relation
between them. The approach avoids the theological conundrum of God's
universal providence giving way to the favoritism that is inherent in election.
It remains only to ask how Kaplan justifies Israel's claim to *Eretz Yisrael*
over the claim of the Arabs. Again, given his premises, Kaplan cannot
produce a writ of ownership which would uphold the Jewish claim to *Eretz
Yisrael*. Indeed, from a naturalistic, humanistic perspective, all peoples can
have only tentative claims to their lands. Kaplan can have recourse only to
history, out of which he makes a reasonable case for Jewish right to the land,
and for the fundamental needs and human rights of the Jewish people. His
position would be strengthened by a more empathetic and realistic appraisal
of the plight of those Arabs who were buffeted around between the world's
powers, in the internecine power struggles over Palestine that have gone on
between the Arab states, and in the confrontation with a dynamic Jewish
national development. Kaplan's analysis lacks the depth which can come
only from a full awareness of the evolution of Palestinian consciousness.
True, he mentions several mistakes made by the pre-state Jewish settlers,
but while his writings on the subject reveal some moral concern about
treatment of the Arabs by Jews, he fails to grapple with the intricacies of the
Arab claim. Kaplan writes at one point:

Jews should have realized that they have to live with the Arabs, and should not have attempted to build a Jewish economy by discouraging employment of Arabs. They should have tried to develop a single high-level economy in which exploitation of both Arab and Jewish labor would not have been precluded. No effort or ingenuity should have been spared in devising ways and means of effecting a *modus vivendi* that would have been satisfactory to all who have a legitimate interest in the land.[22]

This passage opens the door to an examination of what constitutes a legitimate Arab interest in *Eretz Yisrael*, but Kaplan himself never, to the best of my knowledge, pursued this point.

A Final Comparison

Kook and Kaplan represent two conflicting positions on the doctrine of election. It is impossible to understand what Kook's thinking is about without appreciating his complete acceptance of the chosenness of the Jewish people; it is equally impossible to understand the normative Jewish response to the experiences of Jewish history during the long exile without believing in the premise that Jews believed utterly in Jewish chosenness. In contrast, one cannot fathom Kaplan's philosophy of Judaism without discerning his reasons for rejecting election. Kook and Kaplan, simply put, stand on opposite sides of the theological continuum.

I speak of a continuum because the concluding point of this chapter is that both positions belong within the Jewish consensus. That consensus is formed not out of the logical agreement but out of common realization that *Eretz Yisrael* is indispensable to any program for creative Jewish survival. Kaplan and Kook are united in their love of *Eretz Yisrael*, in their conviction that the Jewish people must sink deep roots in its soil, in their belief that only this land can bring to implementation the nation-building capacity of the Jewish people, and in their vision that the purpose of the Zionist enterprise must be to create a moral Jewish nation. Kook presents us with a model held together by the doctrine of election. Kaplan paints a picture composed of human needs, social reality, and a people's will to live. Kook's view is undoubtedly more poetic, but is his poetry to be believed, as George Santayana might have asked? Kaplan's conception is prosaic, but does it not open doors wide to the exercise of moral imagination?

Notes

1. H. Hirschfeld, *Kitab al Kharizi*. New York: Richards, 1927, bk. 4, par. 17.
2. Ibid., bk. 2, par. 14.

3. Maimonides Hilkot Melakim 5:7-9.

4. In his commentary on the Mishneh Torah, Radbaz (R. David B. Abi Zimra 1479-1573 C.E.) properly reminds his readers that Maimonides himself had remained for a long time in Egypt, but he explains this contradiction by arguing that Maimonides was forced to do so.

5. Mosad Harav Kook, *Orot Hakodesh*, Jerusalem, 1963, vol. 1. p. 52.

6. Ibid., Jerusalem, 1964, vol. 2. pp. 423-424. The point is repeated several times by Kook. See particularly Mosad Harav Kook, *Issrot Harayah*. Jerusalem, 1964, Vol. 1, letter 96, pp. 112-113.

7. Ibid., pp.114f.

8. Mosad Harav Kook, *Orot Hakodesh*, Jerusalem, 1963, vol. 1, p. 4.

9. Mosad Harav Kook, *Olat Rayah*. Jerusalem, 1964, vol. 2, p. 264.

10. Ibid., p. 265.

11. See for example, Kook's obscurantist discussion of the nature of men and women in his *Olat Rayah*, Vol. 1, pp. 71-72.

12. Mordecai M. Kaplan, *Judaism as a Civilization*. New York: Shocken Books, 1967, p. 186.

13. Ibid., p. 188.

14. Mordecai M. Kaplan, *The New Zionism*. New York: Herzl Press and Reconstructionist Press, 1959, p. 71.

15. Ibid., 1967, p. a186.

16. Ibid.

17. Ibid., 1967, p. 71.

18. Quoted by Mordecai M. Kaplan, op. cit, p. 96.

19. Mordecai M. Kaplan, *The Future of the American Jew*. New York: MacMillan, 1948, p. 127.

20. Reconstructionist Press, *Sabbath Prayer Book*. New York, 1941, p. 479.

21. Ibid., p. 483.

22. Ibid., p. 136.

·10·
Jewish Spirituality in the Diaspora

Bernard Berofsky

The Problem of Jewish Identity

The conceptual victory just attained by the Jew of the diaspora who feels the pull of his present homeland as well as that of his ancient one may be pyrrhic. The issue that is of deeper concern to diaspora Jews is not whether they are still entitled to the label "Jew," but whether its application, not ruled out by current national status, matters.

To many American Jews, Jewishness matters. How else would one explain the proliferation of Jewish institutions and activities of all varieties—cultural, educational, philanthropic, social, artistic, political, even religious? If one were to attempt to penetrate the labyrinthine structure of this corporate behemoth, one would undoubtedly discover a complexity exceeded only by the federal government and a vitality reminiscent of a modern dance company. The American Jews expend a tremendous amount of energy, not just because they regard the support of education, political causes, cultural enhancement, and so forth as valuable but also because they believe that support of Jewish education, political causes that favor American and Israeli Jewry, the enhancement of Jewish culture, and so on are all valuable. This commitment then must be inspired by the belief that Jewish culture and identity in some form is worth preserving and has a chance of surviving in America. This belief must, I fear, be challenged.

To fix our ideas, let us put several considerations to one side. It may be that Orthodox Jews—by whom I mean those who are bona fide, committed to a life governed by *Halakhah* and not simply those who happen to be members of Orthodox congregations—constitute the most viable group of American Jews. But, in spite of their recent growth and the interest in orthodoxy among young Americans, the appeal of this group will be quite limited in the foreseeable future, and my remarks will henceforth not pertain to that segment of American Jewry.

One must also distinguish contributions to culture by American Jews from contributions to Jewish culture. One occasionally hears the argument that the scientific and cultural achievements of Jews in the diaspora have, over the centuries, been enhanced by the isolation of the Jew and the tension that resulted from his status as a member of a frequently despised and ostracized minority. Had the Jew the security enjoyed by normal people, he would have been more complacent, less ambitious, and more accepting of a mediocre and comfortable existence. As insightful as this observation is, it is irrelevant. I have no doubt that American Jews will, in the future, contribute more than their fair share of scientific, educational, artistic, and professional achievements in the United States, just as they have done in the past and in spite of the fact that they are, according to the arguments just presented, at a disadvantage that results from their having achieved greater acceptance in the United States than in other countries of the diaspora. But these achievements by Jews have little to do with Jewish culture or Jewish life and can coexist alongside total assimilation. This is, no doubt, overstated. Although there is nothing Jewish about the Salk vaccine but its creator, the nature of other achievements by Jews who themselves may be quite assimilated and perhaps even resentful of their ancestry is permeated with their origins. Literature contains a rich source of examples. (Who can fail to discern the Jewish content of Franz Kafka's *The Castle*, for example?) And the logical and conceptual talents possessed by the author of this article are supposed to have a lot to do with his Talmudic heritage. Again, the Jewish soul surely has found in the sound created by the violin a way to express his spiritual yearnings and frustrations. But we are doing no more than illustrating a general truism to the effect that each group's absorption into the American melting pot does not entirely annihilate the distinctiveness of its contributions to American civilization.

Even if we count the above as part of Jewish culture in America and are content to note the Jewish style and flavor that many of these contemporary products portray; even if we will not be dismayed if strictly Jewish culture and learning languish and eventually die here, we are fooling ourselves. For how many generations can we expect the melting pot to be nourished in distinctively Jewish ways by assimilationist Jews who will eventually lose touch with the springs that nourish their Jewishness? To suppose that Jewishness will survive in ways that will continue to enrich American culture in the absence of a self-conscious effort by Jews to preserve it is to ignore reality and, hence, to be condemned to relive the past. We so easily forget, for example, how quickly the vibrant Yiddish culture, transported of necessity to American shores, became moribund and is now but a relic. Its current contribution to American culture consists primarily of the widespread use, even among Gentiles, of some colorful Yiddish expressions— hardly a harbinger of wonderful things to come.[1] How can we expect the

Jewish consciousness to continue and to infuse its creations when it fails to be nourished by Jewish education? In spite of valiant efforts by some, particularly the Jewish day schools, the general level of Jewish education in the United States is shocking. If active members of synagogues and other Jewish organizations are, along with their children, abysmally, and I might add, cheerily ignorant of their heritage, how can we expect totally assimilated Jews who may be very talented to enrich America in Jewish ways?

The low level of Jewish education and the high level of assimilation are also ominous portents for bona fide Jewish culture. With respect to assimilation, although evidence is not difficult to find, the most impressive recent statistics concern the alarming increase in intermarriage. In regard to education, on the other hand, the growth of college level programs in Jewish studies and related curricular developments, reflecting the general vitality of ethnic and other group identification in America, is a countervailing and, therefore, promising development. (It certainly helps to sustain and invigorate Jewish scholarship.) Such programs ought to be encouraged, if serious, and improved if not, in the hope that we are solidifying a permanent enrichment of higher education and not just hanging on the coattails of another fad. Unfortunately, some of these programs are not serious academic events. These failings together with those in the other spheres of pre-college and adult education appear even more profound in light of the primacy, the absolute obligation, of learning in Jewish tradition. Also, one must not confuse education with its trappings. Every synagogue has an adult education program; but education is hardly the correct word to describe the character of much that goes on. Similarly one may be impressed with the quantity of texts available for Jewish education, until one notes how skewed they are to the elementary level. (It is pleasing to note that, in recent years, this picture has improved somewhat with the appearance of advanced and serious texts in several areas of Jewish studies.)

Americans are fond of regarding themselves as distinctive, as possessing within themselves the power to confute expectations based on historical evidence. "It can't happen here" is, perhaps, more plausible if "it" refers to destruction from without, but has already been proven wrong if "it" refers to self-destruction—to the extinction of Jewish identity by the seduction of the host country and the enthusiastic cooperation of the Jew who will prove himself as American as apple pie. Where are the descendants of the first Jews to arrive on these shores, the Sephardim of Spanish and Portuguese origin? They and their culture perished through intermarriage and assimilation. What provides the *Ashkenazim* in America with the faith that it cannot happen to them? In a chilling tale, "America is not Babylonia," Trude Weiss-Rosmarin shows how Jewish culture in the diaspora has flourished only when the Jews were not assimilated, when they were not genuinely *of* the country they happened to be residing *in*.[2] She compares American to

German Jewry, noting "that if not for a constant influx from Eastern Europe, German Jewry would have become extinct long before the Nazis took over. Intermarriage and apostasy took a frightful toll of German Jewry in the post-Mendelssohnian century and a half."[3]

Can anything be said on behalf of the response that the above reflects a failure to take into account the experimental and innovative character of the American spirit? If Judaism is to live in American soil, it will have to take bold new forms. Moreover, the roads to Jewish self-affirmation may be many and varied. If you look at Jewish life in America with the tired eyes of the traditionalist seeking out the conventional and well-trodden paths to Jewish identity, you will undoubtedly miss the action. Look not inside Temple Emanuel or the offices of the Jewish Federation, but rather at a swinging *chavurah* group in Soho. Otherwise, you will be almost as provincial as the (nonreligious) Israeli who cannot even understand liberal Judaism, who regards the Conservative and Reform movements as American *mishegoss* (foolishness).

Where is the action? Weiss-Rosmarin concedes that there are two outstanding illustrations of Jewish creativity in an assimilationist environment—Philo in Alexandria and the Wissenschaft des Judentums in 19th and early 20th Century Germany. We ought similarly to take note of the first-class Jewish scholarship that thrives in the seminaries and universities of the United States. Weiss-Rosmarin's complaint about these creative pockets—namely that their creations are known primarily by specialists and have little impact on either their contemporary Jewish community or later generations—renders her thesis somewhat less interesting. It is one thing to be told that significant Jewish culture in the diaspora, highbrow or middlebrow, requires a fair degree of isolation from the community at large. But if the products must speak to the masses of Jews as Jews ("Philo was at home in Alexandria, and because of this he could not bring a message to Jews who remained strangers in their many *exiles*"[4]), it is almost a truism that we should not expect this sort of result in a place where Jews are content to be integrated into the populace. I would not want to disparage Jewish scholarship in America on this basis and, in spite of my fears concerning the viability of its future, I am prepared to look on it as a happy highbrow oasis.

What are the actual sources of inspiration for American Jews in their quest for affirmation, unfettered by traditional forms and limits? The answer is depressing and is at the basis of my skepticism. We know that it is not a theological commitment. Most Jews do not literally believe that story—the covenant, the mission, the redemption. And, difficult as it is for philosophers of religion to accept, subtle philosophical reinterpretations that render the story palatable to the skeptical mind do not evoke outpourings of Jewish worship on a grand scale. And, since American Jews have also given up the love of the Torah, or religious study, they are left only with nostalgia and fear as sources of inspiration.

Though nostalgia can inspire, it alone can sustain a strong Jewish presence for only a short period of time. We are then left with fear as the principal force determining the destiny of the Jewish people in America. Yet the American Jew, though a victim at times of anti-Semitism, does not live in constant fear for himself or his fellow American Jew. He becomes pre-occupied in his religious and social activities as a Jew with the fear of extinction of other Jews, for example, Russian Jews and Israelis, and with related emotions retrospectively addressed to Jews who have already been extinguished. These concerns are genuine and important and the results of American Jewish attention to such matters are impressive as is the intellectual and literary response to the situation of the persecuted Jew. Moreover, it is certainly understandable that contemporary Jews possess a strong sense of the fragility of their existence and become so preoccupied with the ugly aspects of minority status. But it troubles me deeply to think that a people is bound together principally by external threats and can provide no positive answer to the question of the meaning of its continued existence as a people. Presumably one wants to preserve not just Jews, but the Jewish people. Yet few are interested enough to study Jewish history, Jewish literature, the Hebrew language, Torah, Talmud, etcetera, to try to discern whether the people are worth saving. Perhaps they are discouraged by their leaders, so many of whom (Elie Wiesel, Emil Fackenheim) tell the same story: The meaning of the Holocaust is that the Jewish people must survive. We do not know why or to what end. But we have a duty to further and secure its existence.[5] But we American Jews are pretty secure now. So what is left but philanthropy or the United Jewish Appeal? Jewish education? If it can be squeezed into the hectic American way of life; it almost never can. Thus, as Robert Alter has pointed out, of the 93 courses in American colleges on the Holocaust, nearly one-half of the institutions involved have no other courses on Jewish history or culture.[6] Instead of learning about the Jewish people and their history as a means of deepening our understanding of this calamity, we prefer to vicariously experience monstrous crimes against it in order to forge a collective identity that is to be determined and shaped by forces alien and totally antagonistic to it. The study and dissemination of information about the Holocaust is of the utmost importance, especially in light of the appearance of such revisionist trash as the *Journal of Historical Review*. Though there may be psychological benefits in detailed public displays, before audiences steeped in material comforts, of the most grotesque forms of human butchery, it is difficult to believe that the future of American Jewry is to be found in the institutionalization of these practices.

In addition, are not these sentiments arising from contemplation of that mass murder a reflection of the pride Jews have always felt about their endurance? Perhaps, though, Marvin Lowenthal, who argues that Jews are not as unique in this respect as they are fond of believing, had a point when he said, "Except for mummies existence is no endurance test. The Jews, in common with other people, live by their works and not by their calendar. They are to be remarked for what they have thought and done (and may still think and do), and not for being always on hand."[7]

There is one other external source of inspiration—Israeli culture. But how can American Jewry build a culture by importing it, especially when it does not speak the language of Israel? One cannot found an American revival on Israeli folk or modern dance, as exciting as these are. This becomes even clearer when one recalls how verbal—as opposed to musical or artistic— Jewish cultural expression has been historically.

The spirit is willing, yet the flesh is weak. I have asked many Jewish parents why they join temples and synagogues when their participation consists exclusively of sending their children to a Jewish school that is at best minimal and often merely a sham. Their typical response is: "So they know who they are." The desire to be identified with the Jewish people is there; but it is not strong enough to initiate a serious program to realize this goal, especially if such a program in any way interferes with either the child's or the adult's other business.

Perhaps the disappointing condition of American Jewish life is due in part to a recognition, rarely conscious or explicit, that, for a group who no longer discerns the eternal verities of the Jewish faith and is not prepared to uproot itself from its native land in order to redefine this faith in national terms, there is no positive goal or meaning in continued Jewish existence.[8] No wonder then that one's energies are directed to humanitarian and anti-defamation work and, in place of Jewish idealism, we have Jewish defensiveness and negativism. Given that six million American Jews are here to stay, this is a depressing psychological fact. It is imperative then that some of them—more cannot be expected—address this question. If meaningful self-expression in the diaspora is possible, then the American Jew is blessed with an opportunity unavailable to the Israeli: namely, to display the fruits of Jewish civilization to the non-Jewish world, to interact and exchange ideas with the dominant Christian culture.

> As American Jews, we are called upon to rise to a far greater challenge—that of unfolding the values of our tradition in the free and open spaces of a nonparochial universal culture. Thus we may render our contribution to the achievement of that synthesis of wisdom which our age is trying so desperately to attain.[9]

There are two hurdles, one internal and the other external. The Jew must be prepared to steep himself in his tradition, in the faith that it has worth and relevance; and America must be ready to share the riches.[10] If that happens, the real *galut* has ended; but the evidence that this is likely to take place is nil.

It would be an error to suggest that the sole barrier to an American Jew's ability to express his Jewishness is his own weakness of will, softened by the seductive character of a totally accepting and alluring environment. The negativism we have found to be at the basis of many forms of Jewish expression in America is, I believe, partly to be explained in terms of the Jew's frustration, not always conscious, concerning the conditions of life in a country he wants to believe is the utopia sought by those victims of religious persecution—his grandparents and great grandparents. Although anti-Semitism in the United States can take some pretty nasty forms, many Jews' exposure to it is minimal. They, therefore, come erroneously to believe that its effect on them is not very personal or deep. They fail to discern the subtle, yet pervasive way it affects so many facets of their existence, coloring their relationships with the Gentile world in all sorts of unhealthy ways. They believe that the herd instinct possessed by even the most assimilated Jew reflects only the familiar minority impulse to congregate with those who share your background and habits and is not based equally on the need to act in a way that will not elicit, in disguised or suppressed forms, reactions to Jewish traits. When a Jew's sensitive antennae pick up signals like "You people certainly are clever (boisterous, sneaky, gluttonous, nasal, unathletic, crass, cowardly, arrogant)"—and I have selected the milder epithets—he responds as any sensitive and fearful member of a minority would, by modifying his behavior, perhaps just slightly, to meet the demand of the Gentile majority, while frequenting synagogues and Catskill resorts in order to save his sanity and let his hair down.

It has even been suggested by no less a figure than Immanuel Kant, the great German philosopher, that

> . . . women, ministers, and Jews do not get drunk, as a rule, at least they carefully avoid all appearances of it, because their civic position is weak and they need to be reserved. Their outward worth is based merely on the belief of others in their chastity, piousness, and separatistic lore. All separatists, that is those who subject themselves not only to the general law of the country but also to a special sectarian lore, are exposed through their eccentricity and alleged chosenness to the attention and criticism of the community and thus cannot relax in their self-control, for intoxication, which deprives one of cautiousness would be a scandal for them.[11]

Nathan Glazer has argued that this explanation is still sound for American Jews—they are, by the way, still sober—if one modifies it to acknowledge that the original motivation, having been transmitted in mysterious ways from one generation to the next, now operates automatically.[12]

Israel as the Solution

We are, perhaps, overstating the case, but even if these feelings exist in an attenuated form, they take their psychological toll on a Jewish psyche that has been trained for centuries to be alert, and they explain as well the incredibly expansive feeling a Jew experiences when he steps on Israeli soil and discovers himself a member of the majority. How exhilarating it is to be emancipated and to learn that no one really gives a damn if you are boisterous, arrogant, or crass. True, you must now learn to recognize all the varieties of Jews, and to discover that you have been victimized by myths about them propagated by Jew and Gentile alike. But in spite of all the deep divisions (religious–secular, Ashkenazic–Sephardic, dove–hawk)—and there is no denying that very powerful emotions are associated with these affiliations— the American Jew is first and foremost impressed with the bonds rather than put off by the rifts.

Another reason for this, I believe, is that, because of its relative homo- geneity, its small size, socialist background, pride in the achievements of its pioneers, and perpetual instability that results from the ever-present fear of extinction, Israel feels like a genuine community. To be sure, there are many Israeli Jews who are exploited by other Israeli Jews, and there are many who take advantage of the system; but compared to America, where individualism has attained epic dimensions, where the false idea of an American community requires artificial transfusions administered by a federal government actually driven by a contrary ideology of pure individualism (an ideology that makes a kind of sense in a wealthy, opportunity-laden, free land like the United States), Israel appears to be a close, organic community.

Hence, even the many Jews who find serious fault with Israel report the feeling of "returning home" there, a feeling that might also be described as the end of the *galut*. After all, home is a place in which you don't have to wear a mask, where everyone is related to you in some way, and where everyone loves you as you are, faults and all. Home is the place where people try to make life easier for you by eliminating barriers to personal fulfillment. Whereas in America any form of Jewish observance requires a constant struggle (unless, like the Orthodox, a self-imposed exile is the means to this end), in Israel one observes as a nation. Who can fail to be awed at the excitement that pervades Jerusalem on Friday morning as everyone rushes to get ready for *Shabbat*, or to be deeply touched by the quiet that pervades the city as *Shabbat* begins and thousands of candles appear through the windows of flats everywhere, in the homes of Sephardim and *Ashkenazim*, doves and hawks, atheists and members of Neturei Karta. Many Jews do not light *Shabbat* candles; but they all know what day it is, and herein lies the secret and the hope of Israel.

Somehow, in the reunion of religion and nation, Israel may write a new and exciting chapter of Jewish history. That chapter has not yet been written. The American Jew who, in his frustration, contemplates *aliyah* as his personal solution must recognize, therefore, that the problem of self- definition is not resolved by emigration. On the contrary, as a member of the majority in the spiritual center of world Jewry, the problem is even more pressing, although the persistent concern with survival renders reflection on these grand matters a luxury. In spite of the fact that Jewish history, the

Bible, observances and rituals have become a national heritage in Israel, they can be celebrated in an empty way there just as they can be anywhere else.

Although many aspects of Israeli life are very difficult for immigrants from Western lands, the handful of American *olim*. both religious and nonreligious, report that compensation is provided by an atmosphere that permits, and therefore makes easy, Jewish self-expression, a central dimension of personal well-being for these people. American Jews, except for this handful, are more than willing to tolerate the aspects of spiritual *galut* alluded to above[13] because they accept the compromise of their Jewish expressiveness demanded of them by the American way of life. *Shabbat* goes by the board so that the children can participate in Little League; letters can be mailed with reasonable assurance they will reach their destination; one need not set aside three hours to go to a bank that may in any case be closed due to a strike, or in commemoration of a recently discovered Hasmonean religious site unearthed by Israeli anthropologists, or because it is Tuesday afternoon; and one can afford various conveniences, like a car, color television, washing machine, etcetera.

Although idealistic reasons are the primary ones motivating American Jews to undertake *aliyah*, these can be as varied as the reasons offered by the Zionist thinkers prior to the establishment of Israel. Discontent with Jewish life in the United States can take many forms. A religious skeptic, for example, who, like a junkie, finds himself drawn periodically to an Orthodox *shul* in order to participate in a service his rational self tells him is meaningless —to watch a dozen or so old men mumble rhythmically, to absorb musty and stale odors, to be enthralled when, at the conclusion of the service one of these old men shakes his hand and smiles at him, obviously delighted to see someone under 70 in *shul*, and to leave, refreshed and ecstatic, in order to rejoin the Gentile world, hoping that "they" never learn of this strange addiction and the "fixes" required by it—may come to believe that Jewish fulfillment can exist in a form that permits a far greater degree of personal integration. Although that form is being molded all the time, one fervently hopes that it adds up to more than defensive pursuits combined with irrational bouts of nostalgia.

Perhaps it is naive to suppose that nationhood can play a role in the development of personal Jewish integration beyond that of providing an anxiety-free (external threats aside) and more comfortable atmosphere for all the diverse pursuits in which Jews, like other people, engage. Certainly the idea of a philosophical synthesis—a Jewish creed—that will unify Israeli Jews, atheists, and Orthodox alike, is inconceivable. Even Orthodox Jews are not required to believe anything. Here, in the awesome respect of the Jew for the individual intellect, lies a crucial difference between Jews and Christians that makes the task of defining the uniqueness of some Christian state an easier one.

The idea that the Jews are not a creedal civilization has been expressed before. Their spiritual consciousness is wedded to action. The covenant with God requires of them righteousness, justice, love, and compassion. The personal and communal responses demanded by this covenant have both differed and been interpreted so widely over the centuries that a modern thinker, sensitive to this history and the liberal atmosphere that prevails at present, proceeds with great delicacy and tact in the task of modernizing these demands. In truth, many are content to let a thousand flowers bloom. We return again to the idea that Jewish survival has some point or other; but no one will say what. Each Jew must struggle personally with the tradition and be respectful of differing interpretations.

Some major thinkers who have adopted this line have concluded that this task can be carried on just as easily and meaningfully in the diaspora as in Israel. Jacob Agus talks about a "Jewish family of communities"[14] all over the world, each one of which is devoted to his native land and deeply attached to Judaism. "Jews need not fear that their heritage will be diluted and adulterated by the alliances they forge with members of other families. For a spiritual heritage is not impoverished but enriched by the influence of other cultures."[15] He is positively buoyant regarding American Jewry claiming that "the process of assimilation may assume benign as well as malignant forms. If people acquire from the general culture of their country its best elements and blend them with the historical tradition, they assimilate well. If they choose unwisely from among the elements of their own tradition and from the prevailing culture, preserving the dross and neglecting the pure metal in both cultures, they assimilate badly."[16] But tolerance has its limits if one is concerned at all about Jewish survival in other than a merely physical sense, bad assimilation becomes, at some point, spiritual death. The doubts about American Jewry expressed above, the reference to failures of personal integration by American Jews, and the psychological comparisons of spiritual *galut* with the exhilaration of homecoming, must sound like the paranoic ramblings of a Chicken Little to those who sympathize with Agus's outlook.

I do not want to impose an interpretation of the Jewish heritage, but it is difficult to believe that the confluence of forces comprising the soil of *Eretz Yisrael*: an awareness of Jewish history, and creations as national products, citizenship of a nation that acts on behalf of the Jewish people, the daily use of the holy tongue, a legal commitment to be a haven for any Jew, cannot but be conducive to the deepest and most creative interpretation of Jewish identity by a people whose experience and reflection on that experience are in constant interplay with these elements.

Notes

1. There is a revival of interest on the college level in Yiddish culture.
2. Trude Weiss-Rosamarin, *Mid-Century*, Harold U. Ribalow (Ed.) New York: Beechhurst Press, 1955, pp. 467–478.

3. Ibid., p. 477.

4. Ibid.

5. Although I would stand by this statement, I do not mean to dismiss all philosophy of religion in such an offhand way. It is not difficult to understand why this would be true of philosophical accounts that depersonalize God. As Eugene B. Borowitz says, "Religious devotion is either taken deeply or is meaningless, and most men find it difficult if not impossible to become personally involved with a God who is impersonal to them." (Jewish faith and the Jewish future. In Abraham Ezra Millgram, (Ed.), *A History of the Jewish People*. Cambridge: Harvard University Press, 1976, p. 322). Religious apologetics strikes one often as rationalization and may then evoke cynicism rather than commitment.

6. Robert Alter, Deformations of the holocaust. *Commentary*, LXXI (2), February 1981, 49.

7. Marvin Lowenthal, Don't you believe it! In Ribalow, op. cit., p. 372.

8. A philosopher would undoubtedly shudder at reading this sentence in virtue of the unanalyzed use of the notion of the goal or meaning of a group's existence. My apology consists entirely in acknowledging the necessity of a separate paper on this topic.

9. Jacob B. Agus, Building our future in America. In Ribalow, op cit., p. 284.

10. I might have expressed this thought in terms of the terribly overused term "dialogue."

11. This quote is from Kant's *Anthropologie* and appears in Nathan Glazer's, Why Jews stay sober. In Ribalow, op. cit., p. 422.

12. Ibid., p. 426.

13. An insightful discussion of the psychological toll of exile in Arthur Hertzberg's, Is the Jew in exile? In Millgram (see footnote 5) pp. 281–300.

14. Agus, Jacob B., *Jewish Identity in an Age of Ideologies*. New York: Frederick Ungar, 1978. p. 394.

15. Ibid., p. 396.

16. Ibid., p. 398.

·IV·
Living a Diaspora Life

The Jewish Diaspora and the Middleman Adaptation

Walter P. Zenner

In this chapter I will point to the contribution that a comparison of different ethnic diasporas can make to our understanding of the development and survival of the Jewish people in an exile which has lasted for several millennia. I will focus specifically on the relationship between dispersion, and the tendency for Jews to be concentrated in what have been called middleman roles. In conjunction with such other factors as the religious separatism of the Jews, such middlemanishness has made possible the unique type of diaspora that typifies the Jews—a diaspora without a hinterland. It is assumed in this chapter that dispersion is a natural phenomenon, not an aberrant one.

Middlemanishness

Similar to many sociological concepts, that of middleman minority lacks precise definition. The core of the concept is that of a minority ethnic group which engages in trade and related endeavors in disproportionate numbers, usually on the basis of self-employment, or employment by other members of the group. Characteristically, small family firms are the basis of their economic activity. While such occupations as merchant, shopkeeper, and peddler are those most typical of such minorities, medieval tax-farmers and modern self-employed professionals can also be classified as middlemen.[1]

Despite such apparent heterogeneity, the comparison of different groups on the basis of similar occupations makes it possible to examine the effects of the group's predominant occupational roles on other aspects of their internal lives and interpersonal relationships. Social scientists have formulated many hypotheses, although there is no consensus on the conclusions. For instance, the literature suggests that groups which are successful in small-scale commerce are able to maintain discipline within the group, especially by means of the kin network. This makes it possible to assure credit in various forms, a necessary prerequisite for business. There may be advantages for majority group members in doing business with members of an "alien" ethnic group, because intimate ties among kin are not present and do not interfere with business arrangements. On the other hand, the economic success of strangers can engender envy and fear, thus stimulating violent reactions on the part of the majority. Such hypotheses are formulated to explain the economic successes of such diverse minorities as the Indians in East Africa, the Lebanese in Ghana, the Armenians in Turkey, the Chinese in Southeast Asia, and the Jews in Central and Eastern Europe. At the same time, they attempt to establish a connection between achievements in the economic realm and expulsions, genocides, and other "final solutions" which have pursued such middleman minorities. Obviously a simple analogy is not sufficient. Care must be taken to point out significant differences as well.

While the Jews have indeed constituted a middleman minority, there are differences between their diaspora and that of other middleman minorities, such as the Overseas Chinese and Parsees. It is worthwhile to briefly examine some groups which cannot be considered middlemen in any sense, to see what we can learn by contrast. It is also of value to look at the advantages and disadvantages of the Jewish adaptation of the middleman motif.

THE JEWISH DIASPORA AND "AN EPICYCLE OF CATHAY"

From a sociological viewpoint, a serious criticism of the comparison of middleman minorities is that most of the groups which are compared with the Jews, including Overseas Chinese and Indians, Armenians, Greeks, and Arabs, have relatively short histories as diasporas. This critique was presented most forcefully by Maurice Freedman (1975) in an essay faulting simplistic interpretation of Overseas Chinese culture. Freedman was both editor of the *Jewish Journal of Sociology* and a sinologist. He recognized that the usual popular examples "rest upon a much broader conception of what is common to Jews and *Hua-ch'iao* (immigrant Chinese), or at least they are apt to excite in the reader's mind a fuller range of common features. Jews/Chinese wander about the earth; they are people of ancient culture; for the most part they work their way into intermediate positions in economy and society, as constrained to do so by the restrictions placed upon them; they are disliked and persecuted; as rootless cosmopolitans, they look to Zion/China."[2]

Freedman cites a quotation at this point from an authority who alludes to the idea of chosenness, à la Deuteronomy. Then Freedman continues:

> Well, the analogy has of course broken down at this very point. The Chinese are not a chosen people. They have in fact no Almighty God to choose them. In reality they have not wandered the earth for centuries bereft of a home and keeping to themselves in the name cf a religious duty. The people who left China centuries ago have few descendants now who think of themselves as Chinese. The Chinese "diaspora," by comparison with the Jewish, is an illusion created by a mere hundred years or so of history.[3]

He then goes on to point out that most Overseas Chinese communities can be expected to assimilate in the foreseeable future, although remnants in Malaysia and elsewhere in Southeast Asia may persist. Of course, the expulsion of Chinese in 1979 from Vietnam and other Indochinese countries, and the refusal of most Southeast Asian nations to accept these refugees is an apparent disproof. Still, most authorities would see the process of assimilation in Thailand and some other countries as irreversible.

The basic question raised by Freedman, however, is worth considering; can one fruitfully compare the relatively shortlived phenomenon of an interposed immigrant group with a millennia-old dispersion? Most middleman minorities belong to the former category. Such groups consist of recent sojourners and immigrants and their descendants over a period of three or four generations. After the fourth generation, the descendants of the original immigrants tend to assimilate and no longer identify with the group, although the group may persist because it is replenished with new immigrants.

While the evidence is not complete, such a tendency is certainly evident among the Overseas Chinese and Lebanese, such ethnic groups as Greeks, and some Armenians (as in Lebanon), and Portuguese and Spanish immigrants in Latin America. In some countries, of course, there is more persistence than in others. The policies of the Dutch and Indonesian governments retarded Chinese assimilation in Indonesia, while Thai policies encouraged it. It is also the case with some groups that our evidence is too weak, because the immigration of the group was too recent and its subsequent history was in an environment which encouraged segregation, as with the Indians in South Africa or Guyana. Even some groups that are seen as having a centuries-long history as a diaspora like the Armenians may, in fact, depend on replenishment from a homeland. If one looks at dispersed middleman minorities, one finds that most have had peasant or peasant-like hinterlands. The former type includes the Greeks, the Armenians, the Chinese, the various Southeast Asian groups, the Arabic-speaking Christians in Syria, and the Copts of Egypt.

The Parsees

The group which seems most like the Jews, having a long history in a diaspora and engaging in mercantile occupations is the Zoroastrian group in western India. This group, generally known as Parsees, is notable as a middleman minority which has had a relatively peaceful history.[4] Like the Jews, the Parsees or Zoroastrians left their original homeland centuries ago and acculturated exceptionally well to their new homes in western India; they spoke Gujerati and wore Indian garb like their neighbors. Unlike the Jews, however, they have been concentrated in one corner of the sub-continent rather than having a wide continental dispersion.

Before the British conquest, the Parsees were cultivators, small rural merchants, and liquor traders, as well as urban traders and craftsmen. No specific evidence of anti-Parsee violence at that time is recorded by Kulke.[5] The situation of the Parsees changed dramatically with the arrival of the Europeans, especially the English East India Company. At that time, Parsees became brokers for the European trading companies. The Parsee brokers started a pattern of collaboration with the British which lasted throughout the colonial period. By 1864, Bombay had become the center of Parsee culture in India, and they were the most urbanized minority in India. By 1864, large numbers of Bombay Parsees were engaged in trade, money-changings, auctioneering, real estate, government service, and the new skilled professions. The Parsees pioneered in establishing European-style schools, entering the fields of law and medicine, and establishing modern textile factories in India. They were instrumental in founding newspapers. Internally, they made extensive religious reforms within the community comparable to those of the Jews in Europe. A large number of the civil servants whom the British attached to the courts of the rulers of Native States were Parsees. Thus Parsees can be viewed as a middleman-entrepreneurial minority and as a minority which provided retainers to the ruling class, resembling Jewish status in European countries.

The Parsees generally saw their political role as a minority in terms of loyalty and dependency on the ruling authority. In previous times, they had striven to keep "themselves as far as possible out of tensions and conflicts between various groups and powers in the state." Most Parsees from the establishment of the British Raj until 1947 saw British rule as a government which had brought them peace, security, modern education, and prosperity.[6] The Parsees were one of the Indian communities in closest commercial and intellectual contact with the British.

The Parsees, however, did not respond homogeneously to British rule. They were politically active, particularly in the local politics of Bombay City and to a lesser extent in India as a whole. During the moderate and secularist phase of the Indian nationalist movement in the late 19th Century, there were several prominent Parsee politicians. By the early 20th Century, however, most of the Parsees had withdrawn from visible leadership. While some Parsees continued to be active in the Congress Party, most Parsees supported conservative pro-British and communalist activities. By the 1920s, many Parsees were afraid of independence under a Hindu majority. The social dissociation of the Parsees from Indian society was followed by a turning of many Parsees to an Iran-oriented nativism. Many defined themselves as a "pure white race" rather than as Orientals. As independence grew closer, the Parsees sought a separate Parsee electorate, but the Congress Party opposed such communalism and the Parsees were too small a minority, even in western India, to be able to achieve their demands.

Despite this coolness to independence, anti-Parsee violence was minor. There were several anti-Parsee riots in the 1870s (initiated by Muslims) and again in 1923, at the height of anti-British demonstrations. Although such incidents were minor, Parsee fears of independence were substantial. After Independence, many Parsees emigrated and they became politically inactive, even locally.

Two features make the Parsee case interesting, one being that they have clearly been a middleman minority, and the other that this period in their history was fairly peaceful. The features of Indian society help explain this. In the Indian caste system, acceptance of a division of labor along ethnic and religious lines is acceptable. The ethos of Hinduism is relatively tolerant. Not only the history of the Parsees of Bombay but also that of the Jews and Syrian Christians of South India have been peaceful. The eruptions of violence in India have come in response to those who challenge the hierarchy implicit in the caste system or its religious basis, as in the case of Untouchables, who refuse to accept the inferior status imposed on them, and the case of the Muslims.[7]

Noncommercial Minorities

Many of the middleman minorities become such only when they leave their rural peasant environment, as in the case of villages in Southeastern China which were the birthplaces of most Overseas Chinese, or the villages in Lebanon from which the Syro-Lebanese diaspora spread. It is indeed likely that until the 7th Century (C E.) the Jews of Palestine, Mesopotamia, and even Egypt were primarily agriculturalists.[8] We ordinarily do not think of peasants in the context of a diaspora, but many peasant populations are ethnically and religiously diverse, and are interspersed among neighbors who do not worship as they do, nor speak the same language. Certainly the Druzes, Maronites, Alawites, Shiites, and other sects of Syria and Lebanon live in such a dispersed fashion, although today they all share the Arabic language. In some parts of the Middle East, we also find speakers of Arabic, Turkish, Armenian, and Syriac-Aramaic living in close proximity.

The so-called colonial Germans of Eastern Europe and their Pennsylvania Dutch and Russlander cousins in North America also include large numbers of cultivators. Sects such as the Amish, the Mennonites, and the Hutterites can certainly be seen as a kind of Anabaptist diaspora; many of these communities are descended from people who left Germanic lands over 200 years ago but who have maintained their language and religion as cultivators.[9] It is likely that they have been able to maintain their communal and egalitarian ideals because they remained largely rural. While they also have a literary religious tradition, their dispersion has a very different character from that of the Jews.

Groups which have persisted in dispersion without a settled hinterland include the Romany Gypsies and other itinerants. The Romany Gypsies are differentiated from other people by languages and dialects, as well as by a unique way of life which has persisted throughout Europe and the Middle East for centuries.[10] Other itinerant groups who are less distinct from the populations among whom they wander have also had a long history, such as the Sleyb (Saluba) of the Arabian peninsula and the Irish Tinkers.[11] These groups, however, differ from the Jews in that regular wandering is an important ethnic boundary for such people, whereas Jews are actually sedentary. There have been Jewish itinerants, like the lower class of German Jewry in the 18th Century who were not allowed to settle, and the Bahutzim of North Africa,[12] but such groups did not persist for long. The Gypsies and similar groups differ from the Jews in their nonliteracy. In addition, they lack a great literary tradition, as well as an ideology of a covenant with God or a mission in history.

This statement may seem ethnocentric, but one can admire the unique resilience of the Romany and the Tinkers, recognizing that these groups have qualities distinct from those of the Jews. In former times, both Jews and Sleyb served the camel Beduin as craftsmen, performing despised but necessary tasks. The Sleyb, who were generally illiterate, did this in North Arabia, while Jews, among others, performed such jobs in Yemen and elsewhere. Some Jewish communities in this region were largely illiterate, but the Jewish craftsmen of North and South Yemen were able to read and to perform such complex ritual tasks as kosher slaughtering. They also maintained permanent homes. The men of Habban, the eastern-most outpost of Yemenite Jewry in what is now South Yemen, wandered as silversmiths among the oases and tribes of that region for months on end, but once or twice a year they did return to their homes in Habban.[13] Even in Jewish communities like those in Kurdistan which were not considered learned, there was an effort to teach simple Hebrew reading, unlike the Gypsies who do not view education as a sacred obligation.

The Jews and the Gypsies are alike, however, in being the victims of hostility, and in having been stigmatized as people without honor, as scoundrels, cheats, and sorcerers. There is a basic similarity between the blood libels leveled against Jews and the popular belief that Gypsies steal children. Both myths contribute to the kind of fear and abhorrence which pushed large numbers of both Jews and Gypsies into the gas chambers of Nazi-occupied Europe.

The Jews as a Middleman Minority

The characteristics of middleman minorities do fit most diaspora Jews: trade and other monetary exchanges between people defined as "strangers"; self-employment or employment by others within the group; or personal service in the retinue of powerful members of the ruling elite. These elements are found to be characteristic of most Jewish communities from the period of the early Islamic states to the present. Most Jews during this millennium and a half were not subsistence cultivators nor were they generally accepted as members of the ruling elite. The presence or absence of some Jews engaged in agriculture does not refute this generalization for the region from Europe through the Middle East to India. The silversmiths of Yemen, the peddlers and craftsmen of North Africa and the Fertile Crescent, the moneylenders, used-goods dealers, and cattle traders of Circum-Alpine Europe in the post-Renaissance period, the innkeepers of 18th and 19th Century Poland, even the garment workers of Lodz and New York City who were employed by Jews, fit the pattern noted above. For that matter, many of those Jews who did engage in agriculture such as the chicken and truck-farmers of New Jersey during the early 20th Century were specialized cultivators and were not subsistence farmers.

How were the original Jewish peasantry of Palestine and Mesopotamia transformed into an essentially urban people? Apparently those Jews who had emigrated from Palestine tended to enter urban crafts and trades. There were also certain restrictions on Jewish ownership of slaves after the Roman Empire became Christian in the 4th Century, which may have limited large-scale agriculture on the part of Jews. It seems, however, that the "bourgeois revolution" of the 8th and 9th Centuries, as Goitein has called it,[14] resulted in the urbanization of the Jews. After the Arab conquest of the Fertile Crescent, heavy taxation was imposed on the non-Muslim peasantry.

This taxation resulted in the impoverishment of the peasants. While the government of the early Muslim rulers strove to prevent peasant flight from the land, unrest in the 8th Century encouraged such emigration. Many moved into the new cities and became a cheap labor force there. As a result of the booty resulting from Muslim conquests, and the creation of new towns, a market for luxury goods was created, and the new roads built for military purposes resulted in improved communications. All of this contributed to the creation of new classes and new values centered on urban life, and in turn to the rise of a capitalistic ethos.[15]

The Jews evidently joined this flight from the land, although they were by no means the only ones who became urban craftsmen and merchants. Indeed many became craftsmen and officials, which during this early period of Islamic history were occupations shunned by Muslims. Occupations during this period were not segregated ethnically. Both Jews and Gentiles participated in all occupations, though not necessarily proportionately. The new opportunities created by the conditions of Islamic conquest and city-building opened up niches which were filled by the often non-Muslim ex-peasants. The fact that mercantile activity was open to all was a characteristic of an expanding economy marked both by large-scale mobility and relative openness and tolerance.[16]

The formation of the Jews as a dispersed middleman minority without a hinterland occurred in the early Islamic period (9th and 10th Centuries). From that time up until the present, the pattern was practically self-perpetuating. Obviously there were shifts from one dominant occupation to another. Sometimes most Jews in a particular place were craftsmen; at other times, the retainers of the nobility, like the Court Jews, were the main group; at still other times, pawnbrokers and dealers in second-hand goods were predominant. This variation in occupations shows the inherent adaptability of the Jews to different environments, but analytically it shows similarities in that the Jews were involved in trade and economic ventures, estranged from the majority population and its elites, and exhibited a tendency toward self-employment.

Abran Leon argued that when Jews abandon these niches, they lose their Jewishness and assimilate.[17] The examples he cites in support of this idea are those of such individuals as a medieval Jewish banker who received land and as a landowner was forced to convert to Christianity. The same argument has been revived by S. N. Rhee who connects the complete assimilation of the Chinese Jewish community to the entry of Jews into the Chinese civil service (mandarinate).[18]

Like Leon, Rhee sees the assimilation of the Jews as a function of occupational change. Most estimate the arrival of the Jews in China from West Asia to have occurred around the 9th or 10th Centuries, parallel to the Middle Eastern bourgeois revolution. They came as merchants. The only community of which we have any continuous record is that of K'aifeng, a major trading center, and briefly a Sung capital. The Jewish community built its first synagogue in 1163. The last rabbi died around 1800 and the community was completely assimilated by the early 20th Century.

The assimilation, both on the identity and the behavioral level is attributed to the complete isolation from other Jews, and to intermarriage. Rhee points, however, to a crucial turning point in the history of the community beginning in the 14th Century, that being the increasing participation of Jews in the Chinese civil service. Participation in the civil service was valued much more highly in the Chinese empire than was mercantile activity, which was despised. To participate in the civil service, however, required conformity to the Confucian way and learning in the classics, as well as assignment away from one's birthplace and kindred. The former encouraged heightened behavioral assimilation, while the latter contributed to the dispersion of individual Jews throughout China. Thus, many family members could no longer participate in the community. Given the isolation from other Jews, cessation of immigration from the West, absence of anti-Semitism preventing further civil service participation, and intermarriage, the community's decline was inevitable.

Some would argue that the proletarianization of Jews in Eastern Europe, as well as in Western Europe and the United States during the late 19th and early 20th Centuries, constituted a similar break with the middleman pattern. For a variety of reasons, including governmental actions against village Jews in the Russian empire and a rapidly growing Jewish population, poor Jews were forced into urban areas. Many found employment in the new industries, especially clothing, first in cities like Lodz in Poland and then in the industrial centers of the West, including New York City and Manchester, England. They provided a cheap labor force for these industries.

In some ways, this change had an element of continuity. Most Jewish workers continued to work in shops owned by Jews. The factories were relatively small and there was a sense of community. This was a pattern that had persisted since the Middle Ages.[19] In another sense, this new large-scale employment introduced contradictions into the old middleman minority pattern. There was a clear distinction between employer and employee. Even the small sweatshops were larger than the old domestic workshops of the earlier period. Despite common religious and cultural backgrounds, most employers and employees did not have kinship ties. It is therefore not surprising that Jewish communities both in Eastern Europe and the West were rent by severe class conflict through a series of strikes. Sometimes such confrontations led Jewish employers to prefer non-Jewish workers to their co-ethnics.

For a time, the majority of Jews in the large urban centers of Eastern Europe and the United States could be considered proletarians rather than traders, but proletarianization was a phase of modernization that did not last. In Eastern Europe, of course, the Holocaust intervened. In the United States and Britain, this mode of employment did not last much beyond the third generation. By the post-World War II period, most Jews had ceased to be clothing workers and were either self-employed or worked in white collar jobs.[20] The change here was through transformation, not assimilation. Leon saw a continuity between trade and small commodity industrial production such as the garment industry, which is not an essential contradiction of his thesis. It is hard to predict whether or not the entry into bureaucracy, which Jews in both the United States and the Soviet Union have begun, will result in a repetition of the Chinese pattern.

THE ADVANTAGES AND DISADVANTAGES OF URBAN COMMERCIAL OCCUPATIONS

From the viewpoint of the survival of a dispersed ethnic group, there are both advantages and disadvantages of being specialized in urban-based commercial occupations. From the viewpoint of traders, there were also advantages to be had through membership in a small minority.

ADVANTAGES. The advantages are predicated on the toleration of the minority by the dominant majority, even when such toleration is characterized by oppression. Under the Romans, Islam, and medieval Christiandom, the Jews were such a tolerated group. While there were pogroms and expulsions, extermination of Jews because of their practice of Judaism or ancestry was rarely state policy. On the other hand, heretical sects of Muslims and Christians were fair game and did not generally survive in urban concentrations. In the Middle East, for instance, Jews and Orthodox Christians have tended to be concentrated in urban, often lowland, areas, while sects like the Nestorians, the Jacobites, and the Maronites, among the Christians and the Druzes, Alawis, Ismailis, and others who have Islamic ties, are generally found in mountainous rural areas.

Urban concentration permits a minority to establish such central institutions as a school, a synagogue, a ritual bath, and a printing press. It is true that many of the towns in which Jews lived in the past were small by modern standards, but they were generally of a more urban nature than the tiny villages and hamlets of the peasantry. Judaism, as a religion of the Bible, utilized its urban centers to the fullest. While many Jews did live in small towns, much of what we associate with the Judaic tradition flourished in cities like Warsaw, Vilna, Frankfurt, Livorno, and Baghdad. Sages like Maimonides and the Vilna Gaon were supported by an urban population. Urban concentration had a disadvantage in pre-19th Century times. Urban populations suffered from plague and famine. Here the broad lateral range of the Jewish dispersion was instrumental in providing a quasi-hinterland.

While most Jews lived in permanent settlements, the skills which they developed in the variety of middleman roles were portable and assets were readily liquidated. They were able to have sufficient wealth and power, so that institutions like the *yeshivot* of Eastern Europe could develop. They could also migrate in the wake of a disaster and reestablish themselves in a different city, region, or country, as happened on innumerable occasions. Unlike peasant populations, Jewish groups had skills which stood them in good stead under agrarian and industrial regimes.

Out of necessity, Jews on many occasions were forced to move into social roles which others shunned, or which were obsolescent or new. This filling of roles has been called "pioneering" or "filling the status-gap." The different terminologies express different aspects of such strategies. Pioneering is one feature, as Baron has pointed out:

> Pioneering has indeed been a major keystone of all Jewish history. It was natural for a permanent minority entering any new area to find that all normal positions in the economy and social structure of that area had already been occupied. Simply to make a living, it was absolutely necessary for these new arrivals to find new openings by exploiting certain hitherto undetected possibilities, and to widen . . . the crevices in the body politic of the host nations into regular fields of endeavor.[21]

"Filling the status gap," the more sociological term, describes a situation found in feudal Europe around the 10th Century, when there were two major classes, a nobility which controlled land and cavalry, and a peasantry under their protection and subject to their exploitation. The burghers were just beginning to develop. In this situation, Jews as traders filled a gap which had developed in the body social.

In this regard, it is worthwhile to discuss the reasons why a dispersed small minority often plays an important role in the development of trade. In pre-modern long-distance trade, there are problems which include the exchange of information about supply and demand, speedy transport of goods, and, above all, the organization of trust and credit over long distances. The hierarchically organized modern corporation did not and could not exist in the period before the communications revolution which began in the 19th Century. Instead, long-distance trade centered around family firms and often ethnically and culturally homogeneous groups. Common ancestry, language, and religion provided the basis for a moral community which could enforce ostracism (for example, boycotts, excommunication) when no common territory existed. Even today, ethnically homogeneous middleman groups play an important role in certain lines of commerce, such as the rubber trade of Malaysia and the diamond businesses of South Africa, Israel, the Netherlands, and the United States.[22]

The fact that such a moral community over long distances supports trade also reinforces the diaspora as a whole, since the survival of the group depends on having communications, distinctiveness, and a way of enforcing its norms over great distances. Being involved in an occupation with other members of one's group means that your livelihood depends on your fellow kinsmen and co-ethnics (co-religionists) and makes leaving the group more difficult. In late 19th Century Damascus, when a number of Jewish youths sought to become Christians at the behest of a Protestant missionary, they found that they would be unable to find employment among Jews if they were to convert.

A high degree of ethnocentrism has its uses for both trade and group morale. Among traders, there is a need to maintain a team spirit and to protect secrets from competitors, a trait that has been noted among long-surviving religious and ethnic groups. Even the Quakers with their pacifism and universalistic ethic maintained separation through their special use of language, their refusal to swear oaths, and their conscientious objection to war. Abner Cohen analyzed a sectarian movement among Hausa cattle traders in Nigeria as a means for these devout Muslims to separate themselves from their increasing number of Muslim neighbors and from other groups.[23] Such separatism is not limited to Muslims, Jews, or Quakers, but has characterized many other people.

DISADVANTAGES. A major disadvantage of group separatism is high visibility to the extent that the group becomes particularly susceptible to the hostility typically directed toward such unarmed minorities.

Here a number of the very features which we have discussed as advantages show their dysfunctional side. As we noted, urban life has its dark side. An urban center or seat of government makes the minority even more prominent, even if the majority of its members reside elsewhere. Economic success, again characteristic of small numbers, is often conspicuous and excites envy. When envy is coupled with the negative ethnocentrism of the majority, and combined with a belief in the diabolic quality of the minority, a potent compound has been brewed. It is not surprising that during periods of discontent, such as war, plague, and famine, violence toward an ethnic minority results.

In addition, the maintenance of a group boundary under conditions of geographic dispersion makes the group vulnerable to desertion. It is difficult, if not impossible, for a stranger to join the group, and internal conflict may result in fission and conversion to the majority. Jewish history is replete with examples of this phenomenon.

Surviving Without a Hinterland

Earlier we discussed the uniqueness of the Jewish diaspora by virtue of its special features. These included:

1. Specialization of middleman roles
2. Permanent urban settlement

3. Maintenance of a separate moral community
4. Longevity as a diaspora
5. Lack of a permanent hinterland
6. Worldwide range.

Most middleman minorities share features (1) through (3). If they have longevity, however, it is as often as not through recruitment from the hinterland. Without such a rural base there would be no Chinese in Thailand or the Philippines today. The longevity and the geographical range of the Jews is remarkable among minority groups. The Parsees have longevity but never had the range of the Jews. The colonial Germans of Eastern Europe and North America were essentially rural groups until recently concentrated in specific areas. The Gypsies who have had an equivalent longevity and range were completely different as a community.

The persistence of the Jewish diaspora, which is hinted at by such comparisons, cannot be fully explained by the specialization of Jews in middleman occupations. Obviously the religious factor, couched in such terminology as "separatism" and "moral community," played a crucial role in Jewish survival. Still, the kind of adaptation to the conditions of exile which concentration in commerce-based occupations produced, determined some features of Jewish communities. The Hutterites, for instance, are relatively egalitarian communities with rule by religious elders. Jewish communities, on the other hand, have been marked by a split between religious literati and a wealthy secular leadership, often tied to the Gentile ruling elite. The high degree of literacy marking Jewish culture and its products is again related to its urban nature, even in the small market towns of Eastern Europe. The communication networks of Jewish religious life followed those of international trade, as did the transfer of hegemony or cultural domination, to which Dubnow pointed.

The late classic/early medieval development of the Jewish dispersion as a trading diaspora—or middleman minority—determined the future character of the Jewish people. It helped spread them throughout the eastern hemisphere and later into the western as well. It made them an urban people. The middleman motif contributed to the development of the Jews. It is possible to imagine Jewish survival without commercial specialization, but the Jews would be a very different group from what they are today. They might be a sect of peasants like the Yezidis of Kurdistan or the Mandeans of Southern Iraq, living in isolated rural areas; or they might be utopian rural sectarians like the Hutterites, or fighting mountaineers like the Druzes, or itinerant tinkers like the Romany. The middleman role made it possible for a community to evolve which could transmit its heritage and reproduce itself all over the world, escaping adversity in one area by establishing a center elsewhere. Many perished or were assimilated, but the people as a whole continued.

The pattern which developed was adapted to another era. It is a moot question whether it can survive the pressures of modern nationalism and imperialism. The competition of the multinational corporation may squelch the small familial entrepreneur and impair a basis of our persistence. Even the concentration of Jews in a few countries of the world, including Israel itself, narrow our range of possibilities for future survival. Still, the end of the diaspora has not yet been reached. Israel has produced its own diaspora, despite the ingathering of the exiles. Regardless of utopian hopes, exile and alienation are part of the human condition.

Notes

1. For reviews of the social scientific literature on middleman minorities, see: Edna Bonacieh, Middleman minorities and advanced capitalism. *Ethnic Groups* 2, 3, 1980, pp. 211–222; Edna Bonacieh, and John Modell, *The Economic Basis of Ethnic Solidarity: The Case of Japanese Americans*. Berkeley & Los Angeles: University of California Press, 1981; Walter P. Zenner, *Middleman Minority Theories and the Jews: A Historical Assessment*. YIVO Working Papers in Yiddish and East European Jewish Studies Series No. 31, 1978; Theories of middleman minorities: A critical review. In *Sourcebook on the New Immigration*, Roy S. Bryce-Laporte et al. (Eds.). New Brunswick: Transaction Books, 1980a, pp. 313–326; and American Jewry in the light of Middleman minority theories. *Contemporary Jewry* 5:1, 1980b, pp. 11–30.

2. Maurice Freedman, An Epicycle of Cathay; or the southward expansion of the sinologists. In *Social Organization and the Applications of Anthropology*, R. J. Smith, (Ed.). Ithaca: Cornell University Press, 1975, pp. 302–332.

3. Ibid., p. 318ff.

4. Richard A. Schermerhorn, Parsis and Jews in India: A tentative comparison. *Journal of Asian Affairs* 1, 1976, pp. 119–122; and Sheldon Stryk, Social structure and prejudice. *Social Problems* 6, 1958, pp. 340–354.

5. E. Kulke, *The Parsees in India*. Munich: Woflorum Verlag, Arnold Bergstrasser Institut—Studien zu Entwicklung und Politik, No. 3, 1974.

6. Ibid., pp. 133–134.

7. See ibid.; Schermerhorn, op. cit.; and Richard A. Schermerhorn, *Ethnic Plurality in India*. Tucson: University of Arizona Press, 1978.

8. S. W. Baron, General Survey. In *Economic History of the Jews*, N. Gross (Ed.). New York: Schocken Books, pp. 14–24.

9. Ruth E. Baum, The Ethnohistory of Law: The Hutterite Case. Doctoral dissertation. Department of Anthropology, State University of New York at Albany, Albany, N.Y., 1977; E. K. Francis, *In Search of*

Utopia. Glencoe: The Free Press. 1955; John Hostetler, *Amish Society*. Baltimore: John Hopkins University Press, 1968; and *Hutterite Society*. Baltimore: John Hopkins University Press, 1975.

10. J. P. Clerbert, *The Gypsies*. New York: Dutton, 1963; Werner Cohn, *The Gypsies*, Benjamin-Cummings, 1973; B. Quintana, and L. B. Floyd, *Que Gitano! The Gypsies of Southern Spain*. New York: Holt, Rinehart and Winston, 1972.

11. Michael Meeker, *Literature and Violence in North Arabia*. Cambridge: Cambridge University Press, 1979, pp. 21–22; S. B. Gmelch and G. Gmelch, "The Emergence of an Ethnic Group: The Irish Tinkers." *Anthropological Quarterly* 49, 1976, pp. 225–238.

12. Robert Attal, "Bahuzim." *Encyclopaedia Judaica* 4, 1971, pp. 102–103.

13. Laurence Loeb, "Jewish life in Habban: A partial reconstruction." In *Studies in Jewish Folklore*, F. Talmadge, (Ed.). Cambridge: Association for Jewish Studies, 1980, pp. 201–218.

14. S. D. Goiten, *Jews and Arabs*. New York: Schocken Books, 1955 pp. 8, 100.

15. S. D. Goiten, op cit., pp. 96–112.

16. S. D. Goiten, *A Mediterranean Society*. Berkeley and Los Angeles: University of California Press, 1969, p. 72.

17. Abran Leon, *The Jewish Question—A Marxist Interpretation*. New York: Pathfinder Press, 1970.

18. S. N. Rhee, Jewish assimilation: The case of Chinese Jews. *Comparative Studies in Society and History* 15, 1973, pp. 115–126. We are concerned with Rhee's thesis here, not the correctness of his explanation, which differs in some particulars from those of Leslie (1969) and Sharot (1974). Leslie, who has written the most recent synthesis of Chinese Jewish history, lays more emphasis on the sheer isolation of the Jewish community. The three explanations, however, may in fact be complementary rather than contradictory (Leslie, 1969). Donald D. Leslie, *Survival of Chinese Jews: The Jewish Community of Kaifeng*. Leiden: Brill, 1972; Stephen Sharot, Minority situation and religious acculturation: A comparative analysis of Jewish communities. *Comparative Studies in Society and History* 16, 1974, pp. 329–354.

19. Werner Cahnman, Introduction. In M. Wischniter, *History of the Jewish Crafts and Guilds*. New York: T. Yoseloff, 1965.

20. Simon Kuznets, op cit., and *Economic Structure of U.S. Jewry: Recent Trends*. Jerusalem: Hebrew University, Institute for Contemporary Jewry, 1972.

21. S. W. Baron, *History and Jewish Historians*. Philadelphia: Jewish Publication Society of America, 1964, p. 31.

22. Janet T. Landa, The economics of the ethnically homogenous middleman group: A low-cost club-like economic organization for economizing

contract-enforcement and information costs. University of Toronto Institute for Policy Analysis Working Paper Series No. 79-84, 1979.

23. Abner Cohen, *Customs and Politics in Urban Africa*. Berkeley & Los Angeles: University of California Press, 1969.

·12·
The Death Taint and Uncommon Vitality

Eugene C. Wiener

There are existences which seem to be tainted in some ominous way by a kind of living death. These attenuated lives can occasionally be amazingly vital and creative. It is our aim to explore briefly, and in very broad outline, one of these vital but attenuated existences — the case of the Jewish People.

In its essence, the continuity of the Jewish People is a heroic, unprecedented, existential hyperbole, a tour de force of religious cultural and national assertiveness. And the State of Israel is one of its most impressive recent achievements. Israel, even with its present existence a certainty, still *seems* unlikely. It is based on what may appear to be excessive resoluteness, unique claims about the continuities of national consciousness, and an exaggerated expression of collective will to reembody religious culture in national identity. It is a strange phenomenon. Because while statements about facts are sometimes exaggerations, facts themselves generally are not. The factuality of this latest manifestation of Jewish resoluteness — Israel's existence — still has not dispelled lingering doubts about the possibility of its verification in reality. In this sense it bears the same stamp of unlikelihood — of being and yet not quite being — of life and death, that characterizes all of post exilic Jewish existence. From all that we know about historical processes, social dynamics and group psychology, Israel's existence is highly improbable (Valery, 1962), but it does exist. The shadow of unlikely existence has darkened the reality of Jewish history over the course of the centuries, and it has not been dispelled by the creation of the State (Neusner, 1973). This is the case even though a great deal of the motive force that brought Israel into being was based on the desire to irrefutably establish and normalize Jewish existence.

133

The Aspiration for Normality

Is the aspiration for normalization of existence desirable, or does a death-tainted existence have an inherent vitality of its own? This question has been and continues to be hotly debated. It is our intention to analyze this debate in light of its larger implications for the general question of group longevity. There are two points of particular interest: (1) The existence of the death taint is openly acknowledged, by opposing sides of the question — especially by those who argue for measures to abolish it; (2) The issue is a matter of public discussion. This situation constitutes a most unusually clear illustration of a group struggling with the vitalizing potential of death and its possible contribution to corporate existence and group survival. One can see in the debate the monumental struggle of a group to make the best of a grim and tragic reality. The relevance of the debate has been heightened by the particular circumstances in which the State of Israel was established. If ever group life was manifestly vitalized by death, it was in this case.

As Walter Laqueur has indicated: "The war in Europe was over, the world had been liberated from Nazi terror and oppression, peace had returned. For the Jewish People it was the peace of the graveyard. Yet paradoxically at the very time when the 'objective' Jewish question had all but disappeared, the issue of a Jewish State became more topical than ever before . . . The victors in the war had an uneasy conscience as the stark tragedy of the Jewish People unfolded before their eyes. It was only now that the question was asked whether enough had been done to help them and what could be done for the survivors." (Laqueur, 1972). The possibility of using the graveyard as the means to launch a more vital existence had already been under discussion, by the Jewish People, for a long time, even before World War II. Indeed, one can find traces of such a thrust in the thought and action of the Jewish People as far back as one has historical records of them. This possibility was conditioned by historical experience and mythic paradigms that sought to tap the vitalizing power of death.

The Living Dead

One of the salient images, used by the somewhat emancipated Jews of the 18th and 19th centuries to indicate their own unlikely existence, was that of the *living dead*. They saw in this uncanny and ambiguous condition the starting point for the revitalization movements that they were partial to. In their own condemnatory and critical attitude toward it they bear eloquent, albeit reluctant witness to the powerful grip it held over their consciousness.

As Pinsker, that prescient spokesman of the new Jewish national rebirth, wrote in 1882:

"Thus the world saw in this people (The Jews), the frightening form of the dead walking among the living. This ghostlike apparition of a people without unity or organization, without land or other bond of union, no longer alive, and yet moving among the living—This eerie form scarcely paralleled in history, unlike anything that preceded or followed it, could not fail to make a strange and peculiar impression upon the imagination of the nations. And if the fear of ghosts is something inborn, and has a certain justification in the psychic life of humanity, is it any wonder that it asserted itself powerfully at the sight of this dead yet living nation? Fear of the Jewish ghost has been handed down and strengthened for generations and centuries. It led to a prejudice which in its turn, in connection with other forces . . . paved the way for Judeophobia."

Pinsker developed a theory of anti-Semitism based on the notion that "for the living, the Jew is a dead man." The way to deal with the moribund condition is to "devote all of our remaining moral force to reestablish ourselves as a living nation so that we may finally assume a more fitting and dignified role." Pinsker, like many of the proto-nationalist figures of the late 19th century, acknowledged the aptness of the image of the living dead Jew. That some of the proto-nationalists wanted to transcend this eerie condition does not take away from the extraordinary reality that the description seemed appropriate to them. In their zeal to infuse a less eccentric and, in their eyes, a more bountiful life force into the Jewish People, they gave short shrift to a rather extraordinary life force in its own right, that of the death taint. For if there is one characteristic of the Jewish People that seems constant in its four thousand year history it is that it is forever being perceived as moribund, and consequently, continually the subject of a premature obituary. The British Museum possesses a monument from the 13th century before the Common Era on which it is written, "Israel is desolated, its seed is no more." Some desolation, some seed! Indeed, if the living dead manage to survive with such a spectacular longevity, perhaps this status bears some looking into. Especially by anyone seeking to understand group survival.

The notion of the living dead Jews seems to be composed of two paradoxical and, at times, contradictory ideas. One of these seems to be that the Jews are tainted with death because they have lived too long. The other is that the Jews are tainted with death because they lack an indispensably vital part for living. According to the first of these ideas the Jews are a freakish anomaly of *endurance,* in the other they are a compositional *monstrosity of requisite form* for life. According to this second idea the Jews are without a necessary precondition for life, and yet according to the first idea, they are abnormally lively and vital without it. The anomalous death taint implies both functional and structural defects. The fact that these two notions contradict each other seems to have bothered no one. For how it is possible to live at all, not to speak of an extraordinarily protracted life, if life is defined as the possession of certain vital parts — and they do not exist? Their mutually contradictory implications did not prevent these notions from reinforcing and supplementing each other in practice. In one sense the Jews are the living dead because they have lived too long anyhow, in the other they are the living dead, and not fully alive, because they have a mortal defect.

The Influence of Christian Theology

There are two other attitudes that appear to have reinforced these two primary ones. They were held by Christian theologians, for the most part, but that did not prevent Jews from accepting their basic truth and finding more suitable reasons to support it. Indeed, it is an open question just how much the Jewish explanations of Judeophobia are influenced by Christian theology. First, the Jews were stigmatized not only because they did not acknowledge the proferred savior of the world but, even worse than that, they allegedly crucified him. To be responsible for the death of a God is to provoke forces that are mysteriously threatening to one's own future existence. In a sense killing God is murdering life. The mortal punishment to oneself may be temporarily postponed but its advent is regarded as a certainty. Second, the living Jews were witnesses to recurring murderous attempts to annihilate them. They were mistreated victims whose continued existence reminded *those capable of empathy* that they were always the potential targets of murderous intent. The image of the living dead Jew — murdered in the past, and potential murder victims of the future — colored the perception of the Jews even by sympathetic outsiders.

Furthermore, the notion of the living dead became a social stigma with all the force and power that accrues to its successful imputation. The death taint stigma as applied to the Jewish people was different from the ordinary sense in which every living being is marked for ultimate death. It is not in this natural constitutive sense that Jews were marked with the taint. It was, rather, in the sense in which some people are marked and singled out for an immoderate, indelible, particularly unseemly taint. These people are the living who in many ways are more dead than alive. They are symbolically dead by virtue of having *sentenced identities*. Among individuals they can be convicted murderers who have been sentenced to death and awaiting execution, or sufferers of fatal diseases who have been diagnosed and pronounced incurable. These sentenced identities seem calamitously spoiled and atrociously injured. Among groups, they can be uprooted, displaced tribes of natives, phased out organizations or conquered nationalities and ethnic groups that have been assigned to extirpation, decimation or annihilation.

In the case of individuals the death taint is (as Lifton, 1973 and Cassell, 1972, have pointed out) a relationship between the self and the body which is an "injured one," in which "the self remains shackled to a body seen as somehow already dead, or permanently injured in some inexplicable way." It is "a relationship seen as fundamentally incompatible with life, between two independent, indispensable parts of existence," one of which is irrevocably defective. On rare occasions a sentenced identity can be transformed into a *reprieved identity* if the sentence is annulled or found to have been inappropriately pronounced, but that is rare. In that infrequent case the injury is somehow repaired and the defective part of the existence is remedied. But for the most part sentences are executed, and most sentenced identities expire. Until they do, however, their bearers suffer the taint of their ultimate (somehow future yet present) mortal end.

Sentence-Deferring Identities

There is another kind of identity other than the sentenced or reprieved; it is the sentenced identity in which the mortal sentence seems never to be executed. These are *sentence-deferring identities*. These identities have the taint of death upon them already, but their fatal sentence, instead of being executed, is instead continuously and unaccountably deferred. The possessors of these identities exist in a kind of dubiously protected limbo. Theirs is the remarkable but unenviable power of life. Such is the case of the Jewish People, at least as viewed frequently by other than Jews, and on occasions by Jews themselves (Yehoshua, 1972).

In this instance the death taint is so indelible that ever renewed efforts at revitalization are themselves unaccountably characterized by it. The very thing that could disprove the existence of the taint — a renewed, or more natural form of life — is itself regarded as unnatural. In regard to the Jews one of the main reasons for the persistance of the taint, no matter what action is taken, is that throughout much of history the collective life of the Jew has been regarded as obscene. By obscene is meant: an offense to modesty, decency, involving the overstepping of some limit of propriety. In some historical periods the more archaic meaning of the term has been appropriate: lewd, abominable, disgusting or repulsive. In a certain sense it would be as if one of Lifton's Hiroshima victims, the Hibakusha ("The explosion-affected person: Those who permanently encounter death) would have his defect genetically transferred to his death tainted progeny, and they would never die out. Who would be interested in discovering the secret of their group longevity and emulating their lives? Their longevity, rather than being a meritorious achievement would instead, no doubt, be regarded as a somewhat obscene form of protracted and merciless doom.

A convincing proof of the reality of the imputed death taint among Jews is demonstrated by the fact that they are rarely given credit for heroic endurance. Considering the fascination that longevity generally ellicits, this is very strange, for if there was indeed anyone called Methusalah, and he did actually live 969 years, he most likely spent most of his time answering questions about how he managed to live so long. At least after his 120th birthday. This is probably so because there is to be found in most cultures an idea of what constitutes a reasonable life span versus an extraordinary one. When the limits of that reasonable span are exceeded, it is usually the subject of intense and frequently excessive interest. Witness the many expeditions by physicians and physical anthropologists to Andean villages, Pakistani settlements, or Caucasian farms to locate and examine the extraordinarily long-lived. And the interest evinced is usually not only scientifically motivated. It appears to have the quality at times almost of hero worship. It is as if an uncommon endurance marked with perceptible signs of continued vitality is intrinsically heroic. Its very existence is an encouraging testament to the hopeful possibility of successfully doing battle with inevitable decay, decomposition and death.

But the Jewish People are not the recipients of any such adulation, for there is another side to the issue. A person hoary with age, who spectacularly surpasses a reasonable life expectancy, is not only venerable, he can be, and frequently is, . . . ridiculous. An uncommon old age is viewed frequently not only as incredible, but also as an incredible absurdity, a bit preposterous. Time has been borrowed from death's domain for an unnaturally prolonged and persistent duration. What should be defunct is freakishly vital and what should be deceased is queerly vigorous. It is because of this that an unnatural endurance can itself become an indication and omen of the death taint. Keeping death at bay is not only a heroic feat, but if it is done too persistently and immodestly it can be obscene. It is not only death that has a pornographic potential but so, too, does an uncommon vitality. And so it is that there is no automatic moral grandeur that is associated with endurance, if such endurance is tainted with death.

Resolving Ambivalence

The predisposition to value the particular kind of life that is prolonged resolves the ambivalence toward an uncommon vitality. In the case of the abnormally long lived Jewish People there is frequently no such positive predisposition. It has always seemed strange that the Jewish People are rarely (except by themselves) given credit for existing so long. Remarkably long as far as nations, religions and civilizations are concerned (Elazar, 1969). The great civilizations have, with rare exceptions, rarely continued to exist for longer than a millenium, and most of them a good deal less. In the case of the Jewish People we have a group that has an unbroken connection with its own cultural past for many centuries; a connection *relatively* unadulterated by extrinsic foreign influences. It is one of the very few extant civilizations where the cultural forms developed millenia ago and those existing today are easily recognizable as being substantially the same — whether this be language, values, norms, customs, literature or myth. Where are the paeans that are invoked to sing artful praise for this heroic achievement of endurance? Who is trying to emulate the Jewish experience? On the contrary, in the eyes of many this ability to endure is a questionable virtue.

It is not only because of the immodest relationship with time that Jews have been frequently regarded as having "outlived life," but also because they have existed for much of their history without one of the alleged necessary requisites for national life — a land. Their own land. It is the lack of a land of their own for much of Jewish history that made the Jewish people archetypal wanderers whose dismal journeys and imperiled settlements forever underlined their vulnerability (Roshwald, 1972). But strangely enough, that very vulnerability seemed to emphasize their bizarre talents at survival. For how could a nation so lacking the ecological prerequisites for life be so long-lived? It was different to conceive of a people continuously existing without a land of their own — it was as if there was a kind of congenital structural morbidity that was rooted in this strange group's corporate being that refused to buckle and crumple.

Jewish People and Jewish Land

How did the Jewish People manage to live without this vital part of group life for so long? In a sense the normal death of the Jewish People by losing its land was prevented by its abnormal birth. From its very beginnings the Jewish People had an unusual relationship to its land. Even when the land was inhabited by the Jews the relationship was ambiguous. Its attachment was not simply based on the usual fact that they were born and raised on it. It was a special type of connection.

In the biblical account of the corporate birth of the Jewish People, be it the covenant of Abraham or the revelation at Sinai, the context of birth is alien, the promise is home. In other words, home is not a taken-for-granted reality where being *starts* but rather, according to the mythic account, it is a promised goal to be attained, where being may be *enhanced*. Attaining the title to the promised land is perpetually achieved and constantly legitimated. Achieved through obstinate striving and legitimated through virtuous action. It is a project to *enhance* an imperfect existence rather than a taken-for-granted *given* of reality. Home is not where you come from according to this view, but rather where you are going. Even if you are there already. The promised land is an intrinsically unfulfillable promise — that is, if fulfilling a promise is seen as a once-and-for-all-time matter. The most convincing proof that it is an unfulfillable promise is that the promised goal remained relevant even when the Jews were living in the land. Part of the reason for that relevance was the tenuous hold on the land, since there always were powerful enemies seeking to dislodge them from it. There was never a period when Jewish settlement in the land could be taken for granted. It if wasn't radically threatened by enemies from without, it was threatened from within. Consequently, there was hardly a period in Jewish history when a leader could justifiably claim that the promise to the land was unambiguously fulfilled. For this reason the Jewish People can be accurately described as a group of perpetual home-comers. The Jewish religion as "a religion on wheels" as Isaiah Berlin has characterized it, was already that way at its inception. One of the first cor-porate acts of group commitment for the Jews was a willingness to travel *toward* the land. And the movement does not stop with death. One of the eschatological visions of the 'final days' has the bones of the Jewish dead rolling under the ground toward the promised land. It is not only the liv-ing that are mobile, but also the dead. They are homecomers, all. Jewish bones, especially the ones not already brought to the promised land, are mobile bones, according to the mythic vision. Thus one has from the very beginning a group of people with a double relationship to land, able to cohere as a group without it, but defining their most deeply sacred voca-tion as a legitimate striving to achieve it. And once achieved, however ten-uously, it must be enhanced and perfected constantly, otherwise there will be dire results.

What dire results?

Death.

It has always seemed safer to the Jew to die in the promised land, or be buried there, than to live there. For there is always the grim and not un-likely possibility that in life one will be consumed by the very promised land that is supposed to supplement an imperfect existence. The land was not only an elusive and desirable quest, it was also an inherently danger-ous one. It was hard to say whether the Jew was safer with or without it. For the actual settlement of the land was defined as conditional and con-tingent for the most part, on proper conduct.

The settlement of the land was and is forever being constrained by the fact that it is a holy land above all else. It is filled with both benevolent and malevolent powers, like most things holy. These powers could be activated by behavior that was not in accord with the revealed Divine Will. It did not belong to the Jewish People alone; it was held in trust by them but dependent upon God's promise. It was theirs as long as they were God's. They had their part of the bargain to keep. So long as they were faithful to their mission their connection with the land could persist. Should they be unfaithful, then the land would spew forth its decimated survivors from it. They would be purged from it, amidst death and plunder. For like themselves the land was set aside for a purpose. It was to be the scene for great and extraordinary happenings. This, too, was the meaning of a holy land. Should the Jewish People fulfill their divinely appointed purpose, the land would be the scene of their elevation and apotheosis. Should they betray that purpose, then the very land would consume them. And so, while the land was infinitely desirable it was also mortally dangerous. As if to underline this, one finds in the biblical narratives the constant connection between land and death (Brichto, 1973). The first title to the land was originally for the express purpose of burial. It was Abraham's desire to bury Sarah; that was the first overt act of the Jewish People to take steps to acquire the land.

The land is not only a place to live, it is to a significant degree a place to achieve a desirable entombment by being buried well. But it was a desirable entombment that was not easily had. The desire to find a resting place was forever being confronted by the prophetic warning that improper conduct would result in the undignified death of a large number of people, and the expulsion of the remainder from the land. It constituted the prototypical admonition to remind the Jews of the need for single minded loyalty to their national religious vocation.

At times these death warnings and threats of expulsion became actual. It was the actual destruction of a large part of the people in 722 B.C.E. by the Assyrians, the decimation of the population and expulsion in 586 B.C.E. by the Babylonians, that gave added credence to the prophetic threat. The memory of these two great premontory exiles, the Assyrian and the Babylonian, served to strengthen the credibility of the prophetic threat that a break between the people and the land was possible. But in addition, these cultural memories served as prelusory forewarnings of the Great Exile to come. By the year 70 C.E., when the great dispersion started, embedded in Jewish consciousness was a memory of a number of mass killings and exiles that ended, for the most part, with the resettlement of the land. These previous premonitory exiles had provided the people with an opportunity to develop the means to deal with exile and mass death as a *conceivable* part of their national life. It was as if almost from the beginning of its history this group prepared itself for a most deprived existence. These historical precedents and the particular structure of group consciousness which developed in response to them made it possible, in very large measure, for the Jews to exist for two millenia without a land. The ability to compensate for its loss, and not to be demoralized, is certainly to be regarded as an extraordinary instance of collective elan.

Fear and Creativity

In spite of the anomalous death taint and corresponding functional and structural defects, the Jewish People, throughout its history, have been extraordinarily creative and alive. Everything written thus far hardly prepared one for an appreciation of these achievements. How is it that a people so dead can be so alive? Living on borrowed time, without the necessary means for a proper group life, has proved to be a most surmountable hinderance. Indeed, it is questionable whether it was a hinderance at all.

Rawidowicz in a brilliant, polemical and largely ignored essay has argued, I think convincingly, that it was precisely the imminence of collective death that activated and energized latent creative collective impulses.

"Yet making all allowances for the general motives in this dread of the end, it has nowhere been at home so incessantly, with such acuteness and intensity as in the House of Israel. The world may be constantly dying but no nation was ever so incessantly dying . . . as Israel . . . I am often tempted to think that this fear of cessation in Israel was fundamentally a kind of protective individual and collective emotion. Israel has indulged so much in the fear of its end, that its constant vision of the end helped it to overcome every crisis, to emerge from every threatened end as a living unit, though much wounded and reduced. In anticipating the end it became its master. Thus no catastrophe would even take this end-fearing people by surprise so as to knock it off its balance, still less to obliterate it — as if Israel's incessant preparation for the end made this end absolutely impossible . . . As far as historical reality is concerned we are confronted here with a phenomenon which has almost no parallel in mankind's story: a nation that has been disappearing constantly for the last 2000 years, exterminated in dozens of lands, all over the globe, reduced to half or one-third of its population by tyrants ancient and modern, and yet re-equips itself for a new start, a second and third advance — always fearing the end, never afraid to make a new beginning, to snatch triumph from the jaws of defeat, whenever and wherever possible. There is no nation more dying than Israel, yet none better equipped to resist disaster. . . . (Rawidowicz, 1966).

In contrast to Pinsker's description of the Jewish People as one tainted with death, pleading for a normal existence, we find in Rawidowicz's description a different emphasis. It is not that death has invaded Jewish existence. It is not that the Jews are constituted by a peculair morbidity. On the contrary, what is characteristic of the group is its extraordinary *fear* of death. It is an inordinate fear which leads to anticipatory preventive measures of a most peculiar intensity that serves to prevent the end from ever coming. It is this fear, and the anticipatory measures it triggers, which is the real defense against disaster.

What is stressed in Rawidowicz's analysis is the appropriateness of preparations for the death-dealing onslaught, while in Pinsker's treatment this is of no import. What is important, to Pinsker, is the *discarding of the tainted status*. What is primary is the need for a normal, more whole and complete existence. A living death can only be remedied by a full life. For Rawidowicz a full life devoid of this inordinate death fear constitutes the greatest peril for continued survival. For if group death has been defeated time and again by anticipation however morose, but nonetheless based on proven realities, who is to say what would happen to the group without it. To relate this position to a known parable: the Jewish People have cried: "Wolf, wolf," but they have done so *tirelessly*, believing it most every time, making necessary precautions, and then have had the experience of having the wolf come with devastating frequency. Rawidowicz believes in the positive value of the 1) warning, 2) collective belief in the warning, 3) the taking of precautions against the threat, and 4) assumption of the inexorable continuation of threatening realities. For him living as "an ever dying people" is the surest guarantee for survival; that which provides security and quietude is itself the ultimate threat. Not so for Pinsker. The contamination of the death taint prevents a proper existence, it is a kind of curse, a fate to be deplored and if possible remedied *completely*. It is the aspiration for a new life, not the fear of death which is to be the primary motive force which energizes.

What we have revealed in these two attitudes is not simply an incidental polemic on the way in which reality was grasped by the Jewish People — instead, we see in them the modern manifestation of a basic, centuries old, dichotomous response of a longevous culture to its difficult situation. Of the two, it is the second, that described by Rawidowicz, which appears to us as the most dominant life response of the Jewish People to its reality. But the first, the aspiration for a new birth was, nonetheless, preserved in messianic aspirations and embedded in the corporate imagination. To live a half-life yes, but refusing to give up the dream of the full one. This aspiration for the full life frequently made the half-life bearable. But it was the ability to lead the half life that made possible cultural and historical continuity. What this may indicate is that for a culture to exist it may have to develop anticipatory institutions and attitudes to survive and flourish in morbid conditions. This evidently is difficult for a culture to do, as Benjamin Nelson has indicated:

"Civilizations do not end with a bang or a whimper. Civilizations generally die laughing. The more closely great societies approach the point of checkmate, the deeper the indulgence of great numbers in their favorite games. In fact, the worse the situation the more hectic the abandonment. It is when all is fun and joy, on the go-go, when the dancers in the charades are on the edge of ecstasy and frenzy, that the hoped for oblivion prevails. At this juncture, treasured elements of the legacy of civilizations slip unnoticed out of focus" (Nelson, 1973).

Life as Crisis

While Nelson's description may be apt for most civilizations it is not true for the Jews. It was precisely their ability to anticipate the "point of checkmate" and allow for another move — just one more — and another and another that characterized them most completely. It was the refusal to allow a forgetful and reality-denying ecstasy that was the most typical of Jewish responses to disaster. Life itself was viewed as a context of real and potential disaster — and the main task was to prepare for it. Prepare for it by: a pervasive philosophy of trust that God would never let the end come within historical time; by not making one's survival dependent on things that could be taken away; by developing a theodicy of defeat that justified any misfortune; by building one's basic institutions so that dispersal would not compromise them; by preserving the maximum of autonomy over one's own communal affairs; by having symbolic escape-valves to express aggression against one's oppressors and thereby resisting premature, adventitious and self-defeating uprisings; by prolonging the crisis-mentality, through the enactment at regular intervals of an elaborate social drama of religious ritual that had as its major theme ultimate return to the land; by encouraging near universal literacy so that these lessons could be rehearsed by the individual in his own private study; by assiduously protecting boundaries of membership, so that no matter how dispersed it was always clear who was and who was not a member of the group; by staging very frequent gatherings of members: daily and weekly so that the group has a reality for all to see; by regarding oneself as superior to one's oppressors no matter how powerful and intellectually impressive they were; by remembering one's past glory and making the memory contemporarily relevant; by believing in the group's ultimate vindication; by being devoted to continuity of the tradition but having social mechanisms to interpret and decide extraordinary events; by regulating as much of the intimate life of one's members with rules and regulations as possible; by developing a repertoire of strategies to handle various kinds of disasters; by finding protectors whose self esteem and self interest is served and enhanced by the very existence of your half-life; by regarding endurance and continuity in time as the real test of culture rather than power and influence; by appealing to the conscience of even those who have killed your members, to help you continue living. These are only some of the means that were used to preserve this remarkably enduring yet fragile group existence.

The question for the Jewish People was never "to be or not to be," but most frequently it was, how to be while not quite being. It was preparation for, accommodation to, and temporary acceptance of that state of not quite being that contributed to their extraordinary longevity.

The question that has concerned us is how a culture relates to the possibility of its own demise. The usual question that is asked is how cultures relate to the death of its members. This has not been within the focus of our concerns, though it is an interesting question. The Jewish People was concerned with the larger question, from the very first formative moments of its collective being. We have tried to indicate that this fact contributed to its prolonged existence. I believe this to constitute the fundamental meaning of the sacrifice of Isaac story in which a father, the promised progenitor of a people, is at the same instant assured a fruitful posterity — and commanded to destroy the agent of its realization (Isaac). His willingness to endanger the manifest guarantor of the promise (his only son) and live an endangered half-life — in which he has only his failing flesh to rely on, proves his worthiness. We have in this treatment purposely not dealt with the Jewish belief in immortality, resurrection, martyrdom and other death theories in Judaism — since they are relatively well documented and above all are related to other types of questions. Nor have we attempted to deal with the complex social and religious factors and circumstances that helped to structure various kinds of responses to the belief in the ever dying Jewish People. We have attempted to make plausible the more general thesis that the extraordinary longevity of group life is dependent upon, and intimately connected with, a willingness to live a diminished existence — at least in the case of the Jewish People.

References

Brichto, H.C., "Kin Cult, Land and Afterlife — A Biblical Complex," *Hebrew Union College Annual*, Spring, 1968.

Elazar, D.J. "The Reconstitution of Jewish Communities in the Post War Period," *Jewish Journal of Sociology*, Vol. XI, No. 2, Dec. 1969, p. 187.

Cassell, E.J. "Being and Becoming Dead," *Social Research*, Vol. 29, 1 Spring 1972, p. 537..

Demske, J. *Being, Man and Death*, The University Press of Kentucky, 1970.

Heidegger, M. *Being and Time*, tr. by Macquarrie and Robinson, E., N.Y., Harper and Row, 1962.

Laqueur, W. *A History of Zionism*, Weidenfeld and Nicolson, London, 1972, p. 561.

Lifton, R.J. "On Death and Death Symbolism: The Hiroshima Disaster," in Wyschograd, E. (ed.) *The Phenomenon of Death,* Harper and Row, N.Y., 1973, p. 71.

Nelson, B. "The Games of Life and the Dances of Death," in Wyschograd, E., *The Phenomenon of Death,* Harper and Row, N.Y., 1973, pp. 113–132.

Neusner, J. "Now We're All Jews Again," *Response,* Winter, 1973–4, No. 20, pp. 151–55.

Pinsker, L. "Auto-Emancipation, 1882," in Hertzb erg, A., *The Zionist Idea,* Harper and Row, N.Y., 1966.

Rawidowicz, S. "Am-Holeh Vamet," (Hebrew) Metzudah v–vl (1948).

Roshwald, M. "The Idea of the Promised Land," *Diogenes,* No. 82, Summer, 1973, pp. 45–69.

Valery, P. "The Crises of Mind" in *History and Politics,* Pantheon, N.Y., 1962.

Yehoshua, A.B., in public address, May 1972. Conference Commemorating the Death of Lt. David Uzan, Haifa University, Haifa, Israel. Cf. his comments in Ezer, E.B. *Unease in Zion,* "Let Us Not Betray Zionism," Quadrangle, N.Y., 1974, p. 335.

·13·
Jewish Self-Definition and Exile

Bernard Berofsky

Exile can take two distinct forms, conceptual and spiritual. I feel that it is far easier for the Jew of the diaspora to rebut the charge that he is conceptually in exile than it is for him to show that he is not spiritually adrift.

A particular version of the Zionist challenge to diaspora Jewry represents the members of this group as logically incoherent, that is, as committed to a body of assumptions that can be shown to be self-contradictory.[1] Although a charge of illogicality is not likely to goad a person into action in order that he may demonstrate that his present course of action is contrary to interests other than the avoidance of contradiction, the premises of this argument are worth exploring.

One premise, that the Jewish people constitute a nation, has been convincingly defended by many modern historians. Certainly the Jews as well as their hosts so regarded them prior to the Emancipation. The natural challenge of this claim would take the form anticipated by the participants in the Paris Sanhedrin of 1807. The benefits of emancipation can only be purchased by a redefinition of the Jewish people that would sever the hitherto indissoluble link between religion and nation. From that point on, Jews, like any other religious group, would be able to abide by the laws of the polity and discharge all civic duties so long as the state provided the Jew with the security to which all citizens are entitled and did not interfere with religious practice, a private or social activity now conceived as free of political connotations. To be sure, the Orthodox Jew might still literally believe in and pray for a return to Zion that would be effected by the Messiah. But such dreams did not then appear to constitute a political threat.

147

A *prima facie* strong case on behalf of such a redefinition can be constructed. Moreover, this case need not be utilitarian; that is, it need rely only on the advantages of political equality, especially the security and freedom from persecution that citizenship was supposed to bring.

Jews as a Nation

The (Zionist) argument we are examining claims that Jews constitute a nation. Proponents of this position, therefore, are committed to block attempts at redefinition of the sort we have just described. The point, here, is that the burden of proof is upon those Zionists to show that contrary conceptions of the Jewish people are unacceptable and not simply unfounded or arbitrary. If the Jews are a nation, they are one whose members enjoy, as their favorite intellectual activity, reflection on their status as Jews, on "the Jewish question." Alongside the standard accounts of Jewishness—whether these be religious, ethical, national, ethnic, racial, or genetic—are the anti-conceptions. Some, like social psychologist Kurt Lewin, despair of capturing the essence of Jewishness:

> It is rather difficult to describe positively the character of the Jewish group as a whole. A religious group with many atheists? A Jewish race with a great diversity of racial qualities among its members? A nation without a state or a territory of its own containing the majority of its people? A group combined by one culture and tradition, but actually having in most respects the different values and ideals of the nations in which it lives? There are, I think, few chores more bewildering than that of determining positively the character of the Jewish group. It is not easy to see why such a group should be preserved as a separate unit, why it has not entirely given up its will to live, and why the nations have refused to grant Jews full assimilation.[2]

A similar stance, one certainly motivated by the failure of the Jew to conform to more standard treatment, is taken by those who would confer membership on anyone who professes to be a Jew even if he fails to satisfy any other traditional criterion. A variant of this idea, suggested by Sidney Hook[3] and Jean-Paul Sartre,[4] and earlier by Melville Herskovits,[5] would confer this authority on either the person or the community of which he is a part. (No decision procedure is provided for resolving disputes in the event of conflict, for example, in the case of a person who disavows his Jewish status in a community that insists upon treating him as a Jew. After all, no fact independent of the fact that an assertion or denial of Jewishness has been advanced is deemed relevant as a criterion for membership in the Jewish people.) This position is better interpreted as a nonposition—as a refusal to offer a definition of the Jew. If one conceives the task of such a definition as providing the essential characteristics of Jewishness, I shall soon express sympathy for the nonposition based on skepticism about this idea of the essence of Jewishness. But if we are to suppose that this stance is to be judged like any other definition, it is a failure.

> Let any Catholic Irishman or Boston Brahmin or Southern aristocrat move into a community in which he is unknown and pretend he is Jewish only to the extent of saying he is Jewish, and he will be treated like all other Jews including those who do not say they are Jewish but whom the Gentile community regards as Jews."[6]

Hook's conclusion, that such people *are* Jews, does not follow at all. If these people all pretended to be Republicans, they would be similarly treated as Republicans even though, in their heart of hearts, in, perhaps, the registries of the Democratic Party, and in the privacy of the voting booth, they demonstrated their allegiance to the Democratic Party.

Hook's awareness that Jewishness is not conferred just by choice is illustrated by his remark that "elementary decency and dignity demand that in some sense they accept themselves as Jews."[7] If Jewishness is entirely a matter of being regarded as Jewish, what constraint can there possibly be on opting out? If the denial of Jewishness is indecent and undignified, the reason can only be that the person is being untrue to himself, that is, he is denying the fact of his Jewishness. This fact, therefore, is objective and independent of attitude and treatment. Its existence explains why it might not be undignified for the aforementioned Boston Brahmin to deny his Jewishness. After all, he is not Jewish.

It is a difficult matter, though, to determine what the fact is and to defend an account that will do justice to Hook's justified skepticism regarding the essence of Jewishness. One of the curious aspects of these introspective exercises, energetically carried on by Gentile thinkers as well,[8] is the relative clarity of the extension of "Jew," that is, the overall agreement by Jew and Gentile alike, as to which people are and which people are not Jews. Having familiarity only with these discussions, a rational Martian would conclude that the concept of Jewishness is like the concept of mental health, creativity, success, or the state of being a dilettante. With respect to membership in these cases, one person's estimate is as good as another's, and disagreement is rife. To be sure, there are individuals and groups who disagree about their Jewishness. But in some cases—the Ethiopian Falashas for example—the dispute is based on factual ignorance. If the historical links between this group and the Jews of the pre-Exile era could be traced, doubts about their status would be eliminated. Thus, some uncertain cases do not reflect an imprecision in the concept of Jewishness, but simply ignorance regarding facts that would settle these cases by the application of a criterion, perhaps quite clear in itself, of Jewishness.

However, if this were true, there would be one or several criteria of membership in the Jewish people; yet we know this is disputed. Presumably, in cases like the Falashas, one seeks either facts that support conversion to Judaism or direct ancestral links. But this conception of Jewishness is the *halakhic* one and is bound to be challenged by the non-Orthodox. The Orthodox, for example, do not count as Jews those converted under Reform or Conservative auspices or those members of Reform temples who count themselves Jews because, though their mother is not Jewish, their father is. Such matters do not affect the rationality of determining the status of the Falashas by *halakhic* criteria for, should they fail to meet these criteria, they will also fail the more liberal ones, never having been the beneficiaries of Reform or Conservative conversion.

This is not to say that there is a criterial uniformity for all groups. There were, in fact, borderline groups—the Samaritans, for example—long before the advent of Reform Judaism. In the case of the Samaritans, in fact, there was controversy within *Halakhah* regarding their status.[9] Nonetheless, unless the number of non-Orthodox conversions increases dramatically, or the recent suggestion of some to count as Jewish any who so identify themselves (and thereby to institutionalize the Sartre-Hook approach) is taken quite seriously, it will remain surprising that all this debate remains pretty much on the criterial, as opposed to the extensional, level.

Another explanation of the lack of extensional disagreement that does raise doubts about the clarity of the concept of Jewishness is suggested by Hook's critique of the definition of the Jew in terms of origins. He considers not the Orthodox definition but rather the much vaguer one, "one whose ancestors were of the Hebraic religious faith,"[10] and rightly criticizes it for vagueness. (How many ancestors are required and what relationship must they have to the claimant?) His other objection, that "there are some who are not regarded as Jews, and who do not regard themselves as Jews, whose ancestors many years ago were of the Hebraic faith,"[11] may be applied to the *halakhic* definition. Though we all know that the success of Christianity, due to Jewish intransigence, depended on the conversion of the Gentiles, the Jewish converts to Christianity, of whom there must have been a sizable number, remained, according to *Halakhah*, Jews. So then did their children and their children's children through the next 80 generations. Although we must subtract from this figure the many descendants of those Christian "Jews" whose father married outside the faith to which he was no longer committed and of which he was probably not even aware being a member, we must, on the other hand, add to the figure the many descendants of Jews (including proselytes and apostates) who strayed so far from the fold so as to leave no mark on the consciousness of succeeding generations. There must, then, be millions of Christians who are unaware that Orthodox Jews count them as Jews (if they only knew); many of these people would be horrified at the label and would totally reject it. Whether or not one counts this as conclusive grounds for rejecting the *halakhic* definition, we certainly know why there is no actual disagreement about individuals—we just don't know which Christians are in this category.

Why should this discrepancy between criterial disagreement and relative extensional agreement appear surprising anyway? Is it not common for there to be classes that can be determined by several criteria? The class of human beings can be determined using several criteria—they are rational animals, featherless bipeds, living things that have the capacity to read newspapers, and so on—because either the characteristics just happen to coincide or there are scientific reasons for the co-presence of these traits.

Now where one has this sort of situation, a defender of but one account of Jewishness must be prepared to argue not just for its extensional adequacy because other definitions are extensionally adequate. Though some definitions determine the correct class, he would have to say that they do not express the essence of Jewishness. Let us apply these considerations to the case before us. The Zionist tells us that Jewish identity is essentially a national matter and is, thereby, obliged to reject all competing definitions, some of which pretty well determine the right class, namely Jews, as well as the position of those who deny the possibility of definition. He can score a quick and easy victory by comparing his position only with the religious conception, that is, the view of the Jew as one who professes certain distinctive beliefs and engages in certain distinctive practices. Since many Jews are atheists or agnostics, this account fails miserably on extensional grounds. For an Orthodox Jew, this conception defines a good Jew; but as noted earlier, his definition of Jewishness, converts aside, is a genetic one, based entirely on maternal lineage.

Yet are these really competing accounts? The genetic account provides us with a criterion of membership in the Jewish people; the account in terms of national identity does not. To know that someone is a Jew if, and only if, he is a member of the Jewish nation, does not tell one how to determine during the period of the *galut* whether someone belongs to that nation without invoking a separate criterion, possibly the genetic one. Perhaps, then, the accounts are complementary. After all, the genetic account leads us back to the Jewish nation, our ancestors who were once autonomous in *Eretz Yisrael*. This merger of the definitions is, however, prohibited by the Zionist use of their account to drive a wedge between Israeli and diaspora Jewry. For if the State of Israel is the reestablishment of that ancient nation, a Jew who voluntarily rejects *aliyah* forfeits his membership in that nation. The genetic account, whatever its rationale, would at least permit the Jews of the diaspora to regard themselves as Jews.

The Zionist is again, therefore, committed to his account as the correct one. Even if it fails to provide a criterion of membership in the Jewish people, anyone who is a Jew is essentially a member of a nation and any account that fails to incorporate this feature is *eo ipso* inadequate. Genetic facts, in his view, are not sufficient for membership.

Jewishness

Why must Jews have any essence? Why must there be a trait (perhaps comprised of several more basic traits) that constitutes Jewishness; that is, a trait that, unlike other characteristics, all and only Jews happen to possess, which confers membership in the class of Jews upon those exemplifying it. Those who despair of providing any definition of Jewishness by reflection on considerations pertaining to Jews, Judaism, and Jewish history may be buttressed by general considerations of a philosophical and linguistic nature. Several philosophical traditions merge here to produce a skeptical response. Without attempting to identify the various strands, I shall integrate the results and consider their impact.

It is, first of all, a mistake to suppose that the myriad of intellectual and scholarly activities associated with Jews and Judaism—Jewish history, Bible studies, Semitic languages, Talmud study, sociological studies of the Jews, Yiddish literature—requires that Jews have an essence—Jewishness. These studies may be pursued with equal efficiency on a weaker assumption, to wit, that we know what group we are identifying, that we know about whom we are talking. Any characteristic (or characteristics) that correctly identifies the Jews (or the 19th Century German Jews, or the Jews of the Babylonian exile, or the Jews of New York's Lower East Side), even if it fails to capture their essence, suffices. As the contemporary philosopher Saul Kripke would say, one need only to "fix the reference" of our concepts. [12] Thus, one may wish to use different criteria for different purposes. To take a pertinent example, one may find it useful to define "Jew" in terms of national criteria when talking about the period of the Second Temple— although, in light of the large diaspora during that time, this definition may not fare well—and adopt a different definition after the dispersion. Communication about the Jews, therefore, does not require insight into the nature of Jewishness.

This may not be the case for all concepts. Perhaps terms like "gold," "water," and "human being" identify natural things that possess real essences or sets of characteristics that constitute the underlying nature of individuals grouped in this way and that explain the behavior and observable features of those individuals. Be that as it may, the supposition that Jews constitute a natural kind is a patent absurdity. [13]

Skepticism about Jewishness may be heightened by reflections on elementary considerations pertaining to natural language. Classifications reflected in language are adopted for many different human purposes. Certain objects are grouped together as chairs because human beings are interested in certain common features of those objects and not in others. What could it possibly mean to talk of the essence of all chairs?[14] As Dewey said,

> As far as present logical texts still continue to talk about essences, properties and accidents as something inherently different from one another, they are repeating distinctions that once had an ontological meaning and that no longer have it. Anything is "essential" which is indispensable in a given inquiry and anything is "accidental" which is superfluous.[15]

The essence–accident distinction is a pragmatic, not a metaphysical one. To be sure, this issue is a highly complex one given the claim, vehemently and powerfully argued for by many, that the pragmatic conception does not apply to natural kinds. Scientists have their purposes, too, when they theorize and classify, and these are the discernment of the real essence of the objects studied. Scientific classifications, therefore, though corrigible, at least purport to have more than merely pragmatic import. For example, classifying an object as a chair will tell you something about its use and little else, but classifying it as a wooden object will tell you a great deal about its properties, some of which may and others of which may not be of direct human concern. In any event, as I said above, Jews are not a natural kind. If, for example, (Orthodox) conversion to Judaism makes one a Jew and this fact alone rather than the belief that one is now Jewish or the consciousness of belonging to the Jewish people explains radical and basic behavioral changes and the acquisition of a new set of personality traits, then, perhaps, Jewishness is real. Or, if we may, in order to make a point, adopt the arguable assumption that there are distinctively Jewish lifestyles, beliefs, ambitions, and modes of conduct, then if we found persons who are not aware they are Jewish and who are inexorably drawn to these lifestyles, and so forth, and if, finally, the explanation is *not* provided by such sociological or psychological considerations as the influence of their peers or an unconscious knowledge that they are Jews, we shall have reason to believe in Jewishness.[16]

But if we find two criteria that are acceptable extensionally, one may argue, don't we simply have to consider whether or not we would count someone as Jewish if he or she lacked one of them in order to determine in what Jewishness consists? We do proceed rationally in this way to eliminate some unacceptable definitions. Jewishness is not constituted by a certain physiognomic similarity even if, arguably, Jews (converts aside) share this trait.[17] For we would not want to rule someone out as a non-Jew if he happened to lack this feature. But the reason is not that this feature is different from true Jewishness; it is rather the pragmatic consideration that our classifications are not advanced with such matters as primary nor are they illuminated in any way by citing this feature.[18]

Moreover, the application of this criterion is, in several ways, vague and ill-defined. Do we always know what we would say? How do we block the claim that what we say under hypothetical circumstances may reflect not a deeper understanding of our present concept but rather a change in or extension of that present concept? Why must concepts, adopted for dealing with the actual world, have clear definitions in all possible worlds? In fact, if we take this seriously, it follows that Jews are not a nation. If a Jew prior to the French Revolution posed the question as to whether Jewishness was a national or genetic trait and if the answer to that question depended upon whether individuals would still be considered Jews if they chose to remain in the diaspora at a time when the lengthy exile ended and the national homeland was returned to its rightful owners, then clearly the answer would have been that Jewishness is a genetic trait if it is anything at all. American Jews are still counted as Jews in spite of the existence of Israel.

I conclude, therefore, that a case can be made on behalf of the redefinition sought by those confronting the possibility of emancipation. A cogent argument against this possibility has not yet been found.

The Dilemma

But the story is not nearly over. For the Zionist case we are now examining, though it advances the claim that the Jews constitute a nation, does not rely on that premise. Hence, the above critique can be dismissed as being beside the point. To see this, we may cast the argument in the form of a dilemma. The Jew in the diaspora who personally declines *aliyah* in order to preserve his status as a full-fledged Jew, denies that the Jews are essentially a nation. But he must consider the other horn of his dilemma. In denying a national status for Jewry, he removes the underpinnings of the Zionist case for a national homeland in Palestine. For, only if the Jews are a nation, and not something less, do they have any claim to this land. That one's ancestors happened to sojourn there would not evidently ground such a petition. Only the strong premise formulated in terms of national rights can serve to anchor Jewish aspirations by rendering them *de jure* legitimate. The Jew of the *galut* is impaled on the horns of a dilemma by being reminded that his allegiance to the Jews of Israel demands his rejection of the *galut*. If he affirms the legitimacy of the rebirth of the nation of Israel yet fails to become a member of that nation, he voluntarily casts his lot with his host country instead of with the nation of Israel. If, on the other hand, he denies the legitimacy of this rebirth, he severs the attachment most diaspora Jews feel very deeply and that many consider essential to their self-respect.

Many versions of Zionist doctrine reject the above case by insisting that a Jew is not second-class just because he is not Israeli. Membership in the Jewish nation is distinct from Israeli citizenship and compatible with citizenship of other countries. The Zionist we are addressing, however, claims that *now* the Jewish nation just *is* the State of Israel. Hence, citizenship of that state is a *sine qua non* of continued membership in the Jewish nation.

The Jewish Nation and the State of Israel

We will be better able to focus on the issue before us and not be distracted by matters that only appear to pertain to that question by bearing analogies in mind. A person of Polish extraction who opts for American citizenship voluntarily surrenders his allegiance to Poland. He and others will subsequently often refer to him as Polish; but the term will now identify him either in terms of his ancestry (of Polish extraction) rather than in terms of his present status, or in cultural or ethnic terms. The dilemma we described above would extend this analogy to American Jews, or rather, to Jewish-Americans (compare to Irish- or any hyphenated American). Since they are not citizens of the Jewish nation, their Jewishness is now either a matter of origin or culture. It is important to see just how devastating a consequence this would be for many American Jews, excluding, of course, the totally assimilated.

If an American Jew is Jewish by culture alone, he no more merits this label than anyone else who participates in Jewish cultural life. He is no more a Jew than the Christian who participates in a seder, sings *Had Gadya*, enjoys certain gastronomic delights, or takes a course in Hebrew. We must not, of course, ignore the crucial lack of analogy between Polish-Americans and Jewish-Americans—to wit, the religious dimension. But if religious identification is made the mark of the Jew, not only will many American Jews fail this test, but perversely, citizens of Israel will also.

It would be equally devastating to most American Jews, though less obviously so, to discover that their Jewishness is just a matter of origin. Why should it upset nonreligious American Jews to be told that we are "members of one family, bearers of a common history"?[19] Although Klatzkin believed that the *galut* would not and should not survive, this conception of Jewish peoplehood, with perhaps Israel at its spiritual and cultural center, has been adumbrated and defended by some, most notably by Mordecai Kaplan, the founder of Reconstructionism (see Chapter 4) so that the Jew of the diaspora would have a bona fide and first-class role to play in the ensuing dramatic episodes of Jewish history. Although we shall have occasion to comment upon this idea, we need only note now that it is distinct from and far richer than the idea of the Jew that is exhausted by reference to his origins.

A person who is called a Pole solely because he is of Polish extraction can do nothing to lose this label and need do nothing to merit it. Similarly a person of Jewish extraction is so, come what may. (That is, of course, the *halakhic* or Orthodox conception.) On this account, therefore, a person of Jewish extraction who totally rejects all facets of Jewishness, who has no sense of membership in this family, who retains not a whit of Jewish cultural identity, who converts to a religion of idol worship in a ceremony in which he disavows all ties to his hated past, and who joins and, through deed and commitment, rises rapidly in the ranks of the Nazi party, is as much of a Jew as anyone. (If this is almost, but not completely convincing, imagine that his Jewish mother was just like him!) Certainly, Kaplan would not count this monstrosity as a Jew. (An Orthodox Jew would, however.) A necessary condition of membership in the Jewish people, according to Kaplan, is loyalty to that body.[20] Origin is insufficient, not just for being a good Jew, but just for being some sort of Jew.

Although the point with respect to culture is, I submit, not open to challenge, a case might be made that even the "anti-Jew," just in virtue of origins, is Jewish. Recall, though, that the *halakhic* account must address not only this sort of bizarre case, but the ones described earlier of people who are descendants of early Jewish converts to Christianity. Pope John Paul II, for all we know, might be Jewish. In any event, we can bypass this issue now by recalling that the question concerns origin as a criterion of membership in the Jewish nation. If the Jews had never been a nation, they can never have regarded themselves as a nation in exile. Hence, their nationality is initimately bound up with more than mere tribal and ancestral relations—it has to do, in addition, with allegiance to a body of laws, territorial integrity, acceptance of control by a central governing body over taxation and such affairs as commerce and education, a common judicial system, and an official language (or official languages). The attempt to sustain as many of these features as possible after the loss of territorial integrity is the ground of the conception of the Jews as a nation in exile and the basis for the rejection of mere origin as a criterion of membership in that nation. Hence, if the nation is restored, continued membership is not required of (and may even be barred to) the aforementioned Nazi and other Jews (in the Orthodox view). Israel makes a demand on the Jewish people—to rejoin the Jewish nation— that cannot be met simply by the act of pointing to one's maternal lineage.

An American Jew would then rightly be disturbed by having to concede that his status as a Jew is analogous to the status of that Pole who is also an American citizen. Nor does it help to ponder the possibility of dual citizenship. First of all, since we are considering the intellectual coherence of a set of commitments a person makes, in particular a decision to remain in the diaspora while defending the right of Jews to be restored to their ancient homeland, the state of dual citizenship is not of direct concern to us. For a person can be in this state without having chosen it and cannot, therefore, be judged irrational on this basis. There are, in fact, historical examples, such as the American sailors inscripted by the British during the War of 1812, in which the individuals deny or reject the claim of one country upon them. One can also choose dual citizenship, and it may be prudent or rational to do so under certain circumstances. (A naturalized United States citizen disavows allegiance to all other countries; but a British subject can legally be a citizen of other countries.) But even if membership in the Jewish nation is not automatically precluded by citizenship of countries other than Israel, we still do not have a viable account of the nature of Jewish nationality other than Israeli citizenship. The bare possibility of dual nationality does not entitle an American Jew to regard himself as a part of the Jewish nation. The most we can derive from the possibility of dual citizenship is that, if a feasible conception of Jewish nationality that is distinct from Israeli citizenship were developed (and we have not yet done this), perhaps an American Jew could count himself a part of this nation without surrendering his United States citizenship. This conclusion, however, is evidently compatible with there being no conception of Jewish nationhood other than Israeli citizenship.

Notable American Jews, like Judge Louis Brandeis, have argued not only for the possibility of a vital and meaningful Jewish life in the diaspora but also for the groundlessness of the fears of divided loyalty expressed about American Jews sympathetic with the Zionist dream. Even though he conceived of all Jews, whether in the diaspora or the Land of Israel, as members of a common nation, they can be, if Americans, as patriotic as all the other Americans of foreign ancestry. [21] This claim would be directly relevant here only if it constituted a reason to believe that American Jews are part of the Jewish nation that transcends the State of Israel. But since American Jews are not citizens of the State of Israel, there is no logical reason to be concerned about divided allegiance whether or not they are part of the Jewish nation. On the other hand, scenarios that are far from preposterous can be described that would severely test the loyalty of American Jews to the United States. One type of scenario—in which American Jews are seriously threatened by government-condoned outbreaks of anti-Semitism—could incorporate a justified rejection of the United States for reasons that in no way suggest the idea of a Jewish nation. American citizens are entitled to freedom of religion, due process of law, freedom from fear, and the protection of the government against unjustified attacks on their person and property. Any citizens, Jewish or otherwise, retain, as part of their American heritage, the right to overthrow or reject the government of the United States under extreme conditions. It is commonplace to acknowledge an implicit contract between the government and its citizens and, concomitantly, to deny a notion of absolute loyalty on the part of the citizens to that government; and Jews, like anyone else, might find themselves in a position in which they must avail themselves of such rights. The other type of scenario would describe a conflict between the United States and Israel that is perceived by American Jews as one the United States is attempting to resolve by instituting conditions that gravely threaten not just the security but also the very existence of Israel and the people of that nation.[22] The explanation of the opposition of American Jews to these policies of the United States government—opposition that may conceivably take the form of emigration, civil disobedience, or open rebellion—is evidently constituted by the deep and powerful ties between American Jews and their brethren in Israel. But unless these emotional attachments, founded upon a shared history and religious tradition together with a sense of kinship and mutual responsibility for each other's security, constitute a sufficient basis of nationhood—and this cannot, of course, just be assumed—we again have no reason to believe in Jewish nationhood even if there is some small reason to be suspicious of total Jewish loyalty to the United States.

Let us recapitulate. Though the position that the Jews constitute a nation cannot be rationally established, the rejection of that stance would presumably require the removal of the underpinnings that support the State of Israel. If that is unacceptable, a Jew in the diaspora might still regard himself as a part of that nation if it can be conceived as a larger entity incorporating the State of Israel. However, we have not been able to formulate in a plausible way the nature of that entity and, consequently, the Zionist charge of inconsistency against the Jew of the diaspora still stands.

The Religious Conception Reconsidered

Perhaps our dismissal of the religious account of nationality, based on the undeniable fact of vast indifference to and positive rejection of religion on the part of the Jews, has been hasty. For it is also an undeniable fact that Jews, those who are observant as well as those who are nonobservant, share a common religious heritage even if they differ in their interpretation of that heritage and its value. Moreover, it is certainly worth reflecting on the views of those Zionists who regard the creation of a political entity in which Jews achieve dominance and security as virtually worthless unless it is a step toward a genuine spiritual rebirth and, for some, the long-awaited redemption. What is the point of creating a state for Jews unless Jews as such have a mission; and what can that mission be unless it is identical with or a modern reinterpretation of the ancient mission to preserve God's law and to serve as His witness to mankind? (Even secular Jews who talk of realpolitik, pragmatism, and compromise wince a little when the State of Israel acts as badly as do other nations.) This theme has been passionately and eloquently expressed by religious Zionists of all persuasion, from the Orthodox to the Reconstructionist. Smolenskin's belief that Jewish unity is based on the primacy of Torah over territory or political identity[23] has been restated by the influential Solomon Schechter:

> The brutal *Torah*less nationalism, promulgated in certain quarters, would have been to the Rabbis just as hateful as the suicidal *Torah*less universalism preached in other quarters. And if we could imagine for a moment Israel giving up its allegiance to God, its *Torah* and its divine institutions, the Rabbis would be the first to sign its death-warrant as a nation.[24]

And on the religious left, there is Kaplan's reconstruction of that religious mission as essentially ethical rather than supernatural "The living carrier and vessel of Judaism" is not the State of Israel, as important as its existence is, but rather "the living Jewish people," according to Judah Magnes, the first chancellor of the Hebrew University.[25] He believed that Jews can survive and pursue their mission wherever they exist Even if the State of Israel is or should be the spiritual center of world Jewry, the Jewish nation lives and carries out its divine pursuit as an organic unity whose limbs are spread out over the entire world.

Let us pursue this line of thought for a moment. Logically, we can deal with the nonbelieving Jew who cannot tolerate even liberal religion in the same way that any nation deals with its unpatriotic citizens. One may tolerate them, dislike (or admire) them, even punish them;[26] but they are not exiled or expelled from the nation. To be sure, this means that patriotism is not a criterion of citizenship just as religious commitment is not a criterion of membership in the Jewish people. We are basically invoking an ancestral criterion, but one that zeros in on the religious qualities of these ancestors and their heritage. Perhaps, thus, we can talk of a spiritual nation that embraces all Jewry, observant or nonobservant, in or out of the diaspora.

The danger this doctrine faces is not so much its unpalatability to the unbeliever, but rather the emptiness it bestows on the concept of nationhood. The sentiments expressed above may all be true, including the belief that it is sacrilegious to serve the religious and national dimensions of Jewry by the creation of but another warring and selfish nation-state in a world overpopulated with such anachronisms. It just does not follow that the Jews constitute a nation. To see this, one need only reflect on the fact that a perfectly analogous case can be made that any religious group, for example, Christian, constitutes a nation. Christians all over the world share a common religious heritage, have a spiritual mission, and so on. How abhorrent Christians would regard the creation of a Christian state which had no spiritual purpose other than being a haven for persecuted Christians. If this nation is Christian, its government and people must abide by certain principles. So the fact that a Christian might reasonably deplore the separation of religion and nation implies not that all Christians constitute a nation, but rather that the Christian people are bound by common beliefs and principles. Analogously, the religious Jew's discomfort with Israel's secularism does not mean that all Jews belong to a nation that transcends the State of Israel; it means, simply, that Jews share a common religious heritage and some Jews would prefer the Jewish state to indicate in a more pervasive way its attachment to that heritage.

We must again reiterate the obvious. Whatever a nation is, it is more than a people (defined ancestrally) bound by common beliefs and traditions. A nation must politically embody, or at a minimum, possess autonomy over a certain region at some stage in its existence. To be sure, the term "nation" is vague and undoubtedly is used at times as a synonym of "people," or "ethnic group," or other vague words. But if we adopt this looser usage, then the Zionist case certainly collapses, as I shall briefly demonstrate.

Recall that one horn of the dilemma has to do with the juridical claim of the Jews to the land of Palestine, based on their ancestors having there constituted a bona fide nation, with all that this entails—autonomy, a government and legal system, common language, educational system, etcetera. This claim surely collapses if it is based on the fact that the Jews as a people once resided on that land. On that criterion, the Jews can lay claim to Egypt! Or some Dutch persons can demand a part of New York City.[27] (The Dutch can make even a stronger case than can the Jews for, while the ancient Israelites were slaves, the Dutch exercised political sovereignty over and settled in New Amsterdam.) We need not belabor this point for it will soon be clear, I trust, that the claim of the Jews on Palestine based on the ancient nation of Israel can be rationally challenged. *A fortiori*, the weaker case, expressed in terms of mere occupancy is totally ungrounded. Although the idea of a Jewish nation distinct from the State of Israel still eludes us, a problem for the Zionist has been identified and will be probed further.

Jewish Rights to Palestine

I believe, as was just suggested, that the weakness of the Zionist case under examination is to be found in the claim that the Jew's entitlement to a portion of Palestine rests on the sovereignty his ancestors exercised in that region and the consequent status he now has as a member of a nation in exile. If this is right, then a diaspora Jew is not obliged to regard himself as a member of the Jewish nation in order to remain a Jew. I have argued that a Jew in the diaspora is indeed confronted with a momentous choice if he is a part of the Jewish nation. For *if* such a nation exists, it can only be identified with the State of Israel in which case his membership in that nation demands the rejection of the *galut*—that is, it demands *aliyah*. We argued earlier that, although no proof that the Jews are a nation can be constructed, this conclusion follows from what is apparently the only legitimate way of grounding the claim to *Eretz Yisrael*. But if this grounding fails anyway, the Jew of the diaspora is free to define his membership in the Jewish people in a way that does not make the demand of *aliyah* upon him.

It is important to be explicit about the fact that the freedom of definition just described is severely limited in certain ways. Jews cannot deny that they once *were* a nation, that they *were* for a time a nation in exile, that the people of that nation transmitted to them, their descendants, an important religious heritage that incorporates a special role for and feeling about *Eretz Yisrael*. They are not, on the other hand obliged to believe that that nation in exile has lasted for 2,000 years and has been reconstituted in the State of Israel. In truth, such questions are not straightforward questions about facts. There are no facts that decisively settle the question—though there are, of course, facts that support one side or the other—as to whether these two nations, ancient and modern Israel, are one or two.

ZIONIST ARGUMENTS

To use an elementary philosophical distinction, Zionist justifications for a homeland in Palestine for the Jewish people may be divided into teleological and deontic. Teleological justifications are based on the value such a creation can have, on the beneficial consequences to the Jews, the world, perhaps even to the Arabs, that would flow from the presence of this state. Deontic justifications, on the other hand, are expressed in terms of rights or entitlements to the land, and they are advanced independently of the value or lack of value of the conferral of nationhood—real, not exilic—on the Jews.

TELEOLOGICAL ARGUMENTS. Significant distinctions within each class should be recognized. Within the teleological category there were (and are) those who emphasize the positive benefits to Jews in terms of the possibility of unfettered self-expression; the rebuilding of Hebrew culture; the creation of a model Jewish community that can be emulated by the communities of the diaspora; (for some) the creation of a model socialist community; and, to turn to the more metaphysical characterizations, the reunion of a people with its land and the consequent sense of wholeness that emerges therefrom. Religious Zionists added their own distinctive elements: the fulfillment of the divine mission, the "exalted idea,"[28] that revitalizes the Jewish people and "raises them above all obstacles and hardships and gives them strength to prevail and win out."[29] Alongside the positive benefits are the negative ones, those that were recognized as the deeply urgent ones: the elimination of Jewish suffering and the effects of anti-Semitism. If the world refused to serve as a place for the Jew, let him have his own place. If the world cannot cure its pathology, let the Jew alleviate the symptoms by removing himself from Gentile society. Many saw Zionism as the only way to avoid the "physical and intellectual destruction"[30] of the Jewish people.

There is, then, no dearth of teleological considerations with a variety of appeals, many quite urgent, some more utopian than others, and most quite powerful in force and cogency. A perusal of Zionist literature reveals, I believe, the prevalence of these over deontic appeals. Part of the explanation for this is that such references are far more likely to inspire Jews (and Gentiles for that matter) to action than ones to claims or rights. Another part of the explanation, more pertinent for our purposes, is the greater obviousness of many of the facts appealed to. Israel *is* a haven; Israel *has* initiated a renaissance of Hebrew culture and language; Israel *has* enabled many Jews to feel whole again. Appeals to rights, on the other hand, can be difficult to justify.

DEONTIC ARGUMENTS. There are four categories of deontic justification. The right to a homeland has been alleged to accrue to the Jews in virtue of the near unanimous culpability of the so-called civilized world for the calculated slaughter of approximately one-third of the world's Jews, an event that represents, however unique its magnitude and its monstrosity, the natural denouement of a lengthy chapter in the history of Western civilization. Some Zionists saw that the acceptance of this deontic justification along with several of the teleological ones did not confer a right to Palestine as such—rather it conferred a right to some territory or other. Thus, proposals for a homeland in Uganda and Argentina were seriously entertained by some Zionists, including Herzl.

Some deontic arguments pertain to Palestine directly, for example, those based on the divine promise to the descendants of Abraham of that land. There is, however, a serious deficiency in appeals emanating from a religious stance for they are made in the international arena and cannot be expected to bind those who do not share this stance but who may otherwise be affected. Even if God has bestowed a right to Palestine on the Jewish people, one cannot expect this consideration to count in the arena of international law and politics. One cannot be expected to cede land to any group that declares itself the recipient of divine territorial rights.

A third deontic appeal that is both genuine and directed to Palestine in particular, one that is recognized by many, is based on modern settlement by the early and courageous *halutzim.* One tends to forget that a sizeable Jewish population resulted from emigration that began in the 19th and continued during the early part of the 20th Century.[31] By 1947, Jews constituted about one-third of the total population of Palestine, despite the militant opposition to immigration by the British and others. Thus, a strong case, combining teleological and deontic elements, can be constructed on behalf of a Jewish homeland in Palestine that is independent of any argument resting on the prior existence of a Jewish nation on that land 2,000 years ago.

ANCIENT NATION ARGUMENTS

Everyone is aware that the delicate question concerns the right to Jewish autonomy over regions occupied predominantly by Arabs prior to the founding of modern Israel. The thesis I would like to defend is that the strength of the Jewish case is not substantially or clearly greater by virtue of the fact of the ancient nation of Israel. For example, one factor that weighs against the Arab rejection of Israel that is independent of ancient Israel concerns the actual area envisaged in the United Nations Partition Plan of 1947 and accepted by the Jewish leaders in Palestine. Outside the Negev Desert, it is a miniscule area, comprised of the narrow coastal plain plus the Upper Galilee area west of the Jordan River, and a thin corridor linking the two. More to the point, it was, of course, the area of concentrated Jewish settlement and thereby constituted a satisfactory reply to the Arab concern that a small minority was being granted political hegemony over the vast majority of inhabitants. (It is evidently not our purpose to become embroiled in debates over more specific territorial issues that have arisen since 1947 as a consequence of four wars and perpetually shifting boundaries.)

Since political science is not mathematics, we must, in a discussion of political rights, specify a reference time. There is no analogue in mathematics —or, perhaps, even in ethics—of the fact that *de facto* political control, no matter how achieved, eventually becomes *de jure*. Perhaps this is accepted as true only because of the fruitlessness of denying it and having, therefore, to construct a theory of political rights according to which no existing government is—or, perhaps, has a way of becoming—legitimate. We might, in consequence, ignore arguments against the validity of the State of Israel in 1981 and establish our case against the Zionist argument with great ease. But all of the considerations we have adduced were applicable in 1947 anyway.

One need not cite ancient Israel in order to underscore the fact that the Arabs had not been autonomous in that region for many centuries; the Jews were not wresting a state from the Arabs. Moreover, the Arabs could have cited on their behalf ancient, but more recent, hegemony over that region than the Jews. In other words, if the principal objection to a Jewish state is the Arab one, it cannot strengthen the Jewish case to allude to ancient political control. And why, in light of the aforementioned considerations, independent of ancient nationhood, should there be other rational objections to a Jewish homeland in Palestine?

A rebuttal to the above would allow both Jew and Arab a *prima facie* case for the territorial rights based on political autonomy in the distant past.

Many Jewish leaders were deeply sensitive to Arab rights and some, like Martin Buber and his Ihud movement, pressed for a bi-national state, a goal that turned out to be unrealizable.

It is still true, therefore, that the ancient nation argument does not strengthen the Jewish case, for with it, the Arab case is at least equally strengthened, and, without it, the Jews have a strong case anyway. A key element in the Palestinian situation is the absence of indigenous control from the time such control was wrested from the Ottoman Empire. For unless circumstances are special, it is difficult to imagine conditions under which a people like the Jews can claim national rights to a territory governed peaceably and effectively by the indigenous population or peoples within that population. For this reason, we would look askance at territorial demands based on earlier control when the land in question is unquestionably under the control of the local population. This is part of the reason the Dutch demand for portions of New York City would sound so ludicrous. Nor would such demands gain much plausibility if they were made on behalf of a nation whose homeland had been the territory in question (unlike the Dutch who were colonists). If the current interest in one's roots leads to a rebirth of Visigoth nationalism, we might expect the members of this people, now dispersed through Europe, to demand that Turkey (and Greece) cede to them various territories, including their ancient capital of Adrianople (Edirne) in order to announce the end of the *galut* and to begin the ingathering of the exiles. Multiply this picture by a number of similar groups, just on the continent of Europe, and absolute chaos results.

I trust that I will not be accused of ignoring the deep differences between Jews and Visigoths—such as the actual retention of identity, national or not, on the part of the former group. I mean only to emphasize the fact that the Jews were not displacing a legitimate indigenous government. Notice also that this fact is important whether or not the State of Israel is a reconstitution of that ancient nation. Again Israel's case does not rest on its uninterrupted existence for two millennia.

If these considerations are not convincing, I would draw attention to an important distinction that, I believe, should settle the issue. We are now considering, as I said earlier, whether the Jew's entitlement to a portion of Palestine rests on the sovereignty his ancestors exercised in that region and the consequent status he now has as a member of a nation in exile. But the critic who denies that the nation of Israel existed in 1947, prior to the creation of the State of Israel, need not and would be mistaken to deny that Jews once were sovereign in that region. Even if the claim that one is now a nation in exile makes a stronger demand on the powers that be than the claim that one's ancestors once were a nation in that region, a nation whose inhabitants and their descendants for reasons that are not easy to fathom have retained a powerful sense of identity in spite of the dispersion and eventual breakup of that nation, the latter claim is relevant. I am not arguing that the fact that ancient Israel was constituted on the land we call Palestine is a strong reason for the legitimacy of the current State of Israel, but rather that, whatever force this appeal has cannot be shown to be clearly greater than the force of a similar consideration that takes note of the fact that only the descendants of that nation, not the nation itself, survive. Why should that nation's survival be required for its descendants to claim these rights? First of all, thanks to the powerful forces that have preserved the unity of the people, we know with reasonable clarity who the Jews are. The breakup and dispersion have not created a serious problem about the identity of the children of Israel. Fringe groups aside, there are no other serious claimants.[32]

Second, the desire of this people to recreate a nation is as powerful an argument as would be the desire to restore the ancient nation, assuming implausibly that Jews make this subtle distinction. Similarly, the powerful emotions that bind the children of Israel to that Holy Land are equally powerful whichever construction is adopted.

Just as the stockholders of a corporation retain certain rights after the corporation is disbanded, so may the Jews retain rights even if they no longer constitute the nation whose earlier existence provided them (and their descendants) with entitlement to *Eretz Yisrael*.

The Zionist case is being undermined here by indicating that, although he is required to produce an argument that satisfies the following conditions, it is doubtful he can: establish that justification for the State of Israel depends on the continuous existence of (ancient) Israel (so that all the other cited reasons are collectively insufficient); and retain the force of the argument when recast in terms of the descendants of people who once constituted Israel, an ancient nation that exists no longer.

If we are right, the dilemma argument of the Zionist collapses and, with it, the charge of incoherence against diaspora Jewry. A Jew need not now regard himself as a part of the Jewish nation in order to retain his membership in the Jewish people, where membership may be characterized in several alternative ways. At the same time, he is free to press the case for Israel, including the argument that his ancestors were once autonomous on that land.

Notes

1. See discussion by Étan Levine in Preface, p. vii.

2. Kurt Lewin, *Resolving Social Conflicts* (1st ed.), Gertrud Weiss Lewin (Ed.). New York: Harper, 1948, p. 180.

3. Harold U. Ribalow (Ed.). Reflections on the Jewish question. In *Mid-Century*. New York: Beechhurst Press, 1955, pp. 386–405.

4. Jean-Paul Sartre, *Anti-Semite and Jew*, George J. Becker, tr. New York: Schocken Books, 1948.

5. Melville Herskovits, When is a Jew a Jew? *Modern Quarterly*, IV (2), 1927, pp. 109–117.

6. Hook, Ribalow, op. cit., p. 398.

7. Ibid., p. 401.

8. See, for example, Alfred Jospe, The Jewish image of the Jew. In *Great Jewish Ideas*, Abraham Ezra Millgram (Ed.). B'nai B'rith Department of Adult Jewish Education, 1964, pp. 7–8.

9. See *A History of the Jewish People*, H. H. Ben-Sasson (Ed.). Cambridge: Harvard University Press, 1976, p. 309. The other major religious groups have their borderline cases also. Are Unitarians Christians?

10. Hook, op. cit., p. 397.

11. Ibid., p. 403.

12. Saul A. Kripke, *Naming and Necessity*. Cambridge: Harvard University Press, 1980, pp. 22–70.

13. The only hypothesis under which this supposition would not be an absurdity is that Jews constitute a race. Melville Herskovits argues convincingly against this hypothesis in "Who are the Jews?" in *The Jews: Their History, Culture and Religion* (2nd ed.), Louis Finkelstein (Ed.). New York: Harper, 1955, Vol. II, pp. 1151–1171.

14. The question here concerns the essence of a class, namely, chairs. We are not, therefore, taking a stand on the issue of essences for individuals.

15. John Dewey, *Logic: The Theory of Inquiry*. New York: H. Holt & Co., 1938, p. 138.

16. We shall also have excellent reason to believe in God if these conditions are obtained.

17. See Herskovits, Who are the Jews? op. cit., p. 109ff.

18. If Jews were a race, and the evidence is clear they are not, it might make sense to talk about the discovery of the essence of Jewishness.

19. Jacob Klatzkin, Boundaries. In *The Zionist Idea*, Arthur Hertzberg (Ed.). Garden City, Long Island: Doubleday and Herzl Press, 1959, p. 317.

20. Mordecai M. Kaplan, *A New Zionism* (2nd ed.), New York: Herzl Press and Reconstructionist Press, 1959, p. 112.

21. Louis Brandeis, *Brandeis on Zionism*. Washington, Zionist Organization of America, 1942, pp. 24–35.

22. This scenario is somewhat more imaginable than is the former one.

23. Peretz Smolenskin, It is time to plant. In Hertzberg, op. cit., p. 147.

24. Solomon Schechter, Studies in Judaism. In *Selected Writings*, Norman Bentwich (Ed.). Oxford: East and West Library, 1946, p. 65.

25. Judah Magnes, Like all the nations? In Hertzberg, op. cit., p. 444.

26. I am not, of course, advocating punishment, but rather reminding us that religious nations have in the past regarded this option as their right.

27. That New York City is, despite appearances, under the jurisdiction of an effective government is an impertant consideration

28. Yehiel Michael Pines, Jews will accept hardship only in the Holy Land. In Hertzberg, op. cit., p. 414.

29. Ibid., p. 416.

30. Max Nordau, Zionism, ibid., p. 243.

31. In 1914 there were 85,000 Jews out of a total population in Palestine of 700,000.

32. There are fringe groups, for example various Black Hebrew ones, who claim to be one of several of the lost tribes of Israel.

·14·
The Lessons of Emancipation

Arthur Hertzberg

History of the Emancipation

The emancipation of Jews is now almost two centuries old. The American Revolution was effectively over by 1781 and everyone knew that in the new country Jews would be equal in law. In that very year Moses Mendelsohn persuaded a Prussian official, Christian Wilhelm Dohm, to write a book pleading for "the improvement of the civil estate of the Jews." Dohm argued, in part, that Jews could become good and useful citizens in a Western state, for were not those in North America an admirable example of what the inhabitants of the ghetto could become in freedom?

A century later, in 1881, large-scale pogroms in Czarist Russia brought those hopes of the emancipation into question. Leon Pinsker and Yehuda Leib Lilienblum contemplated these horrors and concluded that the only emancipation that was possible for Jews required that they reconstitute their own nation. After 1881, some handfuls went to Palestine in the first modern *aliyah*. The masses of Jews, two million or more, chose to go westward, mostly to the United States, in search of economic advancement and personal freedom.

In these last two centuries, the Jewish world has been reordered much more radically and fundamentally than anyone imagined at the dawn of the era of emancipation. A European and Middle Eastern people of two centuries ago is now an Israeli–Western people. A once totally unemancipated people now lives everywhere under conditions of equality in law: perhaps three-quarters of Jewry, almost all except those in the Soviet Union, are actually emancipated. To be sure, that equality, both for the nation that is Israel and for the diaspora, has to be protected and fought for again and again. A convincing case can be made for the proposition that even in 'the not a state like any other state," and that even the most powerful of the diasporas—the Jewish community in the United States—is not quite like all other groups in America. Nonetheless, to the degree to which emancipation was conceivable, it has now arrived.

A century after the effective beginnings of Zionism and two centuries after the first signs of the dawning of the new age, it is fair and important that a number of questions be asked: in a world far more turbulent than was imagined a century or two ago, how is the emancipation to be defended?

Jews in an Open Society

There is another question which I think is more fateful. The era of the emancipation has brought Jews out of the ghetto so that their being Jewish, even in Israel, is totally voluntarist. Even the *sabra* (native born Israeli) can choose quite freely to leave for other shores and to forget both Israeli and Jewish identity. That process is even more available in the diaspora, where the open society presents the individual Jew with insistent opportunities and temptations simply to leave his Jewishness without even making a decision to assimilate. The majority of the Jewish people now lives in Israel and in the diaspora, outside the *Halakhah*, with the religious tradition translated either into national memory and group experience or, to be more truthful and exact, to highly personalized sentiment. Under these conditions, now that the emancipation has succeeded, the question needs to be asked: can the Jewish people survive?

ASSIMILATION AND SURVIVAL

Despite the cliché that no lessons can be drawn from history, some lessons can indeed be learned, for there are some recurrent patterns in the response of Jewry to the emancipation. History has repeated itself, and it continues to do so. The fundamental pattern was best stated by a journalist writing in France in 1853: "Our parents," said he, "observed the Sabbath, the holidays and all the rules. We go to synagogue on Yom Kippur; our children do not care at all." This was written 62 years after the final grant of equality for Jews in France by the decree of the Revolutionary Assembly in 1791. At that very time, the grandchildren of the handful of Jews in the American colonies were reaching marital age, and the rate of intermarriage was one in three. This pattern was to recur again in the United States in the 1920s and the 1930s, when the grandchildren of the Central European immigrants reached adulthood. It exists today in a much vaster Jewish community, now that the grandchildren and the great-grandchildren of the hundreds of thousands who came at the turn of the century are marrying.

There are places in the diaspora, such as contemporary France, where the Jewish temperature has been rising because of the recent arrival of the North

African Jews from the last intensely Jewish ghettos in Algeria and Morocco. It is true in several of the big cities of the North American continent, where post-World War II immigration of survivors of the death camps represents an increase in Jewish density. More than ever before, self-ghettoized ultra-Orthodox communities exist in contemporary America. This phenomenon is also to be found in places as far flung as London and Melbourne. It is even possible that this relatively small group, with its high birthrate and its struggle to remain apart from the Gentile and even from most of Jewish society, will outlast the attritions of the diaspora. My own guess is that the future of the ultra-Orthodox will not go quite as well as some of those who romanticize this phenomenon think. Even in the original home of Lithuanian and Hasidic orthodoxies, the quiet and not so quiet continuing losses to the surrounding world were large. In Western Europe before 1933 orthodoxy of the brand of Samuel Raphael Hirsch had a continuity of five or six generations, but its numbers were maintained as much or more by migrants to the West from Eastern Europe as by continuity of its own German–Jewish founders.

It is too early to tell what the destiny of the last stand of Orthodox Jewish separatism, now transplanted to the West, and especially to America, will be. It is, however, not too early to know that the vast majority of the Jews in the diaspora who were last in Lemberg or Vilna, or the villages round about three or four generations ago, are everywhere opting out of the Jewish community at an alarming rate. What makes this phenomenon particularly frightening to those who care about the existence of a discrete Jewish community is that it is happening in the aftermath of the Holocaust, in the very sight of the existence of Israel and the worldwide passion for it, and at a time when there are not East European ghettos or North African *mellahs* left. The few Jews still wearing kaftans in a couple of Rumanian villages, or the defiant synagogues in Soviet Georgia are now remnants and museum pieces.

Therefore, the first lesson to be learned from two centuries of experience with the emancipation, is that a generational clock has ticked over and over again in the open society. Whether in New York and Philadelphia in 1840, in Paris and Bordeaux in the 1850s, in Budapest around the turn of the century, in Berlin and Vienna in the 1920s, and now in the United States, it tells the same frightening thing: the third generation in the open society intermarries at a rate of one in three!

THE SPIRITUAL RESPONSE

There is a second pattern now, more than two centuries old, of Jewish spiritual response to the emancipation. Here the issue is not the era of legal equality, but rather the era of religious doubt, which began even earlier than the 1780s. Here we go back, at very least, to the middle of the 17th Century, to the shaking of the *halakhic* structure from within by Shabbetai Zvi, and from without by Spinoza. These attacks were resisted by *halakhists* and believers, some of whom even understood that the open society was not a boon but a danger. Did not a number of Hasidic leaders oppose Napoleon because they made a conscious choice between the freedom of the Jewish individual and the dangers that emancipation would bring to the inherited Jewish religion? Nonetheless, by the 20th Century, the bulk of the world Jewry is by choice or by economic necessity, living outside the religious tradition.

For the post-Orthodox mass of Jews, the recurrent pattern has been to imagine some substitute ideal sufficiently attractive and compelling so that Jews by their allegiance to it would choose to remain Jews. Early Reform Judaism posited the Jews as the supreme bearers of universal ethical ideals. In the 19th Century, some Jewish Saint Simonians and even an early Socialist like Moses Hess, imagined for Jews a priestly role in the ushering in of the new era of universal brotherhood. In due course, this notion was reiterated by a staggering variety of revolutionaries. Jewish proponents have argued that, since Abraham broke the idols, being Jews means marginality, protest, and being protagonists of the new. A full catalog of these modernisms is beyond the capacity of an individual scholar. He would have to range across the whole spectrum of Western culture—in music, art, history, law, etcetera, to compile such a list.

In the Zionist phase, despite a minority which pleaded for normalcy, most Zionists have hoped that the reconstituted nation would represent, one way or another, "a light unto the nations." The rationale in the diaspora for the Jewish philanthropic establishment which is wideranging and more generous, has been that Jews ought to lead the rest of society toward compassion. Succeeding generations of Jews will then be inspired to associate themselves with so noble a Jewish community. Not so long ago, in America in the 1950s and 1960s, the Jewish community was being told by its leaders that its most important function was to fight for the rights of Blacks, and that, impressed by such nobility, the young would want to remain with their elders as Jews.

There is no need in this context to deal with an intellectual analysis of any of these values and to answer the question of whether they were indeed validly Jewish and adequate heirs of the *gravitas*—the weight and seriousness —of the inherited tradition. This is in itself an important subject which requires special treatment. It is enough, here, to make a point about social history: none of these doctrines, not even those that looked within, like the varieties of Jewish nationalism, and certainly not those that looked without, such as the various revolutionary doctrines, have really provided the bulk of world Jewry with an ideal that has effectively replaced the older religious vision as the grounding for a particularist Jewish existence. Felix Adler, the founder in America of Ethical Culture, a sect in which Jews and Gentiles intermingle and intermarry in the name of ethical ideals, was the son of

Rabbi Samuel Adler, the rabbi of Temple Emanuel, the cathedral synagogue of Reform Judaism in New York in the middle of the 19th Century. Before our eyes in Israel, there is a great and pained outcry about *yeridah*. Whatever may be the truth about the numbers involved, one thing is clear: the most intense Jewish nationalism available, the glory and travail of Israel, has not stopped several hundred thousand *sabras* from opting out. In the diaspora we have taught effectively; all the substitutes for the older religion have been taught with passion, but the erosion in all the diasporas continues unabated.

Jewish Modernity

It is particularly important that we come to terms, more than a century after the effective beginnings of modern Zionism, with the major Zionist analyses of and prescriptions for Jewish modernity. Let it be stated flatly: both Herzl and Ahad Ha'am have been proved wrong by life. Herzl presumed that anti-Semitism would persuade the bulk of the Jews to prefer to live in their own nation. In fact, except for a short decade between the late 1930s and the late 1940s, when almost all the other doors of the world were closed, the bulk of Jewish migration during the whole of the past century has gone to destinations other than Israel. Ahad Ha'am presumed that the existence of a modern Jewish culture in a national center would preserve the diaspora. That center has now been in existence for several generations. It has not stopped the clock of assimilation in the diaspora, or even radically affected it.

It is, of course, possible to maintain that large-scale destruction of the physical being of Jewry has happened before, and that ages of doubt and indifference are not unprecedented. A minority of today's Jews is intensely Jewish in the diaspora—and especially in Israel. It is the saving remnant, reappearing this age as in ages past.

Such a judgment asserts that the problems with which Jews are wrestling are really no different, except perhaps in degree, than those of past ages—*but they are*. The era of the emancipation—the last two centuries—is the first time in Jewish history that Jewish existence, both in politics and faith, has become voluntary. This age is the first time in which secular conversion, rather than the traumatic choice of a change of religion, is the possibility that is open to Jews; and it is a possibility that is widely used. This is the first age in which, effectively, the Jewish people is in its majority post-religious, at least with respect to obedience to norms enforced by some authority. It is this unprecedented community, which has ever less of the anchor of memory in an earlier, more orderly Jewish existence, that is now before us. Indeed, the problem before the Jewish world is not the minority which cares very much, but the majority which cares impressionistically, or not at all. It is for that majority that modern Jewish thought was invented, and modern Jewish politics; and yes, Zionism.

Here too I return to Moses Hess. Writing in Paris in 1860—then the very capital of the emancipation—Hess understood that the forms of Jewish life had to remain congealed and unchanging throughout the centuries of the pre-modern diaspora. He knew very well that the inherited religio-national culture of the Jews was in large part being rapidly destroyed when it left its bitter Shangri-La in the ghetto to face the sun and the wind of the 19th Century. He therefore insisted that this tradition could both change and survive only in its own ancestral home. He detested the classical Reform Judaism of his day, for he saw it as a way-station to assimilation. He had almost as little patience with those who attempted simply to stand aside from their own day and ignore it, for he had read too much Spinoza and had spent too much time being a Socialist. Only in their own land could Jews revive and revise their tradition to make it contemporary. Only there could being Jewish and being human be the same. Only there could Jewry ultimately survive as a people.

Precisely because the patterns are recurrent in the history of the Jews in the last two centuries, there are no better answers today than Hess gave, both in what he asserted and what he did not emphasize. The fundamental problem of world Jewry is not anti-Semitism—it was not in 1860, and it is not in the 1980s. On the contrary, a certain level of anti-Semitism, provided it is not murderous, has acted in the modern era as a preservative, artificially, of the Jewish community, even as it has been losing its inner content. The problem is loss of faith, of commitment, of *raison d'etre*. The diaspora has offered the individual Jew many possibilities. He can find his reason for being at the smorgasbord of the West—in art, music, politics, or, most often, simply in the service of the goddess Success. It is the Jewish people which has, in the open society, no role of its own in the diaspora, unless one defines raising money and political lobbying for the State of Israel as the content of Jewish existence for centuries to come. This, and only this, do Jews now do in the diaspora; to a degree they do it remarkably different than conventional actions of the best-educated elements of the Western bourgeoisie.

THE TRAGIC PARADOX OF EMANCIPATION

At the end of two centuries of the era of emancipation, the Jews have arrived at a tragic and fateful paradox which can no longer be escaped. Those who rejected the emancipation—that small minority which opted out of it from the very beginning—seem safe as Jews in the new age. Those who accepted the emancipation are, in all their varieties, in far more substantial danger. Precisely because they care less about the Jewish component in their existence than do the self-ghettoized, the majority of Jews are today, as before, the ones more in need of radical solutions to their Jewish problem.

There is an answer to the question: is Jewish continuity safe in the open society? The answer is: no. This pessimism does not, of course, apply to the State of Israel, though obviously Israeli society has not yet assumed its stable form and requires radical change in many areas. Nonetheless, after more than a generation of statehood, despite its manifold problems, the prospect for the future of Israel is bright. The problem area is the diaspora, where Jews are by any index, whether economic or cultural, very successful indeed as individuals, but where the Jewish community is seriously at risk.

WHY A DISCRETE PEOPLE

There still remains the question, as yet unsolved and seemingly insoluble of why? Why desire survival as a discrete people? In the name of what? Two centuries of intellectual modernity in all its varieties prove one simple conclusion: universalist ideas such as democracy and socialism have not provided those Jews who have been their proponents with any long-range reason for remaining within a distinctly Jewish community. Ultimately, even if disguised as secular rhetoric, the reason for continuing a distinctly Jewish community has been religious.

I suspect that many more Jews believe in the God who chose them than are willing to affirm that He also commanded them to be obedient to every stricture of the *Halakhah*. Jewish disbelief is not of the variety that asserts "let us be like all the other nations." It wants to assert the divinely ordained mystery of Jewish existence without quite knowing what to do with the inherited law. The true watershed in Jewish life in the modern age is between those who share in awe at this otherness and those who would abandon it or forget it. It is only to the degree to which such a conviction is alive that Jewish existence continues. Those for whom it has died remain at best, or at worst (there is no difference), Jews by situation. Such a Jew has been described at Auschwitz by Jean Amery in a set of moving biographical essays. Amery's Jewishness amounted, even at the end, to the numbers tattooed on his wrist. Sartre knew such Jews in the Resistance in the 1940s; they were people without a Jewish past or future, trapped in a tragic Jewish present.

The Jewish people will not survive in the open society either in memory of the tragedy of the Holocaust or in distant contemplation of the glory of Israel. Of course, those who will choose *alivah* to live in Israel will be secure in their destiny as Jews, but it is clear on present evidence that their numbers, especially those in relatively free and open societies, will not be overwhelming. Even with the help of Israel, to a far greater degree than it obtains at the moment, the question remains open: is there finally enough positive energy in the post-Emancipation Jewish community for it to solve the problem of continuing as a discrete entity?

The problem exists in all its gravity today before world Jewry because now, at last, the momentum of the pre-Emancipation Jewish ghetto is completely spent. The issues of Judaism and modernity and of Jews in an open society are even more open today than they were at the beginning of the era of the Emancipation.

·15·
The Jews in the Soviet Union

Martin Buber

The postulative clarification of one of the most difficult problems of our time—the present situation of the Jews in the territories of the Soviet Union—is attempted in this chapter. By the concept of postulative clarification I mean to indicate that our concern here is neither with the determination of facts and relationships for purely scientific purposes nor yet with the formulation and publication of demands in the political sphere. I do not wish to indulge in either a sociology "free of value judgments" nor in unexamined propaganda: we wish—I believe I may say "we"—through a common effort of the intellect to point out and communicate to the world what is right and desirable in a limited but significant realm of contemporary national life. Altogether it seems to me that this critical moment in history more than ever depends on independent human beings joining to look without preconceptions at contemporary reality and search together, in an unreserved give and take of understanding, for the way out of seemingly unsurmountable difficulties.

But before we begin to deal with the facts and relationships involved in our problem, permit me to point out a circumstance, the understanding of which seems to me indispensable, which until now has been too little regarded. I must ask you first to note that I am expressing only my own personal view of the problem. Moreover: I, whose view I am expressing, do not wholly identify myself with either of the two camps that are engaged in cold war with one another; I am unable to concur with the claim of the one, that it adequately represents the principle of liberty, nor with the claim of the other, that it adequately represents that of equality. If I were a politician, I suppose I would have to call myself neutralist in the strictest sense of the word; but I am not a politician. I am, indeed, a man who carefully and concernedly observes and reflects on the political reality of this hour—but I am not a politician.

As is generally known, the two periods of the Soviet regime that can now be viewed historically—the one defined by Lenin and the one by Stalin—had one thing in common in their treatment of the Jewish problem, different as that treatment was otherwise. They both made their treatments dependent on the question: what actually are these Jews? It is the same question that a century and a half ago occupied Napoleon and the pioneers of Jewish emancipation in the form: "Nation or Religion?" and that reappeared again and again in the discussions within the Marxist camp on the nationalities problem, in the form: "Nation or Nationality or mere ethnic group?" Under the Soviet regime the formulation "Nation or Religion" had, in the nature of things, no longer any validity, even though the law here recognized—and still does—no Jewish institutions other than the purely religious. On the other hand, the question "what sort of national or ethnic existence do the Jews have?" was earnestly discussed—in official and officious circles—even at the very beginning of the regime.

The answer was set out more or less clearly, but finally by Stalin with the greatest exactness, in the form of definition and deduction. A national existence, it was said, is to be found only where an economically independent national unit lives on its own territory. Since these characteristics—this was the deduction—are lacking in the Jewish group, since it can point to no market of its own and therefore no production of its own, it can be recognized only as an ethnic group. But such a group can claim no right to a continuance of its existence, no right to the preservation of its cultural values; it must be integrated into the nation and its nationalities, that is, dissolved in them. In theory, this integration should take place without any coercion, even without any discrimination. In practice, things looked radically different; of this reality the extermination, under Stalin, of the leading Yiddish writers is the most brutal example.

The Limits of Lenin's Understanding

Be it noted at the same time, that however earnestly Lenin thought about the nationalities problem and however precisely he differentiated between the various forms of national existence, he never believed that he could fully master the specific Jewish problem by means of definitions and deductions. What prevented him from holding such a belief was, in the first place, his sense of the realities of folk life; and such a folk reality was, in especially high degree, that peculiar idiom, Yiddish, that succulent mixture of Canaanite antiquity and Central European wanderings, a spoken language through and through, even in its literary products. But bound up with this, too, was Lenin's political instinct, which taught him to distinguish between political opponents whom he must combat and a national-cultural element that desired nothing more than to be allowed to be itself and live its own life.

Where the element of national culture ended, Lenin's understanding also reached its limits. For this reason he set himself against Hebrew, the language of origin with which generations of wandering Jewry kept faith—even while out of the symbiosis with the host nations there arose one idiom after the other. With Hebrew they kept faith, however, not because it was an expression of their folk life in the present but because it was the language of a past when they were rooted in their own land and because it was the language of the promise. Lenin, strangely, associated Hebrew with capitalism and bourgeoisie, whose preservation, following a fatal error of Marx, he connected with the synagogue and its language. He was deaf to the perception that this language had once reached its maturity struggling to find proper expression for the yearning after a real, not merely formal, justice; and that in the Hebrew prayers this very yearning over and over again becomes spoken word, whether or not they who speak the prayers realize it, or whether they do not realize it and pray against themselves. Thus, because Lenin saw in the vitality of Hebrew not an original reality of the life of the people but a political factor, he operated here, in contrast to his procedure with regard to other Jewish cultural values, on the basis of definitions and deductions instead of observation and insight. It is his doing—assisted to be sure by an office that was staffed throughout with fanatically anti-Hebrew Jews—that in the Soviet Union Hebrew is denied all right to existence outside the liturgical realm, and that among all the writings of the Soviet peoples of which representative editions are printed in the Soviet Union, the Hebrew Bible is missing.

The Lenin and the Stalin periods (and the post-Stalin period as well, as far as we can discern its character) thus have in common the rejection of that element of the Jewish spirit, beyond the purely synagogal, that unites the Soviet Jews with those of the rest of the world: apparently because it seemed politically undesirable for this union to be of an overly elemental character. That cultural heritage, on the other hand, which the Russian, and besides them perhaps the Polish, Jews could call specifically their own—Yiddish culture—was under Lenin not merely tolerated but furthered in all its forms: literature, the press, theatre, and education. Under Stalin it was more and more sharply attacked, and finally stamped out with all the means available, apparently because the regime saw in it a suspicious separatism, a suspicious resistance to the "integration" for which the regime was striving. In both periods, definitions and deductions were made to serve—to the degree to which each particular case seemed to demand it—as the points of departure; and actual practice—from simple prohibition under Lenin to elimination by force under Stalin—based itself on these. The trend in the post-Stalinist era, in spite of the appearance of some few Yiddish publications and performances, is still too indistinct for us to be able to judge whether we can speak here of a return—hesitant as yet—to the partial insight of Lenin or merely of a mitigation of the radical solution of Stalin. But there appears to have been no change in the theory of "integration" and in the method of definitions and deductions which it utilizes.

Jewish Religious Uniqueness

The method of definitions of which I speak is based on the premise that a state has the right not only to define the nature of a historic community incorporated in it, but also to determine its individual fate, through the act of declaring that it does or does not belong to this category or that. This method, conceived in such all-inclusive terms, is incorrect. Jewry is atypical. To stamp it an "ethnic group" is misleading, for its essential characteristics are not comparable to those of any known ethnic group.

Even the Napoleonic question, "Nation or Religion?" contradicts reality, for there is no such alternative here. From the historical point of view, and that means from the point of view of the history of the Jewish people, there is in Jewry, as to my knowledge in no other group, a peculiarly dynamic union of nation and religion. There are, to be sure, other nations in which everybody, or the great majority, confess to the same faith; but I know of no other national community in which, from the very day of its foundation, the power of this faith so mightily impressed itself upon the life of society in all its aspects in order to subjugate it to the rule of the Absolute; I know of no other national community in which the great believers stood up so boldly against everything that obstructed the realization of the commandment of truth and justice in the life of the people—against kings, property owners, and, when necessary, the priesthood itself. This dialectic of the simultaneous, this struggle—first of the founding spirit against all that resists it, then of the spirit that has remained faithful to the original command against the forces of political rule and property that have departed from it—this is the true history of Israel from Moses to the last of the prophets and beyond.

Out of the fundamental conviction that what matters is not that one make for oneself any particular image of the Divinity, but rather that one convert into reality, in all the functions of the community, that Divinity's command touching the life of His creatures with one another: out of this fundamental conviction arose the conception of a future in which this labor would find its fulfillment, through a collaboration as it were of that which was intended for the world from of yore and that which is willed by man. All ideas of great building of society into the future derive from this militant faith of Israel.

Let no one suppose that with the end of ancient Jewry's political independence there also came to an end the struggle of the spirit for its realization. Certainly, with the loss of national self-determination there was lost also the possibility of building up a righteous independent society on a basis of righteous relations between individuals and between groups. But the flame from Sinai continued to burn, not merely in the teachings of the sages who demanded that here and now, even in the subjugation of exile, so much of the command of righteousness and mutual assistance should be fulfilled as is here and now capable of fulfillment; it burned on also in the Messianic mass movements whose inner core was not simply the will to return to the homeland, but rather the will to return to it in order there to establish the kingdom of God. And the kingdom of God, in accordance with the ancient tradition, meant a universal kingdom of men and nations living in true community with one another.

This inner flame has not been extinguished nor has the light that radiated outward from it, which the prophet calls "the light for the nations." Karl Marx, that Rhinelander of Jewish stock—he, too, was only a translator of the Jewish faith in the future and will for the future. He translated them with the skill of genius into the language of a pan-technical age, that is, of an age in which the technical dispatch of all human reality comes close to dispatching faith as well. It is not my place here to discuss the question as to whether this can be called a true human language, or whether it must rather be humanized before it can really be adapted to such a purpose.

Linguistic and Territorial Uniqueness

No less than in this realm of national religiosity—one perhaps of little interest to the Soviet Union—Jewry is atypical in the realms which were decisive—the realms of language and of territory.

One of the essential elements of "normal" nationality is singleness of language, and here again Jewry appears as an anomaly, though, to be sure, a significant and fruitful one. The language of the national self, Hebrew, produced almost the whole of biblical literature; but even at the height of Jewish statehood we find at its side, not as a literary language but as a tongue familiar to the educated classes, the dominant language of the West Semitic culture—Aramaic—that language in which later, in Exile, the greater part of the Talmud was written. The great works of Jewish thought were written during the Hellenistic period in Greek, in the Middle Ages in Arabic, in our times largely in German; and in addition to the central language and the varying contact languages, there developed those strange products of Jewish life among the nations, the idioms, of which the most fertile is Yiddish. This multilingualism has a unique background in the psychology of this people: here the will to persevere in what was given from old is combined with a strong and deeply rooted tendency to seek vital contact with the surrounding culture. Every surrounding culture that allowed this double will to work itself out gained thereby.

The Soviet regime in its first phase suppressed the will to persevere in the original tongue, but tolerated or even endorsed the will to contact in the form of Yiddish. In its second phase, the regime, for the sake of radical integration, suppressed all public expression in the contact language of the people as well. What policy it will adopt in its present phase is, as I said, not yet clear.

In regard to the question of territory, Jewry proves no less atypical and unclassifiable than in the question of language, with this difference: that here it became an anomaly only with the end of its autonomous existence in Palestine. Until then it was the singleness of the land that was taken for granted—as the unshakeable reality—even during a period of temporary exile of a great part of the population. With the stabilization of the diaspora, a change occurs: again and again the Jew accepts life in the land to which he has been driven as a serious, meaningful task; but salvation remains bound up with the homeland, for the great faith in the future in which the singular unity of nation and religion manifested itself, the return to the homeland is as an indispensable precondition. There is to my knowledge no other people to whom its own soil was and remained so central, so sacred an object. But the Jew committed himself in his daily life to the land of exile, that is, wherever the host people made it possible. He accepted not merely the surface of his fate, but its depth. He took upon himself not only martyrdom, but also life itself, wherever he was permitted that. In those very lands in which Jewry was later persecuted or exterminated, there existed genuine symbiosis, which would have been unthinkable without genuine loyalty to the lands in question.

Stalin, Marx, and Lenin

Stalin seems to have leaned toward the following deduction: for a national community to be something more than a mere ethnic group without a lasting right to existence it must possess a language and a territory of its own; the Jews living in the Soviet lands have neither their own language nor their own territory; therefore they are nothing more than an ethnic group and thus destined to dissolve themselves, or rather, to be dissolved, in those nations and nationalities in whose midst they live. It is, however, worth noting that within the framework of this method Stalin accorded very different treatment to language and to territory. The Soviet Jews had no language of their own from the moment that this was not conceded them. But the regime adopted quite another attitude toward territory. While the Stalinist regime took note of this grave deficiency (lack of territory), it undertook to remedy it by its own means. The Jews were offered an autonomous territory—Birobidjan—several thousand miles removed from their main areas of settlement. The cultural autonomy which this territory was intended to enjoy was naturally also to include language. Thus the regime was apparently ready to raise the Jews to the status of a nationality and thereby to save them from the fate of integration; more precisely, to substitute for a negative integration through dissolution, a positive integration through annexation of the Jewish people was conceived of as a collective unity and controlled as such. The plan did not succeed. I will not discuss the causes of its failure, but I may indicate one of them as it has to do with the special character of Jewry, of which I am speaking.

One of those Yiddish authors who later lost their lives for unknown reasons was a storyteller of rank who went under the pseudonym "der Nister" (the hidden one); I knew him personally. This author at the time gave an account of the long trek to Birobidjan in which he participated. He described the pioneering enthusiasm of the migrants who believed they were sharing in the "reconstruction of the Jewish masses"; their whole consciousness, he said, was permeated by the realization that their striving for an autonomous Jewish state was not merely not opposed "from above" but given "the maximal assistance." Seen in its historical context, the objective trend which this assistance served proves to be a trend to isolate and eliminate, however. Determined by such a trend, no reconstruction could succeed. For the continuance of the Jewish diaspora depends on the duality of autonomy and contact.

In a famous early work, *A World Without Jews*, Marx, who erroneously regarded the Jews as the historically main agent of capitalism, identified Jewry with the middleman. Out of this extreme oversimplification of the Jewish problem stem all those accusations against the Jews as cosmopolitans, individualists, and the like, which we encounter again and again in the Marxist camp of the East and which have had very far-reaching consequences. Isolated instances which were merely degenerations of that singular Jewish synthesis of a strong will for autonomy and a strong will for contact were generalized into types of gigantic proportions. It was otherwise with Lenin who was a great realist and who knew and understood the environment into which he was born much more thoroughly than did Marx. Lenin indeed destroyed the Jewish bourgeoisie, as was natural, but he trusted the Jewish masses and found in their midst an avant-garde of the fighting proletariat. Stalin, who at the start of his rule assumed the role of Lenin's heir, later departed more and more from his predecessor's line of understanding and trust. At the height of his power Stalin was a man possessed by mistrust, like Nero. In the atmosphere of this mistrust, those accusations of cosmopolitanism and the rest entered into a combination with foreign policy motives; the lack of attachment to the fatherland could then always be interpreted in a suspicious manner and in a direction relevant to current events.

The Need for Realistic Trust

Years ago, in a public lecture in New York, I urgently pointed out that the world crisis, which was even then already approaching, could be traced above all to the universal condition of mutual distrust. I was speaking then to Americans, and my warning was addressed in the first instance to them. But beyond the immediate audience it was addressed to humanity, for I see no salvation for humanity unless it abandons this universal distrust in order to turn to a realistic, sober, clear-sighted, uninhibited trust. Such trust brings out trustworthiness in those whom one trusts. This principle holds good not only for the relations between states but also for the relation of the state to the peoples living within its framework.

What stand does the post-Stalinist Soviet regime take on the point that occupies us here? Has it returned to Lenin's principle of realistic trust? Is it about to return to it—perhaps even on a new, broader plane? What plane could this be? Perhaps among the leading men of the Soviet regime there are some who ask themselves questions of this kind.

I do not see it as my personal task to offer proposals. It was and is my wish to point out that any proposal will hold out promise only if it takes as its point of departure the unique structure of Jewry. But I must still speak to an objection that may well come to mind in connection with what has gone before. Something happened in our era, which observers both from within and from without have called a normalization of the Jewish people: the establishment of the State of Israel. It seems to me that it has been improperly called so. True, there is now an independent Jewish territory, an independent community capable of determining its own way of life, and the children growing up there speak the reborn ancient tongue. Yet the diaspora continues its broadly and manifoldly problematic, though not unfruitful, existence at the mercy of the internal history of the nation-states; and the ingathering of the whole people into its homeland remains, even in this new phase of Jewish existence, a Messianic idea. It is Messianic not in the sense in which political manifestoes appeal to Messianism, but in the original sense as used by the prophets—that is, as something inseparably bound up with the establishment of the kingdom of God in the world of man. And the community calling itself Israel has to do with this genuine Messianism just as much as it contributes to its realization in the relations of its own sections to one another and in its relations to other peoples. Thus, we are again confronted with the peculiar dynamic union of nation and religion in Judaism.

From all that I have been able to say, I hope it has become sufficiently clear that here religion, whenever it is alive, does not endorse power but calls on it to take up its responsibility. It is a fact of no little importance that so many of those who in modern Israel have stood up for a fundamental understanding with the neighboring peoples have done so from religious as well as national motives. The two, nation and religion, here hang together; but even in modern Israel they cannot fuse completely. Some 50 years ago Max Weber said to me that as a sociologist he could take an interest in Zionism only if it were to aspire to a sort of ecclesiastical state. I could not hold out to him the prospect of either a Jewish Pope or a Jewish Dalai Lama;

and so it will remain. Nevertheless, Israel may expect an anormalization of the relationship between nation and religion when the time comes for the appearance of a great new movement of faith from which a new message will issue forth to the world.

Now let us return to our original theme. Any proposals that are to be made must do justice—and it is to this that I have endeavored to call my readers' attention—to the atypical character of Jewry which retains its validity in all circumstances. But the objection may be raised, what positive basis is there for such proposals? If we refer to the realm of religion, the doors of the surviving synagogues are, so to speak, opened before us on a holiday and we are told to note how small the proportion of young people is. If we refer to the realm of linguistic culture, we are confronted with sheets of statistics which record the fact that not more than 25 percent of Soviet Jews gave Yiddish as their mother tongue. Is not this, we are asked, unmistakable indication that integration is taking place of its own accord? And a query may then follow as to whether it can possibly be considered the business of the Soviet administration to revive a dead culture.

What can we reply to such objections? We have after all no expression of the will of Soviet Jewry to which we can appeal for evidence. And yet, I know the heart of a generation of young people who do indeed assimilate, each one out of his individual life impulse, but in whom nevertheless, in their inmost hearts, there exists the desire to be able to meet the original values and forms of the people among whom they live with values and forms of their own. How else could they attain these values except by renewing their ties to the world of their fathers and that of their forefathers? Give them—I would say to those who object—the chance to renew those ties!

·V·
The American Jewish Experience

Strangers
in Paradise:
The American
Experience

Dorothea Braginsky

Surplus People

In every society there are people who, for one reason or another, are not part of its mainstream, who are extraneous to the ongoing functions of that society. They are considered superfluous, unwanted, and unnecessary, and, in some instances, expendable. In an extreme manifestation, the Germans in the 1930s legally declared the mentally retarded to be "useless eaters" and, therefore, expendable. The retarded not only failed to contribute to German society but represented a drain on its resources as well. Their solution was, as we now know, the forerunner to still greater, more extensive atrocities.

A person may achieve the dubious distinction of being surplus in a variety of ways: by voluntarily dropping out and refusing to participate in the mainstream of society (the hippie, for example); by being the victim of an accident that would disable him from participation (paralysis from an automobile collision); by being unable to make a meaningful contribution as the result of his nature (for example, being too young, too old, handicapped from birth); or by being the victim of social forces—economic, political, religious, moral—over which he has little or no control (the unemployed worker, the political radical in right-wing countries).

JEWS AS SURPLUS

This notion is not new to Jews. Indeed, it has been an implicit part of the Jewish condition. Whenever possible, they tried to become indispensable to whatever nation or state in which they lived. The Jewish fear of surplus status and the ramifications that might (and often, did) follow, led to some of the greatest achievements in the secular world. Entire books have been devoted to compiling the accomplishments as well as to listing the names of famous Jews. Suffice it to say that whenever given the opportunity by the society in which they lived, Jews became extremely visible (and seemed numerous) by excelling. Despite their achievements and their integration into society, Jews are keenly aware that with the stroke of a legislative pen they might at any moment revert to their surplus status.

In less hospitable surroundings, Jews went to the other extreme. They dealt with their surplus status by trying to be invisible, by having little or no social intercourse with the mainstream society. They kept to themselves, and when in the company of others, they attempted to keep a low profile. These attempts, we know, were always in vain. In a hostile environment it is simply impossible to be invisible. It is noteworthy that the Jews rarely tried to blend in or assimilate to inhospitable communities. Instead, they became more devout and as a result, stood out even more.

One might argue that in these cases Jews were surplus by choice and that, like the hippie, they voluntarily withdrew from participation in the mainstream. After all, they had every opportunity to convert to the mainstream religion. By not doing so, by choosing to be Jews, they also chose to be surplus. Some did, in fact, take advantage of opportunities to enter the mainstream. It took Hitler to remind them that it was not quite so easy to change identities, and to remind us of the absurdity of such an argument. Being Jewish is not a matter of choice or even of faith. It is a social definition, an ascribed characteristic determined by society. In the instance of Nazi Germany, having one Jewish grandparent was sufficient to be defined as a Jew.

For the most part, Jews have been painfully aware of their expendability and their surplus status in most of the communities in which they have lived. Their lives have been examples of how to survive, replete with creative strategies and intelligent, but not always successful, tactics.

BEING SURPLUS IN AMERICA

Since the diaspora, Jews have stood apart from the nations in which they lived. They were different, regardless of attempts at disguise. They were a minority living among a larger group of homogeneous people. Upon arrival in America, especially during the major immigration periods from the 1880s to the 1920s, Jews discovered a multitude of minorities living in this country—Irishmen, Swedes, Italians, and so on. Moreover, there was no distinct, homogeneous majority that they could see in their immediate environment. The majority had, of course, evacuated these areas when the immigrants arrived. Moreover, they discovered that there was more than enough prejudice to go around, and that each minority group was detested by some other minority, which in turn, was detested by another group. For once, the Jew was not singled out as an object of scorn, but instead was one of many. This was a unique, if not entirely welcome, experience. This indeed was a country of equal opportunity, even with regard to the negative aspects of life.

What was less unique about the American experience was that all of the minorities, to some extent, disliked Jews. It is noteworthy that in America, discrimination among Jews also flourished. The Sephardic Jews, tracing their lineage to a 17th-Century immigration, shunned the upstart, social-climbing German Jews who arrived, by and large, during the mid-19th Century. These educated, cultured German Jews so despised their Eastern European co-religionists that when they began to arrive in great numbers, the German Jews tried to introduce legislation to keep them from these shores.

For the Eastern European Jews there must have been special joy and relief in the knowledge that despite the nasty feelings others might have toward them, they would not be persecuted. There would be no pogroms in America, no violence or threats to their lives because they were Jewish. They had found a haven, a safe harbor in an eternally hostile, stormy sea. Here opportunities existed to transform their surplus, marginal status into that of full, productive citizenship.

Along with other immigrant groups, they were encouraged to Americanize. They filled the night-school classrooms; they manned the sweatshops; they shaved their beards and cut their sidelocks; they broke their Sabbath. Although it was not demanded or required—perhaps because it was not—as they became more American the Jews grew less religious, and the religion grew more American.

The distance from Jewish origins takes us back to basic questions: can Jews today comprehend the experience of their ancestors in any meaningful way? Do Jews perceive exile in similar terms, or for that matter, even see themselves as exiles? Does the return to Israel have any meaning to American Jews?

A Family Profile

Six brothers and sisters had died in early childhood, so my great-grandmother was named *Alter*—Old One—in order to fool the Angel of Death. To further confound this foe, she was married at the age of 13 so that her last name too would be different. My grandmother, Alter's daughter, married at 16. While still in her teens she traveled with an infant in her arms and her belongings on her back to join her husband in America. Despite her native intelligence and her having resided in this country for nearly 60 years, she never mastered English and was a functional illiterate. Although born in

America, my mother too married young and started a family by the age of 20. For a variety of reasons common in that era, she never completed high school, but instead went to work.

Then a remarkable change occurred, one often referred to as assimilation. (Naming the change, however, should not be confused with understanding it.) My father, who came here from Denmark as a very young boy, and my mother had three all-American children, and they moved from a Brooklyn ghetto to an all-American community. I, their daughter, never married, had no children, but became a professor of psychology at a Jesuit university. As Harry Golden would have said, "Only in America!"[1] For better or worse, the social climate here made such a radical break with tradition not only possible but also acceptable. In addition, educational and professional opportunities existed here, especially for Jewish women, that had been undreamed of in the past.

Thus, in a brief span of time on the long continuum of Jewish history—in barely two generations—the transition from the *shtetl* Jew to the urbane Jew was completed: from a great-grandmother whose parents relied on magic to guard her health, and a grandmother who could not read or speak proper English, to their descendant who conducts research, lectures, and writes books. With minor variations, this personal tale is the story common to almost every grandchild of Eastern European Jews.

How, then, can we comprehend the experience of our immediate ancestors, much less those more distant? How can the seemingly unending exile be understood when our places in exile differ so radically? And with what stretch of the imagination can the timeless expression, "Next year in Jerusalem," be uttered with the same longing when with one phone call to a travel agent we can fly there at any time? The voyage to America was, in every sense, a passage to a new world, but the transition has not been as smooth as it may appear. At best we have been left with conflicts and confusion regarding our Jewish identity. Although observers of the Jewish scene remark on the strength and unity of this identity, it is clear that the continuity with the past has been disrupted.

America: A Relative

Because we live in safety and comfort, and because we enjoy great freedom, the concept of exile is alien to most American Jews. Exile is not an objective condition but an experiential one. For most American Jews, the memory of expulsion is academic, refreshed from time to time by the observance of religious holy days. Moreover, another necessary condition for the experience of exile is absent: namely, being unable or forbidden to return to the homeland; we, on the contrary, are all free to go to Israel. Very simply, Jews here do not feel exiled. The closest we may come to that experience is the momentary alienation felt when an anti-Semitic comment is made in our presence, or when we feel ill-at-ease in some social settings. Considering the long and painful history of the Jews in the diaspora, the American experience is one of a stranger in a comparative paradise.

Sensitivity toward and keen insight into discrimination and persecution has been the hallmark of the American Jews. They have been closely associated with civil rights movements and other social causes. Many loudly protest incursions into and violations of civil liberties, be they against other Jews, Blacks, or even American Nazi Party members. Surely there is no lack of comprehension or failure of imagination when it comes to this gloomy arena of the human condition.

Thus, American Jews not only empathize with the plight of others, but also with Jews worldwide. The cause of the Soviet Jews has become one to which many have committed themselves. What is less within our realm of experience is the perception of discrimination in our own lives, either because it really does not exist, or because we are made to feel paranoid if we discern prejudice toward Jews. While American Jews do not feel threatened or persecuted, they seem to know, somehow, exactly how it would feel.

The Return

Because of our experiences here, American Jews are not likely to see Israel as a refuge (a necessary perception for immigrants). Instead, it is perceived as a nation struggling to survive against great odds. Surrounded by hostile countries, the State of Israel is psychologically more reminiscent of the ghetto in the Pale than as the land of milk and honey; the pogroms are full-scale wars and the dangers greater than in the past. There are many Jews today who echo the Talmudic sages in their belief that it is best for Jews to remain dispersed throughout the world so that they cannot be totally and readily annihilated. Although they may not wish to live there, American Jews have a love affair with Israel. Their relationship, however, is analogous to a man and his mistress, rather than a man and his wife. The mistress is given gifts, affection, and financial support. Yet as we know, regardless of the intensity of the passion or the sincerity of his love, the man rarely leaves his wife for his mistress. Thus, we are materially and emotionally generous to Israel but we fail to make the complete commitment to live there and to participate in the struggle. It would, in fact, take the emotional equivalent of a divorce (surely a traumatic event) to leave this country and to return to Israel.

Jews are dreamers, and the dream of *Eretz Yisrael* may have more appeal than the reality of the State of Israel. Despite our detachment from our grandparents' piety, that dream for many may be bound closely to their ideal of the Messianic age. The Messianic nature of Jews, illustrated by their extraordinary involvement in utopian movements, may play a larger role (albeit on an unconscious level) than might be expected. Hearing our grand-parents speak longingly of the Messiah's coming may very well have created a similar, if unconscious, wish. It also, no doubt, brought out the little Messiah in us all: the social, political, and intellectual activist who will help to transform the world. In that case, the wait for the exiles to return to Israel may be long indeed.

For American Jews as well as those living in comfort and safety in other nations the experience of exile and the desire to return to the Land require: surplus status or expendability in the communities in which we currently live; increased attractiveness of Israel so that it becomes too compelling to resist; and/or the coming of the Messiah.

Notes

1. Harry Golden, *Only in America*. Cleveland: World Publishing Co., 1958.

·17·
The American Jewish Non–Community

Daniel R. Hershberg

The Lost Dream: A Diaspora Community

In contemplating exilic aspects of the Jewish condition, I recall a recurring dream which has informed my involvement as an American Jewish activist—that of a genuine diaspora community. And yet I suspect that it is a dream which will not be translated into reality: American Jewry simply will not have it! In our American "gilded *galut*" it is not difficult to find increasing manifestations of our lack of genuine community. In recent years even issues which challenge the very physical survival of the State of Israel have failed to elicit an American Jewish response worthy of being designated as a community action. Among the most common factors cited are assimilation, intermarriage, lack of meaningful identity, and the failure of Jewish education. Yet social scientists demonstrate that these are effects and not causes. Suffice it to say that by any criteria, as a community American Jewry is disintegrating. And this becomes most painfully apparent when one considers the actual condition and potential of American Jewry.

In theory, Jewish communal leaders are correct when they speak about our failure to reach our full potential as a community. This largest and most affluent diaspora community which raises 400 million dollars for the United Jewish Appeal could easily double or even quadruple that amount annually. The American sale of sophisticated weapons to nations hostile to Israel's existence could easily have evoked a powerful Jewish reaction. And the education of Jewish youth could be achieved with little effort, given the resources available to American Jewry. However, there is a widespread mythologizing as to the actual condition of this community. And the reality must be faced if it is to be altered.

Who are the American Jews?

Just as the Jewish people in its dispersion often misunderstood its actual condition in the past, so does this largest of all Jewish communities widely misunderstand its own actual state of affairs. Historically, not every diaspora Jew wanted to be part of the Jewish community, and it is simply unrealistic to assume that some sort of universal bond or identity exists today among all those men and women we classify as being Jewish. First, we must recognize the existence of an ever increasing number of people who no longer consider themselves as being Jewish. Second, we must recognize the existence of a mass of Jews whose sense of Jewishness is limited to a vague moral or ethical definition which is so limited that it stops short of tangible affiliation and participation.

Were these two nonparticipatory groups the only factors to be considered in our reassessment of the American Jewish community, we could still assume enough potential strength to constitute a viable and healthy community in a meaningful sense. Yet there are two other groups of Jews which must be considered; their impact is so great that without significant change in their attitudes, American Jewry is destined for continued erosion.

The first group to be considered are those Jews who vocally support Jewish causes and are theoretically committed to Jewish institutions, but who in fact place Jewish needs at the low end of their priorities. Characteristically, although they do contribute some time, effort, and money to Jewish causes, these are quite minimal as compared to their involvement in non-Jewish affairs. They rationalize this apparent disparity by pointing out the obviously larger number of people who benefit from efforts in the non-Jewish community. Jews should feel honored, they will insist, that the largest American contributors to the arts and sciences are Jewish. Therefore, Jews should feel a real sense of pride that universities and vocational schools under Catholic or Protestant auspices are supported by many Jews.

As but one example of this widespread phenomenon, we may consider the Jewish volunteer at the local hospital who devotes many hours to providing services there, yet objects when the Jewish community asks for help at the Senior Citizen Center or in the Russian Resettlement Program. The personal call from the Catholic Bishop or the Mayor or the Hospital Administrator packs a punch that any Jewish communal leader would envy. The library, the park, the neighborhood association, the country club, and the garden club have all become areas for visible and substantial Jewish support, almost inevitably as alternatives to involvement in things Jewish.

Am I suggesting that Jews withdraw from all these efforts? Would it serve our interests if Jews withdrew and confined their activities to the *shtetl*? Of course I suggest nothing of the sort! But, where are our priorities? It is becoming increasingly popular for many who devote their efforts to the general community to reduce or eliminate their Jewish component. They may argue that there are so many talented, wealthy, and committed individuals within the Jewish community that it can certainly survive without them. Yet this scenario is so widespread that the institutional survival of the Jewish community is now seriously threatened.

The second group of Jews whose actions seriously jeopardize the viability of the American Jewish community are those who limit their connection or involvement to a single Jewish institution or effort. These single-interest Jews narrowly define their participation in the Jewish agenda, thereby excluding themselves from communal efforts. This problem is perhaps even more serious than that group which expends its efforts outside the Jewish community. I say this because we are tempted to count the people in this group as devoted and committed members of our community, whereas their actions in times of Jewish need often belie that trust.

The Effects

Of course many of the most effective Jewish leaders on the American scene devote themselves almost exclusively to a particular institution or group which they believe warrants their intensive effort. Some of these people are also involved in the broader range of Jewish concerns. They do not abrogate their communal responsibility just because they have very important special interests. Their strong advocacy of their special interests tends to strengthen rather than weaken the Jewish community. We must be concerned, however, when significant numbers of talented Jewish leaders devote themselves to a single interest thereby excluding themselves from the community. We must be concerned when the total expression of Jewishness can be tied to the quality of the recreation program at a Jewish Community Center while a campaign for United Jewish Appeal (UJA) flounders. We must be concerned when the most persuasive of our leaders spend all their time recruiting members for their synagogue while the communities' efforts to provide care for the aged is ignored. We must be concerned when Jewish men's organizations find time to help the handicapped but ignore the handicap of Jewish children unable to find an adequate education in their synagogue schools or day schools. We must be concerned when the totality of involvement in Jewish life is measured in the number of bagels served on Sunday morning rather than the number of Jews rescued from Soviet oppression. Similar examples of trivialization are numerous; the effects are cataclysmic.

It is the narrow and increasingly trivial definition of Jewish involvement which takes the greatest toll on the full potential of the Jewish community. It is this tunnel vision which makes us a conglomerate of single interest groups masquerading as a community. It is this group of Jews combined with the assimilated, the lost, the hiding, and those with different priorities who make up the American Jewish noncommunity. Unless significant change is effected in this generation, I believe American Jewry will become little more than a survival group.

Israel and the American Jewish Community

In considering world Jewry as a whole, some people may argue, "What if there were no functioning American Jewish community, so what? Now that Israel exists, doesn't the well-being of Judaism and of the individual Jew depend more on the existence of the Jewish state than on a functioning American Jewish community?" Yet what would Israel be without the support of an American Jewish community? While I have argued that American Jewry is not in the best of shape, it is certainly surviving better and creating more than Jewish enclaves elsewhere in the *galut*. Whether American Jews consider themselves exiles or not is less important than the fact of their existence. The State of Israel is organically bound to the American Jewish community.

While it is certainly arguable that Judaism as a religion might continue without an American Jewish community, it is difficult to imagine that the rich ethnic identification or the body of Jewish tradition and values which bind Jews together would survive. As fragile as these bonds appear to be, they are a necessary component for a meaningful Jewish existence. If one assesses the condition of Jews in exile and finds it hopeless, one must then rate Israel's position as hopeless. It is from this edge of hopelessness that the American Jewish community must pull back. American Jews seem often to have a death wish with respect to their organized community, and this must be fought. We must fight holding actions where necessary, retreat where no option exists, and open new fronts where possible.

The Next Generation

Is the situation hopeless? I think not. Survival is a strong instinct and, properly presented, the condition of the American Jewish community must draw this instinct to the fore. If there is a real hope for American Jewry to reverse its trend it lies with the next generation. I realize, full well, that virtually every complainant who decries the conditions brought about by his own generation relies on the future generation for salvation, yet I believe there is a real basis for this hope.

My conclusion rests almost entirely on the recent revival of intensive Jewish education. Even as many synagogue afternoon schools decline, day schools throughout the country are growing. For a variety of reasons, young Jewish couples are sending their children to schools where they thrive in a positive Jewish environment. They rate as high the need for Jewish survival. They value their Jewishness in general, and their role as American Jews in particular. They learn to translate their love of Israel into tangible support. These young Jews may not be overpowering in their numbers, but their presence is becoming stronger throughout the American Jewish community. It is this minority within a minority that will build the American Jewish community of the future.

18

The Modern Literature of Aparthood

Amnon Hadary

> . . . and we sense that *Herzog* and *The Assistant* will be a long time in occupancy. For it has been demonstrated that intellectuals have a corner on the world's love and compassion; it is probable that they also have a corner on the world's power of survival.
>
> John W. Aldridge

John Aldridge, an American literary critic, is not numbered among the philosemites. One may safely substitute Jews for his euphemistic "intellectuals." One may as surely adduce recent history to belie the incredible claim that the Jews have had "a corner on the world's love and compassion." Yet Aldridge's chagrin is the mandate for this chapter: an evaluation of what is durable and survives and what is transitory in the genre that has come to be called American Jewish Literature. One wonders how much greater the chagrin is now that Isaac Bashevis Singer has been "scandalously" accorded a place of honor—no longer a mere survivor—an impressive corner in the hall of fame.

By now, 20 years after American Jewish writing burst into public consciousness as a remarkable phenomenon, it resides legitimately as a recognized genre, or sub-genre, in the groves of Bloomington, Indiana, in prestigious chairs at Harvard, at UCLA, and elsewhere. Its viability was a matter of concern for actuarily inclined bookmakers in the early 1960s. But by the middle of that decade, with the publication of the two books Aldridge singled out (see quote above) and that were to set the standard by which all subsequent American Jewish novels were to be judged, it was suddenly clear that necrologies were vastly premature. What remains to be assayed, then, is a definition of what is intrinsic and essential to the genre and what accidental. Most such definitions are proven more by what they exclude than by what they try to encompass; for the essential is by its nature a rare commodity. Saul Bellow's *Herzog* and Bernard Malamud's *The Assistant* belong to that category and the burden of this chapter is to indicate why so many of the other books written by American Jewish authors are excluded because they are, in the Aristotelian construction of the term, accidental. The critical strategy to be employed will therefore be ascriptive rather than descriptive.

But first a quandary! How explain the fact that two flourishing sister literatures, modern Hebrew and American Jewish, developed their true excellence in two different modes. Modern Hebrew literature is remarkable for its poetry precisely as American Jewish literature is distinguished for its prose. Yet both came of age, achieved critical—and no less important, popular—success, at roughly the same time. Further, both are related in that they are products of the sons or grandsons of immigrants from the same Eastern European segment of world Jewry, with Bellow being the exception within the exception. Of the three recent Nobel laureates—Agnon, Bellow, and Singer—only Bellow was *not* born in Eastern Europe; but even he was the child of immigrants to Canada from that same reservoir of Jewish culture. True, the practitioners of English had to learn a new language whereas the new Israelis had "merely" to relearn an old one, but there was an equally painful acculturation process for both. This was a process of becoming more than proficiently conversant, of gaining an at-homeness of suppleness and of nuance, the shadings of mode, the unerring exquisite textures which only intuition can bring. Israeli poets have it; American Jewish novelists do too. Each has achieved measures of excellence and of critical acclaim that transcend national and linguistic boundaries. By comparison, Israeli novelists are merely like a good domestic wine that doesn't travel well, and American Jewish poetry is generally a house wine not worth decanting.

Internal Bilingualism

Although language *per se* is not within the purview of this chapter, an aspect of it falls within the rubric of the tools that literature uses. Max Weinreich, the linguist who, perhaps more than any other, was responsible for the maintenance of Yiddish in America claims an "internal bilingualism" for *Ashkenazi* Jews. There were two coexisting living languages to be found among the Eastern European intelligentsia who immigrated to America and to *Eretz Yisrael*: Hebrew and Yiddish. But whereas the first was a mediated language, Yiddish, which was the immediate one, was also precisely the language which both immigrant groups had to cast off as they stepped onto the two littorals of the future. This, then, is what gave an advantage to the practitioners of the new Hebrew—to sing. To sing the songs of Zion in the old-new land.

The fact remains that the novel form is the oeuvre of American Jewish literature, and the poem, despite Yehuda Amichai's declaimer, remains the libretto of Israeli authors. Amichai says:

> *To speak, now, in this tired language*
> *Torn from its sleep in the Bible—*
> *Blinded, it lurches from mouth to mouth—*
> *The language which described God and the*
> *miracles.*
> *Says:*
> *Motor car, bomb, God*
>
> *The squared letters wanted to stay closed*
> *Every letter a locked house,*
> *To stay and sleep in it for ever.*[1]

To be a Hebrew poet, then, is to assume the role of a rude letter-opener, intruding oneself into the square sleep of the language. It costs to accost.

Yet American Jewish authors also paid a price, even for the franchise of expressing themselves in prose, the less exacting of the two media. Two testimonies to this toll can be adduced: one in the words of the British critic Walter Allen and the other in those of Cynthia Ozick, who is perhaps the most quintessentially American Jewish novelist writing today.

Allen calls attention to the coexistence of two lingual strata in Henry Roth's early *Call It Sleep*. But unlike Weinreich's internal bilingualism these are both written "as though" they were English. The one in "quite horrible fidelity" catches "the mutilations of English as spoken by the immigrant slum dwellers, Jewish and others." But when the novel's hero, David Schearl, is at home and his parents are represented by Henry Roth as speaking Yiddish, the English of *Call It Sleep* undergoes a transformation and they "speak a remarkably pure English, the English of people of cultivation." By employing this literary strategy, the novelist makes the reader feel, almost somatically, the degradation of human dignity that was the immigrants' lot as they moved from a society with an enormously rich tradition and highly textured culture to another, flattened one, the much overworked urban wasteland.

But Not All Ideas

Cynthia Ozick, a native-born American Jew, wrote of her plight in an introduction to a recently published short story "Bloodshed": "A language like people, has a history of ideas, but not all ideas; only those known to its experience. Not surprisingly, English is a Christian language: When I write English, I live in Christendom."

This schizoid distillate—the being ill-at-ease in New Rochelle—can be taken as a methodological proof-spirit to determine the true liquor of American Jewish literature. For there are so many books written by American Jews and (since the burgeoning of ethnicity as an almost *de rigeur* of Americanism) so many novels with Jewish content, that one must be critically discontent with any but the most essential definitions. Such definitions ultimately are ascriptions of authenticity for Jewish American literature. Put another way, the only significant question one can ask about the Jewishness of an American novel seeking (or as so often happens, being sponsored for) Jewish canonization is: will it be recognized, say, a century hence as having had something of value to impart to Jews? Such was always the criterion of responsible editors as opposed to chic promoters. Such components as entertainment value, horizon broadening, and instruction on how to be Jewish are not unimportant, certainly not trivial, considerations when evaluating a book. But good American Jewish literature is, first of all, good literature. And one of the most striking things about the few, very few, books which will be dealt with here as measuring up to the strictures of what should properly be called American Jewish literature is precisely the fact that they are "sleepers." As in Henry Roth's *Call It Sleep*, there is always a universal story, there is deep and abiding intelligence, there is something imparted to the reader about *la condition humaine*, and it is administered in such portions as to become habituating. But beyond the universal, or perhaps filtered through it, a design emerges through the openwork to which adheres a tiding that is meant for the *cognoscenti* alone. Call it the *Shema* before sleep. It is ineluctable in the manifest level of the work and must be mined in the latent stratum.

Seek this dimension in the works of Chaim Potok or Herbert Gold, Norman Mailer or Irving Shaw, Herman Wouk or Hugh Nissenson and you will not find it—admirable, widely read, or well-written though they may be. Robert Alter early decried the exploitative tendency of cultural opportunists who write books "sentimentalizing the Jews." Indeed, the tide of books about American Jewish literature is almost as inundating as the output of the novels they consider. Many of these are catalogues: some apply sociological parameters to delimit the embarrassment of riches while others apply the elements of esthetics. Ultimately all fall short. By definition, all American Jewish authors write in English (with the exception of Isaac Bashevis Singer to whom we shall devote an extended caveat). Therefore, the very best among them, if they share Ozick's view, have to contend with English, the very medium they espouse. It has been claimed for Bernard Malamud (most recently in the sociological blockbuster of the Lower East Side—a monument of sentimentalizing the Jews—*Worlds of Our Fathers* by

Irving Howe) that he not only draws upon Jewish figures and themes but that "he also writes what can only be called the Yiddish story in English." Saul Bellow modestly averred that, to the best of his knowledge, he was the last of the American Jewish novelists who could read Sholom Aleichem in the original. But to really parse Bellow and Malamud's inner flow of ideas and angst bordering on fear and trembling, one must hold up the best of the authors of the Christian West rather than Y. L. Peretz, Sholom Aleichem, or Mendele Mocher Seforim. Which is to say that in order to understand what is essentially Jewish in Bellow and Malamud, one must juxtapose those Christian authors who possess the most recognizable—because they are the most essential rather than accidental—attributes of their culture. Only strong drafts of Sartre, Jean Genet, and James Joyce will do.

The Best of the West

In *Making It* Norman Podhoretz, the editor of *Commentary*, maintains that Bellow was Waspish in his early novels . . . dangling in his first novel (*Dangling Man*) between the Jewish intellectual coterie family world of alienation and the vision of a life of larger possibility; "after being 'victimized' in the second novel (*The Victim*) by the spiritual timidity he found in his own Jewishness." So that when he finally hit his stride in *Augie March*, he asserted in the idiom of the novel itself what its opening sentence, in full awareness of what it is saying, makes altogether explicit; "I am an American, Chicago-born . . ." This is what Bellow, the exquisitely sensitive man (who had never forgiven Edmund Wilson for his higher regard for the prose of Robert Penn Warren and the poetry of Robert Lowell as being more American than his writing), is saying. What Bellow the writer is saying is this: "I am an American novelist, born into a Yiddish-speaking household and also educated to use fancy English with the best of them, and the way I speak as a result of these two facts, the way I really speak when I am being myself and horsing around with Isaac Rosenfeld, is a fully legitimate literary language." To appreciate fully the force of this assertion, one needs to recall that 50 years earlier Henry James had come away from a tour of the Jewish ghetto on the Lower East Side of New York with his patrician nostrils, more, his tone-perfect ear, assaulted. He wondered what would become of the aristocratic yet embattled English language when the children and grandchildren of these people come into possession of it. "Whatever we shall know it for," he said, "we shall not know it for English."

Henry James and John Aldridge may claim not to recognize Bellow's Americanism. One wonders whether the Nobel prize was given to him for the Jewishness, the Americanness, or the immaculateness of his artistic conception. Yet no serious English reader can question the exquisite English flexibility of his prose. The man who teaches Melville and Joyce at The University of Chicago can and must be assessed simultaneously as American and Jewish.

Saul Bellow is perhaps the best known of the practitioners of a new language which is the vessel of the American Jewish novel, and Cynthia Ozick is perhaps, unjustly, one of the most obscure. Yet Ozick's quintessence (literally, her embodiment of the fifth or highest essence after the fire, water, earth, and air of the Greeks) lies precisely in her description—prescription of the essential quality of American Jewish literature—its need to write in its "New Yiddish." The only thing it will have in common with the old Yiddish is that it will be the language Jews use when speaking to Jews. Yet it will be something that, to the uninitiated ear, sounds like English. In the best story of her collection *The Pagan Rabbi and Other Stories*, in the story called "Envy, or Yiddish in America," she writes ostensibly about the old, but hints rather broadly at the new Yiddish:

> . . . that our treasure-tongue is derived from others means nothing, 90 percent German roots, 10 percent Slavic. The Hebrew take for granted without percentages. We are a people who have known how to forge the language of need out of the language of necessity. . . .

This language is at bottom liturgical and critical, according to Ozick. Henry James regarded the old Yiddish somewhat less lovingly and, as mentioned above, would not consider the odious possibility of 20th Century English as fashioned by Malamud and Bellow—the New Yiddish—being accepted as a legitimate form, let alone an exquisitely civilized language of the West. He once described a visit to the Lower East Side:

> The denizens of the New York Ghetto, heaped as thick as the splinters on the table of a glass-blower, had each, like the fine glass particle, his or her individual share of the whole hard glitter of Israel.

The New Midrash versus the New Poetry

How that hard glitter has burgeoned! Alfred Kazin writes that just as the writers of the South, who out of their knowledge of defeat and their instinctive irony, were able to speak meaningfully to a chastened American reading public in the 1940s, it is Jewish writers who now represent to many Americans the unreality of their situation. Who more adept than the Jewish intellectual at offering "expert analysis of the complex factors" resulting in "sophisticated explanations. Never was interpretation, explanation, commentary, a vital new *midrash*, needed more." He explains that "definitely, it was not the thing to be Jewish. But in Western universities and small towns many a traditional novelist and professor of English felt out of it, and asked with varying degrees of self-control, if there was no longer a good novel to be written about the frontier, about Main Street?"

This new *midrash*, if it is to be written at all seriously and not remain a hollow boast, must be written in the language of *midrash*. But Susan Sontag and other de-Judaized critics did not want a *midrash*; they wanted a new novel, as new as Allen Ginsberg's poetry. In her seminal essay, "America: Toward Yavneh," published in *Judaism*, Cynthia Ozick describes new poetry as consisting more of "life-style" with its emphasis on "being" rather than on judgment or on interpretation. Ginsberg testified at the trial of the Yippie Chicago Seven:

> What Ginsberg in his testimony called "psychedelic consciousness" is what the Christian used to call grace. At the be-in [an event in a Chicago public park during the Democratic National Convention] a group of ministers and rabbis elevated a ten-foot cross high into the cloud of tear gas thrown by rioting police. When Ginsberg saw this he turned to a friend and said: "They have gassed the cross of Christ." Perhaps for the first time since Rome an elevated cross was on the receiving end of a pogrom, but the fact remains that for the rabbis who carried it and for Ginsberg who pitied it the cross had been transubstantiated from a sign of the real acts of a community into the vehicle of the moment, rich in aesthetic contrast, Christian grace, psychedelic consciousness, theatrical and poetical magic. And love, the kind Bellow calls "potato love" in Herzog.

Take John Updike and his novels, a non-Jew who writes *new* novels. In contrast to a Malamudian or a Bellovian *midrash* novel, it is to be taken precisely like a sacrament, a poem without a history—"which is to say an idol," says Ozick. "It is not to judge or interpret. It is to *be*; it is not to allow anything to *happen* or *become*. 'Happen' implies history, 'become' implies idea"; (she then comes up with a startling example of the New Yiddish and the new *midrash*) "both imply *teshuva*, a turning." What follows in that disturbing essay is the perception that so starkly describes the dilemma of the American Jewish author:

> The commandment against idols, it seems to me, is overwhelmingly pertinent to the position of the Jewish fiction writer in America today. If he feels separate from the religion of Art in the streets he can stay out of the streets. But if the religion of Art is to dominate imaginative literature entirely, and I believe it will in America for a very long time, can he stay out of American literature?—If he wants to stay Jewish, I think he will have to. Even as a writer, especially as a writer, he will have to acknowledge exile.

How can one acknowledge exile through the instrumentality of the New Yiddish by the rivers of Manhattan? The only well-known Jewish precedent relates to the rivers of Babylon. Very few novelists adhere to Ozick's strictures and for them the Tigris and Euphrates are mediated by Dublin's Liffey River. James Joyce was the paradigm of how to rejoice in a foreign land. His strategy enunciated in *Ulysses* was "cunning, exile, silence." This was a triple alienation—from his family, from the Catholic Church, and from the Irish nationalist movement. To the claim of all three he replied in the sacral language of Roman Catholicism (echoing Milton's Satan): *non serviam*; I shall neither submit nor serve.

How to Say No to an Irishman

Saul Bellow's retort to Joyce in *Herzog* is aptly enough rendered also in the language of liturgy, in Hebrew: *Hinenni*. Nor is this a literary coincidence or a derivative conceit. Moses Herzog, Bellow's hero, originated in Joyce's *Ulysses*. There he was a fleetingly minor figment, a leprechaun of Leopold Bloom's imagination. But Moses *qua* Moses was a major preoccupation of Bloom, the half-Jew estranged from his culture, and of Stephen Daedalus, the triply estranged Irishman, who was a stand-in for Joyce himself. Joyce sought to find a panacea to the composite of what ailed both Bloom and Daedalus by proposing that they unite their ebbing Hebraic and Hellenic forces. The "trip" reuniting these two Mediterranean cultures is the odyssey that organizes the plot of *Ulysses*. To that end, Bloom, seeking a lost spiritual son, Rudy, and Stephen, who is meant to' find a new father in Bloom, hold a discussion in the latter's kitchen. Mr. Bloom cites three examples of "post-exilic eminence": Moses of Egypt, Moses Maimonides (these two "seekers of pure truth" have been in Stephen and Leopold's thoughts throughout the course of the day), and Moses Mendelssohn. While this dialogue, which is meant to be the foreplay leading to a union of the two, takes place in the kitchen, Molly Bloom, the daughter of Major Tweedy and a Spanish Jewess, lolls in her bed in the room directly above them. She must be there because in Catholic mysticism the transubstantiation of the father and the son requires the presence, if only as a vessel, of the female principle.

In *Herzog*, Bellow plays counterpoint to Joyce's suggestion of union between Greek and Hebrew. Molly Bloom is reincarnated—pistil and stamen —as the fecundating female principle, Ramona. She affects tweed business suits and is the owner of a flower store in Manhattan. But in order to ensure that the Mosaic element of the Joycean proposition not be forgotten, it is woven into the fabric of the fable Bellow tells in a highly original and entertaining fashion. He has Ramona seduce Moses Herzog in her bedroom whose lampshade is Nile green while the background music is provided by Sidhi Bakher and his Alexandria string quartet (sic!). Bellow does not shrink from driving home the point of what lurks in wait for the American Jewish novelist who would take the conclusion of Joyce as his own starting point: "He was spattered forever with things that bled or stank." This passage is followed by one describing the ritual slaughter of chickens with all the accompanying residual fear and incisive analysis that an observant youth turned into a gifted writer can bring to it.

> . . . he was overtaken one dirty summer evening by a man. The man clapped his hand over his mouth from the back. He hissed something to him as he drew down his pants. His teeth were rotten and his face stubbled. And between the boy's thighs this red skinless horrible thing passed back and forth, back and forth until it burst out foaming. The dogs in the backyards jumped against the fences, they barked and snarled . . .

The dogs of Egypt were silent on the night of the Exodus, we are told by the Aggadah . . . "the shrieking dogs. The man said: 'I'm going to give you a nickel!'" The filth of the nickel he was offered is the manifest layer of *Herzog* and (Joyce) the progenitor of the offerer is its latent layer. Unfortunately, since Bellow was speaking in precisely that New Yiddish which Cynthia Ozick promotes, very few understood the more important of these two strata, what we earlier called the sleeper. Bellow had assimilated Joyce's technique of cunning and silence too well when speaking of exile. One must juxtapose two adjacent portions of the novel in order to realize that the ugly, buggering, dirty old man of the alley is the stand-in for Western civilization as a whole. This literary technique of drawing an inference from a common principle which applies symbiotically to two adjacent segments of text is of hoary tradition and is called *smichut parshiot*: one of the classic means by which Talmudic exposition is conducted. So it comes as no surprise that in the very next paragraph of *Herzog* one finds:

> And later when . . . the good Christian lady came, the one with the button shoes and the hatpin like a trolley-rod, the soft voice and grim looks, she asked him to read for her from the New Testament, and he opened and read, "Suffer the little children to come unto me." Then she turned to another place, and it said, "Give and it shall be given unto you Good measure . . . shall men give into your bosom."

To the great nay-sayer of Dublin Bellow seems to say "no thanks." But, in order to do so, he has to resort to the *suggestio falsi* and the *suppresso veri*, which a leading scholar claimed were employed by Maimonides when he had things of ultimate truth to impart. These truths, far from being self-evident, could not even be spelled out for any but the *cognoscenti*. Just as

Maimonides needed Aristotle in his day to refute the most (to him) attractive element of pagan culture philosophy, and just as Philo the Alexandrian Jew found beloved Platonism indispensable in providing a belief system based on his allegorization of the Bible for fellow Jews quickly assimilating into Hellenism, so too Bellow requires Joyce as a sparring partner to shore up a flagging Judaism confronted with the best of the West.

Malamud's Everyjew

So, too, Bernard Malamud, whose most perfectly achieved work of art to date is *The Assistant*, called for the apogee of modern western culture rather than one of its epigones to make his Jewish point. On the manifest level, the sparring partner is St. Francis of Assisi. But it is Jean-Paul Sartre and Jean Genet on the latent one.

Some evidence corroborating the claim that *The Assistant* really is Malamud's most perfectly achieved work may be in order. To many, *The Fixer* may appear to be as impressive an achievement. What is so impressive about the latter is the almost impossible task Malamud undertook in presenting a fictionalized account of the Mendel Beilis case. The blood-libel perpetrated by the Czarist regime as a warrant for pogroms by the Black Hundreds could serve as the basis of a plot for a historical novel, but only if one decided to give Mendel Beilis a minimal part. He was not a terribly impressive figure even when he was first accused and thrown into the dungeon; indeed, the frame-up by the authorities was quite convincing on this point. Since he was a nobody, he was also everybody—everyjew. Yet if there was nothing of the heroic about him at the start, there was even less that could be usably exploited, for plot, delineation of character, or, for that matter, any of the required composites of a good novel. Malamud's achievement lies in the fact that the fixer, Yaacov Bok, incarcerated in solitary confinement though he is for two-thirds of the novel with no one to bounce off of, grows before your eyes as you read. Not only does he win against the system almost entirely on his own (a departure from the true story told so well by Maurice Samuel in *Blood-Libel*), but the victory is believable. Yaacov Bok the *gornicht* has grown to be a giant, to Aristotelian tragic dimensions, if you will.

NOMEN EST OMEN

As usually happens in an unusually fine imaginative work, there is a mythic stratum subsumed in the novel. Since this stratum is not available to the average reader's cognitive process one could conclude that it is a superfluous ingredient. Not so! Since the latent meaning of a great work is generally the one with the greatest affinity to mythic strata it behooves one to make sure that its geologic contours, the coordinates that orient the work, are properly aligned. Otherwise all one gets is a good read, an entertaining weekend.

This is where the critic comes in. However, the most amazing thing about Malamud's impressive critical success with *The Fixer* is that no one seems to have bothered at all with the question of who Yaacov Bok really is, since obviously he is not patterned on Mendel Beilis. In other words, in the days when the antihero is *à la mode*, Malamud not only has the atavistic nerve to enter center stage with a real live developing hero, but disguises the "last" on which the hero was stretched to that size. The strategy, as in Bellow's case, is *suggestio falsi* and *suppresso veri* and the technique, the vital code, is the name of the hero. This technique is called *nomen est omen*.

One of the most disturbing scenes for Bok in the book is a recurrent nocturnal wrestling match with a spirit in his cell. Initially the spirit is clearly the Czar or his stand-in, but later he describes himself as even higher. "They wrestled beard to beard, in the dark until Nicholas proclaimed himself an angel of God and ascended into the sky." Suddenly, the missing keystone of the overarching pattern that Malamud had been building from novel's start falls into place. Yaacov Bok's heroic stature emerges out of the legends of the Jews. His spiritual progenitor is the patriarch Jacob, who wrestled all night with God's stand-in on the eve of his meeting with his brother, Esau (Genesis 32:25-33). And verse 23 identifies the location of the wrestling match unmistakably as the ford of the river Jabbok. Yet Malamud has so distanced the scene of the action that ultimately the Jacob–Bok crossing is a meaningless —worse—a somewhat trivializing genuflection. For Malamud's hero liberates himself as a freestanding monolith, whereas the best that can be said of Mendel Beilis is that he was a part of a frieze, an altogether not outstanding segment of a bas-relief. Mendel Beilis was released from the Czar's prison only because the mounting pressures of an international campaign indicated to the Czar that he had more to lose on the world scene than he could possibly gain (misguidedly) on the domestic front. World Jewry organized effectively and their impact was no small component in Mendel Beilis's release. But Yaacov Bok fought alone and won a very lonely victory. This, then, is the place where extraliterary considerations intervene and it is in their light that one finds that the novel is a flawed one. It is a poem without a history. If Malamud wants to stay Jewish, if he wants to stay separate from the religion of Art in the streets ("the making of idols"), then even as a writer, especially as a writer, he will have to acknowledge exile. Yet it should have been clear that, from the very selection of locale for *The Fixer*, Malamud elected to *not* talk about exile, at least not the exile in which he himself resides.

One expected more from him for in *The Assistant*, the novel published almost 10 years earlier, he was already able, albeit in "New Yiddish," to declare that the epitaph for exile is *Gevalt*. More, his superscription to *The Fixer* is composed of quotes from two of the better-known poet laureates of the Christian West:

O yonge Hugh of Lyncoln-slayn also
With cursed Jewes, as it is notable,
For it is but a litel while ago—
Preye eek for us, we synful folk unstable, . . .

and "Irrational streams of blood are staining earth . . ."

One must note that Chaucer and Yeats (Malamud's chosen poets) are also known as exponents of anti-Semitism. Yet as the locale of *The Fixer* is at two removes from the experience of American Jewry, Chaucer and Yeats are culturally closer. And yet what Beilis, Chaucer, and Yeats have in common for American Jews is that they all seem to declare: "It can't happen here."

A HALF-LEGENDARY WORLD

In contrast, Malamud's earlier novel demonstrates that not only can it happen here but on the mytho-poetic level it recurs over and over again. In *The Assistant*, Malamud tells the story of three people caught at the edge of violence: Morris Bober, the gentle little shopkeeper whose faith in humanity is so great that he willingly befriends the man who robs him; Frank Alpine, a thief obsessed by guilt, who robs his benefactor and rapes his daughter, the girl he loves; and Helen Bober, who is unwilling to compromise for second-best and thereby is drawn into a passionate love affair with the man who raped her and whom she loves. All this on the manifest—or the dust-jacket—level. But in an early review in *Commentary*, Theodore Solotaroff, who edited *The American Review*, already caught an intimation that "[Malamud] . . . has found the objects and idiom and viewpoint" that enabled him "to create a type of half-legendary world in the middle of New York City." What are the legends of Frank but the phobias of Malamud?

On his own schizoid nature, Frank Alpine reflects that his finer nature, the one he would like to cultivate, is "St. Francis of Assisi . . . when I was a boy an old priest used to come to the orphan's home where I was raised . . . and every time he came he read us a different story about St. Francis." A misleadingly facile transubstantiation would have us read Frank Alpine (*The Assistant*) as St. Francis of Assisi. Yet if Malamud has recourse to the *nomen est omen* technique to explicate his inner meaning, one may legitimately ask whether he has restricted its use to one character only. It can be demonstrated that Morris Bober too is a "nobler" character. In his case the pseudonym is Martin Buber—despite his being a penny-ante grocery-store owner, a miniaturization of the popularizer of I and Thou in dialogue. Why?

The savants who stood at the head of the University of Frankfurt, immediately after the end of the Second World War, cast about for someone to deliver the keynote address at the graduation ceremony for the School of Divinity. Given the still smouldering chimneys, the only one who would do would have to be a Jew, and one of world renown. Martin Buber accepted the invitation and said, more or less, the following: What has just joined our two peoples is beyond human understanding and is therefore the legitimate concern of theology. Neither of us is henceforward permitted to refuse to ponder the divine intent that has just conjoined us as victim and victimizer. I do not forgive your actions but I accept you as a fellow human being. I and Thou are now inextricably bound to one another, in a bond of suffering, suffering in lieu of understanding. Observe the way these very sentiments sound when said by Morris Bober: Frank (Frankfurt?) asks him what his Judaism consists of and in a beautifully reductionist dialogue Malamud gives us: "'What do you suffer for, Morris?' Frank said. 'I suffer for you,' Morris said calmly. Frank laid his knife down on the table. His mouth ached. 'What do you mean?' 'I mean you suffer for me.'" Yet far from accepting what is incumbent upon him by Morris's intimation to him that he recognizes him as one of the two bandits who held him up, Frank continues to steal from the grocer and to rape his daughter.

The true mytho-poetic figure that served Malamud when he undertook to portray the *ur-myth* of Frank, comes from another saint. A paraphrase of Frank's story can be found in the title of Genet's *A Thief's Journal* and his *Miracle of the Rose*. Whereas the affinity to the first of these (theft) is apparent, the derivativeness of *The Assistant* from the second work is revealed in an almost verbatim transposition. When Bober dies, Frank, uninvited, goes to the funeral. Atypically for American Jewish funerals, Helen throws a rose into her father's open grave:

Helen tossed in a rose. Frank, standing close to the edge of the grave, leaned forward to see where the flower fell. He lost his balance and though flailing his arms, landed feet first on the coffin.

Genet's alter-ego in *Miracle of the Rose* is Harcamone, a totally evil, unredeemable murderer. Genet recounts that on the eve of Harcamone's execution he dreamed that the warden, judge, chaplain, and lawyer all wandered around inside Harcamone's deity-like dimensions. When they arrived at the outer precincts of his heart they discovered that his heart was like a huge rose:

. . . the very edge of this pit which was as murky and deep as an eye, they leaned forward and were seized by a kind of dizziness. All four made the gestures of people losing their balance, and they toppled into that deep gaze.

What is Malamud doing in the offal-scented gardens of Genet? One must look to the mediating presence of the priest of existentialism, Jean-Paul Sartre, author of *The Anti-Semite and the Jew*. But as more germane to our treatment we must consider his larger work, *Saint Genet*. According to Sartre, Genet, who was serving a life sentence for theft and for homosexual rape, was not only unjustly incarcerated but should be beatified as a saint. Consequently, he petitioned Auriol, then president of the French Republic, and also wrote a major (670-page) tome which ends in the following words: "Translated into the language of Evil, Good is only an illusion; Evil is a Nothingness which arises upon the ruins of Good." His elevation of Genet to sainthood demands that we accord Sartre a new position; no longer mere priest, he is now high priest of Western post-Christian civilization. To the soap-opera-like question most readers ask themselves at the end of *The Assistant*, "should Helen marry Frank?" the answer is the same as Bellow's rejection of cross-cultural pollination: No!

It ill behooves the Jews to marry—to have congress with—the Franks who imitate, rob, pillage, and rape only to return piously and offer due homage. Arthur Cohen's highly nonfictional *The Myth of Judeo–Christian Civilization* amplifies this thesis which he also set out so startlingly in his novel, *The Days of Simon Stern*.

Malamud and Bellow do not spell this out. Instead, they rely on the New Yiddish to transmit their innermost fears. This is the ultimate benchmark of authentic American Jewish fiction. As such, it creates a waiting-for-the-other-shoe-to-drop syndrome in the reader. We await the days when Aristotle's precept is realized. When American Jewish novelists write like poets even when working a new *midrash* or the New Yiddish. As Aristotle wrote: "It is not the function of the poet to relate what has happened, but what may happen—what is possible according to the law of probability or necessity." That law requires that Moses Herzog own up to the fact that he considers American Jewish life to be like unto Egypt, and Bernard Malamud to think that Western civilization acts as though evil is a mere nothingness which arises upon the ruins of the good. The probability is that the non-Jewish world will continue to behave in Egyptian and in evil fashion. The necessity is that the authors, or at least their heroes, should consider exodus to Israel. Yet, the only American writing (pseudo) Jewish literature to bring his hero to Israel was Philip Roth. Here Portnoy discovered that his membership in the Jewish people withered on the vine when he confronted two Israeli girls, an army officer and a daughter of the *kibbutz*. Portnoy ended up screaming on psychiatrist Spielvogel's couch. He remains screaming there ten years later, reincarnated in the person of Peter Tarnapol in *My Life as a Man*.

Singer Pulls His Punches

The only major American Jewish author who does not write in New Yiddish is Isaac Bashevis Singer; and that is because he writes unqualified, unhyphenated Yiddish. One wonders if it was he that Ozick caught so trenchantly in her short story "Envy, or Yiddish in America." In one of his novels, *The Slave*, Singer had recourse to the very same technique employed by Malamud and Bellow playing counterpoint to a recognized master. In Singer's novel, however, the antagonist was Nobel prize-winning Shmuel Agnon and not a non-Jew. The work whose conclusions Singer wished to debate was *T'Mol Shilshom*. There, Agnon's hero, Yitzhak Kummer, is dispatched by a rabid dog called Balak. Hydrophobia alone did not do it; at core he died for his inability to decide between the robust *shikse*-like Sonia and the devout ghettoized Shifra. In *The Slave* the hero is saved by a dog called Bilaam whose owner is a genuine *shikse* but one who converts. Whatever the merits of the work it is probably the most realistic of Singer's stories. But the language again. This insight of Singer in a polemic with Agnon is only available in the Yiddish original, whereas the English translation (in which Singer was an active partner) erases the telltale signposts. Does Singer pull his punches when translating his own classic Yiddish to Cynthia Ozick's New Yiddish? Singer's original thesis in Yiddish, if indeed it was a polemic with Agnon, seems to say intermarriage isn't only not bad for the Jews, it's good. Did he censor himself when writing in English translation for his American Jewish readers?

If the New Yiddish is to have a chance at success its readers will have to adjust, learn to read it as a new perception. It will be a language that is constantly winnowing and refining obsessions by their transmutation through the Jewish experience. Arthur Cohen writes of Cynthia Ozick that she is a Jewish visionary and warns that a writer has to mind the language when obsessions are at stake.

> It isn't enough to record the experience because the experience is not given. It is wrestled free from the encumbrance of normal perception and wrenched apart, examined like the entrails of a haruspex, and sewn up again differently. For this work all of the literature, philosophical, moral, mythological, and all of the language, its unfamiliar words and its delicious words, have to be used.

Cynthia Ozick does this; would that others of her generation would continue in the tradition.

Notes

1. Y. Amichai, *Selected Poems*. New York: Penguin, 1971.

19

Here I Am;
Here I Remain

Abram Kanof

From the perspective of my 75 years, encompassing my adolescence spent in a Jewish ghetto, subsequent involvement in academia, later years in a largely Christian community, and two world wars, the Holocaust, and the birth of the State of Israel, I ask myself: (1) Why do I choose to remain in exile? and (2) Has Israel affected my status as to, and my feelings toward, being a Jew?

In this "enlightened" age, non-Jews change their nationality easily, abandoning neither their Christian faith nor their ethnicity. The Jew, on the other hand, remains a Jew until he renounces his identity. He must do this in a formal conversion ceremony, and then after one or two more generations his children or grandchildren may be recognized as exclusively American. It would appear that ultimately, to the outside world, religious faith is the factor which identifies me as a Jew. If defined as a religion, Judaism has become somewhat ambiguous. Rabbis and other Jewish leaders constantly refer to the Judeo–Christian tradition, the precepts of the Hebrew prophets having become the common heritage. Religious service is largely a social affair; belief in God and faith in His goodness is considered naive in the best circles. The *bar mitzvah* ceremony, the becoming a son of the yoke of the Torah, has become a rite of passage into puberty.

That which sustains me is a love of Jewish history, pride in Jewish accomplishment, nostalgia, and stubborn indignation in the face of bigotry and discrimination. Since 1948 there is also a Jewish country of which to be proud—a real political state capable of defending itself. But what about my grandchildren? For them there is no nostalgia, and they know the football scores much better than they do the wisdom of Solomon. Their Jewish heritage consists of four years in Hebrew school, three times a week, under protest, with the last year devoted chiefly to grinding out a *haftorah* for their *bar* or *bat mitzvah*. Israel for them is a tourist's destination with a special reason to visit. They will know they are Jews when they encounter anti-Semitism, and then they will wonder why the grandfather who was so concerned with their welfare did not convert in time to spare them the burden. Yet I remain a Jew, with my stubbornness, my nostalgia, my love for Jewish culture, and for Israel, and my habit of attending services and ceremonies. And I remain a Jew who prefers *galut* to *aliyah*.

The reality of the state produced a crisis for the diaspora. For centuries the return had been a Messianic dream in which Jews could indulge without the hope or fear of realization. For many *Eretz Yisrael* was an abstraction, something in a book with pictures. In 1948 Jews were forced to bite the bullet. Some emigrated to Israel, but more opted for exile. Not only were the creature comforts of the diaspora important, but, as was the case for the Jews of Babylonia, Greece, and Spain, life in the West remained preferable. Acculturation has always been a sociological phenomenon among dispersed peoples, but it is especially significant among Jews. After all, Jews have been strangers for a very long time. When my forefathers isolated themselves in the *shtetl*, it was out of necessity, rather than through fear of acculturation. When they moved from a Jewish town in Russia, they went not to the land they had prayed for, but into another *galut*.

Whether or not the mentality of exile is a malady depends on the point of view. The Israeli who looks with contempt at the diaspora comfort of the American Jew sees me as a stranger in a foreign land, spiritually deprived, and in imminent danger of physical liquidation. I see myself in the tradition of the Babylonian Talmudists, the artists of the Dura Europas synagogue, of Rashi, the Golden Age of Spain, and yes, in the spirit of poverty which gave rise to Hasidism. My roots in American culture are as deep as my attachment to Jewish history and my pride in Jewish accomplishment.

I think I know why I prefer exile to *aliyah*. Perhaps it is inertia or the fleshpots of America, but I flatter myself with less material explanations. Exile implies involuntary detachment from the homeland. The very freedom to move I enjoy eliminates the sting of being an exile. In Israel, as we have been told many times, the mere fact of one's presence establishes and instills a feeling of Jewish identity. I prefer being a Jew intellectually, culturally, and in many ways religiously, rather than geographically.

Judaism is flourishing here. There are three national seminaries, numerous *yeshivot*, many day schools, and hundreds of Jewish studies divisions in the universities. There is a very active, 90-year-old American Jewish Historical Society, four important Jewish museums, a foundation for Jewish culture, two Jewish-founded universities, and even two Jewish medical schools. Every large city offers a variety of synagogues, and every town has at least two choices. In the United States, Reform Judaism reached maturity, a Reconstructionist philosophy was developed, and traditionalism flourished in the Conservative and Orthodox sectors. Even Hasidism is on the move, with the *Lubavitcher* reaching into every corner of the American continent. In this country Western culture and ancient Hebrew civilization live comfortably together, and I feel comfortable with both.

In some ways the State of Israel has made being Jewish more difficult both for Jews in the diaspora and in Israel itself. One basic problem is the splits which are developing within Jewry. In Israel the widening gap between the religious and the secular is becoming more and more acrimonious, making it almost uncomfortable to be a Jew in the Jewish state. The politicization of religion affects the relative harmony among American Jews. American Jews live in reasonable relationship with each other. Between different movements there is intermarriage: we visit each other's synagogues, and we unite for charitable purposes. Religious organization in Israel tends to alienate Jews within Israel and abroad, and to give religion a somber face. We see plays for political power and financial gain, unwillingness to assume the responsibilities of citizenship, all in the name of piety. In the extreme cases, differences in religious beliefs become matters to be settled in street fights and on the Sabbath. The two major groups in Israel seem to be the religious minority and the majority, defined by its nonreligious common denominator. Deviation from *halakhah*, traditionally adjustable to people's needs, is viewed with decreasing tolerance, the effects being felt in the United States as well.

The diaspora seems more hospitable to me as a Jew, more in tune with my Judaism. After all, Hillel and Shammai were respected in the same Talmud which records their disagreements. The courteous rabbis of old said kindly that while the School of Hillel determines the Law here and now, Shammai will rule in the time of the Messiah. I do not perceive that spirit in Israel today.

There are also psychological and political factors which have disturbed the harmony of *k'lal Yisrael*. No one loves a rich uncle on whom one is dependent even to a small degree. Diaspora Jews must now separate themselves psychologically as well as politically, and measure with some dispassion their obligations as Jews and as Americans. Some find it difficult to accept Israel's speaking on behalf of all Jews wherever they live. Whereas in the past we had the right to criticize only individual Jews, we now find ourselves able to disagree with a Jewish political party and a Jewish government. We may fight the accusation of split loyalties from without, but how many of us have felt the problem in our bones?

And so I remain a Jew in exile. I hope my faith in American tolerance is not displaced. I hope that "it can't happen here." The many difficulties in the diaspora are balanced by many advantages. My emotional attachment to Israel in no way creates the desire or necessity of being a Jew there.

·VI·
Israel and Judaism

·20·
Religion and State in Israel

Isaiah Leibowitz

In my remarks I shall deal with two subjects which are really one: what can we contribute to the solution of the problems of the world and what can we contribute to the solution of the problems of the Jewish people? These questions are significant only if they are intended to point to what we, for our part, have to contribute. There is no need for the Jewish people, with an organized government in Israel, to take up values, slogans, or teachings which have already been formulated by others and hand them back again to the very same world that is the source of those values, doctrines, and formulations. That is, we must concern ourselves here only with what we ourselves have to offer. This directs our attention to our past.

In my opinion, we ought not discuss Judaism from the standpoint of ideas because ideas are public property and anyone can read anything into them. As long as the disputants are permitted to define Judaism according to the promptings of their hearts, their personal inclinations, and their intellectual or emotional preferences, making Judaism a completely subjective concept, the discussion amounts to no more than exercises in semantics. We must distinguish between Judaism as an empiric-historic phenomenon, on the one hand, and ideologies about Judaism on the other. Our discussion here has nothing to do with the various interpretations—theocentric, anthropocentric, or ethnocentric—which students of Jewish history have attributed to it, nor with the various evaluations of the creations, achievements, and chronicles of the Jewish people; rather it has to do with these creations, achievements, and chronicles themselves. We must understand the term "Judaism" in an objective, empiric-historic sense: the actual embodiment of Jewish reality throughout the centuries. That is to say, Jewish reality in its entirety, throughout the centuries and not in some particular period, not fragmentary revelations, episodic, accidental, personal, and ephemeral.

Now, in what was Judaism actually embodied? What was the permanent foundation on which it was built? What gave it continuity and identity through the centuries? Judaism is nothing but the religion of Israel as actually embodied in the Torah and in the commandments, whose systematic codification is the *Halakhah*. All the different, changing ideas and evaluations in Judaism were only superstructures erected on the *Halakhah*.

Others have already emphasized the central significance of religion in Jewish history and in the problems of our generation. Before we can argue as to what must and should be extracted from the sources of Judaism and from the history of the people of Israel we must first be clear about objective facts and ask a question, the answer to which is empirical and not ideological; namely: what is the essence of Judaism? The answer to this question does not depend on the values, beliefs, and opinions of the questioner or the one who answers the question, and it is not influenced by them. The answer is that Judaism is embodied in the religion of Israel.

Therefore, before we ask what obligation the individual Jew owes to his heritage, we must first put a purely factual, and not a normative, question: what can be extracted from this Jewish heritage? I wish to state as emphatically as I can that the answer to this question imposes no obligation whatsoever. Reality implies and gives rise to reality alone and involves no obligation, and a factual judgment does not bind us to a normative one. I am *not* discussing here what the Jew must or should do. I am merely stating the fact that those things which a Jew can extract from Jewish history, from the 3,000-year-old phenomenon called Israel in all its manifestations and vicissitudes, are nothing but religious values.

The Bible Is Not the Basis

These religious values have taken a definite form in Judaism: a way of life of the Torah and the commandments, whose formulated expression is the *Halakhah*. *It is not possible to erect Judaism on a biblical basis nor on ethics, nor on Messianism.* There are those who offer us bibliolatry as a substitute for Judaism—the Bible itself, not the Bible within the framework of active Judaism and with the meaning given it by Judaism, but the Bible as a document of elevated ethical values and as a basis for secular, human—anthropocentric and Jewish—ethnocentric education. Jewishly, this approach is a distortion, and an absurdity from the human point of view. Bibliolatry is not Judaism. It is a strange and highly paradoxical mixture of atheism and Christianity. It derives from atheism, in that it deprives the Bible of its religious meaning, and from Christianity in that the latter has always clung to the Bible, using it to attack Judaism.

From this point of view we cannot claim to have contributed anything to world culture. There has never been such a thing as Jewish philosophy but

only various philosophies coming from without, some of them even contra-
dicting each other, which worked within Judaism and were either adapted
by it to its needs or rejected by it There has never been such a thing as
Jewish ethics. The religious faith embodied in the Torah and in the commandments does not suffer ethical categories, does not recognize human
conscience nor man's volitional intention cognitively perceived (the ethics of
Socrates, the Stoics, and Spinoza) or felt as an obligation (Kantian ethics). It
recognizes only the worship of God by man; it does not recognize the
obligations of man to man but only those of man to God. As a result, there
have never been specific Jewish political or social ideas, specific Jewish
artistic or esthetic values, nor has there been a Jewish science. The only
specifically unique Jewish creation that has actively appeared in history is
Halakhah, that is, the attempt to organize the rules of human life against a
background of law, the aim of which is the service of God. The world did
not accept this from us. It rejected it clearly and emphatically, and at the time
when this Jewish thought was gaining considerable influence, the world
launched a successful counterattack against it. The counterattack was
Christianity.

Let us imagine that the Jewish people with all that it originated and
created had never existed; it is doubtful if in such a case, anything in the
makeup of the world would have been different from what it is. We cannot
contribute anything of our own to the solution of problems which confront
the world today, for our peculiar approach to the world and man is that of
the Torah and the commandments alone, and this the world has not accepted
and is not likely to accept. Anything else that we may have to say is nothing
but a paraphrase of what others have said in a more original form. The non-
Jewish world does not need us to preach to them the philosophy of Jefferson
and Lincoln—they preach that themselves. They do not need to learn
liberalism from us, nor humanism, nor the rights of man. It is they who
proclaimed the rights of man, and it is they who preach them. There is no
point in our talking about being "a light to the Gentiles."

As for the Jews of the diaspora, most of them, or we might even say all of
them, live in a Gentile world not only in a materialistic but also in a
psychological and intellectual sense, and they are immersed in these world
problems which are, in reality, non-Jewish. Hence, the Law will not go
forth from Zion. What Zion is likely to produce it cannot produce at this
moment, and if it could, the product would be unsuitable for a Jewry which
has decided to live in a Gentile world.

It is not from the prophetic vision nor from the Messianic mission that we
Israelis can draw spiritual nourishment, for these do not constitute the link
between us and Judaism as it actually existed in history. From the standpoint
of historical reality, the people of Israel did not live by the Bible but by the
oral law. A large part of mankind accepted the Bible but did not thereby

become Jews. That is, the Bible is not a constitutive ingredient of Judaism; the Bible alone did not create Judaism. The factors which constitute Judaism —again I state this not as an evaluation but as historical fact—are the *Halakhah* and the prayer book. This alone is the heritage of Jews, and he who accepts them becomes a Jew and is absorbed in the Jewish people. It is the *Halakhah* which made holy scripture out of 24 books that are, in part, second-rate literature and third-class history and philosophy, devoid of humanistic, ethical values. It is not the Bible which made Judaism, but Judaism, as revealed in the oral law, which made the Bible. Only through the *Halakhah* did the 24 books of the Bible receive their holy imprint. Concerning the Messianic ideal and the variants this ideal passed through in tradition, Maimonides, the greatest religious thinker produced by Judaism, says: "Man should not busy himself with legends nor spend too much time on the excesses of *Midrash* and not make them basic, for they lead neither to awe nor love." Judaism, it is true, produced the Messianic vision, but it is not dependent on it. For Judaism in its essence is nothing but the gray prose of the order of man's existence in his daily life, in his time and place, for the purpose of serving God; it is not the poetry of the vision of the end of days, which is merely religious folklore involving no obligations whatsoever.

When we deprive Jewish history of its authentic content and meaning—its religious content—we are creating a new people without historical continuity even though it may continue to use historical slogans and labels. This I also state as an objective fact without passing judgment. We do not have to go far to find an historical precedent. Two hours flying time from here is a land that bears the fairest name in human history—at least in the world from India to the Atlantic—the land called Hellas. Many of us feel that the name Israel is a still fairer name, but this has not been so in the history of mankind where the name "Jew" is a term of reproach. Even today there is a land which bears the name of Hellas. But what has this Hellas to do with that other fair Hellas? It surely occupies the same territory; its inhabitants may even share some of the biological traits of the old Greeks, for they were not physically exterminated but only absorbed other nations; they speak a language which resembles classical Greek and use the same alphabet; they continue to use names like Themistocles, Pericles, Sophocles. There are prospects for the existence of a State of Israel whose ties to Israel will be like those of modern Greece to historical Greece. It would occupy the same territory; the people within it would have inherited some of the biological traits of the Jews of old; it would speak a language more similar to that of Israel than modern Greek is to ancient Greek; it would use the same writing as that in which the oral law and perhaps even the Torah itself, were written; and its sons would be called by the names of Abraham, Moses, and David. Just as the Greeks are proud that Hellenism was cultivated by their fathers, so would we be proud of that Judaism cultivated by ours. Such an Israel is possible, but the state that has been established is becoming a Mediterranean state which is severing its ties with the historic Jewish people.

The repudiation of the actual content of Judaism, the work of the Torah and commandments, vitiates their use as a pedagogical tool. There are those who march under the banner of prophetic Jewish ethics. But Judaism is embodied in religion and this fact by itself does not permit the existence of the category of Jewish ethics. Religious faith, which is incorporated in the Torah and the commandments, does not suffer ethical categories. It does not recognize human conscience; it is no accident that the word "conscience" is not to be found in biblical Hebrew. And it is no accident that not one of the 48 prophets or seven prophecies which arose in Israel ever addressed itself to the human conscience. Human conscience becomes a central, focal point only when man does not recognize God. Ethics as a supreme value is an atheistic category which stems from the view of man as the end of existence and the center of creation. The atheist Kant was a great ethicist, since for him man was God. The prophets placed man against God and never against man. The people of Israel never struggled and never suffered for ethical values and never marched in the forefront of ethical consciousness. We have no right to interpret our fathers differently from the way in which they interpreted themselves. Furthermore, it is doubtful whether ethics can be qualified according to human groupings, whether there can be such a thing as Jewish ethics. It is possible that ethics is not subject to any qualification whatsoever by any adjective derived from human collectivities and possibly from no intellectual, current, or world view.

It is an empirical fact that Judaism is in reality embodied in the Torah and in the commandments and hence cannot be an ethical system. There are only two senses in which ethics can be understood. Ethics is either a volitional effort of man in conformity to his understanding of the truth of existence (the ethics of Socrates, the Stoics, Spinoza) or the volitional effort of man in accordance with his feeling of obligation over against reality (the ethics of Kant). But in the prayer of the *Shema* I and many Jews repeat: "And thou shalt not turn aside to follow after thy heart and after thy eyes" (Num. 15:39). "Not to follow after thy heart" refutes Kant, and "not to follow after thy eyes" refutes Socrates.

A way of life can be extracted from Judaism. The historical reality and the revelations of the tens of generations which have preceded us testify to the fact that it can be done. The religious way of life drawn from Judaism can be differently appraised from the ethical point of view, and on this matter there will be no agreement among us. But it is not possible to extract from Judaism guidance for a secular way of life. If we empty Judaism of its religious significance, we cannot extract ethics from it, for Judaism negates ethics.

The air is filled with slogans of prophetic–ethical vision—the Messianic mission—the redemption of humanity through Jewish ideals but, since these concepts have been deprived of their religious meaning, the result must inevitably be cynicism and nihilism. I do not deny that it is possible to educate without religion—but not from Jewish sources. There have been and are societies, advanced from many points of view, not founded on religious principles and not embodying religious content, but rather based on secular values of their own. The attempt to teach secular ethics from sources of Israel must necessarily lead to Kfar Kassim.

We should forget about these pyrotechnics of being "a light to the Gentiles" and look at ourselves a little more closely. It is fitting that in a discussion of the essential nature, tasks, and obligations of Israel, mention should be made of Kfar Kassim so as to enable us to pause and examine more closely the nature and essence of our existence as it is in actuality, and not as it is seen in the light of the Messianic mission which is, after all, a cheap thing, entailing no obligations whatsoever.

Religion and the State

A number of official representatives of orthodoxy, rabbis and leaders of the religious community, stress the religious significance of the political events of our day. I deny it. God did not reveal Himself in nature or in history but in the Torah. You cannot put a halo of holiness around such a political–historical event as that of the establishment of the State of Israel. Judaism has a number of interpretations of the concept of the Messianic mission, ranging from folklore fancy to the conception of Maimonides, but in every Jewish conception of Messianism, without exception, the redemption of Israel is linked to the perfection of the world or man, at least man in Israel. But the state was established not only without this perfection but, unlike the Hasmonean Kingdom in its day, without a basis in, or impulse from, the Torah. Whether we define ourselves as Orthodox or not, we have established a state as patriotic Jews, and Jewish patriotism like any other patriotism is a normal human phenomenon without any implication of holiness. There is no holiness except in the fulfillment of the Torah: "And thou shalt be holy to thy God." We have no right, therefore, to see the establishment of Israel as dependent on the Messianic mission, in any possible sense of this idea. We do not know whether this state is the first flowering of our redemption and whether it arose through Divine Providence: we do know that it is an achievement of Jews who grew weary of exile and of foreign rule, and that we did what we could, in the light of our understanding and on our own responsibility, not from an impulse derived from the Torah or its teachings.

The argument for religion based on its usefulness and advantages for man in general and for the people of Israel and the state in particular is a kind of desecration of religion. It makes religion an instrument for the satisfaction of human interests, and it makes faith a mercenary love. He who conceives of himself and the events of his life and the destiny of his generation as dependent on providence and sees the finger of God in all things is pitiful from the standpoint of religion itself. The problem and task of religion is to live the life of Torah and faith, a life of awe and love, in a generation "of the eclipse of God" as is ours, in which we, with the strength of our hands and in the light of our understanding and responsibility, succeeded in establishing ourselves as a national state.

It is for this reason that I myself support the separation of religion and state, so as not to make the religion of Israel an instrument in the service of the state (our state but still a secular one), so that religion will not become a governmental office in a bureaucracy.

Between this state which embodies secular values and the religion of Israel there is a need for a clear confrontation. Such a confrontation is not possible so long as religion tries to be a function of the state. Every attempt to take stock of ourselves and to find a way to the world of values obligates us to rise above this two-sided falsification which is symbolically embodied in the "Rock of Israel," in the Proclamation of Independence. The "Rock of Israel" in the prayer following the *Shema*—the "Rock of Israel" of King David and of the prophet Isaiah—transcends Israel, human values, all human categories. The "Rock of Israel" of the Proclamation resides in Israel, is Israel itself, is the national genius of the people of Israel. The insertion of the "Rock of Israel" in the secular document of our Proclamation was nothing but a conspiracy—the bribe that the secular community gave to the religious community which, in its turn, did not hesitate to accept it. Against this background one can have no confrontation between the world of religious values and the world of national, secular values; and no real struggle between them is possible.

But the fateful, transcendent spiritual struggle—which alone can yield us values and from which alone we can derive normative laws for our position as Jews—is possible only through a clear confrontation between this state of ours, which at the moment is secular, and religion, which demands an altogether different quality of political organization of the people of Israel. Religious institutions established by the secular state; the religious seal affixed to secular functions; positive and negative religious commands included as exceptions in the total array of secular laws, as a result of an understanding among various interested groups which share the powers of government among themselves; a secular authority which forces an arbitrary selection of religious manifestations on the community, not for the sake of Heaven but for political expediency; and a religion which enjoys the help granted by secular power—all these things are travesties of reality, perversions of social and religious truth, and the sources of intellectual and spiritual corruption. The state and secular society must speak their piece without hiding behind the skirt of religion; then we will see whether they have anything to say as a Jewish state and as a Jewish community. And religion must say its piece without hiding behind administrative skirts; then we will see whether it is the Law of Life. Only through such a confrontation can vital cultural values grow out of Jewish sources and flourish for us and our sons and daughters, and also for the diaspora.

In order to solve the fateful problems of the triangle—the Jewish people, the state of Jews, Judaism—two formidable obstacles which prevent the conjunction of these three factors must first be removed. The first of these is the artificial administrative connection between the secular state and religion, which makes a genuine link between them impossible. The second is the fundraising drives which do not unite but separate the state from the soul of the people in the diaspora. Every serious attempt and every effort to create a conscious, true spiritual relationship between this state and the Jewish people, in order to rescue diaspora Judaism from vanishing through assimilation and to rescue the state by making it a state for the entire Jewish people— every such attempt and effort founders on the factual rock that the Jews of the diaspora pay a ransom in the form of gifts of money which absolves them from fulfilling their obligations to Judaism and to themselves as Jews; at the same time, by receiving money from others, the Jews in Israel and the state itself find it possible to free themselves from the task of creating a political and social rule that has the dignity of independent existence. It is clear that as long as the Israeli community is dependent on others for the satisfaction of its needs it will not be induced to make the effort required to change this situation.

Until Israel frees itself from basing its existence on the spiritual enjoyment and gratification which it confers on other Jews who are neither interested in, nor see any need for, personal participation in its fate, it will not be able to be a source of spiritual or ethical influence, not to speak of religious influence. And until the Jews of the diaspora are deprived of the very attractive opportunity to fulfill their Jewish obligations by gifts of money to Israel, there is no prospect that a spark of real Jewish feeling may be kindled in the diaspora nor that a spiritual or religious Jewish revival may take place there under the influence of the State.

21

The Next Step

Mordecai M. Kaplan

Ideology in Jewish History

Each time our ancestors in formal assembly knowingly and deliberately accepted certain principles and duties as governing them as a people, Judaism entered upon a new stage in its career. Whether those principles or duties were of long standing and self-evident or of recent illumination, the very act of deliberate acceptance transformed them as a people and had the effect of a spiritual metamorphosis. We should therefore not be surprised, if as a result of a fully developed Zionist ideology that would be generally accepted by the Jewish people, it would experience a genuine renaissance.

In Jewish history, the outstanding case of a formal public act that transformed the Jewish people into a new kind of human society was the covenant by which the Jews, in the days of Ezra and Nehemiah, bound themselves to keep the laws of the Mosaic Torah. They became also a *Knessiah*, or ecclesiastical body, which served later as a model for Christendom and Islam. We might, perhaps, also treat the various covenants prior to the one in Ezra and Nehemiah's time, namely the one which Moses enacted at Sinai, Joshua reenacted at Shechem, and King Josiah at Jerusalem, as cases of public adoption of a way of life. Having been solemnly subscribed to and accepted as an act of choice, the way of life so adopted functioned as a bond of unity among our ancestors, withstanding the disintegrative forces of time.

Except for the Karaite schism during the period generally known as the Dark Ages, neither the unity nor the status of the Jewish people was a problem. The Jews constituted a nation, in the ancient sense of an ethnic or kinship group. Their being exiled from their homeland and dispersed among other nations in no way altered their status.

During the last two centuries, however, events have rendered the Torah tradition inoperative as a uniting factor among the majority of Jews. Consequently their group status has by this time become an enigma. Insofar as we Jews are nowadays without a definite group status and a common basis of unity, we are without a pattern of ideas, or way of life, to direct and regulate whatever cooperative efforts we have to engage in, whether it be the building of Zion, the organization of general life in the diaspora, or the fostering of an identifiable and distinctive way of life for the various segments of our people throughout the world. Whatever has been achieved is the result of impulsive reaction to danger rather than of planned and purposeful initiative. Without an ideology or way of life, how long can we be expected to exercise the will to continue living as one united people and to transmit to our descendants our common cultural and spiritual heritage?

Zionism owes its existence to one of those critical events in the life of our people which almost cut its history in two. Each of those events placed our people at the edge of an abyss, nearly putting an end to its career, but, fortunately, at each such critical juncture a new idea emerged and served as a bridge that carried our people across the abyss. Each such idea may be termed "salvational," in that it saved the Jewish people from extinction and provided it with a new awareness of its destiny.

The Four Crucial Events

The first event was the migration of Jacob and his family to Egypt. Ordinarily that would have put an end to the existence of the patriarchal group and to the tradition that had grown up in association with a deity named *Shaddai*. This outcome was prevented by the advent of Moses who came to the Israelites with the mission from the God of their fathers to redeem them from Egypt. The fact that redemption came from the God of the fathers saved the patriarchal history from oblivion and confirmed the destiny to which it pointed.

The second event was the destruction of the First Commonwealth. The exile which followed might have put an end to the Jewish people, had not the prophets anticipated it with an idea which interpreted that exile as only a temporary hiatus.

The third event was the destruction of the Second Commonwealth. That, too, would have marked the end of Jewish history, had not Yohanan ben Zakkai conceived the idea of "a portable state," by making of the Torah a substitute for the state. That is a form of self-government known as nomocracy.

The fourth event was the confluence of modern nationalism and modern naturalism. An offshoot of modern nationalism has been anti-Semitism: an offshoot of modern naturalism has been materialist secularism. The one has sought to destroy the body, the other to disintegrate the soul of the Jewish people. Once again a salvational idea has come to the rescue. That salvational idea is Zionism.

Thus at each critical juncture in our career as a people, whenever some cataclysmic event threatened to end that career, a new idea emerged. It not only spelled the resurrection of the Jewish people, it also elicited from it new creative powers that had lain dormant. It is therefore not unreasonable to look to Zionism as the salvational idea that will give our people in its present crisis a new lease on life. To meet that expectation, however. Zionism has to be viewed from a much larger perspective than that of the establishment of the State of Israel.

The Second Stage in Zionism

What Zionism has achieved thus far is basic and indispensable, but is only the first half of its task. Were it to stop at this point, it might undo the good it achieved and bring on new dangers to Jewish survival. We should heed the warning sounded by the British Zionists at one of their conventions not long after the establishment of the State of Israel:

> The State of Israel solved the problem of the homelessness of the Jewish people. On the other hand, there is now the real danger that the existence of the State might divide Jewry into two separate camps, the Jews of Israel on the one side, and the Jews of the *golah* on the other, with each camp speaking a different language and entertaining different ideas from the other, and absorbing cultural influences independently of each other. Should such a situation develop, it will be possible to say that while Zionism succeeded in creating the State, it has lost the people of Israel.

Nahum Goldmann in his keynote address put the matter less bluntly but in effect expressed a similar warning when at the First American Zionist Assembly, held in New York in December, 1953, he stated:

> It may sound paradoxical, but it may be true, nevertheless, that Zionism will hereafter be judged by its efforts for Jewish survival outside Israel more than by its efforts on behalf of Israel . . . no less than our obligation to see Israel through its difficult period is our obligation to defeat indifference, arrest assimilation, combat disintegration, for these dangers are more imminent today than in any previous period in our history.

Thus the second stage in the fulfillment of Zionism has to be as revolutionary in spirit as was its first stage. It has to reconstitute the Jewish people, to reunify it, and to redefine its status vis à vis the rest of the world. To do that, Zionism has to release world Jewry from the inhibitive influence of the traditional conception of redemption. That is the conception which pervades all our traditional writings, from the Bible down to modern times, and which is summed up in the prayer which Jews have been reciting for the last two thousand years: "Gather us from the four corners of the earth and lead us proudly to our land." Were Jews to take that tradition seriously they would have to regard themselves as aliens in every country of the world outside *Eretz Yisrael*. The fact is that it is not taken seriously by Jews who are citizens of other countries and who are treated there as equals with all other citizens. Nevertheless, that tradition is potent enough to stand in the way of world Jewish unity and the needed reconstruction of Jewish people-hood.

Prior to that era of the Jewish emancipation, Jews accepted the status of alienage without demur. With the granting of civic rights, however, that status was no longer tolerable. The problem then arose as to what was to become of their status as exiles, which their religious tradition expected them to retain. The Reform movement tried to solve the problem by breaking not only with the tradition concerning that status of Jews, but with the tradition concerning the return to *Eretz Yisrael*: that solution has proved completely mistaken. What has Zionism on its part had to say with regard to the exilic status of Jews outside *Eretz Yisrael*?

The truth is that there is nothing in Zionist ideology as hitherto formulated that challenges the traditional belief concerning the impossibility of a normal Jewish existence outside the Land of Israel. To attempt to read into Ahad Ha'Am's cultural Zionism the idea of a permanently normal Jewish life in the diaspora is entirely unjustified. All Ahad Ha'Am had in mind was the restoration of *Eretz Yisrael*, as more than a haven of refuge for displaced Jews and as nothing less than an instrument of a thoroughgoing Jewish renaissance, calling for a process of reeducation of the Jews in the diaspora. The spiritual radiation from *Eretz Yisrael* on which he counted was to serve as a means of awakening the national spirit which had been dormant for centuries in the diaspora. That awakened national spirit would then impel the Jews in the diaspora to migrate to *Eretz Yisrael* and qualify them to contribute to the Jewish renaissance there.

The weight of Zionist opinion throughout the world and in Israel is emphatically on the side of the "negation of *galut*." The reason is certainly not reluctance to deviate from a long-standing tradition. Breaking with the supernaturalistic idea of a miracle-working Messiah required far more cour-age than breaking at the present time with the traditional negation of *galut*. There is, it is true, a dangerously mistaken notion that harping on this will accelerate the secure establishment of the State of Israel. It is no doubt true that the security of the State of Israel requires as large a Jewish population as the land can absorb. At present the required and feasible number is said to be four million Jews. Likewise, it is essential that many Jews from free countries who are expert in forms of modern technics migrate to Israel. While all that is true, the assumption that by stressing the hopelessness of trying to salvage Jewish life in the diaspora Jews will be persuaded to settle in Israel, is a tragic illusion.

Zionism's Negation of the Diaspora

Zionists who promulgate the doctrine of *shelilat ha-galut* (negation of the diaspora) usually supplement it with the warning that even in the United States anti-Semitism might reach the proportions it attained in Europe during the Nazi regime. How little such arguments can prevail might well be inferred from what happened in Europe itself before the rise of the Hitler regime. Despite all the evidence pointing to the inevitability of what Herzl foresaw as the outcome of the growing Jew hatred on the Continent, Zionism, even as a salvaging movement, made very little headway in Central Europe. Only East European Jews who had a taste of pogroms and boycotts took Zionism seriously and responded to Herzl's appeal. How unrealistic, therefore, is it to expect American Jews who constitute more than half of world Jewry to be intimidated into migrating to Israel by warnings of a possible outbreak of anti-Semitism in America? All that is true, independent of the question as to whether or not the American environment is so radically different from the European as to make the violent outbreak of anti-Semitism even thinkable. Besides, if, God forbid, the cedars catch fire, how can the hyssop by the wall escape?

If the purpose of the doctrine of *shelilat ha-galut* is to prove to Jews that Judaism cannot possibly survive outside Israel, all that it will accomplish will be to discourage those who are making herculean efforts to keep Judaism alive in the diaspora. The Jewish layman on the whole is ignorant of Jewish tradition, not worried about the future of the Jewish people or its religion. The Jewish future, whether in Israel or outside, is a matter of active concern only to about one-fifth of the Jewish population. Their rabbis, teachers, writers, and social workers know from firsthand experience that Jewish life has not yet taken root in the free world, nor has it as yet given evidence of being able to thrive in the modern climate of opinion outside *Eretz Yisrael*. The so-called religious revival in the United States, with Jews as well as with Gentiles, is true to Mark Twain's description of the Platte River as "a mile wide and an inch deep." Fewer and fewer Jews are entering the fields of Jewish service and leadership. Far more disintegrative of Jewish life than any of the external forces in the free world is the suicidal procedure whereby each of the four denominations—the Orthodox, the Reform, the Conservative, and the secularist—is sectoring itself and becoming completely estranged from the other three, so that we do not have one Judaism but four.

Nevertheless, telling diaspora Jews that their efforts to maintain Jewish life are sure to fail will not help matters. It will certainly not bring about a greater influx of American Jews to Israel. On the contrary, it will definitely lessen the interest of American Jews in the fate of the State of Israel, to say nothing of reducing the likelihood of their migrating to Israel. It will only add to the growing spiritual crisis of diaspora Jewry. No sensible doctor ever tells a patient that it is useless for him to exert his will to live, even if he has only one chance in a thousand, particularly if the ailment is one in which the will to live is a determining factor. In the matter of Jewish survival, the group will to live is a determining factor. Instead of trying to discourage it, common sense dictates that it should be reinforced by whatever legitimate means are at hand or can be contrived.

Jews in Israel make a serious mistake when they keep on reminding the Jews in the diaspora that in failing to bear the brunt of the struggle and the dangers incurred in Israel they forfeit their share in the destiny of the Jewish people. Israeli Jews should recall the story in the Bible concerning David's fight against the Amalekite bandits who carried off the women and children and considerable booty from the village of Ziklag. When David returned to Ziklag, those who had fought the Amalekites refused to give those who had remained behind a share in the booty. But David ruled: "As is the share of the fighting man, so is the share of the man who stays by the stores" (I Samuel 30:23ff). The Jews in the diaspora have served, so to speak, in the capacity of staying by the stores, and they will not be denied their share in the achievements of Israeli Jewry.

But, of course, a greater issue is at stake than that of sharing the credit for the achievements of the Jews in Israel. The real problem is how to prevent the Jews in Israel from being so blinded by shortsighted considerations as to write off the diaspora Jews from a share in the future of the Jewish people because they insist upon remaining where they are. The Jews of Israel should be made to understand that in the long run the future of the State of Israel itself is bound up with the future of world Jewry. Israel will for a long time to come have to count for its security and growth upon the manpower, the resources, and the influence of diaspora Jewry. But if they are to be counted upon, diaspora Jews will have to see evidence in the Jews of Israel of a reciprocal feeling of fraternity and spiritual kinship.

Such feeling of fraternity and spiritual kinship cannot last or be an active factor in Jewish life, unless there be a common understanding on the part of the Jews both in and outside Israel with regard to the ultimate character and destiny of the Jewish people. The purpose of our coming together here is to explore the realities—particularly political and spiritual—and to determine upon the basis of those realities what kind of social structure or pattern the Jewish people must adopt in order to be able to maintain a genuine sense of continuity with the people of the Book.

That We May Be a People Again

Without going far afield into the cultural, economic, and nationalist forces that have been breaking up or transforming ancient peoples and calling into being new peoples, suffice it to say that each one of those forces carried to its logical conclusion is a threat to Jewish survival. Fortunately, however, they never operate in disparate fashion, and when they interact, as they must, they are liable to neutralize one another, as far as their injurious effect on Jewish life is concerned. That fact has been amply demonstrated in general life by the failure of the attempt on the one hand, in the 19th Century, to isolate nationalism as the all-decisive factor of human groupings, and in the 20th, to isolate economic determinism as the decisive factor. During the early decades of this century similar potency was ascribed to culture, as was the case with those who promulgated the principle of political minority rights. In Jewish life Dubnow was the outstanding advocate of that principle.

When, in addition, there enters, as has been the case with the Jewish people, the factor of deliberate choice and commitment, all attempts to base any predictive judgment on this operation of cultural, economic, or social forces have proved entirely futile. This does not mean that we can afford to ignore the disintegrative influence upon Jewish life, particularly in the diaspora, of the cultural, economic, and nationalist forces that dominate in the world today. But reckoning with them does not mean submitting passively to them. Given the will of Jewry as a body to win for itself a place in the sun, those very forces can be mastered and made to serve that will.

In the past we constituted a unique kind of society that possessed an intense self-awareness. Every individual in that society was permeated with the sense of unity and mutual responsibility. That feeling was the substance out of which were molded our beliefs, our values, and our hopes. That feeling is by no means dead. It is our task, however, to revive it, so that we may again become what we were in the past, a people as described in a statement by J. Pedersen:

> A people is not a collection of human beings, more or less like each other. It is a psychical whole, and in so far an ideal quantity. "The people" is not visible. All common experiences are merged into the common soul and lend to it shape and fullness. Thus a psychic stock is created which is taken over from generation to generation, being constantly renewed and influenced by new experiences. It is lived wholly in every generation, and yet it is raised above it, is something which is given to it and makes claims to it. The connection between the generations of a people is just as intimate as that between the generations of a family. The soul of a people and the soul of the family belong equally to the individual; only their subject matter differs.[1]

The prayer recited every fourth Sabbath ushering in the new month concludes with the statement: "All Israel form one fellowship or community." According to the description of such a community by Henry Wieman, an American philosopher, it

> includes both intellectual understanding of one another and the feeling of one another's feelings, the ability to correct and criticise one another understandingly and constructively. It includes the ability and the will to cooperate in such manner as to conserve the good of life achieved to date and to provide conditions for its increase. [2]

The leaders of the Zionist movement, both those in Israel and outside Israel, should enlarge the scope of the movement, so that it embraces as its objective not only the security and growth of the State of Israel but also the reaffirmation of the unity of the Jewish people throughout the world, the redefinition of its group status, and the revitalization of the Jewish spiritual heritage as a bond to unite the scattered Jewish communities with one another and with the Jewish community in Israel. These larger purposes of the Zionist movement require a radical change of heart towards diaspora Judaism and a release from the assumption, whether based on tradition or on mistaken expediency, that the refusal to migrate to Israel, when one is in a position to do so, constitutes an act of spiritual disloyalty.

Zionism's primary function is to call those Jews in the diaspora who are of adventurous spirit, who are expert in some practical or theoretical technique, to come to Israel and help in its upbuilding. But it should also seek to motivate those who remain behind to perpetuate their Jewish group individuality and foster their spiritual heritage. They should be encouraged to resist in their communal life the operation of forces which tend to break up minority groups. Traditional Jews, to be sure, do not need such encouragement. They merely have to be asked to live up to what they profess. But the ones who need encouragement are those who are wholeheartedly eager to find a way of keeping Judaism alive wherever they happen to be but who cannot come to terms with the traditional version of Judaism. They constitute by far the majority of survivalist Jews. If their adherence to Judaism is to be retained and their Zionist interest kept alive, they have to be made to realize that no matter where they live, they need the Jewish people and the Jewish people needs them.

Aliyah *and* Diaspora

To exercise that mutual need the following considerations have to be kept in mind.

Diaspora Jews need the Jewish people because the state of which they happen to be citizens does not claim to provide its citizens with the affiliations which are essential to their being morally and spiritually oriented. One such type of affiliation is the family, the other is the religious community. The state leaves it to the individual citizen to choose the one as well as the other. No normal-minded Jew however, can possibly satisfy his need for moral and spiritual orientation in any non-Jewish group. He must naturally look to the Jewish people to serve him in that capacity.

That is to a large extent equally true of the Jews in Israel. The State of Israel is at present already far removed, in its relationship to religion, from the type of state represented in Spain, Italy, or any of the Catholic nations in South America. It is modeled largely on the type of democratic states like England, which recognize an established church but grant equality to other churches. Whether in time state and religion will be completely separated in Israel as in the United States is questionable. However, the democratic character of the State of Israel is enough to preclude it from being able to provide even its Jews with the affiliation that is essential to their being morally and spiritually oriented. That kind of affiliation only the international Jewish people which has its core in Israel can provide them.

For the Jewish people, however, to serve Jews in that capacity both in and outside Israel it should offer them something more than an ancient tradition of a credal religion. It cannot afford to echo Eugene O'Neill s despair (from *A Moon for the Misbegotten*): "There isn't any present or future, there is only the past over and over again now." It has to provide them with the ability to make of its tradition a civilizing and humanizing force not only in interpersonal relations, but also in international relations. To do that, two conditions must be met: (1) The core of the Jewish people must be situated in its own homeland, in *Eretz Yisrael*, and (2) the tradition has to be made relevant to the very ideologies, cultural, economic, sociological, which challenge it. Out of those ideologies there can well arise—to use an analogy from music— both a harmonic and a contrapuntal system of ideas concerning God, men, and the world, which would continue the tradition, enhanced in content and vision. That would then be the tradition that would mark the renaissance of the Jewish people and render it morally and spiritually indispensable to the individual Jew, regardless of where he lived.

The Jews: A Religious People

On the other hand, it does not require too much coaxing to convince the individual Jew that the Jewish people needs him, that its chances of survival are lessened if he deserts it. If the Jewish people is to have a claim on the individual Jew, it has to submit to the process of self-renewal to spiritual needs and complexities which happen to be without prece tradition. If the Jew has his mentality formed by the Torah tradit come to feel what the Jewish people has always felt and to think always thought, he may even disapprove, deny, and repudiate m has been communicated to him, without severing his spiritual kinship with it. On the contrary, his very dissent may contribute to the scope and depth of his oneness with his people.

If the Jew is to realize how much the Jewish people needs him, it must not demand exclusive possession of his personality, by insisting that he reside in *Eretz Yisrael*. It should grant him the right, if he so chooses, to live in two civilizations, in the Jewish civilization and in that of the state of which he is a citizen. The spiritual allegiance he would owe to the Jewish civilization would necessarily have to be of universal scope, and would therefore be entirely compatible with the political allegiance he owes to the state of which he is a citizen. "The attachment of Jews throughout the world to Israel," said Premier Ben-Gurion "is based on a joint spiritual and cultural heritage and on a historical sentiment toward the land which was the birthplace of the Jewish people and of the Book."[3] It devolves upon Zionism now to recognize that attachment as a spiritual or religious bond which can exercise a dynamic and beneficent influence wherever and whenever it expresses itself.

A people in which each individual is fully aware that he needs the people for his moral and spiritual well-being, and that the people needs him for its self-perpetuation and the achievement of its destiny, is, in the truest and deepest sense of the term, a religious people. Hitherto it was assumed that to constitute such a religious people its members had to abide by a uniform code of beliefs and practices. With the rise of the demand for freedom of thought and the right of individual self-expression, a religious people will have to find ways and means of achieving unity without uniformity. That should not be difficult for the Jewish people because of its inexhaustible tradition which, however diversely interpreted and applied, can nevertheless function as a unifying influence. That means that Jewish peoplehood is not a political category but a moral–spiritual category and has to be accorded the same status as that of the world religious bodies. The Jewish people will thus constitute an international people, whose spiritual center—since it has no political center—is to be located in its ancestral home.

In an article in *Hapoel Hatzair*, Israel Cohen described the first Zionist settlements. He calls attention to the experiences of the early settlers in Degania. "They could have failed completely," he says,

> had they not possessed the fundamental trait of pioneers, that of rejecting conventional ideas which had behind them the authority of the most illustrious leaders of their own people: similarly, they emancipated themselves from Socialist principles which also had behind them the authority of great masters of economic theory.

I would add that we now should revive that trait and shake ourselves free from the traditional assumption that the boundaries of the State of Israel are essentially the boundaries of the Jewish people.

All our endeavors to find solutions for our problems as Jews are bound to be frustrated, unless we possess the courage to create new concepts which can help us deal with conditions that are without precedent in our history. We should not expect Jewish life under conditions of dispersion in the past, even those during the so-called "golden periods," to serve as a precedent for the future. In the past, Judaism was all of one piece because of the uniformity that obtained in the thought habits of Jews. This situation cannot be repeated. I, therefore, propose that we discuss the possibility and legality of a Judaism that lends itself to various degrees of one's identification with it, that is a Judaism which, in its home in Israel, finds its embodiment in *all* aspects of life, from those of politics and culture to religion and everyday affairs, but which, in the diaspora must, of necessity, omit some of those aspects, without thereby losing the right to identify itself with the Judaism of history. All this means that the type of people, community, or fellowship which we Jews have to constitute henceforth is a novum, both structurally and ideologically. Structurally, it has to resemble a hub with spokes. The hub is to be the Jewish community in Israel; the spokes are to be the organic Jewish communities in the diaspora. Ideologically, the rim which is to hold together the entire structure must itself consist of different strands of belief and practice which have their source in the Jewish tradition.

What the Jewish tradition means to the Jewish people has been realistically set forth by Buber. "We Jews," he writes,

> are a community based on memory. A common memory has kept us together and enabled us to survive. This does not mean that we based our life on any one particular past, even the loftiest of the pasts, it simply means that one generation passed into the next a memory which gained in scope—for new destiny and new emotional life were accruing to it—and which realized itself in a way we can call organic. The expanding memory was more than a spiritual motif; it was a power which sustained, fed and quickened Jewish existence itself. I might even say that these memories realized themselves biologically for in their strength the Jewish substance was renewed.

Religion in the Free Nations

Of particular relevance to the group status of Jews in the diaspora is the place that the traditional religions occupy in the policy of modern nations. Some nations like Russia and its satellites officially repudiate the traditional religions altogether, not only because they are traditional but also because they are international. They therefore ban whatever activity Jews living in other countries engage in to assert their corporate individuality. In all our efforts at survival and enhancement of Jewish life we must reckon with the understanding and good will of those nations which have worked out a modus vivendi between the traditional religions and their own ways of life. Most of them, like England and the Scandinavian nations, recognize as preferred some particular traditional religion and as permissive all others, and some like the United States show no preference, but treat all traditional religions with respect. These various accords between the modern national ways of life and traditional religion are actually compromises between conflicting ideologies, one based on naturalism and this-worldly salvation and the other on supernaturalism and other-worldly salvation.

Apart from the question as to whether or not these compromises are satisfactory and permanent, it is a fact that only those nations which have adopted them have granted full civic rights to the Jews in their own countries and unqualified recognition to the State of Israel. The fact has to be borne in mind when we wish to find an appropriate social category for our international Jewish peoplehood. Any solution of our problem which would ignore those compromises entirely would hardly contribute to our being understood by the nations upon whose good will we depend for our well being and survival as a people. If, for example, Zionism were to spell the radical reconstruction of the Jewish people into a secular nation confined to *Eretz Yisrael*, with no room whatever for traditional religion with its supernaturalism and other-worldly salvation, or if it were to go to the other extreme and spell the revival of a theocracy with the restoration of the Temple, the priesthood, and a sacramental cult, or if it were to adopt the position that it is impossible for any fruitful life to thrive in the diaspora—if Zionism were to adopt any one of these three ideologies, it would undermine the good will of the western nations upon which it depends both in and outside Israel.

The western nations are the only ones whose political structure and ideologies are such as to be compatible with the will of Jews to constitute an international people with its core in *Eretz Yisrael*. Communist nations do not tolerate the international character of Jewry. That is why it is important for Jewish peoplehood to be identified as a religious category, and for the Jewish people to be known as a religious community. Only as such a community can it fall into the familiar pattern that smooths the way for friendly intercourse with those nations without whose friendship we would find ourselves completely isolated—a condition that must be averted at all costs.

The question, of course, is: how is it possible for a group to be designated as religious which is not based on a uniform system of belief and practices? The answer is that it is not only possible to find a common element in various manifestations of a religion, but that the common element is actually the essence of the religion and that it was the passionate purpose of all our prophets and sages to call the attention of people to that common element. I refer particularly to the attitude of mutual responsibility which unites individual men and women into a group and obligates them to strive for the achievement of freedom, righteousness, and peace in the world. That attitude of mutual responsibility is bound to find expression in feelings of holiness and in acts which symbolize those feelings.

The feelings of holiness are those which give rise to the concepts of divinity and Messianism. Evidently, one must expect that there would be a difference between the way of life of those who conceive divinity and Messianism in keeping with our tradition, and the way of life of those who conceive those concepts in terms of modern thought. Nevertheless, if the leaders of our various parties and denominations are animated by the desire to fortify the unity of our people, wherever it happens to live, they will be able to find the way to retain the individuality of their respective groups, without tearing the body of our people into tatters. We should not ask them to break down completely the fences that divide one group from another. All that they have to do is to permit openings to be made in the fences. Those openings would make it possible for the members of the different groups to work together as one body for purposes which transcend all partisanship and which are cherished by all Jews.

How Zionism May Unite Jewry

Our aim should be to formulate the specific: *halakah* or way of life, which might help our people to live and grow as *one* people throughout the world. With that in mind, we should give heed to the concluding statement made by Bailik in his well-known essay on *Halakah versus Aggada*:

> A people which is not trained to translate its *Aggada* into *Halacha* delivers itself into (the power of) endless illusions, and is in danger of straying from the only direct path that leads from willing to doing and striving to achieving . . .
>
> A Judaism which is only *Aggada* is like iron heated in the fire but not cooled thereafter in water. Yearning of the heart, stirrings of the spirit, profound love— these are beautiful and helpful provided they lead to action that is steeled and to duty that is stern.
>
> If you really wish to build, do what your ancestors did (in the days of Ezra and Nehemiah). *Make a firm covenant and write it . . . and lay obligations upon yourselves.*

The Jews of the diaspora definitely refuse to serve merely as the scaffolding of the House of Israel. They insist on constituting an integral part of that entire house. The time has arrived when we must realize that one God has created us, one past has formed us, and only one future has preserved and will preserve us. If we will live up to that realization, the words of the prophet Malachi will come true: "Your own eyes will behold, and you yourselves will say 'The greatness of the Lord is manifest beyond the boundaries of Israel'" (Mal. I:11)

——————————————————————————————————— *Notes*

1. Johannes Pedersen, *Israel: Its Life and Culture*. New York: Oxford University Press, 1973. Rep. of 1926 ed., p. 475.

2. Henry Wieman, *The Source of Human Good*. Carbondale: Southern Illinois University Press, 1964, p. 64.

3. *New York Times*, June 26, 1957.

22

The Jewish Condition After Galut

Jacob Neusner

The State of Israel has ended (for all time, I hope) the political exile of the entire Jewish people; wherever they live, for now, wherever they are, the Jews are there by choice. No Jew needs to be a refugee. So far as *galut* stands for being homeless or where one does not wish to be, that sort of *galut* is now over. What is left of the idea of exile, however, is a rich and evocative picture of the human situation. For *galut* may have been principally a political condition, but it was not only that. Today, as I said, it is not that at all. It is once more a symbol for the condition of the world in its flawed relationship to the Creator of all life. So far as *galut* is deemed a locative category, it is no longer relevant to the life of the Jewish people. So far as *galut* is understood as utopian and existential, an account of alienation, then we deal with a vivid and provocative mode of insight.

Exile and the Jewish Condition

Galut as an approach to the interpretation of American Judaism is politically irrelevant, socially pernicious, economically dysfunctional, religiously meretricious, but essentially correct. For *galut* essentially speaks of alienation, disintegration, and inner strife. American Jews politically, socially, and economically stand within the corporate limits of society; they do not see themselves as temporary residents, people who really belong somewhere else. Their homeland is America; its turmoil is theirs; so too its tragedy and triumph. To allege that in the *eschaton* (end of days) they will magically be lifted up and transported on eagles' wings to some other place is to present

American Jews with a useless fantasy. One might as well tell them stories of Sinbad the sailor and call them theology or history.

But speak of alienation and one addresses the center of the Jewish situation. American Jews are in *galut*, exiled from the joys and glories of Torah. They have lost the art of dying, the public pleasure of celebrating together, the glory of a day of rest together, the splendor of perpetual awareness of the natural cycle, above all, the capacity for atonement and the certainty of forgiveness. They have no shared myth within which to explore life's private mysteries, through which to locate the meaning of public events and of felt history. Their mythic life is insufficient. Their most abysmal exile of all, therefore, is from the human quest for meaning.

The existential dimension of *galut* encompasses the situation of American Jews as modern people. Having lost the unself-conscious capacity to participate in tradition, the modern Jews—whether here or in the State of Israel—find themselves lost and virtually helpless. They cannot go backward, but they see no way forward. The insights of tradition into the human condition, while sound and perpetually correct, come in symbols to which they cannot respond, garbed as absolutes to which they cannot submit. So they pathetically limp from cause to cause, ideal to ideal, drawn in the currents of searching humanity from one headline to the next. This is the contemporary counterpart to the wandering of the Jewish people from land to land, the former incapacity of Jewry ever truly to settle down. Political *galut* is a paradigm for the existential *galut* of our own time. And both mirror a deeper side to the human heart—the soul's incapacity to ever fully accept, love, not only the other, but, to begin with, the self. If in former times the collectivity of Israel saw itself as alien to its situation but at home in its religious community, today nearly the whole Jewish people has exchanged political *galut* for one that is more comfortable and secure, if in a measure also self-pitying and narcissistic: alienation from the art of living. But these reflections on *galut* have carried us far from the accepted range of discussion. Let me give blunt answers to the questions on the conventional agenda.

The traditional concept of *galut*, phrased in either historical, political, or metaphysical-*kabbalistic* terms, does not and cannot characterize American Jewry. It would be pretentious to elevate the banal affairs of a bored, and boring, ethnic group, unsure of its identity and unclear about its collective purpose and meaning, to a datum of either metaphysical or even merely historical hermeneutics; American Jewry simply does not add up to much. Its inner life is empty, its public life decadent. So to whom shall we ask the ultimate questions of meaning? To what shall we apply the transcendent symbols of exile and alienation? To *bar mitzvah* factories and bowling clubs? It would be not merely incongruous but derisive.

At home in American or Western civilization? Alas, as much at home as anyone. Why abstract ourselves from the generality of man? What choices do we have? In all the world, who aspires to something other than our civilization, our way of living? Shall we repudiate jet planes or penicillin or liberal democracy? For what? The oxcart, the medicine man, and the Messianic general? Do these improve the human condition?

And if we were to migrate to the State of Israel, what gain should we hope for? To be a Jew in America is no harder than to be an American in Israel, but, whichever one is, he or she remains in the situation of exile. Only propagandists seriously ask us to interpret *galut* so crassly that its effects may be washed away by a trip across the oceans. No baptism there, nor a new birth in a new world. The new creation, new heavens, and new earth—these are harder to attain.

It follows that Jews, whether at home or in the State of Israel, cannot repudiate their millennial history of *galut* any more than they repudiate their truncated history of "enlandisement." Having, and not having, a land of our own—both are integral to the Jewish experience of history. The felt history of the Jewish people is single, unitary, integrated: the experience of one people in many places and circumstances, not one of them barren of meaning and insight. They all of them constitute the Jewish testimony on the history of mankind, with most of which the Jews are co-extensive. Shall we now be asked to say the lessons of the Land are true but the lessons of *galut* are false? Are not the great monuments of our spiritual and intellectual history both in the Land and outside of it? And do we not give up our responsibility to stand outside of and to judge the history and works of mankind, if we repudiate our own creation within that history and among those works? And that creation is in a measure the capacity to live as strangers at home.

Galut has nothing to do with whether or not the Jews are fully accepted as human beings, for it is not created by the world and cannot be changed by it. But for my part, if I am accepted as a human being and not as a Jew, I do not accept that acceptance, for I aspire to no place in an undifferentiated humanity and hope never to see the end of significant differences among men. The only acceptance worth having is of myself as I am—first, last, always a Jew, son of my people as I am son of my father and mother; and, I hope, progenitor of Jews as well. Take me despite my Jewishness and there is nothing to take. Overlook what is important to me and you obliterate my being. Of that sort of acceptance we have had enough in the liberal sector of American society. It has yielded self-hatred and humiliation, and, for Jewry at large, an inauthentic existence. So acceptance of Jews fully as human beings not only intensifies but also poisons the awareness of *galut*. It denies us our dignity, our loyalty, our right to be ourselves. Nor does anti-Semitism do much good, for exactly the same reasons.

Granted, *galut* ends with the living of an authentic Jewish existence, but that life is not to be defined by where it is lived. What matters is how. By "authentic" and "Jewish" one may mean many things. To me an authentic

Jewish life is one of joy and gladness, a life that fulfills the many-splendored hopes of humanity with the light of Torah. And Torah illumines the world, no one part more than another. American Jews will have attained an authentic Jewish life when they look forward to Sabbaths of contentment and festivals of rejoicing, when they celebrate natural glories and share the human pathos, when they have so educated themselves that whatever happens enters into Torah and also explains its meaning.

The end of our exile—and the exile of Jews wherever they may be—will come with the end of alienation, disintegration, and inner strife. On that distant day we shall be at one with ourselves, at one in society, and at one with God. We will know the joy of Torah in the private life and for the public interest, and Torah shall open the way to God. And the first step on that long, long road is the start of the search for the joys of being Jewish— trivial, humble pleasures, such as welcoming the sunset on the eve of the Seventh Day and singing songs about the Lord, master of the world, rock of whose goodness we have eaten, the honored day. Song without belief, to be sure, but the song contains all the belief we need. Our voices, our words, our melodies—these resonate as one—the echo of our ultimate unity, the end of our exile from ourselves, the beginning of the inner peace we seek.

The Jewish Condition and the Human Condition

It is time, therefore, for the sons and daughters of the *golah* to give up that dishonest pose of apology we have played out before our Israeli counterparts. Without apology or restraint they proclaim our faults: "You are disappearing through assimilation. Anyhow, the *goyim* are going to kill you all. So your destiny is to die in gas chambers, singing *Silent Night.*" In utter silence we bypass theirs. Out of embarrassment we refrain, too, from declaring what we believe we have to cherish in the experience of *galut.* But there have been lessons. The framers of radically locative Israelism, in which only being Jewish in the State of Israel is authentic, and being Jewish anywhere else is inauthentic, may well be reminded that we have learned lessons they have not learned. These lessons have the power to make us into significant exemplars of precisely that Judaism that is shared among us all. Let me therefore describe what I think being a Jew in the *golah* has taught me— lessons Israelis might well attempt to learn as well.

The Jewish situation in the *golah* endows me, first of all, with a long and formidable perspective. It forces me to see myself as part of a continuum of time and of space, as heir of some of the most sublime and most foolish men that have ever lived, and as friend and brother of people who, in days past, lived almost everywhere humanity has been. I cannot therefore accept provinciality, either temporal or spatial, or see myself as rooted forever in one culture or in one age.

Thus the Jewish situation in the *golah* is international and cosmopolitan, and never wholly part of one place or time. This is both a blessing and a curse. It is a blessing because it assures me of ultimate detachment, of a capacity to contemplate from without, to think less fettered by rooted attachments than can other men. It forces not only detachment, but to some measure, an act of selection and judgment also, for, not being fully committed anywhere or ever, I am forced to perceive what others may stand too close to see, and in perception, to respond, to judge. I must therefore learn to love with open arms, to know that this land, this people are mine, yet not wholly so, for I belong to Another as well. Thus, to be a Jew means in a historical and more than historical sense to be always homeless in space and in time, always aware of the precariousness of people, of the possibility, by no means remote, that I may have to find another place.

But the Jewish situation of homelessness, of detachment, has provided me, secondly, with the awareness that what is now is not necessarily what was nor what must always be. Being able to stand apart because of an inherited and acquired perspective of distance, I realize the people have choices they may not themselves perceive. There have been and are now other ways of conducting life and living with others, of building society and creating culture, than those we think are the norm. Being able to criticize from the perspective of other ages and lands, I am able to evaluate what others may take for granted, to see the given as something to be criticized and elevated.

Third, the Jewish situation of living with a long perspective imposes upon me a terrible need to find something meaningful, truly eternal in human affairs. If I see that all things change, and that only change is permanent, then I need all the more a sense of what abides in man, of what endures in human civilization. If one says, with Sinclair Lewis' men of Gopher Prairie, that to build the emporium that is ours, Washington weathered the rigors of Valley Forge, Caesar crossed the Rubicon, and Henry stood at Agincourt, then one declares his faith that what is here is truly the zenith and the end of Western history. But we Jews know differently, for we know of cities once great and now no more, of civilizations—and we too have built civilizations—that prospered and were wiped out in time. We ask, therefore, because we need to ask: what abides, what is permanently meaningful in life? We want to know where history is moving, because we know that history does, indeed, move.

Fourth, out of this need, this thirst for meaning in kaleidoscopic life, we Jews have learned that something in humanity is indeed eternal. We use the words of Scripture, and say that "man is made in the image of God," but underlying these words is a mute and unarticulated awareness that humanity prevails, and some achievements can endure. We know, moreover, what will live: namely, the intellect, the capacity to learn. We have, therefore, dedicated our best energies to the cultivation of the mind, to study, enrichment, and transmission of man's insights and ideas through the ages. We have held that that part of humankind which may think, know, believe, hope, love—that part is divine and endures, and whatever part of it endures from another age is ours to know, love, and cherish. Therefore, in other ages, our monuments have been books, the school house, and our heroes have been people of learning and of mind.

Fifth, because I am a Jew, I understand how important to the world are compassion and our capacity to transcend the animal base through acts of love and fellowship. The Jewish situation imposes this understanding in two ways. First, because we were slaves in Egypt, we know how important is an act freely done, freely given, that at its most elevated is represented by compassion. Because we have suffered in history, we have learned how important is the opposite of cruelty and oppression: namely, kindness and love. Second, because we see ourselves as human, neither animals nor God, neither wholly objects of nature and history nor wholly subjects of nature and history, we see our human duties and capacities as neither wholly passive nor on the other hand wholly active. We know, therefore, that we may do little, but that we may do: and what we may do as an act of our own will is to act decently, compassionately, justly, for free will permits us to choose compassion. The larger part of life may be conditioned and ouside of our power, but that precious corner of freedom to act by one's own will remains, and will at its most virtuous is goodwill—in Hebrew *hesed* (in the abstract, compassion) and *gemilut hasadim* (in the concrete, acts of compassion).

Sixth, more concretely, the Jewish situation imposes on me an intensity of human relationship, best embodied in the family, that others see as clannishness. Seeing the world as we do—a lonely, insecure, transitory place—we look within it for places of security and evidences of permanence, and these we find, as I said, in the abstract in compassion, and in the concrete, in human relationships of love and deep acceptance. We know that death is always near, and that each man and woman goes a separate way to death. But we find in this knowledge not only separateness, but also union of the generations. Death is the experience that brings together the generations that have gone before and those that will come; it is the one experience we share in common, and the Jewish forms of death—the sanctification of God's name in this one stark moment when we are forced to recognize that His power and His will abide to unite the generations. This is the source of veneration of our past and our capacity to continually live in it, and the foundation of our love for our people, wherever and whenever they are found.

Finally, the Jewish situation has as its foundation a continuing confrontation with the reality of God. Until now, one may have wondered: where is the theology of the Jewish situation? Beyond the theologies of Jewish religion, and before them all, is the simple sentence, "In the beginning God created the heaven and the earth." That is our fundamental affirmation, and all else must be built on that fact. We affirm that God, who made the world, did so purposefully, and ultimately that purpose is revealed in the course of human history. All that I have said about our long and formidable perspective —our awareness of the frailty and transitory quality of man, our thirst for permanence, through dedication to the mind and reason, to love and compassion in the abstract and in concrete terms—all this is founded on our fundamental attitude toward the world and ourselves, both of which we see to be the objects of divine concern, divine purpose, divine compassion. Both humankind and nature are objects, not subjects, of reality. Both are profane, and the only sanctity lies beyond the world and humankind. Hence our concern for history and its movement, for humanity and conduct in society arises out of our awareness that in the objects of creation we see in pale reflection a shadow of the subject.

Because of this awareness, we are not ashamed of our history, of our frailty and inconsequentiality as a small and insignificant people among the peoples of mankind. We know that those great nations that ruled the world like God perished like men, while we who have patiently endured in hope endure today. Therefore we do not reject our tragic past.

Very little has been said here to distinguish Jews from other men. It is hardly necessary to be a Jew to understand the Jewish situation. The existential qualities I have described are those that Jews may know best and longest, but that others know too. We have words for our situation, such as *galut*: exile, *rachmanut*: compassion, *yosher*: righteousness, and *bitahon*: faith, trust in God; and these words, though ultimately not translatable into any other language, are in fact shared existentially by every other people today.

An age that is threatened by the total destruction of entire civilizations knows what it means to be Jews, who suffered the destruction of their entire European civilization in our time. An age that knows no security knows what it means to be Jews, who have lived for thousands of years without security. An age that finds itself almost powerless to change the course of history, in which individuals find they are almost impotent to affect events, knows what it means to be Jews, who have lived as outsiders, standing always on the wings of history and never in the spotlight. An age that suddenly realizes it is in the grip of past events knows what it means to be Jews, who have seen themselves forever in the grip of events they have not caused, and ultimately, in the hand of a Providence. An age that now knows the danger of nationalism and provinciality knows what it means to be Jews, who have lived internationally before there were nations.

If this is so, perhaps others will learn from us the affirmative lessons of our situation: our quest for meaning in events; our consecration to the human intellect and capacity to think, to create and preserve culture; our appreciation of the preciousness and sanctity of man's slender treasure of compassion and of love, in the abstract and also in day-to-day human relations in which, after all, we do retain considerable power; and, finally, our awareness of the reality, immediacy, and centrality of God's will, our knowledge that in the end, it is not we but God who determines the history of men and nations, not we but God with whom men must strive for blessing.

A Zionist Affirmation

My purpose now is to offer ideas which will make possible a Zionism both true to itself and relevant to American Judaism. An entire, large community of Jews—the largest and humanly most accomplished and powerful in the world today—stand committed to the sustenance of the Jewish state. This it perceives not only as a political refuge for those who need it but also as a source of enduring meaning for Jews throughout the world. That commitment is not only rich in ambiguity and—let the truth be said—the potentiality for hypocrisy and self-deceit. It also is profound in its power to move people and to shape their program for themselves as Jews. And it is a source for the definition, too, of the character and content of the American version of Judaism. So, in all, the ideological work is not of negligible consequence.

Alas, it also is not easily done. To turn the nationalism represented by Zionism into an ethnic assertion, to speak of "the Jewish people" as a homeland, is to evade the fact of the Jewish state. It is a typical sleight of hand: to ignore the State of Israel and to traduce the simple assertions of all of Zionism, in all its forms, throughout its history. And yet what is the alternative? It is to speak of a Zionism which one cannot do. It is to construct a system by definition existentially remote from the locus of one's existence. Since Zionism is far more than a set of formulas and a scheme of evocative rhetoric, the issues are not readily resolved within the iron frame of social reality as contrasted to imaginative perception.

One surely may affirm the peoplehood of Israel, the Jewish people, without the territory of Zionism, outside the realm of politics altogether. One may deem the Jews to be a people, one people, and ignore the Land, the one and only Land of Judaism and of Israel, the people, for all its history. But this is not what we of the *golah* maintain; therein is the pain. American Jews affirm it all: the Land, the nation, the tingle down the spine, tears when they hear the song and see the flag. But they have another nearer land, another nation, the one they support and defend, and they sing its songs and with everyone else they salute (or, alas, sometimes burn) its flag. Once more the bone of emigration sticks in the craw. Again the matter of exile makes for choking. Zionism may be locative or utopian, not both.

But the metaphor of the State of Israel as our spiritual center is useless. It solves no problems. The basic objection is not the wrongness of the metaphor but its altogether too broad relevance. For, in truth, everyone everywhere is always in the center of the world—as he or she perceives the world. It is natural for Israelis to see themselves in the center of the Jewish world: it takes little for them to conclude they form the spiritual center. It is equally natural for American Jews to see the world from the American perspective. Any other would be not merely unnatural but distorting. So a metaphor of perception and vision proves useless. Instead of evoking a sense of its own self-evidence, justness, and rightness, it provokes awareness of dislocation. The locative metaphor denied, we try for a utopian one, a metaphor of time, which is universal. The locative metaphor is vertiginous for all but the center.

Yet there are ample grounds for a Zionist affirmation within the framework of a self-respecting American Judaism. Let me list them: First, the State of Israel stands as a source of pride to world Jewry, with our community as its head. Its accomplishments as a society and its capacity for social, cultural, and political greatness attest to the character of the whole Jewish people. If all Israel stands as pledges for one another, then the State of Israel is the rightful guarantor of our good name in the world.

Second, we perceive that, just as we need the State of Israel and a constant, close relationship with Israeli life, so the State of Israel and its social and cultural life benefit from the ties with American Jewry. The relationship is entirely mutual and wholly reciprocal. We are their equals, as they are ours, and we can accept no other definition of the relationship.

On the material side, let us not evade the fact that now and for some time to come, the State of Israel requires the support of the diaspora communities, American Jewry most of all. It simply cannot solely rely on its own resources for the development of its own society. Moreover, the State of Israel acts on behalf of the whole Jewish people in bringing to the homeland those Jews who want or need to go there. What happens to Jews in other lands must be subordinated to those in Israel; Israel must have priority in resources, commitment, and capacities. It is the only place. It is open. It regards each Jew as precious. It wants the Jews. But without our doing our share, the State of Israel cannot carry out the task.

Moreover, the State of Israel requires the political support of world Jewry in gaining a hearing for its cause and in winning steady support for its security. The realities of a world of superpowers are such that American

Jewry's presence and modest influence in its own country have to be regarded as nothing less than providential.

Thus, in a worldly way, we need the State of Israel for the benefit of our own community, and the Israelis need us for their interests as well. But that relationship does not exhaust the spiritual potential of either party. For world Jewry, in important ways, the State of Israel constitutes the spiritual center, just as Ahad Ha'Am and Mordecai Kaplan said a long time ago.

What are these ways? First, the State of Israel is the greatest Jewish educational resource at hand. For us it is a classroom in Jewish living and in living Judaism, a classroom without walls. There is the best place to learn the meaning of the Sabbath. There is the place to recover our roots in our own past, the past of the Hebrew Bible and the Talmud. If we make appropriate provision for our own educational requirements and not simply dump our young people on Israeli institutions lacking an understanding of their educational and social character, we may derive from the State of Israel educational benefits simply unavailable to any previous generation.

The State of Israel has become the spiritual center for world Jewry because it plays a decisive and central role in the Jewish mind and imagination, in shaping the Jewish identity, and in the revival of the Jewish spirit in the present, not only the past generation.

But in some important ways Zionism is not enough, for it is part, not the whole, of Judaism. The State of Israel cannot serve as American Jews' spiritual center. For being Jewish constitutes not merely a national, ethnic, cultural, and social experience. It also is meant to supply an orientation toward life, a mode of being human, a perspective on man, on history, on what it means to die and to live. And those aspects of being Jewish which pertain to the nature of human existence cannot be wholly separated from the particularities of everyday life: the actual, concrete situation in which one is Jewish.

Our perception of ourselves and of the world and the meaning of life begins in our own situation, and that is a complex one. For our lives are shaped by the experience of being Jewish and being something else, many other things. We are not wholly Jewish. Our values are derived from sources other than solely Jewish ones. One perception of life encompasses a society quite different from that of the State of Israel. Our search for abiding values takes place in a personal and cultural setting in important ways unlike that of the State of Israel. The life for which we seek meaning, for good or ill, is a life in the *golah*, a life in at least two civilizations—if not more than two.

We are marginal in our situation. The Israelis are at home in theirs. We are, in a measure, alien; they are never strangers. They perceive reality close at hand. Our perceptions are one stage removed from the center of things. For us the given is something to be criticized and elevated, for we do not take perceived reality at face value. For them things are very different. At the very center of our being is an experience unavailable to the Israeli.

American Judaism, a way of viewing the world and forming a way of life relevant to the distinctive existential condition of American Jews, is a system removed from participation in the world, a detached and noncathectic way of living in the world. This kind of Judaism does not mediate reality, interpreting and shaping a meaningful mode of human existence. It stands as a barrier between direct and personal participation in Judaic existence. The logically necessary conclusion of the matter is to contrast the material reality of the State of Israel with that condition of alienation which is normal, though which can never be normative, for the Jew of the *golah*. For the formation of the State of Israel is the greatest political event in the history of the Jewish people since the last coins of the 2nd Century B.C.E. which read, "Israel's freedom, year one," and "Israel's freedom, year two." Anyone who proposes to reflect on what it means to be a Jew, on the ideology of Jewish being and the theology of Judaism, has both to begin and to end with the reality and presence which are not ideology or theology but prior to both, definitive of the agendum of both. To me these statements are self-evidently true. They present facts.

As a Zionist of the *golah*, therefore, I do conceive that Zionism solved those Jewish problems which it addressed and claimed to be able to solve: assimilation and self-hatred. That is why I am a Zionist. And yet Zionism brought with its success intractable problems of ideology and even of theology. So Zionism constitutes a problem and a dilemma for Judaism. As a Judaist too I have to reckon with these painful matters; I cannot ignore them and I have no solution for them. So there are these two sides to the matter: the Jewish problem, solved by Zionism, and the Zionist problem, addressed to Judaism. Still, the last word is other than ideological. It is personal. But it is no less relevant to others.

The State of Israel, beyond all theories of Zionism and theologies of Judaism, confronts the contemporary Jew in all of its powerful, glorious reality: its frailty, imperfection, vast failure—thus its material humanity. American Judaism lives a life separated from reality by a veil. American Judaism offers a life constructed around symbols which invoke other times and other places, a *Heilsgeschichte* (sacred history) discontinuous with itself.

The concrete and unmediated everyday Jewish life of the Israeli Jew stands in contrast to the Jewish way of compromise and self-restraint, of small self-deceptions, petty pretense, and little achievements, of the Jews of America. American Judaism is founded on the living of life through the lives of other people. It accords the status of a remarkable, puzzling mode of existential being to that same frame of mind which brings to football games people who never exercise at all. With the recognition that, at its foundation,

American Judaism is the existential counterpart to a spectator sport, we reach the end of that argument beginning with the simple assertion of the commonality and humanity of that circumstance which, for Jews in this country (and for much of the world), produces Judaism of the American kind. Beyond this point we cannot go: the recognition that for American Judaism, existence comes mediated and masked. That is how people want things. Perhaps that is how they should be. I do not think that is how they have to be.

·VII·
Unease
in the
Promised Land

·23·
Unease in Zion: The New Israeli Exile

B. Z. Sobel

The Emigrés

The scene has by now become commonplace: long lines at the United States Embassy at Tel Aviv vying for both the hard-to-get immigrant visas or for the easier (but still difficult to obtain) tourist visas which can—as often as not—be finagled into a green card and ultimately, permanence in America. An advertisement in the Israeli press placed by a South African firm asking for 50 technicians is answered by some 1,500 job seekers. News reports about Israeli "wetbacks" wading the Rio Grande from Mexico into the United States, or sneaking across the Canadian border into Alaska and then flying on to Los Angeles on a domestic flight, are not uncommon. Much less common, but certainly shocking, are the occasional tales of Israeli "boat people"—young Israelis who jet to the Bahamas and then rent fishing boats for the trip to Miami, stepping ashore at the first convenient marina. Israeli neighborhoods are springing up in the world's major cities like Amsterdam, London, Munich, Frankfurt, Johannesburg, and, of course, New York, Los Angeles, and Montreal. Fictive marriages with citizens of various countries in order to get permanent residence or citizen status. Israeli doctors staffing, at times, full departments in foreign cities; Israeli engineers prominent in various industries; Israelis driving cabs, waiting tables, baking bread, and, in some cases, engaging in considerably less savory occupations. Israeli artists and musicians, *kibbutznikim*, and *moshavnikim*, from east and west, native and immigrant, religious and secular, educated and uneducated, army veterans and shirkers, rabid nationalists and peaceniks, academics and carpenters —all represented in the great movement outwards. A mere three-and-one-half decades after the establishment of the State of Israel following upon the greatest tragedy to befall the Jewish people in its history, the third Jewish commonwealth is challenged by the most prosaic and ironic of threats to its continued viability—a growing lack of will on the part of tens of thousands of its citizens to stay within it. Furthermore, and at a time when almost any Jew in almost any land can, if he chooses, come home and plight his troth with the Jewish people in its own land, a mere 20 percent have so opted.

As the Yiddish adage has it "Exile is bitter." But if recent immigration and emigration figures and trends for Israel provide any valid indication, then exile is at worst bittersweet and clearly the preferred mode of the vast majority of the world's Jews. Not only has Israel thus far failed to spark any significant voluntary move of Jews to its shores, but something of the reverse seems to be gaining ground with thousands of Israelis opting for a new exile and an almost innocent—sometimes it appears triumphant—return to the *galut*.

A recent news item quoted an Israeli government statistician to the effect that for the past two years emigrants have outnumbered immigrants to the Jewish state. Immigration figures are (with the possible exception of those of 1953) the lowest in the country's history—about 11,000 were expected last year—while emigration is at around the 20,000 mark. Somber as these figures might be, they can be viewed as even more so when one realizes that while the figures for immigration are more or less correct, those reflecting emigration are probably underreported. While accurate figures are difficult, if not impossible, to attain with respect to emigration, all sources agree that a minimum of 300,000 Israelis have left since 1948. The above figure is government supplied; independent estimates range from a low of 400,000 to the frightening and seemingly absurd figure of 700,000. But whatever the true numerical dimensions of the phenomenon, there does exist widespread agreement among observers that the trend is upwards and likely to increase rather than decrease.

WHY ARE THEY LEAVING?

One is constrained to ask very simply at this point: why? What has happened which can explain not only the reluctance of Jews in the *galut* to come but also the apparent lack of reluctance of so many already in Israel and part of Israel to leave? Has A. B. Yehoshua struck a resounding chord of historical and sociological truth when he asserts of the *golah* that, "We foisted it upon ourselves. It should be regarded not as an accident or misfortune, but as a deep-reaching national perversion." Is the phenomenon to be explained perhaps along less existential, less cosmic lines bearing less relatedness to "national perversion" than to such here-and-now pragmatic, measurable, easily definable, and totally understandable factors as the constant physical threat to their existence under which Israelis live, an unpromising economic situation, an absence of career possibilities, reserve duty, high taxation, an inflexible and capricious bureaucracy, and so on? I would aver that even if the thrust of evidence suggests the centrality of all or some of these pragmatic variables, the serious question posed by Yehoshua retains its efficacy. If perhaps not "perversion," then at the very least a deep-seated peculiarity or idiosyncrasy which conditionally determines collective roots and national existence is deserving of exploration, and Yehoshua's phrasing becomes both felicitous and controlled. That is to say, if indeed thousands of Israelis are leaving because of this or that lack or failure of the national enterprise; if thousands weigh their commitments on a scale of measurable devices moving themselves to the left or the right, to staying or leaving based on ephemeral variables, does this not suggest a most peculiar relatedness to normal national existence?

One must keep in mind that the thousands who are leaving Israel now are not penniless emigrants, displaced rural peasantry, an exploited proletariat, a frightened oppressed minority seeking freedom to live its own life and culture according to its own lights. The overwhelming proportion of Israelis leaving the country are at the very least literate, in a significant proportion of cases professionals of one kind or another, and if not wealthy, certainly far from the penniless prototype Jewish immigrant of the somewhat lachrymose and romantic image of the 19th Century. I would, with respect to this latter point, venture a guess and suggest that at least in the case of the United States, the Israelis presently arriving represent the most gilded of immigrant groups to reach American shores in this century. Unlike the Greeks or Italians, the Israeli arrives not from the depressed Peloponnesus or the grinding poverty of southern Italy but from all parts of the country, all walks of life, all economic strata and with savings resulting from the sale of an apartment or an automobile in Israel's overcharged and inflationary economy. Not only are the majority of emigrating Israelis not escaping personal economic distress of any objectively serious dimensions, but they are, in addition, leaving a flourishing country with a high western standard of living; a place where at least on the material plane, a certain ease in Zion has been achieved. Visitors to the country are constantly amazed at the number of autos clogging Israeli roads, the stylish dress of the women, the plethora of banks in every nook and cranny, the stereo shops, the color TVs, the phenomenon of one-half million Israelis going abroad for summer vacations, the "villa" sections growing now even in development towns like Ma'alot and Carmiel. One notes, either with dismay or satisfaction, depending on one's view of the enterprise, the vigor demonstrated by the Israeli Stock Exchange, the high level of personal saving, the existence of diversified and sophisticated portfolios, the "instant" million-aires whose wealth springs from everything from admitted commercial and technical wizardry to land speculation. Opportunity exists, clearly. The goods of this life can be attained in Zion! No Sicily, no Peloponnesus this.

Thus we are faced with something of a dilemma, a conundrum; a land of milk and honey, a country with a constantly growing and expanding economy, a fine climate, a free political atmosphere; a country still enjoying the patina of romance engendered by its remarkable rebirth, astounding growth, breathtaking victories in war; the only country which both in actuality and potential can provide the sustaining valence for the development of rooted Jewish culture—witnessing instead of an influx of tens of thousands of Jews from the four corners of the earth, an outflow of tens of thousands *to* the four corners of the earth.

I would suggest the following modest formulations for exploration:

1. While the material dimension in Israel is comparatively satisfactory, it does not or cannot answer the expectations of many thousands of its citizens who aspire to more. Thus the prime factor underlying emigration is economic in nature.

2. The quality of life in Israel (and by this I refer to everything from the threat of war to an intrusive bureaucracy) is so lacking when compared to other Western lands as to readily loosen ties to the mother country giving rise to emigration. Or to turn it about—the quality of life in other lands is perceived as so far and away superior to what is presently available in Israel as to exercise an unparalleled attractiveness.

3. The persistence of some deep-rooted, seemingly intractable elements in Jewish history and culture which persistently work to undermine developments leading to autonomy and an independent national life.

Economics

There can be little doubt that the economic element, the desire to earn more, buy more, have more, runs like a red thread through the current (and past) emigration wave. Jews have never been marked by undue abstemiousness in the material vein (perhaps no people are so noted); and Israel has, since the early 1960s, followed an upwardly curving line of expectations, fueled by a high level of intense economic development and no little achievement. From a scant 20 years ago when a two-and-one-half room apartment, one week a year at the seashore, and sufficient food on the table (with some luxuries like a radio and a refrigerator) represented the norm of expectation and hopes, we have entered the promised land of luxury flats, trips abroad, stock options, fine automobiles, and the like. Needless to add, most Israelis are not rich, as most Americans are not rich, but the revolution in expectations is relatively fresh in Israel and the resulting growth in appetite and panic at missing out or being left behind is palpable. Observers, friendly and otherwise, have taken note of the seemingly rampant materialism in Israel, contrasting this development with the very recent and recallable past when Israel was (rightly or wrongly) held up as an example of puritan, indeed spartan, egalitarianism. "Making it" in terms of goods and wealth is not easy in contemporary Israel. The possibilities, realistically as well as mythically, are more evident and indeed more probable in foreign parts—especially in places like the United States, Canada, and South Africa. But how is one to explain the thousands of Israelis who leave with tens of thousands of dollars resulting from the sale of their apartments and cars only to start up again in a new and, for most, strange environment abroad? A large proportion of those leaving have "made it"—at least in Israeli terms. Does greed among us know no bounds? Are we (or more correctly are many among us) more committed to money and goods than to Zion? Are Jews a rare breed readily willing to trade roots for cash? I don't think the evidence available supports the supposition.

In dozens of interviews with departing emigrants carried out during the latter part of 1981 and the early months of 1982, I was repeatedly struck by the following:

1. Most emigrants would leave even if by so doing they do not significantly improve their economic situation. Most, however, said they wouldn't if it meant lowering it.

2. Most (at least of those who emigrated formally and officially as opposed to those who use circuitous routes) own apartments, appliances, autos, and have well-paying jobs. My estimate is that disposable property ranges between $40,000 and $50,000 for a significant proportion of emigrants.

3. Failure to put aside enough cash for an apartment or for luxuries motivates only a small minority to emigrate and is not even extensively resorted to as a legitimatizing device.

4. Joblessness is not a significant factor, although lack of job satisfaction might be.

5. Emigrants are willing, at least temporarily, to fill any job abroad though not in Israel—the exception being sanitary workers.

The Elusive Grail

I do not suggest that a dream of affluence does not play some role among most emigrants. It does! But, if the evidence available to me suggests anything, it is that the matter is infinitely more complex, involving a gnawing dissatisfaction of a more general kind. Government leaders and establishment figures in Israel would prefer to explain the departure of so many thousands as resulting from material lust alone, thus avoiding blame and culpability. How after all, can we compete with America? they ask. But I am convinced that it is a kind of floating, almost aimless seeking of an elusive and hard to define grail rather than greed with which we are dealing here.

Not all Israelis who leave achieve wealth abroad. Most probably don't, and yet they stay abroad and do not and will not return, no matter what blandishments are extended. Why? Do Israelis not feel love for their mother-land, their language, the familiar landscapes of their youth and young adulthood? The evidence suggests, if anything, powerful and potent attach-ments to all of these and yet they do not return.

The suggestion has been made (with a dollop of wistfulness) that they are ashamed to come home nonmillionaires and thus continue to lurk in the fleshpots until the proverbial nest egg is sufficiently larded to avoid shame. Perhaps! I am more persuaded by two additional and unrelated thoughts: (1) The chimera of opportunity is knocking more readily abroad than at home—even though it tarries—and thus must be waited out; and (2) not-withstanding the elusiveness of success, it's just easier to live outside of Israel.

The Endless Workday

Repeatedly one hears it said in Israel (and not only by those who leave or who are contemplating departure) that life is difficult in the country. One hears this from academics who claim an inability to write at home, from housewives who assert that the day is never done, from workers who suggest that they do nothing but work, leaving little time for leisure or other activities. When pressed for an explanation, one is told it has something to do with a six-day week, the need to work at more than one job to make ends meet, the relative absence of such household machinery as dryers or dish-washers, and so on. On a purely objective plane, these assertions are weakened by the fact that the workday is not particularly long; Israel in effect works a five-and-one-half-day week (and perhaps less); religious and national holidays do not lag behind any viewable western norm; washing machines, mixers, gas or electric stoves, and vacuum cleaners are widely owned.

There exists, notwithstanding, this perceived notion that the workday never ends, and I would assert that this results from a climate of "nudgerie" which seems to permeate the atmosphere. Shops are not open at hours convenient to the buying public, government and other offices are not efficient or, on the whole, marked by a climate of civility, public discipline is low, and suspicion of one's neighbors' intentions seems somehow pervasive. This last comment becomes palpable on viewing Israelis queued-up, where one notices that not a millimeter of separation is allowed to intrude between queuers; this is not for any reasons of desired intimacy but simply for lack of trust that an inch will not develop into an opening for line jumping.

I don't know if a relaxed society exists, and I am certainly unconvinced of its desirability, but I *am* certain that Israel is not an exemplar of the type. There is indeed an edginess abroad in the society; tempers flare, and verbal violence is rampant. A large proportion of those interviewed for my study, upon which this chapter is based, have been abroad, or were born or raised abroad, and in almost all cases reference is made to the fact that "people are nicer in *chutz la'aretz*. Strangers wish you a good day as they make change or pass you on the street, whereas at home you can consider yourself fortunate to receive minimally civil treatment. One woman interviewed, when asked why she was about to take the drastic step of emigration laughed almost hysterically, and shouted

> Why? Why? Because over there (in the United States) I am a child of God, a child of God. I am treated like a human being wherever I go. I am not shouted at or abused. I am not automatically suspect. Washerwomen in the supermarket don't command me to watch my step. Why?

Another respondent (an immigrant from the United States who had been in Israel for 12 years) broke down and wept, repeating over and over the word "garbage"—"People here are garbage, garbage. They're hateful. I hate this place." When asked to explain, a long list of minor cruelties—more lapses of good taste than anything more evil—were adduced.

Repeatedly, in the case of respondent after respondent, life in Israel was invidiously compared with life abroad. People are politer over there, merchants are more honest over there, government is more benign over there; the weather is better, the quality of goods higher, the opportunities wider, and so on.

One can justifiably assert that these responses reflect a legitimizing device for what is essentially viewed as an illegitimate or questionable act. One must explain one's own side of the matter. I am not deserting the ship; the ship has failed me.

Decisions to Leave

There exists scant doubt that this legitimizing factor is present. But I am equally convinced that a pre-emigration set of perceptions and feelings is present here which has played a role in the decision to leave. Thirty-five years after the establishment of the state, there exists a wide and deep pool of dissatisfaction with the nature of what has been wrought. And while tangibles like high taxes, reserve duty, the threat of war, the high cost of housing, the absence of civility all play a role, there is, in addition, a more inchoate, less tangible, less apprehendable substratum of dissatisfaction which, in the long run, must be viewed as infinitely more troubling than those factors already alluded to.

There is unease in Zion and its elements are varied. Life in Israel, for many, presents a sense of being "locked in," of not having an adequate scope of free choice. This ranges from one's body (army service, war) to government (unresponsiveness) to job choice (limited). Israel to thousands of its citizens is a blocked society. Israel is not an undeveloped or rural society, and its people are not reflective of an emerging peasantry. But the constraints noted above are those associated with an underdeveloped or even authoritarian structure, while the myths and expectations are otherwise.

DISAPPOINTMENT

For a good proportion of the new emigrants disappointment with Israel seems so total as to raise questions with respect as to whether any normal society would satisfy them. One might posit the thought that a putative theme of the classical Zionist design—normalcy—does not, in fact, represent a deep commitment for many. Not a "city on a hill" but "the city of God" has been sought and found absent or difficult to achieve. We are, it would appear, what we have been; a people comprised of reluctant Messianists reflecting a continued and debilitating struggle between what is and what can be, between worship of the golden calf and the explosive shout of *Naaseh V'Nishma*, between the temporal, here-and-now relativities of normal existence and an illusive perfectability. In this sense, Israel is an impossible undertaking. It is a conditional homeland where the very nature of the term homeland rejects conditionality. It is perhaps, as one observer noted, ultimately a question of grammar; it all revolves around "if." "If" Israel is this, that, or the other thing, "if" conditions are good and propitious, "if" we are true, good, and beautiful—I will stay. If not—I will go elsewhere.

HISTORICAL PERSPECTIVE

Alternatively, however, one may not lose sight of the existence of some more tangible, more historically rooted aspects underpinning the new Exile. There exist decided sociological limits to the length of time wherein collective enthusiasms or ideal visions can be maintained in a central societal position. While the simple dream of national revival and the excitement of creating a state and society can sustain for perhaps one generation—if that long—it will not suffice much beyond. Deep rootedness and binding ties to place are not (in contrast to our naive expectations) created overnight. When a collective ideal is buffeted by a sense of smashed dreams, broken promises, false leaders, a moral vacuum, the tenuous and fragile ties which bind unravel. It would appear that 35 years of statehood are both too much and not enough: too long for the dream to remain untainted and too short for expanding and deepening roots.

Especially, and not only for Israel, is this the case for nations reaching independence at this particular juncture of world history, when communications are dominated by television and the not unconnected Americanization of the planet. The global-village theme suggests nothing if not interchange-ability—why here rather than there—and the web of expectations is spun in Hollywood and on Madison Avenue.

Thus, a constantly recurring emotion emerging in the responses of emi-grants is "What difference does it make where I live? I am just as much an Israeli in New York as in Tel Aviv." This interesting conclusion is further supported by the evidence that at least in the case of Israeli emigrants to the United States a certain critical mass has been achieved. With hundreds of thousands of Israelis living in the United States, a satisfying degree of Israeliness—language, foods, friendships, and family links—has indeed be-come a movable and interchangeable feast sustaining those already here and beckoning others to follow.

And they will follow! Not because Israel is extraordinary, but rather because it has become, in the consciousness of so many, ordinary and hence lacking in definition. Thus, choosing to live elsewhere is no longer desertion, and certainly not a crime. Earlier emigrants were wont to explain themselves, to justify, to assert undying fealty to the dream, to swear an early return home. This justifying tendency has declined precipitously and it is increas-ingly acceptable to emigrate and leave it at that. Indeed, there are some discomforting signs that not emigrating or at least going abroad to live for a period of time suggests a certain lack of vigor or ambition among the stay-at-homes.

Underpinning this new attitude toward leaving is a growing sense among Israelis of completion or closure in terms of the creative aspects of state building or Zionism. A corollary is the breaking down of a feeling that one must "just hang in" when in fact the state is built, Zionism is realized, and the country is more or less secure. The time seems propitious to tend to one's own garden, to pursue individual paths to fulfillment, and this, it would appear, is for tens of thousands of Israelis best achievable or solely achievable in the "world" rather than in Zion.

This seems to reflect a disturbing skein of continuity with the Jewish past. We are if not rootless (who is to say that roots are so easily defined as to be circumscribed within a land or a society alone), then certainly with thinner ties to the temporal Zion of this earth than we were willing to admit. The small proportion of the Jewish people who returned to Zion can be said to have done so (largely) kicking and screaming, while the departure from Zion is taking place, seemingly, with ease and almost lightly. Lest this be dismissed as idle subjectivity it should be noted that for significant numbers of Israelis Israel represented a way-station, a point of interrupted migration rather than a final goal. Thousands arrived in the early years of the state more as a result of lack of opportunity to go elsewhere than out of passion for the cessation of exile. One might, therefore, see in the new departure a move toward completion of an essentially interrupted process, rather than an out-of-the-blue response to suddenly changed objective or ideational circumstances. In some cases, it is the emigrant who is himself continuing on. In other instances, it is the children who are completing the process.

Exile versus Redemption

Do we prefer exile to redemption? We are probably unsure as to which is which, and in any event we seem to need the dispersal as a sort of antidote to the seemingly unbearable intensity of our group existence. We seem to desire marginality in preference to autonomy, other lands in preference to our own.

But if this is perverse, perhaps we Jews are not alone in our perversity. I am fascinated—if not solaced—by the appended quote from the journal of John Winthrop written in the middle of the 17th Century and with reference to non-Jews—albeit a people with a sense of constituting the "new Israel."

[September 22, 1642] The sudden fall of land and cattle, and the scarcity of foreign commodities, and money, etc., with the thin access of people from England, put many into an unsettled frame of spirit, so as they concluded there would be no subsisting here, and accordingly they began to hasten away, some to the West Indies, others to the Dutch, at Long Island, etc., (for the governor there invited them by fair offers,) and others back for England. . . .

. . . . They fled for fear of what, and many of them fell into it, even to extremity, as if they had hastened into the misery which they feared and fled from, besides the depriving themselves of the ordinances and church fellowship, and those civil liberties which they enjoyed here; whereas, such as staid in their places, kept their peace and ease, and enjoyed still the blessing of the ordinances, and never tasted of those troubles and miseries, which they heard to have befallen those who departed. Much disputation there was about liberty of removing for outward advantages, and all ways were sought for an open door to get out at; but it is to be feared many crept out at a broken wall. For such as come together into a wilderness, where are nothing but wild beasts and beastlike men, and there confederate together in civil and church estate, whereby they do, implicitly at least, bind themselves to support each other, and all of them that society, whether civil or sacred, whereof they are members, how they can break from this without free consent, is hard to find, so as may satisfy a tender or good conscience in time of trial. Ask thy conscience, if thou wouldst have plucked up thy stakes, and brought thy family 3,000 miles, if thou hadst expected that all, or most, would have forsaken thee there. Ask again, what liberty thou has towards others, which thou likest not to allow others towards thyself; for if one may go, another may, and so the greater part, and so church and commonwealth may be left destitute in a wilderness, exposed to misery and reproach, and all for thy ease and pleasure, whereas these all, being now thy brethren, as near to thee as the Israelites were to

Moses, it were much safer for thee, after his example, to choose rather to suffer affliction with thy brethren than to enlarge thy ease and pleasure by furthering the occasion of their ruin. . . .[1]

The parallels are apt if not exact: the language is familiar, the behaviors known. Would that the outcome be similarly fortuitous!

Notes

1. J. K. Hosner, (Ed.), *John Winthrop's Journal*. New York: Scribners, 1908.

·24·
Israel:
The New Diaspora

William Freedman

Defining Exile

As defined by the *Oxford Universal Dictionary*, exile is "enforced removal from one's native land according to an edict or sentence; banishment also, prolonged voluntary absence from one's native land." Clearly the first part of the definition is not applicable to us. The diaspora Jew has not been removed by force from his native land. The edicts or sentences, broadcast in very different tones, make a powerful appeal for his immigration, his *aliyah*, for his return to the Land of Israel. The edict or sentence that keeps him away, that holds him in such countries as the United States or Canada, Argentina, France, or Britain comes from within. It is a question not of force, but of choice. The exile is voluntary, which takes us to the latter part of the definition where we encounter the term "native land." Is Israel truly the Jew's native land? It is the land of his ancestors, but how far back does one go with such genealogies? How deep does one follow the roots of the ancestral tree? Russia too is the land of my ancestors, Lithuania and Latvia to be more precise. France is the native land of more English than will hear of it. And who is to say where my people were before they came to what is now Israel, Judea, or Palestine?

All this, in a sense, is a lexicographical quibble and more entertaining as such than it is profitable as an object of inquiry. But in another sense it is profoundly pertinent when we address the question, under whatever heading, of the Jew's relationship to Israel, his sense of belonging, permanence, or home. It raises the critical issue of arbitrariness or, more precisely, choice as a crucial determinant of native land. One can establish roots, stop and remain almost anywhere one likes for as long as one pleases. There is no irrefragable definition of "native land," neither for the Jew in particular, nor in a general context. "Native," of course, comes from the Latin *nativus*, "born," and from that point of view the only self-exiled diaspora Jews are the native Israelis who have left Israel for the sweeter climes of Los Angeles or the taxi routes of New York City. Nearly all of the ten million other Jews who live outside of Israel were born in the diaspora. According to this criterion, Israel is not their native land and they therefore cannot be exiled from it.

Nevertheless, for more reasons than we can analyze or assess here, they may consider it their home, even in some sense their native land. The significant point is the element of choice, not in some natural, biological, or self-evident sense, but in regard to feelings, attitudes, preferences, and beliefs. The motivations that keep at least a few non-Israeli Jews in the diaspora, and that have sent many native-born Israelis to it, are not as apparent or as susceptible to easy dismissal as some would like to think. It is deceptively simplistic and convenient to claim that they all opt for the easy life by remaining in Boston, Sydney, or San Francisco. How disturbing, and therefore unthinkable, that something else may hold or pull or drive! Perhaps it is a question of values.

VALUES

Having said this, I have kicked the sentimental tripwire, uttered the giveaway term. "Values" is the secret word, and the one that wins few prizes and much scorn these days. I even wish to speak at some length of what it means, both to myself and in relation to the question of exile and of home. I refer less to the concept of home, than to the *sense* of home, for once again what matters, I believe, is not the *numina* only authors of flyers and tracts seem to experience directly, but the phenomena we all live with, our shifting but nonetheless determinant and undeniable sense of things.

The question for the modern Jew in the diaspora as we know it is not a question of exile, for he has not been exiled. Unless he is an Israeli, he has probably not even exiled himself from the land of his forefathers' dreams. He is simply, or not so simply, *not there*. The question is one of home, for exiled or not, he may be looking for a home, may not feel at home in the place he calls home, may regard that beautiful, homely, distant land as home, and yet not be there. The real question, it would seem, is not "what is exile for the Jew?" or "can living in exile be legitimate?" but "what is home for the Jew?" or "can living away from home or one's sense of what is home be legitimatized?"

DEFINING HOME

I will return to the question of exile, but we have some basic discrepancies to deal with. The same dictionary, after running through the more obvious definitions—dwelling place, abode, one's own home, etcetera—arrives here: "A place, region, or state to which one properly belongs, in which one's affections center, or where one finds rest, refuge, or satisfaction. One's own country, one's native land; the place where one's ancestors dwelt." Which will it be? When the Jew living, let us say, in Odessa, says, "Israel is my home," what does he mean? The place where he properly belongs? The place where his affections center? The place where he imagines he will find refuge and satisfaction? Or the place where his ancestors dwelt? If he comes to Israel and discovers, as some have, that he is not entirely welcome there, that his immigrant benefits are resented, that the people are not united as he had believed, that they are not idealistically committed to the ingathering of the people or to one another or to the realization of goals or principles that are important to him, will he continue to regard his newfound land as home? That depends, of course, on which definition of home is the most fundamental to him. It is still, to be sure, the land of his ancestors—at least of the few oldest he can trace or posit. But will he find rest or refuge or satisfaction here? Will this remain the locus of his affections? Will he feel, indefinitely, that this is where he properly belongs?

My own belief is that he will not, and that this, not ancestry, is critical. The question, in other words, for me at least, is not where were my ancestors born? More important is the question, where do I properly belong? And the answer to that, I believe, hinges on the related questions: Where do my affections lie? Where will I find rest, refuge, or satisfactions of a very basic, often intangible kind?

The answers to these questions are, in turn, contingent on many things— on economic and cultural factors, on whether one can make a decent and satisfying living in that place, on whether one can identify with, comfortably adopt, or as comfortably ignore the identifying traits of folk culture: the way natives dress and speak, the foods they eat, the things they know and care about, the subjects of their jokes and conversations, the way they ask the time or board a bus, offer or decline information. These answers are also functions of shared or unshared values—and again we speak of perceptions here, and absolutes. They are determined or influenced by what one believes in and cares about, by what one is ready to do and the limits which he will not transgress; by how one regards the rights of others and how he settles conflicts between those and his own; by his concern or indifference for friends and strangers, foreigners and enemies. Where he probably belongs, in short, is in large measure a function of what he regards as good and evil, permissible and impermissible, right and wrong.

What is a Jew?

Again I leave myself open. I am one of those bleeding hearts, those soft-headed liberals, those ethical idealists who believe such values are somehow connected with their Jewishness. In a recent, handsomely written and provocative book, Hillel Halkin, a man I know and like and respect, reads the "obsession with social justice and a passion for ideas" out of the role of Judaism. "Ethical idealism and the philosophical mind, as Jewish traditions indeed," he fairly spits, "as if these were the distinguishing marks of historic Jewish existence rather than the very symptoms of its degradation in modern times!"[1] He writes these lines in disdainful response to a friend, real or imaginary, who claims he will not come to live in Israel because he believes (a) that these are eminently Jewish virtues, and (b) that they are both more prevalent and more easily cultivated in the diaspora than in Israel. Halkin concedes the latter point as though he has conceded nothing—nothing because he refutes the former. It is no problem for him to show contempt for such values because they are not, as so many of us falsely believe, historic Jewish virtues at all, but 19th Century German Enlightenment wallpaper slapped over the cracks and gaping holes of orthodoxy.

I will not enter the historic dispute. Let us concede the possibility that for every ancient Jewish text expressing compassion for the enemies of the Jewish people, one may cite ten exulting in their suffering and destruction. Let us concede that in "the Jewish view," that is, the ancient, tribal, or classically Orthodox Jewish view, "social justice in the world is anything but the proper worry of a Jew."[2] Let us concede too that the idea arises, or at least gains currency, with the mid-19th Century German Reform movement. And then let us notice that Zionism too, the basis for the reestablishment of a Jewish state in Palestine, arises at approximately that same time and largely in response to the same secular impulses that generated that movement.

> In all the founders of modern Zionism, there appears again and again the same phenomenon: they did not come from a traditional, religious background. They were all products of European education, imbued with the current ideas of the European intelligentsia. Their plight was neither economic nor religious. . . . Those Jews who were seeking mere survival and economic security emigrated to America in the wake of pogroms and pauperization. Those who, on the other hand, went to Palestine were seeking self-determination, identity liberation within the terms of post-1789 European culture and their culture and their own newly awakened self-consciousness.[3]

The sense of the restored homeland and what it might or should be like, in other words, is enlivened, animated, even determined by these "symptoms of modern degradation."

Let us add to that a touch of evolutionary relativism. Halkin is reluctant to generalize about *the* Jewish view, knows it is a selection, and yet he himself does. He makes his own selection because he feels comfortable with it, and because it is what he can or chooses to live with, and because (less important, I prefer to believe) it serves his argument. It helps him convince his American Jewish friend that one need not be Gentile to be indifferent to humane values or social justice. A Jew is still a Jew, if he can divorce himself from such nonsense. Granted he is more likely to be such a Jew in Israel than in the diaspora. Given Israel's military and economic pressures and the dreadful realities of its perpetual near-extinction, he is less likely to have time, mind, or heart for such *goyishe* or modernist luxuries. Since these have nothing to do with Judaism per se, they are irrelevant to the question of where the committed Jew is truly at home.

It is, you see, a matter exclusively of ancestry—the most distant one can find. The Jew at bottom, where his roots and definition lie, is an Old Testament Jew, a medieval Jew, a patriarch, a tribal warrior, a monotheist in the desert. I sound sarcastic, but I do not mean to. It is only because I am so saddened by this view. I am an Israeli myself, born in Newark, New Jersey 29 years before I came to live in Israel just after the Six-Day War in 1967. I am saddened and angered, because this view is not by any means Halkin's alone. He wears it well, better than many, I dare guess, because he was born in the diaspora, is afflicted by an overlay of that same ethical idealism he drums out of Judaism.

I reject the drumroll and wish to sound my own. I say this: that indeed is one kind of Jew and one conception of Judaism, but it is neither my own nor that of many of my fellow Jews. This is largely because the Jew has come to recognize that only where liberal codes of justice have prevailed can the Jew himself survive and, with luck, flourish. "Freedom and social concern," as Balfour Brickner observes, "are values as Jewish as the Jewish belief in God. When any aspect of freedom is threatened, Jews have an obligation to protest as Jews. Nothing could be more Jewishly elemental than this. Jews, thank God, still seem to feel this way."[4] "Social liberalism," adds Irving Howe in his contribution to the same symposium on Liberalism and the Jews, "has been defined as the 'secular religion' of many American Jews, the precious salvage from their immigrant and East European heritage, the embodied value of a major segment of Jewish experience."[5] And finally, as Neal Kozodoy, the executive editor of proudly illiberal *Commentary* magazine, acknowledges,

> . . . the essence of the liberal social doctrine, which amounts to charity rationalized, is coincident in every important respect with the oldest and deepest principles of Jewish communal life. So instinctive and reflexive, by now, is the Jewish identification with this ideal of social obligation, so ingrained in habits of action and attitudes of mind, so in tune with long-sanctioned impulses and religious precept, that most Jews today would be hard pressed even to conceive of any other model of civic virtue than the model bodied forth by the catechism of liberal reform . . .[6]

The facet of Judaism to which Halkin has recourse may be hoarier. The other may come later, may come in part to paper over cracks in the shaky facade of historic Judaism. It too has its roots in orthodoxy and tradition. If it is wallpaper, the wallpaper has stuck. It is now the pattern on these walls. It is how I recognize these rooms and quite frankly it is how I like them. It is with this I feel at home, not with the harsh glaring yellow of the desert walls beneath. One cannot stop the development of Judaism where he pleases and say, "This is where it ends, here the corruption and the artifice begin." Or rather, one can do that, but only for himself, not for others. He can say what it means for him to be a Jew. But he cannot do it for me. He cannot do it for Judaism.

One may not be able to determine for himself the defining criteria of his own Jewishness. In Israel the Orthodox rabbinate relieves us of the burden. Elsewhere Gentiles often do, sometimes at far greater cost. But we can choose for ourselves the strain of Jewishness to which we belong. Or rather, we cannot do that either. The distinction is flaccid, but you will know what I mean and we will avoid a muddy dip into existential philosophy if I simply say our natures choose it for us.

One branch of Jewishness may be older, but neither is "more Jewish" than the other. Neither has an inherently greater claim on us. The kind of Jews we are, in turn, will determine where we feel at home, will determine in fact what *is* home; for unlike the label "Jew," "home" does not stick to us. It is not a matter of maternal lineage or persecution. Home, as the definition says, is not only our native land or the place where our ancestors dwelt, but where we properly belong. And while others may tell us where we do not properly belong, whatever our naive delusions, no one may do the contrary; no one may tell us that despite the alienation of our affections, despite the deprivation of rest, refuge, and satisfaction, this is where we properly belong, that this is home.

Israeli Emigration

For me and other Jews like me, that sense of home is complex. It depends on more than shared ancestry. It depends on a sense of shared values, a sense of being cared about, welcomed and wanted, a sense of being accepted as a member, a dweller in this home even when those values are different, a sense, nonetheless, that those values, if not identical, are basically reconcilable. The clear and present danger in Israel today—I write this in the summer and fall of 1981, just after the most corrosive election campaign in Israel's history—is that for many of Israel's Jews, *sabras* and immigrants alike, that land may cease to feel like home, may already have begun to do so. The most transparent manifestation of this change is the growing exodus from the state, typically among native-born *Ashkenazis*, the increasing dropout rate of Russian emigrants, and the decline to near zero of western immigration. Self-exile from the Land of Israel is a more complicated matter than it is often made to seem. Economic reasons are usually cited, the greater ease with which one finds suitable work and comfortably supports his family in the USA (that is the usual destination) than in Israel. According to a current survey, 88 percent in the *yordim* questioned reported that their income in the US was adequate to most of their needs. Only about one-third said the same of the income they had earned before leaving Israel. Comforting as it may be to ascribe the growing exodus exclusively to insurmountable economic disparities, there is more to the departure than this.

> When ideology was more central to people's lives, they were less bothered by the material shortcomings of Israeli society. With the decline of ideology, it has become permissible for Israelis both to question the necessity of continuous belt-tightening and to acknowledge a more self-centered concern with such things as advancing their careers, bettering their standard of living, providing for their families, and so forth. Once these concerns are acknowledged—and legitimated—the decision to go elsewhere in search of greener pastures becomes more than logical.[7]

CHANGING VALUES AND IMAGES

The reason for the rise in emigration may be in large part economic, but in no small measure it is a matter of changing values. The problem of contemporary Israel—certainly one problem—is the justification and solidification of the Zionist vision of Israel as a homeland for all Jews, at least for those who wish to come. The problem, I believe, will never be adequately dealt with, let alone solved, as long as the causes of declining immigration and rising emigration are comfortably described as economic. Jews leave Israel for many reasons, economics high among them. One of those reasons is also an explanation for why other Jews do not come, and it goes beyond a mere decline in ideology. The moral image the nation has begun to project—as an occupying power determined to cement its occupation: as an increasingly iron-fisted occupying force (though there have been recent efforts to soften this hand); as a fierce avenger diving to the moral level of its attackers; as an increasingly divided nation of bitterly opposed and frequently aroused factions; as an increasingly antidemocratic populace headed by an increasingly autocratic and theocratic government—is unattractive, even repugnant, to some.

This is not to say anything special about this much maligned nation and its people. Only that its own specialness begins to erode. This is not to say that Israel is worse than other nations, certainly not than its enemies. For in many ways Israel remains a far more humane and vastly more democratic society than that of the nations and peoples who surround and threaten it. It is only to say that we have begun to resemble them too much. There has been a cry in Israel for many years that the burden of being Chosen People is too onerous, that the weight of even the attempt at ethical superiority is too heavy, and that we would be happily relieved of it. "Let Denmark carry it for a while," was a remark one often heard, spoken only partly in irony, several years ago. "Let the Canadians be the Chosen People for a while." This is all very arcane so long as one speaks of concepts such as a divinely Chosen People. It is all very witty so long as one speaks wearily and as much in jest as in frustration. It becomes very disturbing, at least to me, when it begins to become a reality, when we do indeed sink to the condition of the overwhelming majority of the world's nations.

I hope it is evident: there is something proud, though I hope not arrogant, in my conception of Jewishness, in my view of Jewish history and values, in my understanding of Zionism, and in my sense of what Israel has been and may yet be; I am the kind of Jew who still points with a kind of possessive pride at Einstein, Freud and company, at the disproportionate number of Jewish conductors, writers, and first violins; and at the traditional Jewish identification with social causes and social reform; and at the general tenor of Israel's history from its inception to the Six-Day War. Hillel Halkin, in the book discussed, closes his argument with an imaginative analogy between the Jewish people and the koala bear. The point of the comparison is that Jewish survival is not a matter of the preservation of specialness or greatness, not a matter of the persistence of certain ethical norms or laudable achievements, but a simple matter of biological continuity. Just as the koala bear has a right to live and climb eucalyptus trees and feed on their leaves, so we, the Jewish people, have an equivalent right to live in our own national forest and to nibble our kosher, or even our unkosher meats. There is nothing particularly admirable or commendable about the history or habits of the koala. They are simply and uniquely his, and he is entitled to exist no less than are other creatures—the Dutch, the Pakistanis, or the Sioux—to perpetuity.

The analogy is charming and valid on its face, but it settles for too little. Its principal appeal is to those who do not or will not mind becoming koalas, though I had thought we were a little more ambitious than that, that we had achieved and striven for a little more. We by no means forfeit our right to survival when we begin to imitate and duplicate the behavior of others—no more than Iraq, Syria, Libya, or a hundred other equally unadmirable nations have forfeited theirs by carrying on a long and bleak tradition. But does that mean we are obliged or content to ask so little of ourselves? The raven too has a right to protection and perpetuity. May he live and fly in predatory peace, but I do not have to reduce my claims on the world or on myself to ravenous terms. Nor am I obliged to justify my ravenous behavior when I am guilty of it. The problem with the koala bear analogy is that the koala's history is relatively undistinguished, even as eucalyptus eaters go. His survival is of profound importance to him, no doubt, and that should be enough. To others, and in external or objective terms, it is chiefly an ecological issue. Love him as I do, I do not wish to form a moral alliance with the humpback whale.

Ethical Alternatives

Zionism is not a tree with many branches, but rather, more accurately, it is one with many branches in search of the roots that became the nation of Israel. Two of those branches are relevant here, for they embrace the ethical alternatives. For some of Zionism's founding fathers, Israel had no special mission beyond its own establishment and survival as a locus for the ingathering and protection of the Jewish people. That, embellished with an overlay of anti-Arab, antilabor, and expansionist sentiment, is the view adopted by Jabotinsky and his disciple Menachem Begin. It is quite evidently the driving ethos of the current government of Israel and, in all probability of the majority, perhaps the abundant majority, of the nation's people. But there was and remains another Zionism—the Zionism of Hess, Gordon, Syrkin, and Borochov. In this view the Zionist objective was not simply to establish a viable Jewish state in the Holy Land, but to make of that state and in that state a better society, a society predicated on spiritual and social ideals, on principles of democracy, social equality, concern for one's neighbors and cohabitants, and conciliatory rather than retributive justice. The idea, in short, was not simply to found another state, not to make Israel a nation like all other nations, but to make of it, if the dream were possible, something a little less familiar, something nearer to the stuff of moral fable. "It was in this area," as Gershon Winer writes, "the socioeconomic, that the message of Zionism sounded the universal note in its national theme. Espousing world socialism, a classless society, peace among nations and harmony within them, the Zionist pioneers undertook to lead by example."[8]

It was the latter vision that provided the dominant ethos for most of Israel's early and recent history. I will not attempt to assess the degree of its fulfillment. Palestinians no doubt will scoff at the notion that it was even begun, and there is substance to their scorn. As I speak mainly out of critical and almost resentful disillusionment with today's Israel, allow me to cite a single exhibit in its behalf and to show thereby from what level we begin to fall. Israel has fought, since its inception, by some counts three, by others five, wars with surrounding Arab nations sworn to destroy it. Israel itself has a substantial Arab minority, about 12 percent of its population, yet despite its far more serious and prolonged external threat, Israel has no stain on its record comparable to the American treatment of its Japanese citizens during World War II or even to the less organized hostility toward German–Americans. Its record on the treatment of its Arab citizens is badly blemished, but no nation in similar or comparable circumstances can match it. For all its lapses, no nation surrounded by a vastly larger and more numerous enemy, containing within its boundaries a substantial minority of ethnically related peoples has, to my knowledge, acted with such humanity, tolerance, and restraint. All of it, I might add, demonstrably earned by that minority.

Facts like these, I believe, are what Israel has most to be proud of. Not merely its military victories, but its behavior in most of these victories; not the occupation, certainly, but, until a few years ago, the relatively benign nature of its occupation; not the power implicit in the fact of occupation, but again until these past few years, its relative reluctance to occupy. Such traits and practices are of course not exclusively Jewish, no private ethical bailiwick of this people. But races and ethnic groups, like pencils and automobiles, are not defined exclusively by their uniquely possessed characteristics. They are defined by that congeries of attributes, whether unique or widely shared with others, which they most typically exhibit, by those qualities and values with which they identify and for which they strive. A pencil is not the only writing instrument, an automobile not the only motor vehicle. But these are, nonetheless, components of their definition and would be even if they were not originally conceived or invented for these purposes. Ethical idealism, the democratic ethos, social justice and reform, and a passion for ideas may not be exclusively Jewish traits. Thank heavens they are not! They may not have formed the dominant strain in its original composition, but in the eyes of many that is what Judaism has come to stand for and be identified with. Having been nurtured on such an identification, it is also what many of us feel at home with and feel exiled from when it is taken away.

Dangers in Israel Today: Territorial Theocracy

The danger, as I've said, is that contemporary Israel begins to take this away. In doing so, it begins to deprive some of those who have lived there, either all or part of their lives, of a sense of belonging and of home. Recent expressions and events make it painfully clear that to a growing and ever more powerful segment of Israel's population, I and others like myself should not regard their nation as our own. There is a numerically small but disproportionately powerful neo-fascist organization on the campuses of Israel's universities that finds a resounding echo in the society at large. It calls itself *Yisrael Shelanu*—Our Israel—and it means what it says. I have said earlier that others, if there are enough of them or if they speak loudly and forcefully enough, may tell us, if not where we do belong, where we do not. The Germans, the Poles, and the Czechs, for example, did so quite eloquently to the Jews some 40 years ago. The analogy ends there, but the members of this organization make it eminently clear that their Israel has room neither for those who support PLO terrorism, their ostensible target, nor politically verbal or active Arabs of any oppositionist stripe, nor those who believe in a more conciliatory approach to the question of Palestinian rights, nor those who actively oppose continued settlement on the West Bank or its populated areas, nor those who favor the establishment of a separate Palestinian state in that region, nor even for those who believe too ardently in the rights of free speech and free assembly. As the recent election campaign made clear, they are not alone. To a substantial number of the present leadership's more vociferous champions, chanting in the streets for "Menachem (Begin) King of Israel," their king's opponents are *bogdim*—traitors. A recent and ominous poll showed that 30 percent of the population currently favors the replacement of democratic with more autocratic rule. The new autocracy, one assumes, would deal harshly with these traitors.

Such Israelis, although they are still a minority of the population, are a growing minority and a gathering force. And what they are saying, sometimes explicitly (I have heard it more than once), sometimes implicitly by advocacy, deed, or indirection, is that a certain other kind of Israeli, a certain other kind of Jew, does not properly belong in this land. A significant number, though by no means all, of these would-be exilers are Sephardim— Israeli Jews of North African origin. Objects themselves of discrimination and neglect by the ruling *Ashkenazi* class for these 30 years or so, defined into an unkempt corner as the "Second Israel," some of these Sephardim, with understandable anger and alacrity, have begun to rearrange the seating in the bus, at least on paper. Unable to reverse the inequitable distribution of wealth or power in their own favor, they ventilate frustration by crying out for and proclaiming a new distribution of rights. It is not they who are the outsiders, for now their leader—ironically a Polish *Ashkenazi* (Menachem Begin) who has done little or nothing to improve their lot—guides this vehicle and determines its direction. No longer is it they, who, for reasons of cultural differences, do not belong. Rather it is these others, including former leaders and their supporters, who for reasons of attitude, political affiliation, and belief, have become traitors to the security and well-being of the state. It is they who do not belong in this new nation. It is they who, compelled to trade places with the until-now disenfranchised Sephardim, are made to feel they are not, whatever they may have thought, at home.

One does not have to be labeled a traitor or invited to leave a nation to feel it is no longer in the richest and most vital sense his home. One may be reminded, in fact a dozen times a day, that this is his home, where he was born or has chosen to live, that these are his people, that the Law of Return guarantees to every Jew citizenship in this once great state, and yet he may doubt his address. This has begun to happen to me and, I suspect, to a fairly substantial number of other Jews of comparable attitude or mind. It accounts, I believe, for more of the emigration from Israel than has been acknowledged. It contributes too to the sharply declining percentage of Russian emigrants who select Israel in preference to America. And it accounts, at least in part, for the virtual termination of western emigration to Israel. Economic factors alone, however important, simply cannot account for these phenomena, all markedly intensified since the election of the Begin government and the realization of what his election portended and entailed. Frenetic inflation notwithstanding, life in Israel is not, for most of us, significantly more difficult in economic terms than it was in most previous years. Buying power and the standard of living are not markedly depreciated. If all one cared for were financial comfort and security, he would be almost as likely to find it in Israel today as he would have five or ten or fifteen years ago; yet fewer stay and fewer come, because fewer are or would be genuinely at home in this altered setting.

An American, unless he has come, as some have, to settle in Hebron or in other Arab cities on the West Bank, is not likely to hear upon his arrival that he has come home and that he is welcome there. If he is politically silent he will probably be told, quite simply, that he is a fool for having come, for having given up what looks like so much for what Israelis have come to feel is so little. If he is politically vocal and dissident, he will probably be told he has not yet earned his right to speak and he will be invited to return from whence he has come. Ironically, the people of Israel, on the verge of reconciliation with Egypt, find themselves for the first time since leaving it, awash in a divisive sea that threatens to engulf it. The nation is divided—between *Ashkenazi* and Sephardi, between secular and religious, between immigrant and *sabra*, between Arab and Jew. The occupation has been devastating to the nation's soul. Crossing over from ideological democracy toward territorial theocracy, Israel is caught in a rising tide of bitterness, frustration, and antipathy, of increased intolerance for dissent, of depleted empathy or concern for the Arab minority or the Palestinian cause, of participation in the universal thirst for territory, and of relative indifference to the suffering of innocents caught between combatants. The tide has not swept over us yet. It has not submerged or drowned us. But it is shoulder-high and rising, and in such a sea a certain kind of Jew, wherever he may live, cannot feel at home. I spoke earlier about the irrelevance or inapplicability of the term "exile" to the recent Jewish experience. The irony of all this and the point toward which I have been aiming since the start of this chapter is that for many of us, Israel itself may be the new diaspora, another seat of it at any rate; and this is indeed a matter of exile—exile not from his land, for the Jew is in his land; not from his people, for nominally he is among his people—but exile from the concept most early Zionists and settlers spoke and wrote and dreamed of, exile in the land of the Jews from the values and ethos he may identify with Jewishness, exile from what for most of the past two centuries has in large measure defined the Jewishness he identifies with, admires, and would cling to.

Israel as Diaspora⁹

The Jew, whose values and ambitions were basically harmonious with the theoretical underpinning and early character of the state, was an unwelcomed outsider, a suspected alien in his own land. These are intriguing ironies, bitter in obvious ways, perhaps promising in others less evident, and characteristic of certain Jews in Israel today. Like the Jews of Western Europe and North America, this Jew is viewed as disproportionately wealthy and powerful, too sharply visible in universities and among the intellectual class, too stridently audible in the media. The present government is currently weighing the introduction of a second television channel, on the condition that it will prove less hostile to its policies than the current one. Like the Jews of another diaspora he is viewed as elitest and condescending, as one who tends and caters exclusively to his own and is slighting or disparaging to others. Like the diaspora Jew he is seen as arrogant and self-righteous, an annoying purveyor of lofty morals and blind ideals who assumes a pose of moral superiority, judgment, and critical dissent. Like many Jews of America, Western Europe, and the Soviet Union, he is suspected of divided loyalty. To his accusers, the ruling party, and its constituency, his beliefs suggest a sacrificial internationalism. He demonstrates an unnerving willingness to give important place to the needs and moral claims of others—Palestinians, Lebanese civilians and refugees, for instance—even at the expense of immediate national self-interest, at least as conceived of by those in power.

There are of course important differences between this and the other diasporas. One is that unlike almost all earlier diaspora communities, that of the marginal Jew in Israel today is distinctly more secular than the prevailing culture. Until recently, despite the invariably disproportionate power of the religious parties in Israel's coalition governments and therefore in the country, theocracy kept pretty much to its corners—its traditional bailiwicks of birth, marriage, divorce, and death. The influence of Orthodoxy was evident, in addition, in compulsory Saturday closings, in the restriction of public transportation on the Sabbath and Holy days, in the laws of *kashrut*, and elsewhere. Nevertheless, the one of national life and the thrust of government policy were distinctly secular. That is changing. Orthodoxy begins to take precedence over national security and economic welfare. According to the recent coalition agreement that enabled the participation of the radically Orthodox *Agudat Yisrael* party, the national airline will no longer be permitted to fly on Saturday, Israel's ports will be closed on that day, and vast sums of previously unavailable money will be funnelled into Orthodox *yeshivot*. Conscription will also be altered, man- and woman-power shortage notwithstanding, to exclude all married women and all newly Orthodox Jews who opt for sacred study rather than national service. The education ministry has fallen into the hands of the other religious party, and the government's settlement policy is quite thoroughly in line with that party's biblically grounded designs on the greater Land of Israel. The diaspora Jew in Israel, therefore, is not the anachronistic figure in the black coat sweeping through the narrow crooked streets of his *shtetl*. Rather, he is the *apikorus*—the westernized apostate (again the betrayer)—in an increasingly anachronistic, increasingly theocratic society. The adherent to the basically humanistic Jewish values on which the State of Israel was constructed is being gradually set aside, relegated to the role of outsider in the land his ideals and standards helped to found.

There is danger in this to the community of which we speak. Jewish humanism, it would seem, does not have the strength or coherence, certainly not the proven tenacity and perseverence of orthodoxy. Where the latter could survive insularly intact for centuries, in nations devoted to no or other gods, the persistence, resilience, or resistance of the new diaspora community is less assured. Less well insulated than their Orthodox ancestors who, in tandem with other forces, now begin to exert powerful and unwelcome influence over their daily lives, less bountifully blessed with protective certitude about the utter rightness of their way, they are likely first to accept, then to see virtue in the changed society that once was theirs. Greater than the threat of assimilation is the temptation of exodus. Since most of these Jews are educated, middle-class, and connected by family or other ties to the West, they are unusually mobile. As Israel continues its accelerating drift, as these Jews are made to feel increasingly alien and inappropriate in their country, as their hope for a restoration of Israel to something more hospitable to their own sense of Jewishness and self declines, more of their number will emigrate to more comfortable diaspora settings.

That this is a secular Jewish community dwelling in the land of an increasingly potent and assertive Jewish orthodoxy distinguishes it from earlier diasporas. The critical distinction, however, is that the Jew in the Israeli diaspora and the new Israeli Jew who begins to wrest the nation from his hands are—and the point is of overwhelming importance—both Jews. That fact contains a promise. Whatever else may happen in this sadly divided land, Jews will not be slaughtered because they are Jews—not by other Jews at any rate. They may be envied or despised because they are a certain kind of Jew, but not because they are Jews; and when the knock on the door is heard at midnight, it will more likely be a draft call to fight a common enemy than a roundup for the trains. That may sound like small or superfluous comfort, but it is, after all, the indispensable if not the only raison d'etre of the state, and to the Jew such a guarantee is neither trivial nor assumed.

Moral versus National Survival

The fact that Israel at present remains a predominantly Jewish nation has other ramifications as well. One is a debilitating confusion of loyalties between peoples and ideals, far more serious than any faced by Jews in more conventional diaspora settings. It is one thing to be torn between American national interest—oil interest let us say—and devotion to Israeli security and the preservation of that state. In such a dilemma, if that is what it is, survival of the other is pitted against economic comfort for oneself and neighbors, the commitment to life set against the desire for pleasurable well-being. In moral terms at least, it is not a wrenching choice. If the American Jew perceives those oil interests, however, as indispensable to American security or to its continuity as a positive force in world affairs, one comes closer to the dilemma of the diaspora Jew in Israel. The latter is asked, and will be asked at every turn, to choose between those values he has come to identify as the core of his Jewish character and actions which may, just may, be vital to the security or preservation of the state. What if dropping bombs on terrorist targets where hundreds of civilians are known to reside does turn the population, in fear, against those terrorists and deprive them of a protective setting from which to attack and invade? Is it then justified? Can one then sanction such an act? What if an iron fist in the territories really does intimidate violent opposition and reduce terrorist incursions from that base? It has in other occupations. It is largely a matter of how much repression one is willing to enforce. Would efficiency thus defined justify such a policy—one of collective punishment, for example? How iron does a fist have to become before it is more cruel than what it would prevent, and less tolerable? Do we have a right to be in these territories at all? Possibly not, but what are the possible or likely consequences of withdrawal? Not to some distant or abstracted other, mind you, but to ourselves—to other Jews, however unlike us in all other ways, and to ourselves.

Almost every choice, it seems, raises the issue of moral versus national survival. Almost every choice threatens to pit the preservation of one's moral integrity, the values by which he has come to define himself and his Jewishness, against the security of the Jewish people in a nation of its own. Ideally, of course, the two are compatible; and perhaps they often are. But it is *luftmenschkeit* of a higher order than any of us can afford to imagine they always or inevitably are. And this newly exiled Jew, with his commitment to ethical ideals and his passion for ideas recognizes, when he is functioning most efficiently, that not every viable idea is ethically ideal and that many such ideals may, at least, be very dangerous ideas.

The Promise

These are a few of the dangers, but in them also lies the promise. Like it or not, the Jew as I know and wish to preserve him has fared and flourished best in the diaspora. The specialness of the Jew, in which I persist in believing, is not a matter of divinity or genes. It is, I believe, a matter of condition. One does not have to be an Actonite to recognize the erosive faculties of power. One need not be a Tocquevillian to acknowledge the dangers to the soul of majoritarianism. One need not see with Samuel Johnson patriotism as the last refuge of the scoundrel to be aware of the corrupting ethos of nationalism and the dangers of the chauvinism it drags behind it. The Jew, alas, has proven no exception to these rules of spiritual corrosion. The establishment of his own state, his cultural dominance within it, and his military supremacy in the region have done wonders for his pride and no little for his preservation on this earth. But there has been a price. It was the folly and naivete, perhaps, of the Zionism reflective of the Jewishness I extoll and fear for to believe that the Jew could succeed where others had so dismally and consistently failed, to believe in the compatibility of power, nationhood, and a high order of ethical integrity. We did it, I think, with at least some measure of laudable success for almost 30 years. Under the pressures of constant war, economic stress, and human inevitabilities, and under the leadership of those who never placed ethical norms on the same plane of importance with expansion, nationhood, and strength, we begin, sadly if ineluctably, to bear out the familiar axioms of sovereignty and dominance.

The danger in all this is that Judaism at its best, the Judaism that transcends not only koala bearism but, in my perhaps immodest view, too much that is human besides, will be the price of the nation it began. In a provocative book written more than a decade ago, Georges Friedmann forecast "The End of the Jewish People." [10] Since Jewry in the western democracies was rapidly succumbing to assimilation, and since the Jew bred in Israel was a different brand than we had known since perhaps Bar Kochba,[11] the Jewish people as we have come to know it is threatened with extinction. The emergence of a new diaspora, in of all places, the State of Israel, may steal the credence from that prediction. It may also offer hope for an unforeseen revival in a promising new form. In the land of his ancestors and closer to that land than any other diaspora Jew, he may draw on his history of promise, sacrifice, and faith, on the people, the ideals, and the values that are still there to be found if the archeologist is sufficiently tenacious. Stimulated and challenged by external threat, by the need to battle it if it comes alive, by the need to defuse it if he can, he is at the same time freed of the debilitating impotence that accompanies the mortal fear of a hostile and potentially lethal citizenry. As a result, he may turn his energies to this double battle while reserving more for a third. He may battle the downstream current of his own nation at a cost high enough to test and hone him but short of drowning. The waters that threaten him are the assimilation I spoke of, accession to the devalued standards by which the nation has begun to act. There is some comfort in the knowledge that even in assimilation there is a basic preservation. The Jew in the Israeli diaspora knows what no other homeless Jew can know: that his people, though they may be diminished, are not depleted by his absorption into the mass. He may yet, should he turn his back, give birth to a generation that will confront what he fell prey to, who will identify once more with what he has lost, with the finest strains in the Jewish tradition—and in the State of Israel no less. The idea of a Jewish diaspora in Israel is in significant ways a concession of defeat, but recognized, properly understood, and adventurously grasped, what a promise it holds.

If he can resist the temptation to abandon the challenge for a more luxurious and conventional diaspora; if he can resist the temptation toward assimilation into the increasingly autocratic, theocratic, and often harshly pragmatic majority; if he can maintain his vision of the values that have energized and defined his people through most of its modern history; if he can balance his ideals with an enlightened sense of the real that does not compromise them mortally—then perhaps, he can become a realistically modified version of what he was ostensibly chosen for: not a light and a way unto all nations, perhaps, for that is too awesome a burden for such a fragile race, and the price is too high, but a light unto its own. It will not be easy. He will almost certainly not be heeded, and he will be neither liked nor appreciated for his efforts. But then again, isn't that what it has always been about?

Notes

1. Hillel Halkin, *Letters to an American Jewish Friend*. Philadelphia: The Jewish Publication Society of America, 1977, p. 87.

2. Ibid., p. 88.

3. Shlomo Avineri, *The Making of Modern Zionism*. New York: Basic Books, Inc., 1981.

4. Balfour Brickner, Liberalism and the Jews: A Symposium. *Commentary* 69(1), 1980, p. 25.

5. Irving Howe, ibid., p. 48.

6. Neal Kozodoy, ibid., p. 51.

7. Drora Kass and Seymour Martin Lipset. Israelis in Exile. *Commentary* 68(5), 1979, p. 70.

8. Gershon Winer. *The Founding Fathers of Israel*. New York: Bloch Publishing Co., 1971, pp. 14–15.

9. I hope it is evident that here and in much of the discussion that follows I use the term "diaspora" not in its literal sense of geographical dispersion, but as remoteness or exile from a spiritual home or sense of home. "Emigration to Palestine," wrote A. D. Gordon, "without radically revolutionizing Jewish social structures, is nothing else than a transference of Exile to the Land of Israel." I use "diaspora" as Gordon uses "Exile" and I would amend his proclamation thus: Domicile in Israel without a tenacious adherence to Jewish social values is nothing else than a transference of diaspora to the State of Israel. A. D. Gordon, *Kitbe A. D. Gordon*. Tel Aviv: Hasifriah Hazionit, 1952.

10. Georges Friedmann, *The End of the Jewish People*. New York: Doubleday, 1967.

11. Bar Kochba was the leader of a revolt against the Romans in the year 135 C.E.

·25·
Zionism and the Legacy of Exile

Nehama Lyn

What is Jewish Statehood?

Despite its impressive successes, the political movement to end Jewish exile has paradoxically been a movement working counter to its own ultimate purpose and avowed interests. With the perspective of almost 100 years behind us, it is becoming increasingly evident that the Zionist movement largely failed to grasp the implications of the term "Jewish state."

Quite understandably, the driving force of Zionism was the cessation of exile and the establishment of a political entity. Yet this single-minded goal produced, in large measure, both intentional and nonintentional neglect for the inherent nature and characteristic features of that state. Throughout the decades of the 20th Century, the Zionist drive for statehood purposefully (and perhaps wisely) avoided the pitfalls and detours of overdefinition. Specifically, it avoided an ideological definition of "Jewish statehood" beyond that of ending Jewish political exile.

Zionism as a Structural Ideology

In part, this was a natural reaction to the historical contradiction implicit in "Jewish statehood": throughout the long centuries of exile, Judaism was not characterized by a territorial or political structure. The perceived incompatibility of Judaism and statehood was resolved, to a great extent, by simple neglect of the issue: an issue which would become more and more crucial as the state became established. And of course, if Jewishness and statehood were seen as being mutually incompatible—in fact, a virtual contradiction—then the state could not be, in any significantly cultural or valuational sense, Jewish. Thus, almost by necessity, with structure becoming the all-consuming goal to the exclusion of content, Zionism could not adequately create a political structure nurturing and nurtured by Jewish civilization in its organic, traditional forms. The culture built up during the diaspora period was almost summarily dismissed.

The Radical Rejection of Diaspora Judaism

From its very inception, Zionism was a radical movement; rather than attempt to modify whatever existed in the way of Jewish autonomy and self-determination, Zionism categorically rejected anything short of complete Jewish political independence, for the Jewish people for almost 2,000 years had suffered from the lack of a protective political structure. And only a Jewish nation–state could provide the physical safety, psychological health, cultural insularity, and demographic strength necessary for genuine Jewish peoplehood.

Certainly the Zionist message was correct, as 20th Century history has underlined in blood red. However, the error to which we have all fallen prey was the supposition that Jewish lack of form was a necessary corollary to the intrinsic content of Judaism. And it was this fallacy which largely legitimatized the rejection of Jewish culture on the part of many early Zionists. It is not surprising, therefore, that the driving force of Zionist ideology was not toward creating a state which would be unique by virtue of its Jewish dimension, but one which would be, in large measure, an imitation of existing nation–states. And to this end, the Zionist movement has succeeded, and continues to succeed. Increasingly, however, we are hearing voices, both inside and outside of Israel, who see this success as something hardly to be celebrated.

Given the complex of desperate circumstances and historical perspective in which Jewry found itself throughout the late 19th Century and thereafter, it is not surprising that Zionist ideology developed as it did. A situation of desperation invariably produces a drive for radicalism; the more radical the proposed solution, the more it seems to address the immediacy of the problem.

Zionist Nationalism versus Diaspora Particularism

As a radical departure from the particularistic confines and self-definitions of Judaism, Zionism substituted its own antithesis. A romantic humanitarianism and nationalism became its theology. Of course, universalism was in fashion in the most sophisticated intellectual circles of the West. And the

Zionist movement was affected by these cultural winds, and was swept along. However, passion is invariably specific: there was no way that vague universalism could support a lasting passion. Therefore, before long there came the warning signs that Zionism had no sustaining energy other than the power generated by its own momentum. In brief, cut off from its own diasporic cultural roots, there was no life force adequate to meet the demands of a sustained effort. Although one can appreciate the general goal: "to be a nation like all other nations," passion cannot be nourished by the universal. Passion cannot be abstract: it demands a focus. Passion is specific by its very nature: there are no impassioned generalities. The comfort of the universal is antithetical to the intensity of passion. A State of Israel which conceives of itself as simply being a nation like all other nations except for its having a demographic Jewish majority, cannot help but fail to elicit the ongoing loyalty and commitment of its citizens to a degree greater than the citizenry of other states.

The Self-destruction of Jewish Distinctiveness

In retrospect, the early Zionist avoidance of both defining and celebrating Jewish peoplehood and Jewish civilization has created a sad paradox in which Zionism may well prove to be a formulation for their extinction. To a significant degree, Zionism has weakened and diluted the substance of that which could have filled the vacuum it itself created: that diaspora culture which had the potential of being part of the bedrock of a truly Jewish state. Many Zionist thinkers had been convinced that Jewish civilization, and the so-called diaspora Jewish mentality, was its worst enemy. And this concept has taken such hold that in many ways they have, in fact, ceased to function as sources of strength and direction in modern Israel.

In analyzing the Jewish condition, we face the stark reality that much of the Zionist impetus has collapsed in the face of the very goal it established initially, that was—the creation of a Jewish state. As a radical ideology it burned brightly in the Jewish breast for a brief period, and then began to be extinguished in the very state in which it should have flourished. The establishment of the State of Israel has created a milieu in which Jews live as a majority culture. Yet this has not inspired an increasing or even enduring sense of Jewish peoplehood, nor a belief in the unique purpose of the State of Israel. Perhaps, as some critics claim, it is the absence of external pressure that has resulted in our loss of internal creative energy. And, it is true, in the past oppression and challenge did function as a source of Jewish cohesion and particularity. But woe to us if these are the sole bases of our distinctiveness.

Addressing the Dimension of Purpose

As we examine our new home and our new life in our new home, we must be moved and guided by positive reasons: knowing who we are and what we want to become. We must look outward at the community of nations from a point of self-knowledge and a sense of our individual self-worth. Otherwise we will be constantly juggling an everchanging image and self-image, becoming a caricature of others' perceptions and expectations. The difficult question that all concerned Jews must face today is: is Jewish commitment to Israel basically a reaction to negative stimuli? In other words, can we, as a people, marshall energy even when we are relieved of oppression and opposition? Do we have faith in the worth of our apartness and uniqueness?

In Israel, we have increasingly come to conceive of ourselves as basically another state in the family of nations. We don the national trappings and adopt the behavior of other nations as we have observed other nations do. And in this basically imitative fashion, we prove to what degree we are novices in the art of statecraft and the science of self-definition.

The Diaspora Tradition of Self-Denial

Ineptitude in the creation of a Jewish state—by any definition of the term—may be excused, in measure, as being a function of time and inexperience. Yet at the same time that we have turned our backs on diaspora Judaism as being anachronistic and inappropriate, we cling tenaciously to certain traits, habits, and thought patterns of the diaspora which are counterproductive for any independent state. For example, ever since the establishment of the State of Israel (in fact, even prior to 1948), we have projected a readiness to concede on territorial issues. Our essentially defensive attitudes have helped to create a separate standard in the international community by accepting treatment which benefits no sovereign nation. This is a direct throwback to our diaspora mentality: we accept this near-pariah status and this uniqueness of liability because on some level we know that we are expected to bear a burden of supposed guilt. After all, didn't we always live it in the past? And thus we balk at confrontation; we hesitate to change that which is a characteristic attributed to us by others. We continue struggling to project the image that others have of us. As a nation we carry within us the self-denigration of *galut*: the self-image, hence the image of the petitioner.

Obviously, self-criticism is a valuable asset, be it for an individual or a nation. But exaggerated self-flagellation and self-denial is pathology, not ideology: in a context where these *galut* illnesses should have been healed, we continue to see them thriving. We seem to have transplanted and internalized this most unfortunate characteristic of exile. In our dispersion we found pariah status abhorrent; are we now to impose it on ourselves?

No people having the depth and breadth of historical experience and the tenacity of spirit to emerge triumphant from its own rebirth can allow itself to establish a posture of apology, defensiveness, timidity, and compromise on basic issues. Yet we fail to recognize and assert our uniqueness and our statehood.

To Remain Unlike Other Peoples

It is true that the basic Zionist ideal—the motivation to be a nation like other nations—still elicits loyalty and commitment today. But there is a fundamental flaw: it is impossible for a Jewish state, however defined, to be a nation like all other nations. To the extent that we strive to be like other nations we deny our own uniqueness and individuality. And the criterion by which the Jewish people traditionally defined itself as a nation was not what it had in common with other peoples, but how it differed, how it was distinguished from other nations. Surely this can deteriorate into self-congratulation, chauvinism, and even racism, yet without a firm sense of who we are and where we want our path in history to lead, we must, perforce, flounder.

The birth of the State of Israel constitutes one of the most noble, spectacular events in all of recorded history. So much of the Zionist success is almost unbelievable, just as Jewish history in its entirety often seems to be an incredible tale of recurrent impossibilities. The State of Israel exists today by virtue of the uncommon effort, heroic devotion, uncompromising love, and untiring faith of the Jewish people. But now the time has come for all who care, whatever their orientation may be, to come together and grapple with the next phase of the Zionist dream and the Zionist reality: part of our people has come home; now we must build our house.

·VIII·
The
Israel–Diaspora
Brotherhood

·26·
What We Want of the Diaspora

Golda Meir

I should like to try to give my answer as to what we want and expect of Americans and what, in my opinion, you ought to bring to the attention of your friends and of American Jewry in general.

I think I found that answer while reading a letter today. The woman who wrote it described the first performance of the Israeli delegation to the Moscow Youth Festival. She did not dwell on the artistic standards of the performance. She began with the words: "He cried." When I first saw that opening sentence, I thought she was referring to some Russian Jew who had been deeply moved by the performance—and I myself have seen Russian Jews weeping. But this time it was a young, stalwart *sabra* she was describing; a second-generation Israeli *kibbutz* member who knows no Yiddish and certainly no Russian, and who had probably never before been out of the country. According to the theories we have heard here, this young man should have had a very narrow Jewish outlook and been concerned not at all with Jews in the *galut* but only with the small country of Israel or even only with his own small *kibbutz*. Yet it was this boy who was moved to tears on seeing his brethren in Russia, with whom, supposedly, he had nothing in common—neither language, nor past experiences, nor suffering.

If I were to state in one sentence what it is that we want and expect of you, it is that your children, too, shall be moved to tears on meeting Jews in a *galut* like that of Russia. That is all. Present-day Jewish youth, outside of Israel, is not capable of that. Our children are neither more handsome nor more precocious nor more wise than yours; they have no more remarkable abilities than yours, but they have one great quality: they are free and healthy, normal and independent Jewish children. They know what it is to build and to fight, to struggle for their own existence. They have seen their comrades die for them and for their own land. They are not the only Jewish youth who have died in war, but they alone have fallen on Jewish soil.

If our youth were raised in an atmosphere where it did not matter whether Jews lived in Israel or in the diaspora, that boy would not have wept in Moscow that evening. He wept because, in his own simple way and in the atmosphere he had breathed since his childhood, there is something that revolts against life in the *galut*.

We must be quite frank. I confess that when I visit my hometown in America and see my old friends and comrades doing well, their children older than mine, their grandchildren older than mine who live in the desert— I confess I pity them when I think of the difference between the ways my grandchildren and theirs are raised.

We have nothing against Jews in the *galut*. It is against the *galut* itself that we protest. And I don't understand the state of affairs in which we are not allowed to say what we feel because someone might misunderstand us and believe that we are interested only in the small and narrow confines of Israel.

What Is Zionism?

Likewise I fail to understand when people say that there is danger for Israel if we continue hammering into the minds and hearts of Jews in the diaspora that they must come hither. If we tell our fellow-Zionists what we experienced during the scores of years until we reached our present stage; if we say to them that Zionism means not only to work for *Eretz Yisrael*, we are told that by this emphasis we make our world so narrow and our culture so short-sighted that we may—heaven forbid—become Levantine. In my opinion, anyone who takes that view denies the very principle of Zionism.

We have always believed, and I personally have thought, that the foundation of Zionism is more than geographical independence. I have always believed that Zionism means Jewish emancipation in every sense, including the spiritual and cultural, so that a Jew who creates cultural values may do so as a free man. It may be an assumption on my part, but I believe that there is no Jew in the *galut* creating as a free man and as a free Jew. Only a Jew in Israel can do so. If a Jew lives in Israel and creates as a free Jew and as a free man, writes about various problems in the world, about Jewish life and non-Jewish life, about science, art, and literature, his writing will not be less universal than that of a Jew who lives in the *galut*—in every *galut*, even in the best of them—for there he must, willingly or unwillingly, consciously or unconsciously, adapt himself to his surroundings. Then he is not free.

In these discussions ways and means have been sought to make possible double loyalty and to prove that it is not dangerous to the countries of which diaspora Jews are citizens. But is double loyalty a danger only to those countries? Is it not a danger also for Jews? Is it not a danger to Judaism if a Jew must feel loyalty to two sovereign ideals? Must we only see to it that

Americans who believe that double loyalty is not good for America should feel comfortable? Is it comfortable for Jews?

I must confess that sometimes I am led to believe that my Zionism may be imperfect, for I fail to understand what we have often heard during the past ten years—that the State of Israel is not the final goal of Zionism. Sometimes this is said by people who previously urged a definition of the final goal of Zionism. If you maintain that the State of Israel cannot be regarded as the final goal of Zionism so long as there are not millions of Jews living there, I agree. But what exactly is meant by the statement: "The State is not the final aim of Zionism"? What did we understand by the "final aim of Zionism" before the State emerged, when we had to devise devious ways and means of bringing Jews over to *Eretz Yisrael* and had to adapt ourselves to the reality in which we lived? Zionism wanted Jews to gain independence in their own land, have their own language, and create all the social and cultural ideas which Tabenkin enumerated.[1] It would certainly be foolish to say that Zionism means that once we are a people of close to two million in Israel, the aim is achieved. There are many Jews and many Zionists in the lands of the diaspora who would like to talk us into believing that we must be satisfied with that. We disagree. At least, we urge you, do not claim, and do not bring up a young generation in the diaspora in the thought that, though the State of Israel is a good thing in itself, it is not Zionism. What then is Zionism?

I should like to ask you something. Jews in all generations strove for *Eretz Yisrael*. It is immaterial how we define that urge, whether religious or not. But that urge for *Eretz Yisrael* was one of the fundamentals—the main power—that kept us alive and maintained us in the world. Jews wanted *Eretz Yisrael*, and so they prayed to God and mourned and lamented and fasted on Tisha b'Ab. And that desire of theirs had an extraordinary influence and was a decisive factor in Jewish life. But was *Eretz Yisrael* created thereby; did *Eretz Yisrael* become a tangible fact through that? Wherein lay Herzl's great achievement? It was in the fact that he gathered Jews together and told them that their yearning and urge for *Eretz Yisrael* must not remain only a dream, something for which one must weep and pray, but that it be something which could be accomplished—if they actually wanted to accomplish it. And so the Zionist movement came into being. And the Zionist movement in its own fashion aspired and worked for the creation of a Jewish state and Jewish independence. The Zionist movement said that if we wanted our state, it could be achieved. These Jews achieved the state.

Now I should like to ask you: how is a Zionist who does not personally go to Israel to build the state more important than a Jew who is not a Zionist, who on Tisha b'Ab sat on the ground and wept with all his heart and mourned the destruction of the temple, as though it had happened only yesterday? I do not underrate such weeping and mourning. But how is a modern political Zionist, who does not go to Israel to help build the country with his own hands, how is he more important for the state than those Jews who shed tears on Tisha b'Ab? Why are we not allowed to say that after the emergence of the state a Zionist is only he who packs his bags and comes to Israel? What else can a Zionist aspire to?

It is suggested that we should be partners. I am the last to underestimate the tears of sorrow or the tears of joy of the Jews in America, and I have seen both. They wept at moments of great danger for Israel and they wept at moments of great joy for Israel. They wept from afar, and I shall be the last to think lightly of it because I know that they wept from the bottom of their hearts. But I cannot be satisfied with that, despite the great value I attach to it. My dear friends, there is a great difference that we dare not underestimate, the difference between the family that lives here and whose son or daughter went out to fight in Sinai, and a good, sincere Zionist family living in New York or in Buenos Aires or in Johannesburg that looked on from afar. Yes, their hearts beat warmly, I am convinced of that, and in their own fashion they prayed to God for our success; but there is a difference, and one cannot do away with it. One must not try to do so.

The Two Great Tasks

I was always under the impression that after the rise of the Jewish state we would have to undertake two tasks and that we would have to try with all our energy and understanding to find ways to reach all Jews, so as not to leave any of them out. Possibly the two tasks may be welded into one. They are to build up and consolidate the Jewish state, and to preserve and guard every Jewish young man and woman, every child in the diaspora so long as they have not come here; the goal is not to create all types of theories saying that it matters little if they remain there. One must constantly demand that they come here, but in the first place, one must guard against the great danger that we may not be able to understand each other. The spoken language is immaterial, for at times one fails to understand one's fellow even if the same language is spoken. I have always thought that since the emergence of the Jewish state there are no Jews, apart from the Council for Judaism and the Communists, whose hearts do not beat for Israel. But that is not enough for us.

We speak of the free world. The free world is also free to assimilate, and the danger is by no means small. I have always been of the opinion, and I still am, that as far as the Jewish state is concerned, work should not be vested in organizations, though certainly they have had great importance in Jewish life and for the State. Jews, Jewish communities as such, Jewish groups without special tendencies, must now be concerned with two things: to build up and strengthen Israel and to work toward *aliyah*. We lament every day that passes without Jewish life, without Jewish education, without the Hebrew language, without preparation for work in Israel. Not one day, not one hour must be wasted in that respect. One must not acquiesce in the idea that the diaspora will be permanent.

Whoever talks himself into the belief that the Jewish people in the diaspora can exist as it would in Israel, and that it has a lasting chance of survival there, is deeply mistaken. One must not make peace with assimilation. Assimilation means being cut off from the Jewish people. Whoever becomes assimilated no longer exists for us. Nor must one make peace with the idea of mixed marriages. The children of mixed marriages are not full Jews. It depends on the Christian mother or on the Christian father and whether he or she is large-hearted or broad-minded enough to allow the children to go to a synagogue. The compromise is often to go to neither a church nor a synagogue or to go to the church. At any rate, it is not one of Judaism or of Hebrew or of Israelism. Don't give me instances of things turning out otherwise. I, too, know of Christian women being devoted and wonderful Hadassah workers. They are exceptions, and they simply prove the general rule. Half-Jewish children are not wholly Jewish children, and a mixed family atmosphere is not a Jewish home. One must not acquiesce in such conditions. Their effects in the diaspora are obvious.

Zionism Makes No Compromises

Zionism never made any compromises. No, not even over the Uganda question. Zionism had the courage even to oppose Herzl and to say: "No Uganda, no compromise!" Would you now want us to compromise? And are you offended by our not wishing to accept a situation in which only a small section of the Jewish people, only 14 or 16 percent, will live in Israel, while the great majority of Jews will remain in the *galut* and will, from afar, either take pride in us or criticize us? It matters little and it is all the same which of the two attitudes they take. They will be far away, in either case. Admittedly, they will feel with us and help us to build up the country, but only from afar.

Obviously, as long as the debate continues between you and us; as long as we make demands and you express no opposition to them (I don't want to believe that you are opposed to *aliyah*); as long as we make demands and you say that *aliyah* in itself is a good thing but that we should not demand it, and have no claims upon you; as long as that is the state of things, you will not in your heart of hearts be able to believe that the Jewish people now residing in the lands of the diaspora, in the free countries, will continue to remain a Jewish people. Whether you acquiesce in assimilation or not, it is a fact that

Jews are drifting away. No, it is not we who are pushing anyone off the wagon. They keep falling of their own accord; they slide off; many of them do not even want to make an attempt to get on.

We want the Zionist movement to be the force that harnesses all Jews, that brings them to Israel and, as long as they remain in *galut*, gives them a meaningful Jewish life with a knowledge of Hebrew and a deep Israeli atmosphere in the home and in the upbringing of their children. And if there is talk of a university, it should be the University in Jerusalem and not any other. And if there is talk of a summer camp it should be a summer camp in Israel and not any other.

You say that this is double loyalty, that it means creating a Jewish ghetto in free America. Yes, I should like to see in free America what you call a ghetto—Jewish children brought up in Jewish homes with one goal and one desire and one thought: to be in Israel. I am not so foolish as to think that that can be done overnight. We have not yet reached the stage where we can discuss this with Jewish fathers and mothers. First of all, we must discuss it among ourselves, and realize that this approach is essential.

And another thing that I believe is that every Sunday school in America is a blessing for us. Rather than that children should grow up ignorant of anything Jewish, it is better that they should meet every Sunday for a few hours and that they should be told something about Judaism, even in English. It is better than nothing. But that is not a Jewish education. It is not Hebrew and it gives nothing of the Israeli spirit. It is not sufficient.

Partners—But Not at Long Distance

I know how fully to appreciate the love that Jews bear for Israel; but if we Israelis were to come to you and express confidence in our strength and belief that "the Jewish State will in all circumstances be in a position to fend for itself," I would say the confidence is quite mistaken. With only a certain percentage of Jews in the world here, with only the present Jewish strength in Israel, it is impossible in the world in which we live, in the constant danger by which we are surrounded, to guarantee the state's security. It surely cannot be done by singing songs of praise. Please do not misunderstand me, but every time I hear anyone in New York or in Chicago or in Los Angeles singing Israeli songs, "*Heh Daroma,*" "*Aravah,*" or other songs, my heart leaps up and I am delighted. But by singing songs about the Negev in Los Angeles or in Texas, the Negev will not be built up. Songs about the Negev sung in New York or in Boston are wonderful only if they serve as instruments and a path for the youth to go to the Negev. Otherwise Jews will remain living in America and will continue to sing about the Negev for a few years longer, but the Negev will remain in its desolation.

I agree with those who claim—possibly it's not logical or rational—that Jews will come from Russia to *Eretz Yisrael*. I simply have not the strength to tell myself that these three-and-a-half-million Jews will be cut off forever from us. When they will come I do not know. It may be tomorrow, it may be in ten years time, I cannot say. But Jews in the free world, Jews who are devoted to Israel, Jews who must be brought up in devotion to Israel, they cannot and must not continue to remain afar; they must feel with us, and be partners with us: yes, partners, but not long distance partners. That cannot be. One is a partner and the other is a sleeping partner, and Jews in the diaspora invest not only money but also love and dreams and yearning and pride in Israel. Yes, that is all very well. But from afar it is not possible to irrigate the Negev. And Israel's existence depends on whether or not the Negev remains a desert and on whether or not the Galilee remains a region of barren and rocky hills. It depends on whether Jewish youth who must defend Israel when need arises, are here. I cannot separate the security and the existence of Israel from the presence of Jews in Galilee. One cannot exist without the other; they are inseparable, knit together, and they must be together.

Israel was built not for the chosen few who came here originally from Eastern Europe, not only for those who are forced to come here, and not only for those who cannot come because they are not allowed out of other countries; Israel has been built for all Jews, and Israeli Jews will not give Jews in the diaspora peace until large masses of them come here.

I believe you, and every one of us believes you, when you say you envy us. This must mean that something is being created here which is lacking in America. Why, then, should you take it amiss when we say that you should see to it that your children and grandchildren should not be in a position to envy us but should come here and be with us and share the happiness of our children.

I know that Jews will continue to live in the diaspora for many years to come and that we must be concerned with their life there. Jewish leaders in the diaspora are often told that they must not leave for Israel because their contribution in the diaspora is more important. There can be no greater lack of realism. The more people taken out of any diaspora community, the richer that community becomes. This is paradoxical but true. A Jewish community from which there is no *aliyah* becomes spiritually impoverished. Did the prewar *aliyah* from Poland and Lithuania make those Jews poorer?

No real bond can exist between Israel and the Jews of the free countries without a great immigration to Israel.

Notes

1. Y. Tabenkin, *Debarim*. Tel Aviv: Hakibbutz Hameuchad, 1954.

·27·
A New Outlook for Israel and the Diaspora

Salo W. Baron

We all have a feeling—a correct feeling—that both the Zionist movement and Jewish life generally are passing through a great crisis which calls for solutions not previously offered either by Zionist literature, the Zionist movement, or by life itself. The situation is new and the solutions must also be new.

I shall therefore begin by saying that, as far as can be foreseen, the Jewish diaspora is an enduring phenomenon, destined to last for generations. I am not saying that it is eternal—no one can make predictions as to eternity—but that we are going to have a diaspora for many generations to come. Likewise, I feel certain of the permanence of the State of Israel, so that there is bound to be a continuing dialogue between the State of Israel and the diaspora.

To put the matter paradoxically, let us assume, for the sake of argument, that all diaspora Jews decide unanimously, except for those intending to emigrate to Israel, to vanish out of existence, to liquidate diaspora Jewry. And let us assume even more paradoxically that in order to implement their decision they resolve to adopt the ruling religion, to become Catholics in Catholic countries, Protestants in Protestant countries, Moslems in Moslem countries. Would this mass conversion put an end to the Jewish group?

It is still possible for an individual convert to be absorbed in the majority, though this is now more difficult than it was in the Middle Ages and in the earlier part of the modern period, when a man became a Christian and no questions were asked. Today there is hesitancy even after the man has become a convert, but it is nevertheless still possible for his descendants to become members of the majority group. However, if all Jews were converted simultaneously, according to all historical experience, we should before long

305

witness the emergence of new communities, a Hebrew-Catholic Church, a Hebrew-Protestant Church, and even a Hebrew-Moslem Community. That is to say: there would be the same separate groups, the same Jewish minorities in all countries, but with this difference—that the Jewish tradition, the Messianic idea, the Jewish religion—the fine things that justify the existence of the Jewish minority—would vanish from the world. This process occurred in Visigoth and Almohad Spain, with the Marranos in Spain and Italy, the Donmeh in Turkey. Whenever Jews changed their religion simultaneously, as a group, they were not absorbed into other nations. We have heard repeatedly of Jewish assimilation, cataclysmic assimilation, anonymous assimilation, or whatever other name you wish to call it. Assimilation is widespread, and I shall yet discuss it, but assimilation will not mean complete disappearance. The Jews will remain.

This, then, is our initial premise. The Jews will remain in their various diaspora countries for many generations. True, diaspora communities may be lost through extermination, such as occurred in the Holocaust. No sane person will deny such a possibility. Fifty years ago, the idea of anything like the European Holocaust would have seemed fantastic. It would have been inconceivable that nations in the 20th Century should exterminate their Jews. And yet it happened; it happened on a much larger scale than ever before; and so it is possible. But it has to be made clear that from the point of view of the Zionist movement, a great change has occurred as far as anti-Semitism is concerned.

Anti-Semitism and Zionism

From the days of Pinsker and Herzl to our own days, anti-Semitism has been a main factor in Zionist ideology. We have always stressed the idea that because of anti-Semitism there was no hope for Jewry in the diaspora and that the Jewish state, therefore, was the only solution. Even today there are people who believe that this threat can induce Jewish youth in the United States, Canada, South Africa, or anywhere else to come to Israel en masse.

This belief is sadly mistaken. The threat of anti-Semitism is not capable of influencing many people. Nuclear war constitutes a much more immediate threat: thousands of people fear that such a war may break out in the near future. There have been times of international tension in recent years, when indeed, it seemed almost imminent. Nevertheless, have people in the thousands left New York, Washington, London, or any other city threatened by atomic war and gone to settle in smaller places? I have met only a few—a select few, if I may say so—who changed their residence for the reason of that ever-real threat.

This means that if we speak of mass emigration, I am sorry to say that it is a great historical truth that mass emigration is almost always the result of pressure, usually economic, or both political and economic. One does not have to be a Marxist to know that in such matters the economic factor is the strongest, while political pressure also plays an important part. This was illustrated long ago by the nomad Bedouin tribes of antiquity. When there was a famine in their country, they migrated elsewhere. And so people have migrated at all times under economic pressure. Even in our Zionist history most of those emigrating to *Eretz Yisrael* came from Russia under pressure from the Czars, from Poland under pressure from Grabski, from Germany and other countries under overwhelming pressure from Hitler, and are coming at this hour from Moslem countries under pressure from the Moslem governments. In all these cases, there has been both political and economic pressure.

Of course, there have always been a number of notable exceptions: there have always been pioneers, both in this country and elsewhere, who emigrated from their homes for idealistic reasons, in quest of spiritual values. And I hope there will be many thousands of them both in this and coming generations, who will come to Israel in order to find spiritual satisfaction, not because they are compelled to leave their own country. But to hope that there will be a mass emigration of this type, an emigration of millions—two millions, as Ben-Gurion said—is contrary to all past history, to all experience not only of the Jewish people, but of all peoples.

Therefore, it seems to me that the Zionist movement should abandon its view that anti-Semitism is the main motive for the exodus of the children of Israel. Under the impact of everyday life, the anti-Semitic threat has lost much of its force as a living reality in the minds of the young, whether in the United States or in other free countries.

I will tell you of my personal experience. I came to the United States many years ago. I live in a small community, not in an illustrious Jewish community such as that of New York, but in a tiny place in Connecticut. There were very few Jews there; when my daughters went to school, they were the first Jewish children there in 20 years. I have been living for 22 years in that completely Christian locality, which, moreover, lies in an area considered in that part of the world to be anti-Semitic. Nevertheless, I have told my friends that if I were asked to testify before a Senate Investigation Committee, not from hearsay, but from personal experience, I would have to say that neither I nor my family have been exposed to any anti-Semitic incident or anti-Semitic expression during the 22 years of my residence in that locality and all the 32 years that I have been in the United States. I have read about such incidents in the press or heard about them from others, but I cannot recall witnessing a single thing of this kind.

Not that there is no anti-Semitism here. There certainly is anti-Semitism in America, but hearing is not like seeing. Those who have not had some actual, personal encounter with anti-Semitism will regard it as something remote. There are youngsters in America who may feel they have not been admitted to a certain school, especially a medical school, because they are Jews. This is quite possible. Others may have applied for a job and not obtained it because they were Jews. But even these people are becoming fewer. If, under these circumstances, one tells the young that anti-Semitism is on the march, they will regard it as something remote. It will not psychologically affect them either today or tomorrow.

The Lachrymose View of Jewish History

It thus seems to me that Zionism will do well to leave the matter of anti-Semitism to those organizations which concern themselves mainly with the protection of Jewish rights—the American Jewish Committee, the Anti-Defamation League, and so on. The Zionist movement has a more fundamental issue with which to concern itself. Perhaps I am coming to something even more fundamental: the theme of anti-Semitism and Jewish distress. I have felt increasingly all my life that this emphasis keeps the youth away from us both in Israel and in the diaspora. Present-day youth is tired of hearing that all Jewish history is a tale of woe and nothing more. Present-day youth feels that there is more to Jewish history. Perhaps that accounts for the fact that the youth take greater interest in the Bible than in the Middle Ages or in the modern period. All descriptions of the Middle Ages and the modern period present a sequence of tribulations, of expulsions and persecutions, of what Graetz calls the *Leidensgeschichte* of the Jews. This *Leidensgeschichte*, he says, is the only thing that happened to the Jews, apart from the history of our sages.

Since my early days, I have insisted that the lachrymose conception of Jewish history is not correct from the point of view of historical truth, but neither is it congenial to our generation, a generation not of ghetto Jews, but of Jews living a young, free, and active life in various countries. It seems to me that the sooner we abandon this conception the better it will be both for the understanding of Jewish history and for the education of the present generation. There is much greatness in Jewish history—creative greatness. There was pioneering in every sense in the days of the Babylonian Exile, when many Jews played an important part in the Babylonian economy, and in the days of Hellenistic Egypt; and there were pioneers in Europe and America. Those merchants of the 19th Century, those great nuclear scientists of our days, all these were and are pioneers, pioneers of the mind and the body, who found and paved new ways for themselves and for civilization.

The same analysis applies to the great epic of our martyrs, and as far as I can see, even to the history of the Holocaust in our days. When Shlomo bar Shimshon told of the martyrs of Mayence in his *Scroll*, he spoke of 1,000 victims slain in one day, who silently suffered the fate decreed by heaven. But in the case of the Holocaust of the six million, we hear chiefly of the fighters of the Warsaw Ghetto and far fewer of those who suffered their fate in silence. In fact, I have been told that both in Israel and in the United States it is difficult to find young scholars to study the Jewish history of the Nazi period. They admit that it is an important subject, but it is not one they wish to go into very much. Our great writers both in Israel and in the United States have not yet given us an artistic–literary account of the Holocaust, the greatest disaster in the whole of Jewish history. This, too, seems to me a symptom of a new feeling, a new approach. It appears that we want to create, to be pioneers, to be fighters, to be active, and not a passive Jewry of distress and tribulation.

Hence, the Zionist movement must tread new paths, stressing neither anti-Semitism nor the past and present suffering of the Jewish people, but the great beauty of the new creativeness, the new life that is developing in Israel. It is this great creativeness, which is indeed without parallel, that will captivate the hearts of youth abroad, and it is similar creativeness that will make our Middle Ages and our recent past appear as something vital and attractive.

The Enduring Dialogue

The dialogue between the diaspora and the State of Israel is not something newly arisen. It is what distinguishes Jewish history from that of all other peoples. I will not go into the question of the Chosen People here. These are religious beliefs which one accepts or not; but I have no doubt whatsoever that the history of every great people is something new under the sun. Has there ever been in world history anything like the history of the USA, or the USSR, or the British Empire, or even of the French or the German people? Every people has its own peculiar history. Jewish history, too, is unique, all the more so because it dates back 3,500 years or more. Its importance lay originally in the significance of the religion engendered by it for a large part of mankind. It became still more unusual as a result of the dispersion of the Jewish people throughout the world.

I remember that in my youth several opponents of Zionism came to me and said: "You Zionists are mere dreamers. Can a colony be created without a mother country? If the English, the Dutch, the French, the Greeks, the Sidonites, etcetera, established colonies, there was in each case a mother country behind them. There was an army, a powerful fleet, a government treasury behind them. You wish to reverse the order and have the diaspora build itself a mother country. This is the opposite of what is normal." I said to them: "You are right. It is generally true that colonies are created by a mother country. But in our history, in Jewish history, it has already happened twice that the diaspora built the mother country. The Jews from Egypt built the First Temple, and the Babylonian exiles built the Second Temple. Why should not the exiles of the 20th Century build the Third Temple?"

This is precisely what has happened. We have reversed the order. Why? Because from the very outset, from the days of our ancestor Abraham, there has been a unique relationship between the world at large and this country.

NATIONALISM

I am now coming to the grave and fundamental question of our nationalism. We must remember that world nationalism has undergone a great development during the past 100 years. Gone are the days of Fichte's *Menschheits-nation*, of Mieckiewicz' and Mazzini's Messianic nationalism, that is to say, of nationalism that assigned to itself a cultural task, the task of building up a nation for the sake of mankind, and not a nation for its own sake. When the Zionist movement first emerged at the end of the 19th Century, it was largely nurtured on the Messianic nationalism. It added, of course, an ingredient of its own, something of the age-old, traditional Messianic idea, which represented precisely that same combination of nationalism and humanity. The greatness of Zionism lay in this universal Messianic idea it stood for.

In the 20th Century, nationalism as a whole deteriorated considerably. It became more extreme, more radical, until it reached its peak in Fascism and Nazism, in all the totalitarian slogans of the state, the national state or the racial state, as the be-all and end-all.

I sometimes warn my Arab friends and my friends from the Far East, saying: "See that you do not make your new states purely political bodies, centers of political power and political entrenchment, keeping out the human–cultural element."

I remember that a few years ago an Arab student at Columbia University wrote a thesis on the part played by the Arab states at the UN. While examining him, I remarked: "You have written a whole book about how the Arab delegates have represented their states, doing this and that, almost always in connection with the Israel question, that is to say, in a matter where your own interests were involved. What would you have done if you had had to write such a book on the Scandinavian peoples, who are also members of the UN? They, too, have taken part in every General Assembly, but they have not had such a question, they have not always been concerned with the interests of Denmark or Sweden, for or against which the UN can do very little. You would not have been able to write a book then."

This confirmed to me something that I had known in advance: that the Arab nations were in fact concerned almost exclusively with political questions. This may perhaps be a lesson both for the State of Israel and the diaspora. Let us not forget our own age-old nationalism which has always been both national and human, but which is now appearing in a new shape, under new conditions. The danger of our forgetting it is very close.

Lesson from History

We, who stand somewhat outside, should always remember certain things. Let us not forget that our ancestor Abraham, who lived a long time before Joshua the son of Nun, left Ur of the Chaldaeans and came to *Eretz Yisrael*, left Egypt and returned to *Eretz Yisrael*. In a sense, he symbolizes for us the combination of the greatest cultures of the ancient East—Babylonian, Assyrian, and Egyptian—the cultures which made world history together with *Eretz Yisrael*. When anti-Semites speak of the international Jew, there is something to it. The Jews have been and are scattered all over the world; they were so scattered in the days of the Second Temple, when the greater part of Jewry already lived outside *Eretz Yisrael*. Evidence of dispersion may perhaps be found even in the days of the First Temple. There are numerous indications that some Jews remained in Egypt and did not go to *Eretz Yisrael*: Papyri of the 12th and 13th Centuries show that there were still Hebrews in Egypt then. There were some there again, in Tahpanhas and Elephantine, even before the destruction of the First Temple.

If even during the period of the First Temple, we were not exclusively in *Eretz Yisrael*, in the days of the Second Temple most of the nation seems to have remained abroad. It seems to me that one of the most important things I have to say concerning the period of the Second Temple is that, in my opinion (I am not here following the latest view), two-thirds of the nation lived abroad at that time. These two-thirds, except for those in Babylonia and later in Egypt, did not make Jewish history. They were content to let *Eretz Yisrael* make history. They were helpers, but not partners. They certainly made pilgrimages; they paid the *Shekel*, the holy *Shekel*, to Jerusalem; they collected money and sent it through groups of emissaries to the Holy City. All this was very well, but they left it to the leaders in *Eretz Yisrael* to make fundamental decisions for them, without consulting them. Of course, there were political conflicts even then. In the diaspora, the Roman government protected the Jewish minority; in *Eretz Yisrael* it protected the Greek minority against the Jews. "Divide and rule" was the motto. The difference in Rome's attitudes to the two groups was so great that after the destruction of the Temple, Vespasian and Titus told delegates from Alexandria and Antioch that they did not wish to deprive the Jews there of their equal rights on account of Jewish treason in *Eretz Yisrael*. In Alexandria the Jews were convenient to the Romans, whereas they were not at all so convenient in *Eretz Yisrael.* The position was different later on, during the revolt under Trajan, when the Jews of Egypt rose up in arms.

Historical developments might perhaps have been different if the diaspora had taken a more immediate part in the destinies of the State of Israel in the days of the Second Temple. Of course, it is not worth speculating what would have happened in history in such and such a hypothetical case. But the great tragedy of the Destruction of the Temple is at least half to be ascribed to the split. The Sadducean leaders in Jerusalem, in particular, did not pay attention to the diaspora, and the Pharisees did not stress the State so much as religion. They felt that it was they who understood the requirements of the nation, they who had brought about its rebirth. Let us remember these facts. We can learn no end of a lesson from this historical experience.

The Beginning of Worldwide Emancipation

Last, I wish to tackle one more basic problem, which is bound up with all these matters: the problem of emancipation. If we speak of the assimilation of American, British, or French Jews, the expression is perhaps not strictly correct. Assimilation is a program, a party program, such as there was in Germany or in Poland. But we should remember that assimilation—that is, becoming a part of the people in whose midst one lives—is one of the basic objectives of every emancipation movement. If emancipation has any meaning, it is that from now on the Jews will not be a minority in face of the national majority, but rather a part of the national majority itself. This is a situation the likes of which has never been in Jewish history and which has accordingly led to a great crisis in Jewish life.

In the days of the First Exile, the question was whether Jews would be able to survive without a state, without a country, without a temple. Then Ezekiel came, and later the men of the Great Synod and many others down to Hillel and the Pharisees, and decided that the Jews could live in segregation from the other peoples, be a separate people in the midst of the peoples, a minority, the same sort of minority in all countries, with the same synagogues, the same *batei-midrash,* for which it makes no great difference whether they are in one country or in another. All this ceased in the period of the emancipation.

However, the crisis was only beginning. True, Emancipation was first proclaimed by the American Revolution, by the French Revolution, as early as the 18th Century, but in truth, in historical fact, it is not a reality even today, for it is sufficient to remember that only 50 years ago half the Jewish people lived under Czarist rule, with its Pobiedonochevs and its Porich-kieviches, utterly without equality of rights. Another important part of the people lived in Rumania, in the Ottoman Empire. Perhaps two-thirds of the entire Jewish people did not enjoy emancipation. And as for the free countries where they had formal equality of rights, most of the Jews who lived, say, in 1907, in the United States, Britain, or France had been born and bred in Russia, Rumania, or the Ottoman Empire and were not free Jews in the full sense of the term. A man does not change overnight merely by passing from one country to another. He does not stop being what he is. Even in America, after 100 years or more, the present generation of Jews is the first almost wholly born and bred in the country. This is something new.

There is still more to it. After 1917 to 1918 it seemed that equality of rights would be given to Jews in the whole world. But it was not. Poland did not keep her promises; Rumania did not keep her promises. Then the Nazi movement arose, which not only did not grant equality of rights, but wanted, and proclaimed as its objective, the total destruction of the Jews.

Therefore, future historians will perhaps admit that the emancipation of the Jews, even on paper, did not really begin until 1946. It is a very new phenomenon. Worldwide emancipation has only just begun.

Turning Point in History

Thus, we are indeed faced by a great crisis. We are no longer able to accept the answer given for 500 years, from Ezekiel to Hillel, which was basic to the whole existence of the Jewish people in the diaspora down to our own days. We now have to think of a new life, a life to lead, as Americans and Jews, Britons and Jews, Frenchmen and Jews. This is something new. If this crisis finds no solution, then diaspora Jewry will perhaps indeed, in the course of time, vanish from the world. However, as I said at the outset, there is no reason to believe that for many generations to come the Jews would be able to vanish from the world even if they wanted to. The great majority of diaspora Jews wish to survive as Jews. What, therefore, does this turning point in Jewish history mean? That is the question.

I think it is one of the great tasks of the State of Israel, in partnership with the diaspora, to find new ways in which Jews living in the countries of equality of rights can at the same time be creative and fruitful as Jews. Since historically it was not possible for Jews to vanish from the world, let us not make the mistake of thinking that ways will not be found.

A great degree of pioneering ability has been demonstrated by American Jewry not only in the economic sense, not only in the spiritual, human sense, but also in the sense of communal achievements, new organizational achievements. I have in mind all those Jewish centers, all those summer camps, charitable institutions, all those new approaches of a free people. If it has the pioneering spirit, if it has the will to strengthen the community, it will find the way. Jews in America have in part already found it, not only for themselves, but also for several other diaspora countries.

Conclusions

It would be well for us to make up our minds: first, that both the State of Israel and the diaspora have come to stay for the foreseeable future—not eternally, but for as long as we can foresee; second, that the dialogue between the State of Israel and the diaspora will go on for a great many generations to come, though its form may vary from time to time; third, that the Zionist movement should not lay so much stress on the anti-Semitic menace, but leave this matter, as well as the practical fight against anti-Semitic phenomena, to other public bodies; and fourth, that it must be constantly stressed that the Zionist movement does not regard the emancipation movement as an internal rival but that, on the contrary, Zionism confirms the demand that the Jews in all their countries of residence should enjoy full civic rights.

It has generally been held in Zionist circles that there is a rift between emancipation and Zionism. Ahad Haam spoke of "bondage in freedom," and Pinsker spoke of "auto-Emancipation," as opposed to emancipation. Conversely, many fighters for equality of rights regarded it as their duty to oppose Zionism. Now, in historical perspective, we can see that emancipation and the national movements, including Zionism, are in fact one. It was emancipation that made possible the emergence of a modern, nonghetto nationalism. Moreover, it was only through emancipation that a generation or generations of Jews grew up knowing how to use arms, familiar with industrial technology and government administration. Emancipation has given diaspora Jewry economic plenty and political influence. Without all these things the rebirth of the Jewish state in this form would have been inconceivable.

Actually, it was precisely emancipation that demonstrated the need for a Jewish state, more than did all the Messianic ideas. In our time the greatest danger to Jewish existence was and is the possibility that the Jews may cease to be one people. There was a danger that there would be a separate Jewry in the United States, another in European countries, another in Russia. In fact, in the 1920s, it seemed as if two Jewish peoples already existed, one in Russia, Yiddish-speaking, brought up on Sholom Aleichem, without religion, without Zionism, without Hebrew, without a Messianic idea, but recognized as an ethnic group; and another in the West, educated in English or French schools, mostly not speaking a language of its own, not constituting a national minority in the legal sense, but having a religion, having the Hebrew idea, the Zionist idea, the longing to return to Zion.

If this situation had lasted a long time, different sects might have arisen in Judaism, perhaps more than the 24 which in the opinion of our sages brought about the destruction of the Second Temple. This is the reason why it was particularly necessary that a modern state should arise, a place where it would be impossible for the Jews to assimilate, where they would be Jews, not American Jews, British Jews, or Argentine Jews, but Jewish Jews. Such a place, the only such place, is *Eretz Yisrael*. Even in the days of the Mandate, there was no question of the Jews in Israel assimilating to anyone.

The fifth point I wish to make is that the Zionist idea should no longer base itself to so great an extent on the long succession of our tribulations, but should also stress that which is beautiful and auspicious, the great achievements of the Jewish people in the past as well as those yet to come.

Sixth, the future economic, social, and spiritual achievements of the State of Israel will, without doubt, give it a strong magnetic power even for countries in which there is no political or economic pressure.

Meanwhile—and this is my seventh and last point—let us continue building a great world culture which for all historic antecedents is essentially new, the culture of an eternal people scattered throughout the world, which is at the same time a partner in the world's cultures and a partner—a real partner, not a mere helper—in the political, and even more, in the cultural and religious achievements of that increasing part of Jewry which is concentrated in the State of Israel.

·28·
American Jews and Israel: Strengthening the Bonds

Yitzhak Rabin

I was born and raised in Israel, and my image of the diaspora was essentially of East European Jewry. It was based on what I learned in elementary school and high school, and from Hebrew literature. (I am afraid they still teach that way in Israeli schools.) But in my five years of working and living in the United States, I came to understand the diaspora.

In discussing the relations of Israel and American Jewry, it is well to start with the numerical discrepancy. We are talking about the relations between approximately three million Jews who live in Israel and about six million Jews who live in the United States. And if we take into account the fact that there are also some three million Jews in the Soviet Union, then this triangle—Israel, American Jewry, Soviet Jewry—constitutes the great bulk of the Jewish people. These three Jewish axes reflect the independent Jewish people (the State of Israel), the distressed diaspora (the USSR), and the affluent diaspora (the United States).

The importance of the Jews of the United States in Jewish life is tremendous, in both Jewish thought and Jewish education. Academic Jewish research in the United States may be said to be holding its own vis à vis its counterpart in Israel. The economic and political power of the Jews in the United States enables them to exert considerable influence on American policy with respect to Israel and the Jews. American Jewry also plays the leading role in determining norms and standards of Jewish behavior in all the democratic countries. The nature of the relationship between Israel and American Jewry is therefore of unique importance.

Historical Perspective

The relations of Israel with world Jewry should be viewed in the perspective of Jewish history. I shall mention a few principles which serve me as a point of departure for an examination of Israel's relations with world Jewry, and particularly with American Jewry. Historically, the main goal of Judaism and the Jews has been to preserve the Jewishness of Judaism both as a value and as a physical entity. This has been the aim of the Jewish struggle throughout history.

Through 19 centuries of exile, there were three main forms of the Jewish struggle for the preservation of Judaism. The first was profound faith, the extraordinary attachment to religion, to tradition, and to Jewish values. Without this attachment it is difficult to understand the phenomenon, which has no parallel in human history, of a people that has succeeded in preserving its uniqueness, its character, its religion, and its values—despite persecution, cruel treatment, forced conversion, and inquisitions. The Jews achieved this by regarding themselves as a Chosen People bearing values, not just for themselves, but values that could guide mankind. On the other hand, the belief that "Thou hast chosen us" gave rise to the concept of the Jewish nation being "a people that dwells alone" (Num. 12:9).

A second expression of the urge for Jewish preservation was the yearning and the unrelenting faith that one day they would return and establish an independent Jewish state in their ancient homeland. How could a people— an ethnic group, a religion—preserve this yearning and eventually attain its desire? This too is one of the most astounding phenomena in history.

The third expression was the Jewish dispersion. This was a curse, but it was also a saving factor in ensuring the survival of the Jewish people. There was no situation in which, by destroying some part of the Jewish people in a particular place, it was possible to liquidate the entire Jewish people. In addition, the Jews were imbued with the sense of mutual responsibility toward their persecuted brothers. The principle that "all Israel are responsible for one another" was fostered as a value, and it became one of the unique assets of the Jewish people, enabling it to survive. When misfortune struck a Jewish community in one place, the other sections of the Jewish people did more than any other people in history ever did for its compatriots or co-religionists.

Toward the end of the 19th and in the beginning of the 20th Century, Jewish history (the religious would say "Divine Providence") created a new reality: the Zionist movement which led to the establishment of the State of Israel. This occurred at a time which enabled the Jews to achieve three things: first, it allowed them to build a Jewish national and spiritual center that serves as a substitute for the decline in religion as the main element in the preservation of Judaism; secondly, it is a physical solution for the rescue of

Jews; and third, it is a central core around which Judaism can continue to foster Jewish values, in the context of a progressive 20th Century society.

Today's Issues: Preservation of Values

In exploring the contemporary challenges to the Jew and to Judaism, it is necessary to emphasize both the struggle for the upbuilding of the Jewish state and the building of the Jewish people. I am stressing both—the state and the people. There can be no state without a people and no people without a state. We must, therefore, face both challenges, the upbuilding of the Jewish state and the preservation of the Jewishness of world Jewry. And we will be unable to achieve both aims unless the connection between them is fully understood. So long as we do not understand the connection between the realization of the Zionist vision and the preservation of the bond with world Jewry, with the aim of preserving its Jewishness, we shall endanger both of them.

I realize that in the foreseeable future the Jewish people will continue to be divided into Jews who live in the State of Israel and Jews who will continue to live in the diaspora. People who reject this approach and who interpret the goal of contemporary Zionism as the liquidation of the Jewish diaspora are on very slippery ground. Without a realistic appraisal of the contemporary Jewish situation it will be difficult for us to explore the methods of shaping the relations between the two portions of the Jewish nation.

THE UNIQUENESS OF AMERICAN JEWRY

American Jewry must be understood against the background of the United States and the American people. The American people is a nation of immigrants in which the process of the absorption of the immigrants is not yet complete. The fact that it is a nation of immigrants is a decisive element in its national consciousness. Moreover, in the past few years the ethnic minorities and national groups have been striving to stress their origins and the attachment to their own past.

Anti-Semitism exists everywhere, but the American people lacks that tendency toward national uniformity which characterizes other nations. This enables the American Jew to be an American and a Jew at one and the same time, without becoming entangled in contradiction. Since American society was founded by refugees from religious persecution, there is in the United States an unprecedented degree of freedom, and Jews enjoy considerable opportunities to achieve social, economic, and political success. This determines a pattern of life for the Jewish community in the United States that differs from that of any other Jewish group in the world.

Once, I flew to the United States—it was before I was ambassador—in the company of an American officer, an Air Force colonel. He was sitting next to me, and we began to talk. He discovered that I was an army man from Israel. Toward the end of the flight he was in a good mood, and then he said to me: "You know, I was born in the South. I was not brought up to like Jews, for all sorts of reasons, but above all because they did not fit into my conception of 'American.' True, we are a land of immigrants, there's nothing wrong about being an American and retaining one's attachment to a country of origin. The trouble with the Jews was that they did not fit into my world of ideas as to the nature of Americans. The English did not regard him as an Englishman, the Russians did not regard him as a Russian, the Poles did not regard him as a Pole, and the Germans did not regard him as a German. But now you have solved the problem. You have established the State of Israel. Now I consider the American Jew an American in every respect, since he too now has a country of origin. He is now a normal American as far as I am concerned."

More than anything else perhaps, this story indicates what Israel contributes to the American Jew, and why Israel is important to him, not only in terms of Jewish sentiment, but also with respect to his status as an American. The existence of Israel constitutes a reference point that determines his position in American society.

American Jewry has its own particular textures and structures, and these must be understood when considering its relations with Israel. What is American Jewry? How does it act as a Jewry? To this day, American Jewry has been preserved, for the most part, by living a Jewish life around the synagogue. This is not a synagogue in the Israeli sense of the term. The American synagogue is really a community. In the United States there is no Jewish life on a countrywide scale. Jewish life is concentrated around the nucleus of the synagogue-community and its social activities.

Of course, there are also national movements, political movements, and Zionist movements, but their influence is surprisingly small. The basis of Jewish life always was and has remained the synagogue, in the broader American sense of the term.

The national Jewish organizations are not as strong as the community organizations. And the State of Israel acted wisely when it founded the United Jewish Appeal and the Bond Drive—which have become the greatest instruments of practical activity on behalf of Israel—not as national organizations but as community systems. In fact, the two strongest Jewish national organizations in the United States today (and not only as financial instruments) are the UJA and the Bond Drive.

Shaping Relations, Strengthening Bonds

How should we shape the relations between Israel and American Jewry? What do we want? And what can be expected? Most American Jews are not interested in *aliyah*. In the history of Zionism we never had large-scale *aliyah* from affluent countries. The large waves of immigration were always spurred by Jewish distress. At the same time, it seems to me that there is a danger of a drifting apart between Israel and American Jewry, which may be caused by an estrangement from Judaism. Our common denominator is the Jewish roots of American Jewry. And if I were asked what should be the focus of our main effort today I would say: to develop ways and means to strengthen the Jewishness of the Jews of the United States. *Aliyah* will be a consequence of the success in this area.

I see this as a vital matter for the continued existence of Israel. There is really no need for me to argue that Israel cannot be satisfied with the number of Jews now living within its borders. The Jewish ideal is the existence of a Jewish state that assumes a Jewish mission vis à vis the Jewish communities in the affluent countries, and a Jewish rescue mission to the Jews living in distress.

There are, to be sure, Jews like George Steiner who see an essential conflict between the existence of Judaism and the existence of the State of Israel. Steiner is not the only one. There are extremist groups—*Neturei Karta* on the one hand and communists and other leftists on the other— who oppose Israel. But the great majority of the American Jewish community (as far as I am able to judge) regard themselves as closely linked with Israel.

This stems primarily from two positive factors. The majority of the Jewish public in the United States still wishes to preserve Judaism, as it understands it, and to preserve Jewish values and identity as well as the attachment to the Jewish heritage and religion. Second, there is the unassailable connection which the non-Jew sees between Jews and Israel. The status of the American Jew, even if he tries to repudiate his Judaism, has in the eyes of his surrounding society become inextricably linked with the State of Israel. The Six-Day War restored Jewishness to Jews who had sought to flee from it, because they now realize that they could not escape from it. In the consciousness of most of the American people, the Jews diminished or grew commensurately with the status of the State of Israel. And that is why Steiner and his colleagues in their academic ivory towers are so utterly wrong. The American Jewish community is firmly convinced today that it is inextricably connected with the State of Israel.

ISRAEL'S ROLE

It therefore seems to me that the time has come for us to consider not only what Jews in the diaspora can do for Israel, but what is the task of Israel vis à vis the Jewish communities. There are a number of things that I today consider to be essential:

1. To give full recognition to the realistic aspects of the situation; to be aware of our mutual dependence; and to realize that unless we foster these ties we shall undermine the basis of our existence.

2. To develop the potential inherent in the concept of the centrality of Israel which is today firmly rooted in the Jewish consciousness of most American Jews—as a complement to religion—in the preservation of Judaism.

3. Ways must be sought to strengthen the Jewish educational network. If we do not deal urgently with Jewish education—and I refer to the pre-university levels—we shall undermine the attachment of Jews to Judaism and the ties between Jewry and all Jewish affairs, including Israel.

4. Methods must be found for engaging American Jewry—in addition to *aliyah*—in Israeli and Jewish activities: economic, social, spiritual, and political.

5. The attempt to introduce political content into Jewish activity in the United States on Israeli and Jewish issues is one of the important factors that maintain the Jewishness of the Jews of the United States. When a Jew or the Jewish community in the United States declares, for instance, "As Americans and as Jews we are fighting for Israel, as Americans and as Jews we are fighting for the Jackson Amendment, for that has to do with the persecution of Jews as Jews," this infuses a content without which Jewish life in the United States cannot survive. For without Jewish activism it is impossible to maintain Jewish frameworks, and without Jewish frameworks it is impossible to maintain Judaism. I have not been able to understand the difference between certain persons in the United States who are defined as Zionists, and others who are not described as such. I have not discovered any difference between such groups with respect to their attachment to Israel, to their readiness to work for Israel, to their willingness to do everything on behalf of any Israeli or Jewish matter.

It appears to me that in the American situation there is a basis for a broad network of relationships, which is essential for both sides. Israel is vital for the American Jew, for his status as an American and a Jew. For Israel, the preservation of American Jewry is vital. Even the issue of Soviet Jewry would probably not have developed as it has, were it not for the tremendous importance of American Jewry. It seems to me that it is possible—and essential—to reexamine the network of relations between Israel and American Jewry. I see this as a matter of the utmost importance, second only perhaps to the internal problems of Israeli society. In any case, it comes before many other subjects that are exercising the Israeli public.

I share the belief that the State of Israel is bound to preserve its Jewish character. What we mean by Jewish character is, of course, debatable. To engage today in an antireligious conflict seems misguided. It should not be forgotten that there is a difference between the importance of religion in the United States or anywhere else in the world in the preservation of the

Jewishness of Jews, and the political bargaining that we are familiar with in Israel.

The religious leaders, too, must take into account that they ought to adapt substantial parts of the Jewish legal system which are, in my opinion, only incidentally connected with religious values. The problem for the Jewish religion is that for 19 centuries it was not a state religion. In ancient times there was a struggle between priest and king, a *Sanhedrin*, and a working system that enabled the adaptation of religion to reality. This adaptive ability has been largely lost, at least since the establishment of the State of Israel. Had religious Jews evinced the need to adapt religion to changing realities, I believe that a broad basis for understanding could be found. If not, then in five or fifteen years the clash will come—a clash from which no one will emerge victorious. The Jewish people will be the loser.

Conclusion

The framework of Jewish life in the diaspora will continue to be religious. I have not discovered any concrete suggestion as to how to preserve the Jewishness of the Jews by other means and that is why I do not propose that we now destroy frameworks, patterns of life, or values, before we find better substitutes which will offer an answer to the overall Jewish problem. It is not just that we have no choice. I think that every framework that serves to maintain Jews ought to be strengthened and developed.

I believe that we have been granted the opportunity to concentrate on two issues: building a society (in addition to building a state) in Israel, and strengthening the ties between Israel and world Jewry. If we do not accomplish this, we will miss an historic opportunity which is of vital and lasting importance for the future of the Jewish nation.

·IX·
Israel
and the
Jewish Future

·29·
Identity and Alienation: Zionism for the West

Abraham Kaplan

Adaptation in Exile

Adaptation has for so long been necessary to Jewish survival that it has become our second nature. "If there will be another Flood," we say, "we will simply have to learn to live under water!" We not only adapt; we persuade ourselves that all is for the best. "If life gives you lemon," the proverb runs, "make lemonade." "And make a *brachah*," the Jew adds: recite a blessing before drinking it. In folk humor the *shadchan* or marriage broker presents the bride's shortcomings as virtues: the ugly bride will never give cause for jealousy, the stammerer won't nag, the cripple won't chase after you. If she brings only a small dowry—*nu*, you can't have everything.

For many Jews of the diaspora, exile is just such a bride. The Talmud calls the dispersion of the Jews a blessing to the nations, since thereby we can more readily make converts among them (Pesachim:87b). Yet proselytizing has not been a marked feature of Jewish life; and if Israeli clericalism has its way, conversion will become even less frequent.

The Zohar more realistically describes the Jews of the diaspora as a leaven among the nations (Genesis:244a). Historians have noted, for instance, the decline of Spain after the Inquisition. Germany's fall from scientific leadership after the Nazi era is also seen as a mark of what nations lose if there are no Jews among them. The Talmud goes further: God did "a great favor to

327

Israel" in dispersing them (Genesis:244a). The argument was already advanced by Philo of Alexandria and by Josephus: dispersion makes possible the survival of the Jew—not for the superficial reason that there is no one place where the Jewish people might be utterly destroyed, but because dispersal, in denying the Jew land and liberty, forces him to turn from time to eternity, and there he is indestructible.

The lesson had been learned in the First Exile. The Babylonian captives carried with them a book and a tradition which could endure as long as Jews, however widely dispersed, would cherish them. Emphasis on Torah as the sustaining force in Jewish life was the contribution of Ezra the Scribe; it was said that had Moses not received the Law, Ezra would have been worthy to do so.

In modern times the argument has been extended beyond Jewish survival to Jewish attainment. The historian Simon Dubnow argued that the extraterritorial nationality of the Jews endows them with a "spiritual peoplehood" which, he says, is the highest mode of collective existence, a height to which other people have not yet arrived. "By not being part of any particular environment, the Jews become a universal people."[1] Diaspora Jews are not in exile, but only dispersed; Jews are more truly at home than are those among whom they live.

This rationalization is deeply rooted in Jewish history. There is a tradition that the *Shekhinah*, the Divine Presence, accompanied the Jews into exile (Megillah 29a; Numbers R 7:10, etcetera). "If you have Me," God might say, "what else can be lacking? Better to take refuge in Me than to trust in princes" (Psalms 118:9). Though you are not in a land of your own, who needs it? Though you speak a foreign tongue, yet you may speak freely with Me. While those among whom you live worship strange gods, you may serve Me, and live by My law.

Such assurances are falsified by the history of Jewish persecution. But even persecution has been accepted as a blessing in disguise. The Jewish people, it is said, is like a flask of perfume, which gives off its scent only after being shaken. The hard-boiled egg featured at the Passover table is taken to be a symbol of the Jew: the more it is cooked, the harder it gets.

True, great centers of creative Jewish life have sprung up in the diaspora. What we know as "the" Talmud is the Babylonian redaction, not that codified in Jerusalem. The golden age of Jewish poetry and philosophy, exemplified by Yehudah Halevi, Maimonides, and the Zohar, flourished in Spain. Eastern Europe gave birth to the Hasidic movement and the rich Yiddish culture. Great Jewish commentators lived in medieval France, while modern Germany produced scientific Jewish scholarship and progressive Judaism. The Jew made himself at home abroad.

The difference between dispersion (*tfutsot*) and exile (*galut*) remains. Diaspora is a neutral, geographical concept. Exile implies something involuntary and undesirable. It connotes alienation and longing, a life whose meaning lies in the past or in the future but never in the present. Diaspora is experienced as exile unless there is systematic self-deception or else scarcely a self to be deceived. *Galut*, I conceive, is what Haim Greenberg defined it to be: "wherever Jews live as a minority." In a trivial sense, everyone belongs to some minority or other: left-handers, redheads, or tea-drinkers. It is not trivial if minority status is central to personal identity, which is what it means to *live* as a minority. Exile is alienation when the exile has become a "marginal man" (the term coined by Kurt Lewin, a German Jewish social psychologist who came to the United States as a refugee). At best, being a member of a minority is like what Tevye says about being poor: it's no shame, but it's no great honor either!

Even in the Golden Age, minority existence was deprecated as marginal. The Jewish people of the diaspora, said Yehudah Halevi, is "a body without a head or heart . . . not even a body but scattered bones." His contemporary, the commentator Moses Ibn Ezra, characterized life in the diaspora as "a form of imprisonment . . . plants without soil or water." In modern times the ideologue of labor, A. D. Gordon, declared that in the diaspora "we can have no living culture . . . because we have no life of our own."

The rabbinic tradition is equally emphatic. Some centuries ago Judah Loew of Prague called diaspora "a perversion of the divine order which assigns to each nation its own place." In the early decades of this century Solomon Schechter observed that Jews "go about begging for a nationality—clamoring everywhere 'We are you!'" Rationalization has given way to the defense mechanism of denial: we are not in exile, alienated, marginal—we are not really a minority at all.

The majority does not always persecute its minorities. It has its own patterns of adaptation. Among them is incorporation: swallowing up the minority by denying it a distinctive identity. This is a process in which the minority often collaborates. "Let's put religion back into Christmas," the announcer pleads; "this Christmas, go to the church or synagogue of your choice!" An apocryphal story tells of a member of the American delegation to the United Nations who exclaimed, "Why can't Israel and her Arab neighbors settle their differences like Christian gentlemen!"

Less subtle, but ideologically more respectable, is the majority's toleration, the 18th Century liberal's version of the separate-but-equal doctrine. Tolerance implies something objectionable in what is tolerated, as in tolerance for poisons, and tolerance in the sense of the engineer's acceptable margin of error. It also implies passivity on the part of the majority, an attitude which excludes the minority from full participation in community. Toleration can work against incorporation by emphasizing the distinctive character of the minority in the very act of tolerating the difference.

Toleration may benefit one minority at the expense of another; it may also discriminate against less-favored elements of the majority. Affirmative action originally meant actively seeking out eligible members of a minority and offering special training to all who needed it to become eligible. Now it means preferentially lowering or even eliminating standards of eligibility on behalf of the favored minority. Affirmative action is now negative equality. It reinstates the quota system, by which discrimination, especially against Jews, has long been practiced. For a Jewish applicant to law school or medical school, the outcome is the same whether he is denied admission because he is a Jew or because he is neither a Black nor a Hispanic-American.

Exiles may continue to live as a minority just because they are tolerated as such. When the gates of the ghetto were opened, Jews encapsulated themselves in voluntary ghettos. The medieval Jewish quarter has largely given way to the modern Jewish neighborhood. In the diaspora, while Jews study, work, and shop among non-Jews, their friends and personal associates, remain, for the most part, other Jews. Alienation from the larger society persists. "Life in exile, at best," said Ahad Ha'am, the founder of cultural Zionism, "will always remain life in exile."[2]

By the waters of Babylon Jews sat down and wept, asking, "How shall we sing the Lord's song in a foreign land" (Psalms 137:4)? In modern times, Jews persuade themselves that the land is not really foreign. Initially, this attitude may have been a strategic pretense, like that of the Marranos, the crypto-Jews who accommodated to the Inquisition. Later, in the Age of Enlightenment, it may have been a calculated tactic for personal advantage. In our own day, at work may be the psychology of identification with the aggressor.

Many German Jews returned to Germany after the Holocaust; many Iranian Jews who had left in the first days of the Islamic revolution subsequently returned there. In countries where toleration is deeply rooted, as it is in the United States, emigration is almost unthinkable. Only a fraction of one percent of American Jews attempt *aliyah*. Although it is ten years since I moved to Israel, American friends find it hard to accept the move as permanent, and still ask whenever I am back in the States, "How long do you plan to live there?" My standard reply is "Only a short time—just until the coming of the Messiah!" There is less irony in the answer than in the question. It has been well said that it is easier to take a Jew out of exile than to take the exile out of the Jew.

Assimilation is not necessarily abandoning one's Jewish identity; it is transforming the identity so that it blends into its background. There are many "Jewish Unitarians," and some "Jewish Roman Catholics"; a popular evangelist advertises himself as "the little Jew with the big Jesus." Assimilated Jews need not become "amateur Gentiles," as Horace Kallen called them. They may remain Jews, while their Jewish identity shrinks to a mere identification. They label themselves Germans, Frenchmen, Americans, or whatever, "of the Mosaic faith." What is the distinctive content of this faith if it has been emptied of the history and destiny of a particular people and place?

American tolerance and incorporation have been crystallized in the symbolic triad "Protestant, Catholic, Jew." The military has three sorts of chaplains. At the Jewish university—Brandeis—are three chapels; Brigham Young, Notre Dame, and Southern Methodist Universities do not house a synagogue. Jewish life in the diaspora is in its very nature an exile; the Jewishness must *make* itself at home. That there is something to be done, something to be reached for which does not come naturally of itself—this is the essence of alienation.

The Jew *succeeds* in making himself at home; his love of country is intense and genuine. Patriotism can protest too much, compensating for an element of self-interest. Self-interest makes the patriotism more sincere; it also points to the underlying insecurity which is the mark of the exile. "Seek the peace of the city where I have caused you to be carried away captive," says the prophet (Jeremiah 29:5-7), adding, ". . . for in its peace you shall have peace." Quite understandable is the prayer attributed to the Hasid, Israel of Koznitz, "O God, if Your time has not yet come to redeem the Jews, at least redeem the *goyim!*"

In the meantime, the Jew of the diaspora keeps a low profile. Not always is the pattern so extreme as that of Iranian Jews who celebrated their weddings in London so as not to attract the envious attention of their neighbors. The Jews of the diaspora in the West are not Jews of silence, but they speak in low tones, except when the conventional symbols of tolerance are to be pronounced. The relations of Jew to non-Jew are usually those of quiet diplomacy.

Uninhibited expressions of Jewishness are felt to be in bad taste. The real bondage in Egypt, another Hasid, Henoch of Alexander, pointed out, is that the Hebrews learned to endure it. The golden calf was born of nostalgia.

The problem today for the Jew in the diaspora is how to maintain his Jewish identity. There is widespread concern for the preservation of Jewish identity by the children, particularly in the face of an ever higher rate of intermarriage. Few recognize that we cannot give our children what we do not have ourselves.

Diaspora Jewry copes with its predicament by enlisting the services of increasing numbers of "professional Jews"—rabbis, teachers, social workers, education directors, community center personnel, and the like. Forgotten is the injunction, "Thou shalt teach thy children"; it has been changed to, "Thou shalt have thy children taught." Jewish organizations proliferate: against anti-Semitism and for philanthropy; social organizations, religious organizations, cultural and political organizations. There are many Zionist organizations as well, on behalf of Israel and of those who may wish to go there from *other* parts of the world.

This is not a healthy life but a life of health clubs. Jews of the diaspora devote a great deal of effort to the expression of their Jewishness, matching the great effort called for by adaptation to a non-Jewish society. That is what it means to be in exile. It is why a precursor of Zionism, Moses Hess, declared well over a century ago that the Jewish people cannot be regenerated as long as it remains in the diaspora.[3]

Anti-Semitism and Its Disguises

In many countries the situation of the Jew is precarious. First are the Muslim countries, especially Iran and Syria. Denial of human rights to the Jews of the Soviet Union is notorious. Argentina's atmosphere is ominous; France's is worrisome. Even the United States is disquieting: one-fourth of non-Jewish Americans hold anti-Semitic beliefs; of those with a definite opinion, the proportion is one-third.[4] This is down from the nearly one-half in polls taken a decade ago; it is still disturbingly high.

The situation is clouded by political verbiage, like the campaign pledges of American candidates, and the principles enunciated in the Soviet Constitution in the Helsinki accords. In America, sentimental rhetoric reveals a pervasive belief in the magic of symbols, as do bumper-stickers, lapel buttons, t-shirt slogans, and observances like Brotherhood Week.

Persistent inequalities between Jew and non-Jew are ignored. Jews of the diaspora have risen high in politics; their Jewish commitment has not always been as dubious as, say, Kreisky's. Yet even in the United States—for Jews, probably the most egalitarian society in the diaspora—there are few Jews in the upper echelons of diplomacy, the military services, the automobile industry, and such stereotyped areas of Jewish expertise as banking and finance.

On the world scene anti-Semitism masquerades as anti-Zionism. In the Soviet Union, a Russian who prizes life in his own land, among his own people, is a patriot; a Ukrainian or Latvian with those values is a nationalist; a Jew with the same aspirations is a "hooligan." Jews were once charged with being clannish; today we are smeared as racist. In the past we were attacked for being cosmopolitan; now our offense is to defend our own homeland.

That nothing has changed but the labels is revealed in the selective morality displayed by the United Nations and by its member states—including, at various times, each of the Western states. There are few official condemnations of events in Afghanistan, Ireland, Lebanon, or Iran, though thousands of people are wantonly being killed in those places. But let Israel take any measure of self-defense and the world is in an uproar. The Jew continues to be a scapegoat, especially when he refuses to play the part of a willing victim.

Israel is continually being weighed in the balance and found wanting. There is a worldwide fixation on Israel, a grossly disproportionate amount of attention devoted to her in the General Assembly of the United Nations, and in the world's media. Her enemies accuse her of being at work everywhere, behind every setback they suffer. At a recent international student seminar some college students had the impression that Israel was about half the size of the United States and had a population of fifty million (it is the size of Connecticut and has a population of four million). The Jew looms large in the eyes of others.

The diaspora Jew struggles against this image, for it makes him conspicuous and vulnerable. The struggle is doomed, since the denial itself brings Israel and the Jews once more into the focus of attention. Devoted to Israel as he is, the Jew of the diaspora is caught up in explanations, excuses, and apologies. In my periodic visits to the United States I am challenged as an Israeli, not by Gentiles but by Jews. They are expressing their defensiveness. Every challenging question is meant to be, "What answer shall I give when I am asked why Israel does such and such?" Defensiveness is a mark of the exile; it is not felt in Israel. There, criticism of the Israeli government is the staple of political life; it is not a psychological defense-mechanism.

Jews of the diaspora suffer from an Arab obsession. Every Israeli issue is viewed in its relation to "the Arab problem." Visiting at the home of American friends during the World Series, I was asked what sports Israelis were interested in. "For one thing, basketball," I replied. Maccabbee Tel Aviv had just won the European basketball championship—European because the Asian countries will not admit Israel's teams; even in the European finals in Belgrade, no Hebrew advertisements were to be displayed, since the game was to be televised to countries that would object. Israelis, I reported, were thrilled with their victory, having also defeated the Red Army team on their way to the championship. The Jewish sport lovers heard me out, then asked only, "Were there any Arabs on your team?" (Ironically, there were two American Blacks.)

When I am identified with the University of Haifa, the first questions that I am likely to be asked are, how many Arab students we have, whether there are any Arabs on the faculty, whether there is a program of Arab studies, and the like. It is as though the American Jews I talk to would like to believe that I joined an Israeli university only for the sake of the Arabs, as some years ago a number of American Jewish professors lent their services to Black universities.

Similar questions were once put to me in quite another setting. A year or two before the Islamic revolution I was lecturing at the University of Ahwaz, in Iran; it is not far from the Iraqi border, so that a considerable number of Arab students are enrolled there (Iranians, of course, are not Arabs). After my lecture I was surrounded by Arab students asking about life in Israel. I invited them to come see for themselves, at which they protested that they would never be admitted. Upon my informing them that our university had over 600 Arab students, they were wholly unbelieving. That *they* felt the need to ask about Arab students in Israel is understandable; when the question is asked by Jews in the diaspora, it has a different significance. It is a mark of the exile that Jews of the diaspora are so reluctant to demand *our* just rights, and continue to be so uneasy about what they perceive as the moral issue raised by the continued existence of Israel.

No boundaries in the Middle East predate the present century. The Arab confrontation states were formed from mandated territories just as was Israel. Israel was established on what has been known for millennia as the Land of Israel, not on so-called "Arab lands." As new states emerged after World War II in many parts of the world, over 25-million people were resettled (five million, for instance, between India and Pakistan alone). If the Arabs had absorbed Palestinians in the same proportion that Israel absorbed Jewish refugees just from Arab states, the Arabs would have taken in all the Palestinian refugees 30 times over. They have had 30 years to do it, and billions of oil dollars to do it with. The exile mentality leans over backward; only so can it seriously consider that perhaps 20 Arab states are too few and one Jewish state is too many.

Zionism sprang out of concern for the hazardous situation of the Jew in the diaspora, a situation of which the Dreyfus case made Theodore Herzl aware. The movement began as refugee Zionism, whose aim was to provide a haven for persecuted and homeless Jews. For this reason, one of the early non-Jewish supporters of the movement was the founder of the Red Cross—an organization which today recognizes as an affiliate the Red Crescent but not the Red Magen David. The Holocaust undoubtedly played a large part in the agreement of Western nations to the establishment of the State of Israel. Jewish commentators pointed out long ago that the life of Isaac was saved by the ram caught in the thicket.

At its very outset Israel enacted a Law of Return, which provides that every Jew has the right to be admitted to Israel. Israel is the homeland of all Jews, in the sense of the folk definition, "Home is where, when you come, they have to take you in." Refugee Zionism meant the difference between life and death for hundreds of thousands of Jews fleeing first Nazi, and later Arab, persecution.

It may, alas, make the difference again. The Jew of the diaspora has been seen by many Jewish thinkers as a lamb among wolves.[5] Sooner or later, they believe, the lamb will once more fall prey to its lifelong enemies. "Only one day," says the Midrash, "did Jacob dwell in peace under the shadow of Esau" (Genesis 63:13).

Preoccupation with the danger is understandable, especially in Israel, which is so largely populated by survivors and the families of survivors of

brutal persecution. This preoccupation is expressed ideologically ...
Zionism, an exaggerated sensitivity to every manifestation of anti-Se...
in any form. The implication is that Jews of the diaspora should come to
Israel before it is too late.

Scare Zionism is pointless so far as the diaspora in the West is concerned.
The Jewish people has undergone a severe illness and traumatic surgery; it
need not become a confirmed hypochondriac forever after. There are,
admittedly, fairly widespread anti-Semitic attitudes in the West, and they are
sporadically acted out in incidents of vandalism. It would be rash to predict
anywhere that "it can't happen here." Yet the danger must be put into
perspective. That there are many criminals on the streets does not mean that
we must prepare for anarchy. Shortly after World War II numbers of
Americans were panicked into preparing shelters against nuclear attack.
Builders advertised "Twenty years to pay!" without discouraging buyers.
The threat of nuclear war is a real one; living underground is not a realistic
way to face the threat. *Scare Zionism* does little to encourage *aliyah* from the
West; those it is meant to reach are more realistic than are the ideologues.
The Jew of the diaspora has long prepared himself to take calculated risks.

Zionism cannot rest on reasons for running *from* something. Russian Jews
are desperate to escape Soviet mistreatment, but over 80 percent of those
who do escape run to another place in the diaspora. A half-million emigrés
have left Israel; neither they nor the Russian dropouts can be frightened back
to Israel. The question is, not what the Jew must run *from* but what he can
come *to*. The answer is: an identity.

National Identity

Nineteenth-Century liberalism was internationalist. It envisioned a world
in which men were no longer alienated from one another by divisive
groups—political, racial, and religious. History decreed otherwise. Group
identities of all three sorts are more important in this century than in the last,
more important today than they were a generation or two ago.

National identities have proliferated to an extraordinary degree. Most
nations are in their infancy as political entities. Over half the members of the
United Nations became members after Israel; this includes 11 of the 20 Arab
states.

There has not been a corresponding weakening of the sense of world
community, which is, after all, a community of nations. Groups are not
always divisive. Some groups place fraternity and equality among the
supreme goods and pursue them across boundaries of every sort. That
pursuit is one of the great virtues of the diaspora Jew.

Whether national identity fosters such ideals depends on the kind of
nationalism it embodies. Hans Kohn, a modern historian of nationalism,

usefully distinguished between closed and open nationalism. Closed nationalism is an ideology of exclusiveness and superiority, emphasizing the purity of the national character, the ancestral soil, and a religio-mystical destiny. This was the nationalism of 18th Century Japan and of 19th and 20th Century German and Slavic politics. It is found today among a small group of Jewish extremists, and among ruling majorities in Iran, Libya, Syria, and Iraq. Closed nationalism regards violence as a laudable instrument of policy. Its violence expresses hostility of almost paranoid intensity to those it identifies as national enemies. Closed nationalism is fed less by love of one's own than by hatred of the other. The Arab League is held together by the existence of Israel. Throughout the modern world, a signpost of political morality is: who are the haters and who are the hated?

Open nationalism rests on self-respect rather than on hatred of the other. It pursues peace rather than extolling violence; its ideal is equality, not triumphant superiority. Closed nationalism sets out to destroy demons— "the great Satan" America for Khomeini's Iran, the Trotskyites of Stalin's Russia, the Zionist-imperialist-racists of Arab terrorism. Open nationalism aims, rather, at self-determination, freedom from oppression. It aspires to survival without fear, diversity without hatred, independence without alienation. It is the nationalism of Washington and Bolivar, Garibaldi and Mahatma Gandhi, Bar Kochba and Ben-Gurion.

A movement of national liberation may include elements of both closed and open nationalism, sometimes rivals for leadership of the movement. The movement can be neutrally labelled defensive nationalism. Third World politics has a moral basis insofar as it is a genuine struggle against imperialism and colonialism.

What passes itself off as liberation may be only a replacement of one master by another. Russia has replaced Germany in Czechoslovakia, France in Syria, and Britain in Afghanistan. Foreign masters may also give way to indigenous tyranny, as in the regimes of Idi Amin (Uganda), Moammar Kadafi (Libya), the Ayatollah Khomeini (Iran), and a succession of Central and South American dictators.

Jews throughout the diaspora support open, defensive Jewish nationalism. Issues arise with regard to the political expression of defensive nationalism, for this, some say, rests on the closed ideology. The philosopher Hermann Cohen distinguished "nationality" from "nationhood": the former is ethnic, cultural, religious, historical; the latter is political. Jews, he felt, could preserve their nationality without nationhood—that is, within other states. Diaspora is not exile. Cohen died only two decades before the rise of Nazism.

There are many multinational states, like Canada, Yugoslavia, and India. There are many nationalities without nationhood, like the Kurds and Armenians, dispersed without a state of their own. The majority of Palestinians, incidentally, live in Jordan, and a majority of Jordanians are Palestinian; Jordan *is* the Palestinian state. Even if refugee Zionism is the only effective defensive nationalism for Jews, what meaning can Zionism have for Jews living in a democratic and egalitarian diaspora?

The cultural Zionism of Ahad Ha'am looked to a Jewish homeland as "a home of refuge for Jewish culture," making possible self-determination in language, religion, art, and literature. In Russia, teaching Hebrew is a crime against the state, and such synagogues as remain always include among their congregants government informers.

In the democratic West, where Jewishness is happily free from repression, it must nevertheless be a minority culture, continuously struggling against being swallowed up or transformed. Taking up an appointment as visiting professor at an American university, I was confronted by the symbolic circumstance that my classes were scheduled to begin on Rosh Hashanah and to meet also on Yom Kippur. I was free to reschedule them, and can say wholeheartedly, "God bless America!" But the calendar keeps me in exile.

An Israeli tourist guide, the story runs, was asked by a visitor to the Wall why it is so suitable a place for Jews to pray. He replied, "From here it's only a local call!" That is the answer of closed nationalism. Open nationalism would say, "Here we are no longer on a party line!" At the inauguration of Sir Rufus Isaacs as the last British Viceroy of India, he interrupted the ceremony when he noticed that the Bible on which he was to take his oath contained the New Testament as well as the Scriptures he held sacred. An aide stepped forward, ripped out the pages of the New Testament, and the inauguration proceeded. Zionism means that we want to have at hand our own editions, instead of tearing up the books of others.

Authenticity is inseparable from autonomy: if I do not live my own life, it can scarcely be called living at all. The God of Israel identifies Himself to us, not as the Creator of heaven and earth, but as He who brought us forth from bondage in Egypt. We became a people in journeying to freedom in our own land.

Ironically, Palestinian nationalism owes its existence to Zionism, both in imitation of Zionism and in hostility to it. Demands for (another) Palestinian state—in Judaea, Samaria, Gaza, and the Golan—date only from 1967, when these territories came under Israeli administration. During the preceding 19 years, when the "Arab lands" were already in Arab hands, not a single voice proclaimed Palestinian nationalism. Jerusalem, too, became politically important to the Arabs only reactively. It has never been even a provincial capital during centuries of Islamic rule; it was the capital of a Jewish state for 1,000 years. Jerusalem is mentioned over 600 times in the Bible, not once in the Koran.

The Messianic ideal of Judiasm does not have an other-worldly reference; its content is earthly peace and freedom. Says the Talmud. "This world differs from the Messianic era only in respect of the servitude of the Diaspora"

(Sanhedrin 91b). The daily liturgy includes a blessing extolling God for redeeming Israel; the blessing is not recited aloud to the very end because the redemption is not yet complete. Exile is still a basic fact of life for the Jewish people—a large majority of Jews, three-fourths or more, still live in the diaspora. The blessing does not trail off into silence on only one occasion—on Passover, the celebration of the exodus from bondage.

For the Western diaspora Israel does not have the significance given to it in refugee Zionism and defensive nationalism: Jews of the West are neither refugees nor under attack. What Israel means to all Jews is *kibbutz galuyot*— the ingathering of the exiles. One-fourth of the Jews of Israel are immigrants; these, together with the children of immigrants, make up one-half the population.

For some months I had feuded with a new neighbor whose parking slot adjoined my own because his car often encroached on my space, making it impossible for me to park. When we met at last to thrash things out he apologized, explaining that since they were newcomers from Morocco, his wife did not know how to drive very well and often had to wait for him to straighten the car. I, in my turn, explained that, coming to Israel from rural Michigan, I was not used to having neighbors crowd in on me. "Avraham," he rejoined, taking both my hands in his, "but you and I came to this country in order to *be* neighbors!"

Zionism has the significance of the long voyage home, the return, the resurrection. The Zionist dream is the prophet's vision of the valley of dry bones—the dispersed remnants of the House of Israel which are to live again (Ezekiel 37:3). In the fulfillment of the dream, Gentiles as well as Jews can find meaning. "The day when the Jewish tribes return to their fatherland," wrote Moses Hess, "will mark an epoch in the history of humanity." The rebirth of a people and a land is symbolic of the new world in the making. "Great is the day of the ingathering of the exiles," says the Talmud, "as the day of creation of heaven and earth" (Pesachim 88).

At the first Brussels Congress for Soviet Jewry a prisoner of Zion declared, "We have been imprisoned for a dream—not for crimes against the State, but for a dream of life in our own land among our own people." Another such dreamer proclaimed when he was being led away to imprisonment, "If I forget thee, O Jerusalem. . . !"—a vow harder to make there, the Prime Minister of Israel commented, than by the waters of Babylon.

I once gave a lift to a student whose Hebrew, though spoken in a strong Russian accent, was flawless. On learning that she had been in Israel only a year or so, I remarked that no doubt she had known Hebrew before coming to Israel. "No," she said, "not a word," then quickly corrected herself. "I *did* know one word," she said earnestly, "—'visa'." The word she used was not the Hebrew *asharah*, but the international term, "visa," familiar to exiles the world over.

Community Identity in the Diaspora

Western Jewry has long had a liberal tradition. This may be one of the reasons for so little *aliyah* from the West. Zionism is suspected of the closed nationalism which liberals so strongly oppose. Zionist extremists have been perceived as Jewish fascists, though there are also anti-Zionist Jewish extremists. Jewish liberals in the diaspora are torn between pride in Israel's achievements and guilt for the assertiveness of national interest which makes the achievements possible. Such inner conflict helps explain the Arab obsession.

Zionism was born in an era when national liberation was a goal of progressives, not reactionaries. Today it remains such a goal for other people; why not for Jews? Why should Jews support demands of Blacks, Indians, Chicanos, and others for recognition of their aspirations but not support comparable Jewish demands? Concern for the other need not undermine acceptance of the self. The Jew has always been both nationalist and cosmopolitan. Judaism makes the history and destiny of a particular people a vehicle for a universal teaching. Nowhere in the Torah or the Talmud is there reference to the "good Jew," only to the "good man"; the Law is for man to live by, not Jew (Leviticus 18:5). This is the ideal conveyed by the Yiddish expression, "to be a *mensch*"—literally, a person, but used to mean a decent human being. The book of Esther introduces Mordecai with the phrase: "There was a Jew in Shushan. . . ," but God is not mentioned in the Purim story. The book of Job begins, "There was a man in the land of Uz . . ."; in justifying God's ways to man, Jews are not mentioned.

The universalism of our day is a pragmatic universalism: if we cannot learn to live together we will destroy one another. Philosophers have espoused a rational universalism: men are united by a common faculty of reason. Judaism promulgates a prophetic universalism: we are all children of the same Father—the brotherhood of man is intrinsic to the human condition.

The Talmud (Megillah 9) relates that when Pharaoh's pursuing hosts had been destroyed and the Hebrews had safely crossed the Red Sea, Moses and the people lifted up their voices in song. The angels, too, joined in, at which God rebuked them: "My creatures are drowning—how dare you sing!" At the very moment of Israel's triumphant national liberation, even those who had enslaved them are to be recognized as brothers.

Zionism has been opposed because of what is thought to be its separatism. Zionism, the argument runs, widens the gap between Jew and Gentile instead of contributing to the integration of the Jew in a non-Jewish world. Zionism rejects diaspora even when the diaspora offers the Jew liberty and equality, if not fraternity. No wonder, say the critics, that the nations view Zionism with suspicion and distrust; these attitudes are only a reflection of how the Zionist looks upon the *goyim*.

Jewish patriotism in relation to the lands of the diaspora often has an exaggerated quality. The arguments of the anti-Semite have been tacitly accepted by the diaspora Jew: Jews must prove their loyalty. Jews who rightly urge separation of church and state in Israel see no incongruity in accepting the intrusion of the state on religion in the diaspora, symbolized by the display of the national flag in synagogues—flanking the ark together with the "Jewish," that is, Israeli, flag—as well as by formal prayers on High Holidays for the well-being of the political authorities. Anxious virtue is as suspect in politics as it is in morals.

Separatism, objectionable both politically and morally, is widely misunderstood. We do not separate ourselves from others merely by being ourselves. We do not accept others only by obliterating the differences that make us other. A work of art can be universal in meaning and worth even though—indeed, because—it is saturated with its own culture. Much of what is being produced around the world today is in the neo-nothing style: without flavor or character and indistinguishable from what is to be found in any other part of the world. The neo-nothing style can also become a style of life.

Community is not identity but recognition and acceptance of difference. When community is confused with identity we pursue the advertiser's ideal of a world rich and creamy with homogenized goodness. The image of the melting pot was of enormous importance for several generations of American immigrants. Today there is in America a crisis of community; ethnic groups, alienated from the rest of society, struggle to achieve identity. It is one thing to be integrated and quite another to be assimilated. For the Jew of the diaspora, the distinction becomes a predicament.

A certain illogic here is common to the thinking of many minorities. Because differences have been made the ground of discrimination, the inference is drawn that we should deny the differences, rather than denying that the differences justify discriminatory treatment. Women demand to be treated like men, instead of demanding changes in how women are treated; unisex fights sexism by giving up sex. Differences in age, race, and religion have been subjected to the same illogic. "After all, they're just like us" is no foundation for social justice; the injustice lies in the assumption that only those who are like us deserve whatever rights are in question.

The counterpart of "just like us" is the insistent, "We're just like you." Shylock's query, "Hath not a Jew . . ." is endlessly quoted, though it is in spirit both false and unjust. I am not you, and will not sacrifice my identity to be rewarded with a share of your rights and privileges.

Even speaking of differences is felt to invite discrimination. Americans have accepted the myth of something called the Judeo–Christian tradition. Differences are obliterated by being ignored. Christianity is nothing if not a belief in Christ as Savior, precisely the belief which Judaism rejects. Judaism cannot countenance a dying and resurrected god. It has no monasticism, and since the dispersion, no priesthood. Judaism is the religion of a particular people and is deeply concerned with the fate of its people everywhere. Many Jewish festivals, such as Passover, Chanukah, and Purim, are national and historical, more like Thanksgiving and the Fourth of July than like Christmas and Easter.

When Bertrand Russell was being jailed as a pacifist in World War I, he identified his religion as "atheist," to which the kindly bailiff replied, "Well, we all believe in the same God, anyhow!" The God of Israel is not the god of any Judeo-Christian tradition any more than He is the god of Islam. Similarities can be traced through continuities of historical development, but differences have also been of historical and sometimes deadly importance; they remain important today. Diaspora is no less an exile for all the pretense that we never left home.

A miscalled ecumenism assumes that each religion would be improved if it adopted something of other faiths. In our time there is much interest in what is common to all religions; this interest is especially marked among those who have no religion at all. The essence of soup is only water. True ecumenism is not the neo-nothing style in matters of religion, but acceptance of differences among faiths, and respect for other faiths with their differences.

Diaspora Jewry defensively adopts an axiom of uniqueness: nothing good is plural. If we have something good, they don't; to acknowledge it to others is to deny it to ourselves. This belief underlies the tactic of ego-imperialism: if it's good it must be mine (Jewish). The tactic is often linked with its converse: the chauvinism which says that if it's mine (Jewish) it must be good. Ego-imperialism and chauvinism claim for Jewry every achievement of the human spirit. The diaspora is far more proud of Israel than are Israelis —it has a more desperate need for pride.

Much of what both Jew and Gentile in the diaspora think of as Jewish is not so. "Jewish names" are Slavic or Germanic; a "Jewish face" can as easily be Syrian or Iraqi; "Jewish dress" is 18th Century Polish; "Jewish delicatessen" is Central European—kosher dill pickles have nothing whatsoever to do with Jewish dietary laws. Gefilte fish is no more Jewish than, say, sashimi or kippers; gefilte fish owes its presence on the Sabbath or festival table to the circumstance that in Judaism at a ritual feast both fish and meat must be served. The "Jewish mother," defined by overprotectiveness and the manipulation of guilt, is as likely to be Italian or Mexican as Jewish.

Jewish culture has borrowed freely from others; borrowings are identifiable in Jewish festivals, customs, and rituals, as well as in the Hebrew language. It has been rightly said that "there never was nor will be an exclusively Jewish culture."[6] The question is always whether what is borrowed is, like food, transformed and absorbed as nourishment, or whether, like a disease germ, it takes over and ultimately destroys its host. Chanukah may derive from pagan observances of the winter solstice, observances marked in many cultures by some sort of lights; a "Chanukah bush," complete with greeting cards and presents from Santa Claus, is scarcely a Judaic version of the Chanukah lamp. The struggle of the Maccabees against Hellenization has been a feature of Jewish life in the diaspora ever since their day. The struggle does not attain its goal either by surrender or by encapsulation in voluntary ghettos. Surrender abandons Jewish identity; encapsulation abandons everything else, freezing Jewish identity in the condition of the ghetto of an earlier age. Choice between surrender and encapsulation makes diaspora an exile.

The predicament is exacerbated by the widespread acceptance of an axiom of comparison: the belief that when values differ one must be better and the other worse. Anti-Semitism and Jewish defensiveness both accept the axiom, differing only in the outcomes of the comparison: for one the Jew is inferior and for the other he is superior. Both deny the Jew the right to be average; both are ego-imperialists and chauvinists.

Self-respect does not rest on invidious comparisons. "What kind of God can be worshipped in only one way?" asks the Hasidic master, the Seer of Lublin. It is hard for the diaspora Jew not to make comparisons because he himself is continually being compared. To live as a minority is by definition to be different, and therefore, by the axiom of comparison, to be either inferior or superior. The minority cannot accept the first alternative nor the majority the second; how are they to live together?

The question confronting the marginal man is how to be what he is without fear of being different, and how to be with others without fear of losing his identity. In the West, the diaspora Jew has answered the question with a series of brilliant improvisations. In Israel, where the Jew is no longer marginal, the question does not arise.

Personal Identity

In many synagogues the Ark has inscribed on it the injunction from the Talmud (Berachot 28b) "Know before Whom you stand!" Socrates enjoined, "Know thyself!" For Judaism each injunction is implied by the other—the precious essence of man's nature is the element of the divine in his makeup: man was created in the image of God. Personal identity, however, is a matter of distinctive individuality. To be identified as a child of the Heavenly Father, or as one of the children of Israel, is not yet to be individuated.

Identifications do not disclose identity; they conceal it. An identification is an external mark by which a particular person can be distinguished from others. Identity is what makes him the individual that he is. Identifications are as intrinsically meaningless as the lines on one's fingertips; identity is the locus to which is referred everything significant in the personality. Identifications are embodied in names and numbers—the "paper identities" we all carry. We can be insured against the loss of our identifications; no one will compensate us for loss of identity.

Alienation is awareness that others relate to us only in terms of our identifications, not in terms of our identity. We are customers, clients, taxpayers, workers; we perform in many roles. What matters to others is only how well each role is performed; no one cares about the performer. Identifications allow others to put me in my place; though I know my place, I do not know who I am.

An answer readily forthcoming in our time provides a negative identity: I am not one of those others. Americans once preoccupied with "un-American activities" had little conception of the positive content of loyalty. There are bigots today who know only that they are "not Niggers," while their Black counterparts identify themselves only as "against Whitey." There are Jews whose Jewishness is encompassed by the fact that they are not non-Jews. Said Mendel of Kotzk, "If I am I only because you are you, and you are you only because I am I, then I am not I and you are not you."

Jewish identity in the diaspora is often a vicarious identity, finding content by linkage with the attainments of other Jews, without regard to the question of what their Jewishness consists. The game of "you know who else?" is widely played: the unexpected Jewish identification of someone in the public eye is revealed, providing the Jewish hearers with a satisfaction to be repaid with another unexpected revelation—if possible, one involving an even greater achievement or a more hidden identification. Only minorities take such comfort in the revelation that "he is one of us." A *landsman* is close to us only when we are far from home. Vicarious identity identifies us as fellow exiles.

Identity is not antecedently existent; it is a creation, not a discovery. It is not bestowed by others; it is an achievement, not an award. Being born a Jew marks when the process began; it is not a manner of its completion. We can remain immature in our Jewishness, as we can in more limited dimensions of personality. For instance, the religious conceptions of many Jews—in Israel as well as in the diaspora—are limited by what they learned in grade school or in preparing for the *bar mitzvah*. Maimonides states as the aim of his *Guide for the Perplexed* "to put an end to the fantasies that come from the age of infancy" (I:26). Someone who never went beyond nursery rhymes and fairy tales cannot be expected in his adult life to take seriously poetry and literature.

Identity is many sided. There is no definitive answer to the question who is a Jew because no identity can be precisely defined. No single, fixed, necessary, and sufficient condition can circumscribe all Jews for all time. The conceptual structure is that of family resemblance: every two members of a family are similar enough in appearance to be recognized as kin, but there is no feature common to all members of the family.

Jewishness may find expression in political life, in cultural pursuits, in social activities, in philanthropy, in sentimentality. There are even in the diaspora "kitchen Jews," who retain a tenuous hold on their Jewishness by a taste for certain foods thought of as Jewish. Religion occupies a central place in Jewish identity, but Jewishness is not to be confused with Judaism; there are secular Jews and even atheistic Jews. Judaism itself is so complex and varied that it cannot be said without amplification to define any identity.

Identity is not only many sided; it has superficial and deeper layers. Part of every identity is an involuntary self, imposed on us by our social environment. There are Jews whose Jewishness is largely involuntary, either concealed or rejected, or else embraced as a gesture of defiance. There is a peripheral self, neither imposed nor chosen but implicated in doings whose meaning lies elsewhere. Peripheral Jews may appear at High Holiday services or contribute to the United Jewish Appeal, not because doing so has intrinsic significance to them, but because it is part of what it means to them to belong to the Jewish community. The autonomous self is the seat of everything freely and wholeheartedly undertaken, with integration and self-respect. An autonomous Jew neither submits to being Jewish nor works at it; he simply *is* Jewish. He is at home with his Jewishness.

Identity is first the result of what has been taken into the self. We are what we have become because of what we have been. Man is his history. The importance of roots is not a Black discovery, nor Jewish either; it is as old as the recognition of the past in the present. In the Renaissance, when the past was just becoming present to western culture, it was seriously proposed that scholars could settle whether or not Hebrew was indeed the language spoken in Eden by isolating a newborn infant and observing what language it would eventually begin to speak. All our meanings are as dependent on our past as is our language.

At the entrance to the Yad Vashem, the memorial in Jerusalem for the victims of the Holocaust, is a plaque bearing a saying of the Ba'al Shem Tov, the founder of Hasidism: "The Exile is forgetfulness; the root of redemption is to remember." Freud once described the aim of psychoanalysis as filling in the gaps in memory. Wherever Jewish identity is more than nostalgia, more than personal memory is important. Much of what has become personal began as communal experience. The *Haggadah* of Passover enjoins each participant in the seder to realize that he himself was freed from bondage. The ceremony is not only a commemoration of social events long past; it also celebrates present achievement of personal identity.

There is nothing here of the vicious notion of racial inheritance. Only cultural inheritance is involved. Culture is nothing other than the product of such inheritance: whatever has been learned in a society from the experience of others. Only human beings have traditions; it is to tradition that they owe their humanity.

When I was a child in America, other children, hearing my name "Abraham," would ask mockingly, "Abraham Lincoln?" I put a stop to it one day by replying proudly, "No, but we were named after the same man!" We were, of course, but only through long divergent lines, ending on my side, as might be expected, with the name of my mother's brother.

Identity links the present to the future as well as to the past. We are what we make of ourselves, what we are becoming because of what we reach for. Identity is defined by emotional investments as well as by introjections. Man is a compound of recollection and vision, memory and hope. The Jew remembers his bondage in Egypt, and looks to the day when the nations will beat their swords into plowshares.

At first, we are what we have been given; later we are what we give ourselves to. The paradox of this giving is that by it nothing is lessened, nothing is transferred away. The more we give the more we have; to give nothing of oneself is to be no one. What happens to another Jew happens to me, not because I put myself in his place, but because he fills my place; it would be empty without him. If I do not continue to demand, "Let my people go!" I myself remain a slave.

There is a superficial universalism which thinks it immoral to give to one's own. Giving to one's own, far from violating morality, is a moral obligation. In all societies kinship conveys special duties. There would be no such thing as marriage if a man were to love all women as he loves his wife, no parental care if adult concern were to be divided equally among all children. Everyone's friend is no friend of mine. All societies recognize that blood is thicker than water and that charity begins at home. Hillel is unanswerable: if I am not for myself, who indeed will be?

A New York bank advertises with the slogan, "You have a friend at Chase Manhattan." The New York branch of Israel's Bank Leumi one day countered with, "You may have friends elsewhere, but here you have *mishpachah*!" I am told that there was a rejoinder: "If you have *mishpachah* there, you *need* a friend here!" We cannot always make friends of our relatives; they remain kin for all that.

Jews have been described as the passionate people; morality is not served merely by spending our passion on strangers. Jews in the diaspora who are passionately devoted to good causes have been uneasy about including Jewish causes in their efforts. Jews know that we need not hate others to be ourselves; not all recognize that we need not hate ourselves to be decent human beings to others. Morality begins with caring for one's own. It is no good loving my neighbor as myself if I have turned away from myself. We are all members of one family of man; we can not do justice to more distant relatives if we are uncaring about our closer kin.

After Adam had sinned he ran and hid; God called out, "Where art thou, Adam?" Martin Buber points out that God asked not because *He* did not know, but because Adam did not know. The answer should have been, "In Exile." Adam drove himself out of the Garden of Eden. Man is in exile the moment he hides from the voice which speaks in his innermost being. The deepest alienation is to be a stranger to oneself.

The more fragile our self-respect the more vulnerable we are to what Buber called group egotism—the ego-imperialism and chauvinism of defensive Jewishness. The enemy within is the hardest to defend against. Jews of the diaspora have more vanity than pride, more concern with how they will appear to others than with their image in their own eyes. They are forever asking themselves, What will the *goyim* think! So-called Israeli "arrogance" is the pride which has replaced the other-directed humbleness of the ghetto.

The diaspora has good reason to be proud. "From Zion shall go forth the Law." In the diaspora the Law was universalized. Social justice became prudent self-interest for a people living everywhere as a minority. The Talmud opens with the question when it is permissible to recite the morning prayers—anytime after midnight, with the first flush of dawn, when the sun has fully risen, or when? The most memorable answer is, when there is enough light for a man to recognize his brother. Jews of the diaspora have long been committed to the enlightenment which recognizes brotherhood; we know well who is murdered in the dark.

The Word continues to go forth from Jerusalem, morality again being sustained by self-interest. Israel gives new relevance to the teaching of the prophets. Political crimes, Israel proclaims to the nations, are not exempt from moral assessment. Ideology has become idol worship, with a terrorist priesthood and the sacrifice of human victims. Acknowledging that ethics stands above politics calls for the moral courage of the prophet saying to the king's face, "Thou are the man!" Israel teaches that those who lack the courage are destroyed.

Jews of Israel and the diaspora both can take pride in the great tradition of Jewish rationalism. Sage and scholar are characteristic Jewish honorifics. From the writers of the Wisdom Literature, the compilers of the Talmud, its numerous commentators, philosophers like Maimonides and Spinoza, down to Einstein, Freud, and countless other Jewish scientists, Jews have extolled the powers of the mind and the role of reason in guiding human affairs. We live in a time of contempt for the intellect, glorification of violence, and license for any feeling whatsoever if it is sufficiently intense. In this age of madness Jews, wherever they are, speak with the voice of sanity. Our existence depends on it.

Jewishness: A Point of Departure

Throughout the history of the diaspora, Jews wrestled with the theological question why God had cast them into exile and how long it was His purpose to keep them there. The question today is empirical rather than theological: why is there so little *aliyah*? More disturbing, why is there so much *yeridah*? If diaspora is exile, why do so many Jews choose to remain there and even to seek it out?

Israel is not "the gate of heaven," as Yehuda Halevi called it (*Kuzari* II:14, 23); the whole earth lies at Heaven's gate. But life in Israel puts an end to Jewish agonizing over identity Those who do not come to live in Israel do not know what they are missing, those who leave it do not know what they already have. The first are unknowing because they have always lived as a minority and so do not know what it is to be at home; the second are unknowing because they have always lived as a majority, and so do not know what alienation is.

When the perversions of meaning in political semantics are dismissed with the contempt they deserve, Zionism today is seen to be what it always was: the return of the people of Israel to the Land of Israel. It is the Jew reestablishing his roots, fulfilling the words of the Prophet: "Say to the desolate, You have come home, to the prisoner, You are free, to those who are in darkness, Behold the light!" (Isaiah 49:8–13).

In Israel the Jewish past reaches up into the present. The lanterns I saw hanging in the sky on my arrival in Israel were not, as I supposed, a gigantic Chanukah lamp, but flares illuminating night exercises of the Israeli Navy. There is a "Samson" cement factory and a computer called the "Golem"; the river Jordan provides water for an advanced irrigation technology.

In World War II America faced the problem of selecting soldiers for service in isolated and confining Antarctic bases. None of the tests used to predict successful adaptation to those conditions was more exact than the one question: Do you like cold weather? The best predictor of successful absorption in Israel is the one question: Do you like to live among Jews? Alienation means to feel a stranger and afraid in a world one never made. There is no need to be afraid if one is not living among strangers.

Large numbers of immigrants fail to adapt; for immigrants from the West the proportion is over one-half. Many native-born Israelis leave—a total of perhaps six hundred thousand since the founding of the state.

In the diaspora it is often supposed that the military threat to Israel produces an intolerable level of anxiety; this picture scarcely fits even the border settlements. Ironically Israel is at the same time denigrated as a militaristic society. Anxiety is less marked a feature of Israeli life than it is of life in American cities.

Economic pressures are more to the point. Israel's rate of inflation is among the highest in the world, as is its rate of taxation; it has the highest per capita defense expenditure, and the highest per capita foreign exchange deficit. Real wages are a fraction of what they are in the West. Ironically, Israel is at the same time denigrated as a materialistic society.

The image of Israel as being good at what diaspora Jews are bad at— fighting—and bad at what diaspora Jews are good at—business—does a serious injustice to both diaspora and Israel. It overlooks the heroism of the Warsaw Ghetto and other Jewish fighters of the Resistance. It also overlooks the overwhelming costs of Israel's defense, of the ingathering of the exiles, and of building a technologically advanced and humane society in a sea of sand and feudalism.

Zionism stands or falls on ideological grounds. The early waves of immigration to Israel were not motivated by desires for a higher standard of living but for a *better* standard. They were responses to events like the Dreyfus case, the Russo-Japanese War, and the Bolshevik Revolution. Large numbers of the early immigrants also left, but not until they had laid the foundations of the future state. In our day, immigration surged after the Six Day War and after Entebbe, not when conditions were eased for bringing in stereos and refrigerators.

"Better is it to lodge in the deserts of the Land of Israel than in palaces abroad," the Midrash declares (Genesis Rabbah 39:8). With less hyperbole we can say that in Israel being Jewish is no longer a predicament; it is simply a fact. In Israel, Jewishness is no longer a goal; it is a point of departure.

Israel has disposed of the predicament; it still leaves problems. Underlying them is an ideological vacuum—the gravest failing of the Israeli establishment. The religious establishment is not occupied—as was the Grand Rabbi of Palestine, Abraham Kook—with rebuilding Zion, but with holding onto its political power and protecting its religious monopoly. The labor establishment is not concerned—as were its ideologues Berl Berelson and A.D. Gordon—with making work more meaningful and enhancing the dignity of labor, but with securing shorter hours and higher pay regardless of productivity. The Zionist establishment does not see itself—as did Theodore Herzl, Chaim Weizmann, and David Ben-Gurion—as an instrument for the fulfillment of a dream, but as an entrenched bureaucracy to be preserved at all costs.

It is easy to criticize from a distance. Two soldiers, from the American and Russian armies, met in Berlin at the end of World War II. Said the American, "When I get back, I can say to Truman, 'Mr. President, I don't like your foreign policy!' That's democracy." "So what," the Russian replied, "when I get back, I, too, can say to Stalin, 'Comrade Stalin, I don't like Truman's foreign policy!'"

The question is recurrently raised whether diaspora Jewry has the right to publicly criticize Israel. The question is more troublesome as concerns Israelis abroad, especially officials, present or past. The proper place for criticism is at home. The maxim, "I will defend Israel as if she had no friends and criticize her as if she had no enemies" balances a fact with a fiction. The unintended harm which can result from unrestrained criticism may easily be greater than that done by what is being criticized.

Reforms can seldom be carried out at long distance and second-hand, "Without you and me," Buber once said, "the most glorious institution is a lie." With you alone it is still only your truth, and remains a lie for me. Criticism of Israel for being militaristic or materialistic attains, at most, only a vicarious pacifism and spirituality, with no more substance than belongs to the vicarious identity it expresses. Even if Israel yielded altogether to the many and not always consistent demands of the diaspora, the predicament of exile would remain.

There is a moral issue here. If ethics stands above politics, how can I say, "My country, right or wrong!" But if I say, "My country—provided it is right!" how is my attitude to her different from that to countries not my own? Love is not blind to faults nor does it excuse them; they are simply irrelevant. We do not love because it is deserved, as if we were paying out something earned. Love knows no reasons because it sets no conditions and makes no demands.

This is not to say that norms and standards are abandoned. To love does not require losing the power to discriminate between right and wrong nor does it require abandoning the commitment to what is right. It requires only giving up weighing the other in the balance, whether or not he is found wanting. Neither teaching nor learning is a matter of good grades; some people—Jews among them—seem to think that Israel is taking the course on a pass–fail basis.

On the world scene Israel is more isolated than ever before. Not only concern for the supply of oil undermines its support. Another factor is the vast purchasing power of oil money. The annual income of the Arab oil states has a dollar value equal to the total annual exports of Sweden, Japan, and the United States combined.

Relative to the Arab states, Israel decidedly remains the underdog. In armament it is outnumbered three to one; in acquisition of additional arms, five to one; in states, 20 to one; in population, 25 to one; in area—including Judaea and Samaria, Gaza and the Golan—600 to one. The double standard of today's international morality adds insult to centuries of injury. Israel does have one priceless asset: the diaspora. Israel is the only country in the world which has three emissaries abroad for every citizen at home. Without them Israel could scarcely survive. The diaspora gives to Israel money, political support, and immigrants—usually in that order of magnitude. Israel's needs are in the reverse order. The money from private contributions is only a few percent of the grants and loans made by the United States government. The Jewish campaign may deflect energies from more important efforts on behalf of Israel. A year of service in Israel may count for more in the long run than the annual UJA contribution.

Financial assistance to Russian Jews is past dispute; but those who leave Russia on Israeli visas might be required to spend a specified time in Israel before they are helped to go elsewhere. If Jews in the diaspora do not choose to end the exile, they need not contribute to prolonging it. The Talmud holds that a Jew may compel his family to come to Israel; no one may compel it to leave Israel or to stay there.

Israel and the diaspora need one another. There are some distressed parents in the diaspora who unhappily think of Israel as a reform school to which they can send their troubled children. The significance of Israel for the diaspora relates to a deeper need: to find meaning and value in existence as a minority. Jewish life in the diaspora has an intrinsic worth far beyond what it can do for Israel. There will always be Jews in the diaspora; Israel can help them cope with alienation.

Even if all Jews were free to come to Israel and wanted to come, immigration and absorption on so vast a scale would be a matter of generations. At its height, the Russian exodus barely kept pace with the natural rate of increase of the Russian Jewish population. The problem for the Jewish people as a whole is not what to do for Israel but what to do for the Jewish people as a whole. In this widest perspective Israel can still be seen to be central.

If Jewish identity is to have any content beyond involuntary identification, then, as Franz Rosenzweig put it, the first step is to know oneself as part of Israel—the people and its land. Jewishness is first and last an indissoluble bond with other Jews—*kol Israel chaverim*: all Jews are comrades. "If I had my choice between Heaven and Hell," said the Hasid, Pinchas of Koretz, "I would choose Hell, so as to be with other Jews. There," he added, "I would teach Torah to those near me; others would come to hear, and so little by little out of that corner of Hell we would make a bit of Heaven."

In a remarkable passage in the Torah (Exodus 32:32) Moses, pleading for the sinning children of Israel, says to God, "If You forgive them [very well]; if not, blot my name from Your book." The Book of Life is meant; Moses was offering himself as a sacrifice. The statement might also be read as a declaration of his unyielding identification with his people, as though to say to God, "If You go Your way, I will go theirs!"

The people of Israel is like the Torah scroll which, made of segments of parchment, becomes holy only when the segments are sewn together. According to Kabbalah, to every Jew there corresponds one letter of the Torah and it is all one Torah. All the generations of Israel are one generation, all Jews one single Jew. The declaration of faith, "*Shema Yisrael*," has "hear" in the singular but "our God" in the plural, expressing individual commitment to collective faith. The converse declaration remains an ideal—"Hear, O God, Your people Israel, Your people is one!" All Jews, says a Midrash, stood together at Sinai when the Torah was given; when they stand together again the Messiah will come.

The identification of each Jew with the whole Jewish people recurrently raises in the diaspora the pseudoproblem of "divided loyalties." It is a pseudoproblem because there are always many loyalties. That a married man continues to care for his mother does not make him faithless to his wife. Diverse loyalties are not always divided. Neither is there a preestablished harmony among our loyalties; painful conflicts—psychological, moral, personal, or political—can very well arise. If loyalties are narrow enough to preclude any possible conflict, the boundaries of the self have shrunk to a dimensionless point.

The realistic question is not how to strip away from the self every problematic concern but how to integrate in the self all the concerns which make our lives meaningful. In one of his poems Yehuda Halevi writes, "My heart is in the East and I am in the West. How then can I taste what I eat, and how can food to me be sweet?" That is the question which makes the diaspora an exile.

Jews are so caring for their own that Jewish philanthropy is a byword; when generosity stops short of giving oneself, we ourselves are being denied. Religious Jews pray daily for the restoration of Zion; when prayer stops short of action we ourselves are to be restored. "The distance between the mouth and the heart," said the Hasid, Simcha Bunam, "is as great as that between Heaven and earth. Yet the earth," he added "is nourished by rain from heaven."

Confidence, Continuity

From the outset Jews have been a stiff-necked people. It is well for us that this is so, or we would never have survived as a people. In Haifa there is on display one of the ships used to bring refugees to Israel at a time when their landing was opposed by barbed wire and guns; the ship is called "Nevertheless." The Arch of Titus in Rome depicts scenes of the fall of Jerusalem; by tradition, Jews did not walk through the Arch until Israel was reestablished. I recently saw there a party of Scandinavian tourists to whom a guide was explaining, in German, a grafitti inscribed on the Arch in Hebrew; it read, "*Am Yisrael chai*"—the people of Israel lives.

One evening shortly after the Six-Day War I was with friends in Jerusalem when someone suggested we go to the Wall. Assured that the site was illuminated after dark, we set out. Passing through the sentry booth I asked casually, "How late is this open?" He answered, "We will never close again!"

Confidence has been an integral component of Jewish life since the exile. "Be of good courage, my people!" said a writer of the Apocrypha; "you were sold to the nations, but not for destruction." Millennia later the historian Heinrich Graetz said of the Jews, "A people which lives, as it were, on hope, is on that very account, like hope, eternal." In Israel today an optimist is defined as one who believes that the future is uncertain.

"It's hard to be a Jew," runs the Yiddish aphorism: hard but worthwhile! Being a Jew in Israel is harder, and more worthwhile. According to the Talmud (Hullin 86a), "From the time that the people of the Exile came up to Israel there ceased to be shooting stars, earthquakes, storms and thunders, their wines never turned sour and their flax was never blighted." Nature is not so benign, but life is as rich as the symbolism intends. It is a life of authenticity, among one's own. A new immigrant, scanning the faces of the crowd at the airport, was asked by the porter, "Are any of these your relatives?" He answered, "All of them!"

On the first anniversary of my mother's death, to share in a memorial service I sought out a humble place of prayer such as she herself might have gone to. When I entered, only the rabbi was as yet present. "*Shalom aleichem*," he said extending his hand. "*Aleichem shalom*," I answered. "Who are you?" he asked. I made the traditional reply, "A Jew." He nodded, pleased. "And where is a Jew from?" I answered, again in the same vein, "From afar." "Why," he now asked earnestly, "does a Jew come from afar to this place?" My answer was, "To say, *Amen!*"

That is not a bad reason for returning to Israel.

Notes

1. Nathan Rotenstreich, *Tradition and Reality*. New York: Random House, 1972, p. 59.

2. Ahad Ha'am, *Essays*. Oxford: 1946, p. 99.

3. Moses Hess, *Rome and Jerusalem*. 1862, p. 166.

4. Los Angeles *Times*, July 29, 1981, p. 10.

5. For instance, Ahad Ha'am, *op. cit.*, p. 214.

6. Kaufman Kohler, *Jewish Theology*. New York: Macmillan, 1923, p. 396.

·30·
Confronting the Aliyah Option

Étan Levine

It is not accidental that the topic of emigration to Israel, or *aliyah*, has been almost summarily dismissed by American Jewish thinkers. *Aliyah* is conspicuous by its absence from the American Jewish organizational agenda. For the fact is that in a profound sense, ever since its inception in 1948, the State of Israel has been an embarrassment to both Christians and Jews alike.

To the Church, Israel's reconstitution as a Jewish state was an embarrassment because it simply could not be! Christian tradition had long held that the Jewish people was destined to eternal wandering, as divine punishment for its rejection of the Son of God made flesh in its midst. The fact that the Pope in Rome now can gaze from his Vatican window upon a sign urging "Fly El Al to Israel" itself constitutes an ecclesiastical dilemma of cardinal proportions. The Jewish state represents a fundamental difficulty for Christian thinkers of all denominations; these have reacted in a predictably varied series of responses.

Paradoxically, the emergence of the State of Israel has proven to be an even greater embarrassment to Jews. For they know that in normative Jewish thought, as expressed in Bible, Talmud, medieval, and even later texts, redemption was defined as a return to the Land of Israel with Jewish autonomy and self-determination. The traditional Jewish prayer book is replete with prayers for the restoration of the exiles and the ingathering of the dispersion. In fact, throughout their 2,000-year diaspora, and despite significant loyalties and attachments which Jews may have had toward their adopted lands of residence, invariably they regarded themselves, and were regarded by their host countries, as a nation-in-exile.

The Jews preserved the language, law, and lore of their ancestral home, their self-identification as an ethnic group, and their nostalgia for their homeland. (They even went so far as to continue celebrating the agricultural festivals of Israel in countries where the climate and crops were totally inappropriate!) Not a Sabbath or festival went by without the Jew praying, "Because of our sins we have been exiled from our land," and beseeching He who underwrites Jewish history to restore His children to their borders. At the close of Yom Kippur, the holiest day of the year, the *Shofar* would be blown, and the community would resolutely proclaim the faith and prayer "Next year in Jerusalem!" Similarly, on the festival which marks the ancient liberation from Egypt, the Jew would save the seder from being antiquarian and anachronistic by declaring that redemption lay ahead: "Next year in Jerusalem!" Then suddenly, after 19 centuries of exile, the 2,000-year-old dream turned into a reality; the prophetic assurance was fulfilled. Whether past generations were fully honest in their espousals of their desires to return to the Holy Land is a moot question. What is beyond dispute, however, is that except for the cases of governmental incarceration, the world Jewish community can no longer honestly see itself as a nation-in-exile. The Jew may perhaps still pray to be returned to his native land, but, in fact, what is now required is not divine intervention but merely a visit to the nearest travel office.

Aliyah *as Joining* "Our Crowd"

If one wants to capture the earliest phylogenetic memory of the Jewish people, a feeling which accompanied this people from its inception, it is the pathos of belonging to a crowd that is wandering through the desert in search of the Promised Land.

> The image of this multitude moving year after year through the desert has become the crowd symbol of the Jews. It has remained to this day as distinct and comprehensible as it was then. The people see themselves together before they settled and then dispersed; they see themselves on their migration. In this state of density they received their law. If ever a crowd had a goal, they had. They had many adventures and these were common to all of them. The crowd they formed was a *naked* crowd; of all the many things which normally enmesh men in their separate lives, scarcely any existed in these surroundings. Around them was nothing but sand, the barest of all crowds; nothing is more likely than the image of sand to emphasize the feeling of being alone with itself which this wandering procession must have had.[1]

Obviously, specifics about the crowd, and specifics about the bonds within the crowd, evolved through the ages. But is it not true that to this day, when a person feels he or she is a Jew that the primary feeling is a sense of attachment to this crowd wandering through history on its way to its Promised Land? Is the Jew's deepest existential attachment to a theology or to a people? Some American Jews have chosen *aliyah*. And after the secondary, tertiary, and totally irrelevant motivations have been discarded, what remains is their longing to join that crowd. Like their ancient forebears, they are idealists and realists: Israel is not the Promised Land, but it is a land of promise. And apparently for them that is enough. As Robert Browning put it, "A man's reach must exceed his grasp, else what's a heaven for?"

The Aliyah Dialogue

Of course, the overriding majority of American Jews reject the *aliyah* option. And in the past, to the extent that the issue was discussed at all, the *aliyah* debate between Israeli and American Jews was distinguished neither by impeccable manners nor by rigorous logic. Perhaps this was inevitable in confrontations between two parties, one intent upon justifying its own decision, and the other convinced that it alone was discharging the obligation which perforce should be met by both parties. In order to transcend the familiar level of recrimination and homiletics, it is first necessary to reevaluate the basic assertions which are posited as self-evident truths.[2]

To posit axiomatically at the outset of the process that if one's fellow Jew is not committed to *aliyah* then he or she is not responding positively or honestly to Jewish history and Jewish identity is to effectively terminate the discussion. An *ab initio* assertion that only one response to the creation of the Jewish state is appropriate, in lieu of examining alternative responses, precludes dialogue. In order for the *aliyah* issue to cease being a deteriorated confrontation of slogans, sermonics, and self-congratulations, and to become a genuine issue, there must be some tension between certainty and doubt. *Aliyah* will then remain a live option as long as there is a Jewish state, and as long as there are Jews in the diaspora who relate deeply to it. And there will never be an unequivocal, categorical imperative for all Jews.

The Physical Survival Argument

Zionist rhetoric generally addressed the diaspora with the warning that "it could happen here." The implication was that self-interest itself—mere physical survival—dictated *aliyah*. But this argument did not move the American Jew. Even granted the obvious truism that "it could happen here," the conclusion is a non sequitur. The American Jew would immediately ask, "Is *aliyah* necessarily the most appropriate response to a theoretical possibility of anti-Semitism, or are there appropriate alternative responses which could prevent, inhibit, minimize, or combat latent and overt hostilities? Further, might not the prediction and heralding of catastrophe actually constitute a self-fulfilling prophecy by causing fright and helplessness among the intended victims and encouragement of their would-be persecutors?" The thinking Jew would ask whether it was very Jewish to program life exclusively in terms of fear, and whether emigration to Israel on that basis is genuinely *aliyah*. In fact, he often protested that the possibility of anti-Semitism in America actually constituted a mandate for American Jews to face the danger by becoming even more involved in those activities, programs, and organizations which are dedicated to Jewish self-defense and communal well-being.

A primary factor making for Jewish survival during the past two millennia has been the very condition of geographic dispersion which radical Zionism sought to end. It was this demographic feature more than anything else which contributed both to the seeming helplessness but unparalleled viability of the Jewish people. Thus, modern military theoreticians stress the survival value of dispersal, as opposed to concentrated masses, with the threat of nonconventional weaponry reinforcing the need for demographic diffusion. In light of these factors coupled with the unnerving reality that there are currently few places as dangerous for Jewish masses as Israel, American Jewry found the argument that *aliyah* is the one appropriate means of assuring Jewish physical survival less than convincing.

The Israel Community Argument

American Jews generally conceded the point that Israel would greatly benefit from massive immigration from the West and improve a situation aggravated by Israel's alarming problem of emigration (*yeridah*). They were also prone to admit that the fullest means of becoming part of the Israel experience in all of its historical romance and significance is by being physically present within the borders of the Jewish state. However, they qualified their concessions with the insistence that the communal boundaries of Israel are quite different from the political boundaries of the state. In fact, thére is a profound difference between community and proximity; the criteria for being part of a community are not solely geographic. Rapidly evolving communication media, commercial organization, travel modes, etcetera, are continuously minimizing proximity as a community factor. Thus, for example, emerging communities in the world today—be these communities of religion, letters, professions, power, ideas, and so on—increasingly are structured on a global, rather than on a national, level. And Jewish intellectuals argued that the Jewish agenda must cope with the global village rather than denying its emergence.[3]

Thus, rather than succumb to guilt or discomfort, many committed Jews stressed the fact that throughout history, even during the period of the Second Temple and Jewish autonomy, Jewish populations throughout the world exerted critical force for the benefit of the Jewish homeland. This was expressed in economic, cultural, political, and military terms, and was a major source of support to the Jewish community in the Land of Israel.[4] And today the Israel community is a worldwide entity. It is the envy of other small nations who are not similarly blessed by such widespread reservoirs of commitment and concern.[5] Thus, when addressing the question of becoming an integral part of the Israel community, the Jew does not automatically conclude *aliyah* as the self-evident response. Rather, he often notes the alternatives in all their complexity, often within the context of how indiscriminate *aliyah* would perforce affect the Jewish people's political strength, economic power, public relations abilities, institutional structures, etcetera.

The Cultural Survival Argument

American Jews, by and large, are quite aware of the problem of Jewish cultural survival. In the modern era, cultural pluralism is an undeniable fact. In an increasingly pervasive world culture, barriers to, and proscriptions against, interethnic communications are being dismantled. In fact, today cultural survival requires the purposeful seeking out of other cultural energy, content, and form. Precisely for these reasons, conceiving of Jewish culture as being geographically defined by the boundaries of the Jewish state is as obscurantist as it is unhistorical. Asserting that *aliyah* is a self-evident precondition for Jewish cultural survival is hardly convincing; what a bleak prospect emerges when one considers an individual Jew or an entire people choosing to withdraw into itself, defensively resisting the creations which humanity is bringing forth! Fortunately, as both Israeli and American Jews know, there is hardly a country as open to, and as sensitive to, the international community as is Israel. Today's Zionist intellectual sees Israel as part of the world, not an escape from it; without world culture sustaining it, there can be no Israel culture.

The thinking Jew today, both in Israel and abroad, is involved in more profound questioning: how is Jewish culture defined? What are the criteria for determining whether specific elements of Jewish culture are worth transmitting, in what form should they be transmitted, and what are the most feasible means of transmission? In the context of these basics, the intellectual deals with the Israel issue: Israel as a locus on the Jewish cultural map.[6]

The Religious Survival Argument

The final unconvincing gambit to Jewishly committed Americans is that *aliyah* is necessary for religious survival: that Judaism as a religion is viable only (or to a greater extent) in Israel. This myth not only ignores the historical reality of Jewish religion having demonstrated remarkable survival power for 2,500 years in the diaspora.[7] It also ignores the fact that one could hardly demonstrate a necessarily greater religious concern on the part of today's Israeli Jew than the diaspora Jew to whom *aliyah* is being preached as a *sine qua non* for Jewish religiosity.[8] Consequently, the American Jew generally denies that emigration to Israel necessarily constitutes a religious *aliyah* or a tactical move for the survival of Judaism. He argues that a noble idea is not limited by national boundaries; a universal religion is, by definition, a universal religion. And neither the Jewish God, the Jewish people, nor the Jewish religion was ever so restricted or restrictive as to require protective constriction. He senses that if Judaism has nothing vital to say to the hearts and minds of men and women in the diaspora, it will say equally trivial things in Israel—albeit in Hebrew!

Since diaspora Jewry is perforce a self-conscious Jewry to which meaningful religious survival is a constant challenge, it is, more than Israeli Jewry, aware of the immediate dangers of assimilation, acculturation, secularization, and the centrifugal forces inherent in the open world culture. It is, as a consequence, more aware than Israeli Jewry of the need to create and positively enhance Jewish practices, institutions, and commitments. The American familiar with the Israeli scene knows that in Israel extensive population groups are unaware (or unconcerned) that assimilation there is rampant. It is not assimilation into the secular Christianity of America, to be sure, but it is a very real assimilation into a Western lifestyle where the most fundamental Jewish practices, ideas, and ideals are dismissed as being incompatible, anachronistic diaspora relics.

Advocating *aliyah* as an indispensable condition for religious survival is, therefore, simplistic in the extreme.[9] That the major energy for the survival and enhancement of Jewish religion will be the State of Israel is not as pat as apologists for *aliyah* claim, and their overstated case make for poor rhetoric and even poorer logic. The Jewish intellectual almost never assented to the proposed panacea of *aliyah*. He preferred to address the issue in its living flesh: what do we mean by Jewish religion? What elements are to be stressed? How are these to be grounded in a program of knowledge, sensitivity, and action? What role can the State of Israel play in the creation of the greater Judaism in the making?

Aliyah *as an Option*

The fallacious dialectics notwithstanding, the *aliyah* option does have a legitimate claim for attention. However, to understand, discuss, and act on the issue, the above mentioned half-truths must be discarded, and a new logic of *aliyah* discourse must be framed.

It is essential to recall that historically, Zionism generally and *aliyah* specifically were never conceptualized as ends in themselves. From the biblical prophets of the return, to the modern Zionists, *haluzim* and *aliyah* groups, there were always articulated purposes and ends for which *aliyah* to the Land of Israel was but a means. Their specific purposes differed widely,[10] ranging from religious Messianism to socialist egalitarianism, but *aliyah* was invariably considered and advocated in relation to specific purposes: individual, Jewish, or universal. Further, the malaise which besets much of the Zionist movement today, as well as part of the Israeli population today, is precisely the fading of these transcendent purposes which once informed those who returned to Zion. Contemporary Zionist dialogue blithely ignores this essential precondition for effective, constructive *aliyah* discourse—hence its virtual failure in the affluent Western democracies.

Aliyah must be considered in the context of the entire question of Jewish relatedness to Israel, and of Israeli relatedness to Jewishness. One must deal with the unprecedented, difficult question of the nature of the Jewishness of the Jewish state, and there is no way that one may circumvent the fundamental issue: the purpose of Jewish existence. This is an admittedly difficult task, but it is both futile and meaningless to consider *aliyah* without a satisfactorily articulated and demonstrated rationale for Jewish existence. In highly compressed terms, the logic of the *aliyah* option may proceed along the following lines: being human, or being Jewish, are nominal, objective states, usually unrelated to choice. Categories of choice are adjectival, that is, to modify the nouns human and Jewish. Thus, one can be Jewish consciously, reluctantly, partially, enthusiastically, happily, intelligently, superficially, profoundly, etcetera. Being Jewish is a given; *how to be* Jewish is an option.

Moving from the theoretical to the historical, it is not difficult to demonstrate that the Land of Israel was the stage upon which the Jewish people enacted heroism, creativity, and romance. It is also apparent that the drama has not ended; new annals of Jewish history are now being written. Every Jew faces the existential decision as to whether and how he wants to be involved as part of that unfolding drama. Israel represents an unprecedented historical experiment: a mighty act of risk, daring, self-assertion, adventure, and thrust back into nationhood of the Jewish people. It is an experiment which may very well fail, with all the horrible, nightmarish consequences of such failure. And each diaspora Jew, as well as each Israeli Jew, is a factor.

Like all acts which flow from loyalty or commitment, *aliyah* involves an element of the transrational; an element not reducible to mere self-interest, either on the individual or collective level. In fact, it is precisely this commitment of transcending narrow self-interest that is most characteristic of Jewishness.[11] It is with the admission that *aliyah* is a complex, multifaceted issue that a discussion of *aliyah* begins.

Advocating Aliyah

One can, in all good conscience and with clear intellectual honesty, advocate the *aliyah* option. But it must be done in terms of what is, in fact, best for the individual and for the community. The following may serve as the rubrics of such an analysis: The self of the Jew, like that of any human being, consists in large measure of the accumulated experiential background of that individual. The self is unique because it is what has been built, since one's life began, through unique experience and unique purpose on one's unique biological structure. This applies too to the selfhood of the Jewish people. And it is not difficult to prove that Israel offers a range of Jewish experiences potentially greater than that offered by the diaspora. Thus, there is (again, potentially) an argument for greater Jewish selfhood in a Jewish state. This self consists not only of the organization of accumulated life experiences, but also consists of how the individual sees himself: his self-image. The essential issue is not simply what he is, but what he thinks he is. And this invariably crystallizes in relationship to others. Again it should not be difficult to demonstrate that a Jewish self-image is more positively, naturally, easily cultivated within a supportive, affirmative, sympathetic Jewish milieu, rather than a non-Jewish context which perforce is alien and judgmental, if not outright unsympathetic and hostile.[12] It is a truism that the self has to be achieved and is not a given. Thus, the Jewish self, like all selves, is achieved primarily through contact, and has to be understood as a mutual relationship in terms of others. The self and the other is not a duality: separation is impossible because neither can exist without the other.[13] And nothing could be more favorable for the creation of a Jewish self than an environment of a Jewish other. To the authentic Jew (a phrase which although it may be difficult to define is not difficult to describe), Judaism is the unifying factor of life. It is not simply the experience of the holy: the experience of the *tremendum* and *fascinosum* as Rudolph Otto would have it.[14] Nor is it equivalent to the ethical as Immanuel Kant would define it.[15] Rather, as Abraham Joshua Heschel repeatedly described it, Judaism is that which is of ultimate significance—or it is of no real significance at all.[16] It is an all-embracing relationship, eliciting Jewish reactions to the totality of life. The State of Israel, obviously, offers the closest approximation of totality: a field, or grounding, in which Jewishness is capable of its broadest expression.

The Jewish self—like any self—is fed by the perceptive process. And it is important to recognize the nature of that process.[17] Perception is necessarily selective, since to perceive all would be to experience intellectual and emotional chaos.[18] Man therefore chooses that which his self feeds upon, and these choices determine the direction of his growth. Thus, experience itself is not enough to account for our lives, for there are infinite objects in our surroundings with which we may have had experience but which we do not perceive. Israel provides a significantly Jewish medium of perception: seeing history through Jewish experience, communicating (and cerebrating with ourselves) in a Jewish language, experiencing the passage of time in a Jewish calendar, etcetera.[19] To take but one example: if thought consists of talking to ourselves, how profound the distinction is if we talk to ourselves in Hebrew! Without further ado, suffice it to say that Israel offers the most favorable climate for Jewish perception.

Finally, the self and its perceptive intake are determined by a sense of purpose. Partially this is on a conscious level, and in part it is less conscious, but nevertheless the self is selective regarding purpose. Just as man is selective in what he feeds himself physically, so is he selective in what he feeds himself perceptually. This too is related to his purpose. What more fertile source of Jewish purpose is there than the Jewish state? Is there a greater Jewish challenge to be found anywhere? Is there a more compelling, more romantic, more demanding, more multifaceted, more ennobling Jewish purpose to which the Jewish self may be linked? Is there any greater source of Jewish heroism both for *the* people and its people? Is there any purpose in which the risks and the potentials are so great? It is almost as though two millennia of Jewish history have conspired to offer the 20th Century diaspora Jew a heroic purpose, mission, and destiny: to participate in a grand adventure yet in the making! These may not, in fact, prove to be adequate motivations for mass *aliyah*. On the other hand, they do, to my mind, frame the parameters for considering and discussing the *aliyah* option.

Postscript

As one who, over a decade ago, exercised the *aliyah* option, I can attest that joining the crowd (to return to the biblical metaphor) is a decision and an implementation not lightly achieved or sustained. For we are, in sum, a crowd of survivors—I don't mean survivors of the Holocaust or murderous traumas of that ilk—but survivors of a long march through history which perforce tried the bodies and souls of even this most loyal, stubborn breed of men and women. And today our crowd is confronted by virtually every challenge, both from within and without, that could face an emerging society.

Disillusionment is a constant temptation when one chooses the *aliyah* option. It always has been. One is often tempted to say, "Six million American Jews can't be wrong!" Living in Israel has its abrasive, frustrating, and debilitating aspects; we are not a pleasant, charming crowd, for history has not yet allowed us the ease and quietude to develop these amenities. Despite all this—and despite much, much more which could be elaborated with specificity—it is good to be back in the crowd. Critics of *aliyah* may, in fact, be right: we may be a naked crowd and no more. But here we constitute an historical existential assertion; in the words of the early pioneers who sang it even on empty stomachs: *'Anu banu 'artzah livnot ulehibanot bah.* "We have come to the land, to build and to be built in it."

———————————————————————————— *Notes*

1. Elias Canetti, *Crowds and Power*, Carol Stewart, (Tr). New York: Seabury Press, 1978, p. 208.

2. For similar argumentation, cf. Étan Levine, Toward a logic of *aliyah* discourse, *Reconstructionist* XXXIV:4, 1968, pp. 1–6.

3. In his popular *Understanding Media* (New York: New American Library, 1973), Marshall McLuhan has promulgated this concept of the global village.

4. Cf. Étan Levine, Israel as Jewish theology. *The American Zionist* LX:4, 1969, pp. 30–33. See documentation in S. W. Baron, *A Social and Religious History of the Jew*, Vol. 1. Philadelphia: Jewish Publication Society, 1952, pp. 167 ff.

5. For universalist concept, cf., Étan Levine, *The Aramaic Version of Jonah*. Jerusalem: Jerusalem Academic Press, 1970, pp. 6ff.

6. See overview in Arthur Hertzberg, *The Zionist Idea*. New York: Meridian Books, 1960, pp. 15–100.

7. On the diaspora scene, seminal questions of this nature were cogently raised by Mordecai M. Kaplan, *The Future of the American Jew*. New York: Macmillan Co., 1948.

8. Cf. Étan Levine, Toward a logic of *aliyah* discourse, op. cit.

9. See G. H. Mead, *Mind, Self and Society: From the Standpoint of a Social Behaviorist*. Chicago: University of Chicago Press, 1974. cf., Étan Levine, Problems in Jewish teacher training. *America* 1969, p. 7ff.

10. Consider the gamut of personages such as Rabbi Yisrael Moshe Hazzan, Rabbi Zvi Hirsch Kalischer, Rabbi Yehudah Alkalai, Moses Hess, Peretz Smolenskin, Moshe Leib Lilienblum, Eliezer Ben-Yedudah, Leonardo Pinsker, Theodor Herzl, Max Nordau, Ahad Ha'am (Asher Ginsberg), Hayyim Nahman Bialik, Micah Joseph Berdichevski, Jacob Klatzkin, Joseph Haiim Brenner, Nahman Syrkin, A. D. Gordon, Ber Borochov, Berl Katznelson, Yahiel Pines, Rabbi Samuel Mohilever, Rabbi Abraham Isaac Kook, Judah Magnes, Martin Buber, Vladimir Jabotinsky, Rabbi Meir Berlin (bar-Ilan), Rabbi Mordecai Kaplan, Chaim Weizmann, David Ben-Gurion, etcetera.

11. See general conceptual approach in Josiah Royce, *The Philosophy of Loyalty*. New York: MacMillan Co., 1914), pp. 99ff.

12. See Earl C. Kelley, The fully functioning self. *Etc.: A Review of General Semantics*, XXIX:4, 1967, pp. 403–417.

13. See ibid., p. 408.

14. For elaboration, see Rudolph Otto, *The Idea of the Holy*. New York: Oxford University Press, 1966.

15. A. C. Ewing, *A Short Commentary on Kant's Critique of Pure Reason*. Chicago: University of Chicago Press, 1950.

16. See A. J. Heschel, *God in Search of Man*. Philadelphia: The Jewish Publication Society, 1956, as well as the description provided in Herbert Marcuse, *One-Dimensional Man*. Boston: Beacon Press, 1964.

17. I have attempted to demonstrate this in Jewish historiography: cf. introduction to Étan Levine, *The Aramaic Version of Lamentations*. New York: Hermon Press, 1976.

18. See pedagogic principles in Weller Embler, *Metaphor and Meaning*. Deland, Fla: Everett/Edwards, 1966, as well as the symbolic equivalent in Harvey Cox, *The Secular City*. New York: MacMillan Co., 1965. The Hebrew writings of Bialik, Ahad Ha'am, and others stress this point with cogency, and the validity has been established in, *inter alia*, the research of J. Bronowski, S. I. Hayakawa, and students of semantics.

19. Cf. Kelley, op. cit., p. 411.

⬧ INDEX ⬧